Chaucer's Sexual Poetics

Chaucer's Sexual Poetics

Carolyn Dinshaw

THE UNIVERSITY OF WISCONSIN PRESS

The University of Wisconsin Press
114 North Murray Street
Madison, Wisconsin 53715

3 Henrietta Street
London WC2E 8LU, England

Library of Congress Cataloging-in-Publication Data
Dinshaw, Carolyn.
Chaucer's sexual poetics/Carolyn Dinshaw.
320 pp.   cm.
Includes bibliographical references.
1. Chaucer. Geoffrey, d. 1400—Criticism and interpretation.
2. Sex role in literature.   3. Sex in literature.   I. Title.
PR1933.S35D56   1989
821'.1—dc20   89-40253
ISBN 0-299-12270-0   CIP
ISBN 0-299-12274-3 (pbk.)

For A. J. S.

Contents

Acknowledgments

Writing this book, creating this text, has been most like a process of weaving—of taking up the thread of an idea, connecting it with other threads, and slowly working up the stuff of an argument. I can only begin to acknowledge the people who have helped in this process, but it is a pleasure even to start. The works of R. Howard Bloch, Lee Patterson, and Eugene Vance have coincided with, inspired, and informed this project from its very early stages; the influence of my teachers, Robert Burlin and John Fleming, goes back even further, and is still strongly felt. I am very grateful for advice and guidance from the many who read part or all of this manuscript at various stages, offering their ideas and encouragement: among these whose influence I have felt are Elizabeth Abel, Janet Adelman, Peter Allen, Paul Alpers, Joel Altman, Christopher Baswell, John Bishop, Charles Blyth, Carol Clover, Phillip Damon, Sheila Delany, the late Donald Howard, David Hult, Sylvia Huot, David Miller, Winthrop Wetherbee, and the anonymous reader for *Yale Journal of Criticism*. Special thanks go to Anne Middleton, for her constant interest and fine readings of all of this material in its many incarnations; to Mitchell Breitwieser, for his patience and acuity through draft after draft; to H. Marshall Leicester, Jr., for the exchange of drafts and thoughts, and for sharing the excitement of working on Chaucer "in a new key"; and to Susan Schweik, for her sharp and imaginative reading and her unwavering support of this project. Thanks, too, to my students at Berkeley, both undergraduate and graduate, for their affirmative subversiveness (or is it subversive affirmativeness?). I thank in particular Frank Grady and Laura King for their help in compiling the bibliography, and Andy Galloway for proofreading.

I thank the National Endowment for the Humanities for a Summer Stipend and the University of California at Berkeley for grants supporting this project. At the University of Wisconsin Press I am especially thankful for the support and enthusiasm of my superb editor, Barbara Hanrahan. Mary Carruthers and Peter Travis read the manuscript for the Press and provided me with perceptive, invaluable suggestions, because of which the book is, I think, a much better book than it would have been otherwise. I thank Mary Caraway, copy editor extraordinaire, for her intelligent and sensitive editing of the final text, and Elizabeth Cunningham, for the index.

Never-final thanks go to my family and to Johanna Gladieux.

Parts of my analyses in Chapters One, Two, and Six had their beginnings in my dissertation, *Chaucer and the Text: Two Views of the Author* (Princeton, 1982; published in 1988 by Garland Press). An early version of Chapter One, now substantially revised and expanded, appeared as "Readers in/of *Troilus and Criseyde*," in *Yale Journal of Criticism* 1.2 (1988): 81–105; Chapter Three, "The Law of Man and Its 'Abhomynacions,'" is reprinted, in substantially unrevised form, from *Exemplaria: A Journal of Theory in Medieval and Renaissance Studies* 1.1, published March 1989, by Medieval and Renaissance Texts and Studies, © 1989 Center for Medieval and Early Renaissance Studies, State University of New York at Binghamton. Chapter Six, "Eunuch Hermeneutics," is a much-revised version of an article of the same name in *English Literary History* 55 (1988): 27–51. I thank the publishers of these journals for permission to reuse material.

Chaucer's Sexual Poetics

Introduction
Chaucer's Sexual Poetics

Adam scriveyn, if ever it thee bifalle
Boece or Troylus for to wryten newe,
Under thy long lokkes thou most have the scalle,
But after my makyng thou wryte more trewe;
So ofte adaye I mot thy werk renewe,
It to correcte and eke to rubbe and scrape,
And al is thorugh thy negligence and rape.[1]

1

"Chaucers Wordes unto Adam, His Owne Scriveyn" offers a brief glimpse of the fourteenth-century poet at work, allows us a rare exposure to the material circumstances and social relationships involved in late-medieval literary activity. In the *House of Fame*, of course, we get a glance of the poet at work when, in book 2, the eagle narrates a detailed scenario of "Geffrey's" eremitic life of study, depicting long hours, silence, and isolation from neighbors. Chaucer's dream-vision narrators are frequently depicted as encountering the old books, "write with lettres olde" (*Parliament of Fowls*, 19), that motivate their poetry; but the process of composition itself is occulted—consider the ending of the *Book of the Duchess*, for example ("This was my sweven; now hit ys doon" [1334])—and the transmission of the written texts is seldom an issue. In "Adam Scriveyn," however, the remonstration of the hapless scribe addresses precisely the problematics of textual transmission and makes it clear that literary production in the late fourteenth century is a social enterprise: this "maker" is unavoidably dependent on the copyist for the accurate transmission and, indeed, the very intelligibility of his works. The texts of "Boece" and "Troylus" have, apparently, been compromised by Adam's carelessness already; in fact, the voice of the maker had knowingly expressed the same concerns at the end of "Troylus" itself. Textual distortion would seem to be all but inevitable in the process of transcription: the narrator in his address to his "bok" at the end of *Troilus and Criseyde* worries

3

about just such scribal mismanagement as is later castigated in "Adam Scriveyn."

> And for ther is so gret diversite
> In Englissh and in writyng of oure tonge,
> So prey I God that non myswrite the,
> Ne the mysmetre for defaute of tonge;
> And red wherso thow be, or elles songe,
> That thow be understonde, God I biseche!
> (5.1793–98)

"Adam Scriveyn" as lyric is conventional enough—it sounds like a classical epigraph—but its tone of exasperation may be understood to express as well Chaucer's deep and lingering concern with the treatment of the letter of his texts, and the appropriate interpretation of that letter.

"Adam Scriveyn" focuses, however, not only on the basic constituent of written literary production, the relationship between maker and scribe, but also on the basic constituent of all social relations: the human body. Chaucer threatens Adam with a future of itchy scabs on his head because he himself must "rubbe and scrape" the scribe's defective work. Literary production takes place on bodies—on the animal skins made into pages, on cursed scribes' scalps—and the rubbing and scraping that must be done to both suggests a figurative identification here between the human body and the manuscript page, the text. It is just such a figurative association of literary activity with human bodies that I want to pursue in the course of this book.

Chaucerians considering "Adam Scriveyn" these days tend to sympathize with the exasperated author and ruefully recall their own experiences with incompetent typists, thus positing the existence of a timeless brotherhood of authors (the masculine significance of that phrase here will soon become clear) and placing themselves, like Dante in Limbo, in the company of the great. Scholars earlier in the twentieth century (Brusendorff, Hammond, and Manly among them) found the search for the "real" Adam, the fourteenth-century scrivener, tantalizing—irresistible, albeit inconclusive.[2] I think the poem does in fact solicit a timeless identification—although not that of critic with Chaucer—as well as invite such reconstruction of the particular conditions of Chaucer's literary production. The poem evokes and exploits the rich implications of what may be simply a particularly felicitous circumstance: the scribe's name is Adam. "The mark of Adam," as the Wife of Bath will later put it, is both the generic sign (derived from the first man) of masculine humanity and the writing that men (such as Adam scriveyn) do.

And that mark, to continue to use the Wife's vocabulary, itself needs to be "redressed." Chaucer castigates here an Adam who is definitely fallen, an Adam whose written letters do not accord with the intent behind them. The first Adam was the first human to use language; indeed, he was, according to Genesis 2:19, the inventor of names: "Omne enim quod vocavit Adam animae viventis ipsum est nomen eius" ("Whatsoever Adam called any living creature the same is its name").[3] Medieval commentators on the original human language—from Philo, in the Alexandrian tradition, to Augustine, to Dante, to late fourteenth-century grammarians—saw it as a flawless language in which the name of a thing perfectly suited the thing's material nature:

> The names assigned are manifest images of the things, so that the name and thing are inevitably the same from the first, and the name and that to which the name is given differ not a whit.[4]

That original, single tongue, undivided in essence from things and undivided as yet into different languages, was constituted of sounds given by God. Dante, in fact, uncanonically assumes that Adam's first word must have been the word for "God" (*El*, the first language being Hebrew) rather than the names of beasts; Adam's first linguistic expression was of his most fundamental being, his essence as *imago Dei*.[5] In addition, some commentators saw Adam as the inventor not only of proper names but of letters. This was not a widespread notion— Moses was most often identified as the inventor of letters, with which the Law was written—but it is consistent with this view of Adam in the originary moments of language.[6]

But clearly something intervened between that originary moment in the garden and this moment of frustration in the scribal workshop. Adam scriveyn is hasty; his attention is divided, wavering, uncertain; his "werk"—the word itself refers to the *modus vivendi* of postlapsarian man—is defective and corrupt. The letters he inscribes apparently do not correspond to Chaucer's intent, his meaning.[7] As the narrator has lamented in the Epilogue to *Troilus and Criseyde*, there is "gret diversite / In Englissh and in writyng of oure tonge," and that diversity of the language imperils the intelligibility of Chaucer's texts. The language that Adam scriveyn uses is a fallen language: when mankind disobeyed God in the garden, the word was cut off from the Word, and the continuity of language and being was disrupted; after Babel, human language was split into many languages and dialects (a common rubric for Genesis 11 was "Confusio linguarum et dispersio populorum"). I shall discuss language and the Fall more fully in later chapters, but here I want to suggest that the situation "Chaucers Wordes unto Adam" delineates—divided attention; corruptible letters; a text that deviates from its author's intention; the necessity of "correccioun" (as the Parson will also put it); "negligence"; and, finally, "rape" (fallen sexuality)—is indeed resoundingly postlapsarian.

The idea that this Adam scriveyn might elicit associations with the first Adam is supported by a very popular Latin lyric of the twelfth century, in which "clericus Adam" sits under a certain tree and writes of "primus Adam":

> Arbore sub quadam dictauit clericus adam
> quomodo primus adam peccauit in arbore quadam.

The remarkable thing to me about this lyric—about fifty-five lines in all, the length varying slightly across versions—is its obsessive proportions: after these two lines, which almost invariably open the poem, follow forty-six lines beginning with the word "femina." It is classic, the paradigmatic poem of the medieval antifeminist tradition:

> femina uicit, adam uictus fuit arbore quadam;
> femina serpenti mox credidit alta loquenti.
> femina deceptos sapientes reddit ineptos;
> femina te, dauid, et te, salamon, superauit;
> femina decepit te sanson, et hoc tua fecit
> femina job; uicit genesis quoque quomodo dicit.
> femina . . .
> femina . . .
> femina . . .[8]

If, as R. E. Kaske also thinks, the words directed to "Adam scriveyn" resonate with figural overtones of "Adam primus," where is Eve, where is "femina," in Chaucer's poem?

She is the condition that motivates the lyric in the first place; she is what has caused its sad necessity to begin with. For, as "clericus Adam" put it, "Femina uicit, adam uictus fuit arbore quadam"; if Adam is the first namer, associated with a language that is unified, perfectly expressive of intent or spirit, Eve is associated with fallen language (in the *Ancrene Riwle* it is Eve's speech that is said to be the cause of the Fall)[9], with the division, difference, fragmentation, and dispersal that characterize the condition of historical language. If the first Adam is associated with the spirit of an utterance, Eve is associated with its letter, divided from intent or spirit, fragmentary, limited, and unstable. I shall locate these associations in medieval discussions of language in a moment; for now, let me note the diction Chaucer uses to admonish Adam: he is urged to "wryte more trewe." "Trewe": this is a loaded word in Chaucer's poetry, one that occurs frequently; among its various connotations in the texts, it is used to enunciate a—perhaps *the*—major problematic in Chaucer's narratives, the problem of truth in love. That problematic is very often focused on woman's truth—her honesty, her fidelity—or her significant lack of it. Men, of course, can be true, and their truth or lack thereof is also problematized in Chaucer; but unlike a man's fidelity, a woman's truth in love, as I shall argue in my discussion of *Troilus and Criseyde*, constitutes her function within the structure of patriarchal society. Criseyde, like Adam scriveyn, should have been "more trewe" ("Adam Scriveyn," 4); the women in the *Legend of Good Women* are, in contrast, "trewe in lovynge" (G:475); Constance and Griselda are tried and prove themselves "trewe" (2:456; 4:713); the test in the *Franklin's Tale* is a test of Dorigen's "trouthe" (5:759); the Wife of Bath is, in her own words, "kynde/ . . . And also trewe" (3:823–25). The problem of the corruptibility of the letter, itself associated with Eve, is expressed in "Adam Scriveyn" with a word that suggests its implication in a general problematics of the feminine. And when Adam as scribe is urged to be attentive (not negligent), patient (not hasty), "trewe" to his master's intent, conforming his will to that of the "maker," he is not only associated with the fallen letter but is urged to be, in a sense, like a woman—like Constance, say, or Griselda, whose desires, as we shall see, must conform to the desires of the men who possess them in patriarchal society.

But what of the obvious and age-old association of the pen with the phallus, celebrated, for instance, in two of Chaucer's favorite poems, *De planctu naturae* and *Le Roman de la rose*? Alain de Lille's *De planctu*, mentioned in the *Parliament of Fowls*, is noteworthy for the thoroughness with which it makes the metaphorical identification between writing and male penetration of the female.[10] And in the *Rose*—which is enumerated among Chaucer's translations in the Prologue to the *Legend of Good Women*—Genius' vivid exhortation to Amors' barons emphasizes that writing with this special stylus is necessary to the continuation of the human race.[11] The fallen Adam may be feminized, both in exegetical tradition and in relation to the "maker" Chaucer, but there is another lively tradition of sexualized literary discourse at work here with the opposite association. This tradition is activated, I suggest, by the poem's last word, which alludes to another consequence of the Fall and preserves Adam's masculinity: violent sexuality, "rape." This word is univocally glossed by Chaucer's editors as "haste"; the *Middle English Dictionary* cites this very line in its definition of "rape, noun (1)," derived from an Old Norse root. "Haste" is, no doubt, the primary denotation of the word here; but it seems to me that a secondary meaning, or at the very least a connotation, of sexual violation is evoked as well. The word "rape," it is true, occurs very seldom in Chaucer; "ravish" or "oppress" are the words he chooses most often for acts of sexual violation (remember, for example, that Troilus worries aloud to Criseyde in book 4 that Calkas will so praise some eligible Greek man "That ravysshen he shal yow with his speche" [4.1474]). But it seems very likely that "rape" had a sexual denotation by the mid-1380s, the probable date of the lyric.

According to the *MED*, in Chaucer's day two verbs "rapen" were current and idiomatic. One is derived from the Old Norse; this is "rapen, verb (1)"—"to make haste, hasten, hurry; rush, charge," and so on, as attested by citations from the thirteenth century on. The other, a Norman French borrowing that entered the English lexicon later than the Germanic word, is derived from the Latin *rapere* (cp. Anglo-French *raper*, Old French *rapir*); this is "rapen, verb (2)"—"to abduct (a woman), ravish, rape; also seduce (a man); to seize prey; to carry off; to fix (a certain time)," and so forth, as attested in works dating from about 1390. "Rape," the noun derived from this verb, is found in a legal document dating from 1291–92 to mean sexual violation. In the *Romaunt of the Rose* (1929, 6516; if he indeed made these particular translations), Chaucer uses "rape" derived from the first verb. But in *Troilus and Criseyde* he uses a noun derived from the second verb in an unequivocally sexual context: in book 4, Pandarus tries to convince Troilus to carry off Criseyde, saying, "It is no rape, in my dom, ne no vice / Hire to witholden that ye love moost" (4.596–97).[12]

What is more decisive for my purposes here, however, is the *MED*'s "rapen, verb (2) (e)," which defines the verb in an idiom, "rapen and rennen"—"to seize and make off with (something), *perhaps confused with rapen v. (1)*" (my emphasis). The dictionary cites line 1422 of Chaucer's *Canon's Yeoman's Tale* (c. 1395) as evidence: "Ye shul no thyng wynne on that chaffare, But wasten al that ye may rape [variant: rappe] and renne." It is precisely the possibility of such conflation of the two verbs that enables me to argue that "rape," as it appears in "Adam Scriveyn" (c. 1385), can denote sexual violation. The late Middle Ages was a time of great change in the English language, as this very word suggests, and it is entirely characteristic of Chaucer—a poet with a keen alertness to social shifts and changes—to choose to accentuate words that reflect, and are themselves in, transition or flux.[13] Late Middle English "rape" seems to be able to denote either haste, or abduction, or sexual violation, or a combination of these; and here, I maintain, it indeed carries a sexual charge.

If, then, "rape" in this short lyric does indeed connote a sexual act, what does it mean to say that Adam scriveyn "rapes" the text? The phrase's strong and assertively masculine associations suggest the idea that writing is a masculine act, an act performed on a body construed as feminine. I am not concerned here with the genitally focused sexual act but with its abstract gender structure, "gender" referring not to biologically determined sex ("male" and "female") but to sexual identities that are socially constructed ideas ("masculine" and "feminine"). I am concerned with masculine and feminine as roles, positions, functions that can be taken up, occupied, or performed by either sex, male or female (although not with equal ease or investment, as I shall suggest throughout this book). The poem's last word points out that literary activity has a gendered structure, a structure that associates acts of writing and related acts of signifying—allegorizing, interpreting, glossing, translating—with the masculine and that identifies the surfaces on which these acts are performed, or from which these acts depart, or which these acts reveal—the page, the text, the literal sense, or even the hidden meaning—with the feminine. As will become clear in the following pages, the significance and value of the masculine and the feminine in such a model of gendered hermeneutics constantly shift and change in the exegetical tradition and in Chaucer's poetry; Chaucer plays with the gender associations, hermeneutic values, and power relations this structure suggests. Some of the richness of, say, the denouement of the *Miller's Tale* lies in its playful reversal of this model so that the feminized Absolon brands with a hot poker—"writes" on—the naked body of the clerk Nicholas. Some of the Wife of Bath's peculiarly affirmative subversiveness is directed toward a radical revaluation of the feminine within this model. And some of the jolting power of the Pardoner's performance comes from his confounding any certain determination of gender and any interpretive models that depend on stable and distinct binary categories. It will be my project in this book to elaborate the varied and nuanced uses of gendered models of literary activity in Chaucer's works.

But we can already see the suppleness of Chaucer's ideas of gendered poetics, the flexibility and complexity with which language and literary acts, gender, and power are interrelated, in "Adam Scriveyn."

Whoever exerts control of signification, of language and the literary act, is associated with the masculine in patriarchal society—but that position can be seen to be occupied by both Chaucer and the scribe, and, in turn, the feminine is assumed as well by both characters. Adam, writer of a fallen letter, is associated with Eve (with his "long lokkes") and is feminized in relation to the "maker," Chaucer; but Chaucer, in turn, represents himself as the victim of scribal rape: his text, his work, his intent are violated by the pen of the scribe. I shall argue that it is such positioning of himself as feminine, in fact, his extraordinary and difficult attempts to envision fully the place of the Other in patriarchal society—to imagine even the pleasures and pains of a woman's body, be they May's feelings of sexual repugnance on her wedding night, the Wife of Bath's delight in past sensuality and her rueful awareness of present pain in her ribs, or Griselda's resistance to the public exposure of her "wombe"—that motivate, to a large extent, Chaucer's thematic concerns as well as the very forms and structures of his poetry.[14]

It may seem richly ironic that Chaucer should position himself in "Adam Scriveyn" as raped, not as rapist. Perhaps the one biographical fact everyone remembers about Chaucer, if one fact is going to be remembered, is that in 1380 Cecilia Chaumpaigne apparently threatened to accuse him of raping her. Parallel, we might say, to scholarly alacrity in glossing "rape" in line 7 as "haste" is the scholarly eagerness to vindicate the father, as it were, of English poesie of the charge of rape. From the moment of the discovery in 1873 of Cecilia Chaumpaigne's release to Chaucer of all legal action "tam de raptu meo, tam [sic] de aliqua alia re vel causa," debate raged about the meaning of "raptus" in fourteenth-century legal usage, the circumstances that surrounded such a release, the identity of the woman, the plausibility of the charge, even the date of birth and parentage of the "lyte Lowys my sone" whom Chaucer addresses in the *Treatise on the Astrolabe*. Scholarly research and debate over this incident have abated as interest in general in the biography of Chaucer has diminished in the later twentieth century; but the "strange case," as one scholar called it, has not been settled, and no scholarly consensus has ever been reached.[15] It is usually merely passed over as an "unfortunate incident" about which too little is known.[16] Robinson is paradigmatic here:

> It has sometimes been supposed that this referred to an act of physical rape. . . . But it is more generally believed that the case was one of civil "raptus," or abduction. . . . It has recently been argued that

in 1380, after the passage of the Statute of Westminster, "raptus" would have meant "rape," as it is there defined. But the circumstances of the Chaumpaigne case, and Chaucer's connection with them, still remain unknown.[17]

But even by the time of Robinson's second edition, from which I quote here, it had been established that "raptus" in fourteenth-century legal usage denoted either abduction or sexual violation or *both*. [18] The *Riverside Chaucer* (1987) acknowledges this, but emphasizes that although the meaning of "raptus" is ambiguous, "the record, however, is clear; it means that Cecilia Chaumpaigne clears Chaucer of all responsibility." [19] The interpretation of all the documents surrounding this case (the releases by Goodchild and Grove to Chaucer of all legal actions; the release by Cecilia Chaumpaigne to Goodchild and Grove; the payment by Grove to Cecilia of ten pounds) is disputed, but a sexual incident involving Cecilia and Chaucer does seem to have taken place. Legal historian Theodore Plucknett wrote in 1948—in an argument that itself has not been challenged since—that "if only abduction had been involved, the release would have proceeded from the injured party, *viz.*, the feudal lord, parent, husband, or employer of Cecilia." Haldeen Braddy maintains that there is no reason to suspect (as Plucknett does, in a sudden and unsubstantiated reversal of the apparently intolerable implications of his argument) that the charges were brought by Cecilia against Chaucer falsely or in bad faith.[20]

It is mere happenstance that we have this record. Like all the *Life-Records*, it does not mention that Chaucer was a poet. But it is a very felicitous circumstance that it exists alongside the poetry; it reminds us that there are not only *figurative* rapes—the writer's intent raped by the scribe's pen, the text as woman's body violated by the interpretations of literary and exegetical tradition—and there are not only *fictional* rapes—the rape of Philomela, the rape of Helen, the rape of the maiden in the *Wife of Bath's Tale*—but there are *real* rapes as well. It forces us, first of all, to face the literal reality that such a metaphorical identification can obscure, and it keeps in front of us the *difference* between literary activity and sexual violation. To equate reading with rape would be to underestimate drastically the transgressive reality of rape, on the one hand, and to slight the potentially positive value of literary interpretation, on the other.[21] But this fact also invites us to consider causal relationships between gendered representation and actual social relations between men and women; it invites us to consider the relations that form the bases for figurative discourse and that, in turn, are affected by literary representation. In the first chapters of this book, I shall analyze Chaucer's poetry in terms of its allegorical representation of the text as a woman read and interpreted by men; similarly, in the last chapter I shall analyze the poetry as it figuratively represents hermeneutic values in the gender of the Pardoner. But in the chapters on the Wife of Bath and Griselda, and in aspects of my consideration of the Pardoner, I shall suggest that this very representation of literary activity has actual social consequences: it has real, and negative, effects on lived lives.

Thus it is the figurative gender value and implications of literary representation that will concern me, for the most part but not exclusively, in this book. As I remarked above, in treating gender I am interested in analyzing masculine and feminine as positions that can be occupied by either sex; thus I shall speak of "reading *like* a man" in *Troilus and Criseyde* and the *Legend of Good Women* and not "reading *as* a man."[22] Women can and do read like men, and—perhaps more importantly—men don't have to read like men. I shall suggest that the Clerk, in fact, reads like a woman. Cross-gender identifications are not made with equal ease or maintained with equal consequences by men and by women, however; I am concerned, in the cases of the *Wife of Bath's Tale* and the *Clerk's Tale*, to determine what exactly it might mean for a man in patriarchal culture to take up the feminine place. In the case of the Pardoner, I want to discuss the consequences of an individual's not clearly identifying with either gender. Chaucer, I suggest, is alert to the social construction of gender and to the patriarchal power structures that keep these gender notions in place. But, in addition, he shows an important awareness of the difficult relations between abstract or figurative gender formulations and people with real bodies and "sely instruments." The Wife of Bath points to the distance that can open up between clerkly notions (gender) and biological sex; Griselda and the Pardoner both point up the actual consequences, borne on male and female bodies, of gendered hermeneutic formulations. Accordingly, the literal, or real, social effects of gendered literary metaphorics and formulations are my concerns as well.[23]

If this reading of "Adam Scriveyn" should seem too preoccupied with gender and sex—if my reading of scribal practice, of "trewe" and of "rape" should seem to ascribe unwarranted significance to the literary and social relationships represented in this lyric—I ask the dubious reader to consider the language of modern textual editing. Its pervasively moralized, gendered diction, I suggest, explicitly carries into the modern age the tradition I have been describing here, the fundamental correlation between language and literary interpretation, on the one hand, with gender, on the other. We might note in passing that Petrarch, whose literary concerns as humanist can be seen in part as forerunners of modern textual studies, puts scribal practice in a moral framework as he commends a certain scribe for his *castigata* letters—his neat, chaste hand. (Petrarch also, in desperation and with high expectations, as he tells a correspondent, employed a priest as scribe.)[24] But the conventional, moralizing diction of modern textual criticism makes the point clearly enough: scribes "corrupt," they "contaminate"; the editor seeks "fair" copies, seeks "purity" of the text, avoids texts of "mixed" character. As Eugène Vinaver remarks, the term "textual criticism" itself "implies a mistrust of texts."[25] Of course the discourse of modern textual editing is indisputably informed by late nineteenth-century preoccupations—Darwinist theory, to mention one—but I would suggest that there is an older tradition informing this diction as well.

The basic procedure of textual editing as it was practiced in the nineteenth century by Karl Lachmann, among others, consisted of the construction of genealogical stemmata. This fundamental model of textual criticism was thus based on the model of the family. Although stemmatics (and, in particular, classification by shared error) has come to be questioned by some textual scholars, the familial model of cataloging manuscripts is still employed by all editors: they construct family trees, construe family resemblances, hypothesize parent texts, ancestors, and patriarchs. In this context, moral and gender relationships are obviously immanent. One recent historian of textual editing, commenting on the "desire" at "the heart of every editorial procedure," in fact speaks of the "libido" of the model of stemmatics.[26] E. Talbot Donaldson's elaborate sexual scenario of textual editing in his article "The Psychology of Editors of Middle English Texts" thus differs only in its explicitness—differs in degree, not in kind—from the discourse of his colleagues:

> The editor, not unlike a bachelor choosing a bride, selects Line Form A for his text. For a time he lives in virtuous serenity, pleased with his decision. A year or more passes, and then one day it comes to him, like a bolt from the blue, that he should, of course, have chosen Line Form B; in short, he married the wrong girl. She is attractive, she is plausible, she has her points, but he just can't live with her; he lies awake at nights enumerating her faults, which seem considerable when she is compared with her rejected rival, who now appears infinitely preferable. So the editor (who is the least reliable of all possible husbands) obtains a divorce. . . . His marriage with Line

Form B is now consecrated, and he settles down to live happily ever after. Then after a year or so, Wife B begins to prove incompatible in a different and even more annoying way than Wife A. . . .[27]

When Donaldson ponders the question of whether a particular manuscript is "a chaste virgin" or a "scarlet whore,"[28] he is participating in a discourse, I suggest, that Chaucer himself understood intimately.

2

From "Adam Scriveyn," one of Chaucer's "minor poems," we thus gain access to a major nexus of late-medieval ideas concerning literary activity and gender relations. The variety, range, and popularity in the Middle Ages of works which represent literary activity by means of gendered models argue for the fundamental nature of this correlation between the use and interpretation of language, on the one hand, and the social relations and organization of gendered bodies, on the other hand. The models are indeed various: I shall focus on the particular figure of the text as woman's body, but I do so only because of practical limitations of space and time; other sexual metaphorics were commonplace and influential in the literary culture of the later Middle Ages. To mention just a few: the Ovidian recommendation to lovers to use poetry as a seduction (*Ars amatoria* 3.329–46) and Ovid's own demonstration that love follows a rhetoric—that the art of love might be seen more precisely as an art of reading and writing love poetry—informs the romantic use of the book as a go-between (consider Paolo and Francesca's use of the *Lancelot* as a "Galeotto" in *Inferno* 5, and Chaucer's own narrator's offering *Troilus and Criseyde* as an aid to lovers in his audience).[29] The imaging of literary creation as a dissemination, a scattering of seed, may owe something to Matthew 13:3–23 (the parable of the sower); it is perhaps behind Dante's representation in *Inferno* 15 of the author Brunetto Latini, who, as sodomite, scatters seed where it cannot grow.[30] Plowing a field, an image related to dissemination, is used as a figure both for sexual intercourse (see Alain de Lille, for example, in *De planctu naturae*, and the *Roman de la rose*, 19513-762) and for literary creation (Chaucer's Prologue to the *Legend of Good Women* and the *Knight's Tale* both allude to this figure). And "Adam Scriveyn" itself might be read to suggest not just the text as woman's body but, alternatively, the text as child of the "maker," an offspring that has been abducted ("raped" in this sense) by the scribe; such a reading would be supported by the narrator's admonitions to his "litel bok" at the end of *Troilus and Criseyde*. Love, sex, gender, and literary activity are intimately, metaphorically related in the Middle

Ages. That Chaucer's early narrators are all outsiders in matters of love thus indicates something about their literary practice, and erotic models of literary activity provide us with some broadly based ways to read power relations between *auctores*, narrators, and readers.

In fact, literary activity as it is represented in Chaucer is always, I believe, a gendered activity; it is an activity that is represented in terms of relationships between people and that expresses larger principles of social organization and social power. In the earliest of the dream visions, the *Book of the Duchess*, reading is a substitute for a love affair and itself has an erotic valence (and that erotics, in turn, expresses relationships of authority and power between author and reader); in the strange and shifting *House of Fame* the love story of Dido and Aeneas forms one third of a triptych, the rest of which is an anatomy of literary tradition and literary authority; in the *Parliament of Fowls* the act of reading yields a dream of courtship. These varied sexual poetics extend to the *Canterbury Tales*, early and late: in the *Second Nun's Tale*, for example, the desire to demonstrate the fullness of meaning of Cecilia's name is related to the desire to preserve virginity, the purity of the female body; in the *Nun's Priest's Tale* "glossing" is a tool of masculine sexual conquest; and in the *Manciple's Tale* Phoebus, god of lyric poetry, breaks his "mynstralcie" with a gesture identical to the one by which he kills his wife. Throughout Chaucer's poetic corpus, I argue, literary representation is understood in terms of the body—the body as it enters into social interactions, as it functions in social organization, as it is assigned gender value in the transactions that constitute social structure. Even in the *Retractions*, as we shall see at last, the renunciation of fables is performed with reference to a body—to the incarnate Christ, who was sent down to earth in human form in a divine commercial transaction, a holy trade: Chaucer, even in this final redefinition of his poetics, invokes the embodied "Lord Jhesu Crist . . . that boghte us with the precious blood of his herte" (10:1090).[31]

This statement—that literary activity in Chaucerian narrative is significantly represented as a gendered activity—is founded on a broader claim—that Chaucer's poetics is essentially gendered—and, broadest claim of all here—that language (signifying activity) is essentially structured in relation to gender. This claim about language is of course not new: it is widely accepted that language, whether seen from an anthropological, sociological, psychoanalytic, philosophical, or theological point of view, is structured in very basic ways by relations between males and females. Two such accounts of language and gender relations—one by Claude Lévi-Strauss, the other by Jacques Lacan—

will be particularly important to my analysis of Chaucer in the chapters to follow. I shall detail them later; here I shall simply sketch them. Lévi-Strauss contends (as explicated by Gayle Rubin) that society as we know it—patriarchal society—is constituted by "traffic in women," the exchange of women between groups of men that is motivated by the prohibition of incest, and that women function therein, as do empty linguistic signs, in forming bonds between men.[32] Lacan revises Freud, suggesting that the infant enters language—enters the realm of signification—at the precise moment, again due to the prohibition of incest, at which he or she turns away from primary identification with the mother toward the figure of the father.[33]

What is especially important in these paradigms for my analyses is not, in fact, their putative value in describing a universal truth about language but, rather, their specifically patriarchal and misogynistic character. Both the anthropologist and the psychoanalyst here— whose theories of relations between social and linguistic structures are themselves clearly related—make signification dependent upon the passivity, blankness, or absence of woman.[34] I suggest that between the Middle Ages (although it did not originate there) and the modern day there is a continuity of such patriarchal thinking about signifying; I suggest that these modern articulations are inflections of a very long patriarchal tradition of understanding language and literary activity. Such specific inflections vary from age to age, but, I argue, the abstract social forms and structures remain constant. In Chaucer's time, for example, bourgeois wives legally were not property in any simple sense, but the form of the exchange of women does not itself depend upon legal ownership. Lévi-Strauss's paradigm of patriarchal social organization as a traffic in women usefully describes medieval hermeneutic paradigms—and it does so, I claim, because *both* modern and medieval theorists participate in the same kind of patriarchal thinking, the same ideology. Lacan's paradigm of signification elucidates the Pardoner's performance, and that correspondence between medieval and modern has similar implications. I shall argue that Chaucer's works point to a critique of patriarchal conceptions of language and literary activity—conceptions at work in recent criticism of Chaucer as well as in larger theoretical formulations about language, the self, and society—and that they suggest alternatives to such misogynistic formulations.

I maintain, indeed, that the modern theories I engage and the medieval texts and ideas I discuss—Lacanian theory and Augustinian language theory, for example—are related through what might be called a philosophical or intellectual-historical tradition; their relationship, I think, is not only heuristic. Some such relationship has already been acknowledged, in fact, as when Lacan cites Augustine's *De magistro* in stating that "no signification can be sustained other than by reference to another signification," an idea about language that has powerful anxiety-generating capacity in the Pardoner's performance.[35] But the continuity of sexual poetics remains largely undiscussed. An important part of my general critical project, as I see it, will be to describe a medieval philosophical tradition (or, more precisely, the medieval component of what I take to be an ancient philosophical tradition) informing modern theoretical preoccupations and formulations, as I have already briefly done in my suggestions about modern textual editing in reference to "Adam Scriveyn." I want to develop, that is, a more extensive intellectual context for understanding certain modern literary-critical formulations and hermeneutic obsessions than has heretofore been delineated. My discussion of a medieval sexual poetics provides a fuller cultural context for the idea, current in feminist literary criticism, of the text as woman's body, inscribed, read, and interpreted by men;[36] it writes, that is, a history of feminist critical theory. Moreover, it suggests a context for understanding the significance of Barthes's poststructuralist formulation of "the pleasure of the text" and the gender implications of that formulation. Chaucer's literary concerns may sound quite modern in this book, but I would prefer to say that our present-day critical concerns turn out to be quite medieval.

Although it follows from my remarks on the fundamental nature of this tradition that Chaucer is not unique in his constant coordination of poetics and gender, he is nonetheless noteworthy for his penetration, as it were, of these ideas, for the thoroughness, flexibility, and variety of his engagement with and exploration of traditional formulations. I now want to sketch out, roughly and with broad strokes, the medieval literary-interpretive context of Chaucer's sexual poetics. More particularly, I want to outline the context for his repeated, subtle, exploratory use of the figurative identification of the text with woman or the principle of the feminine. The representation of the allegorical text as a veiled or clothed woman and the concomitant representation of various literary acts—reading, translating, glossing, creating a literary tradition—as masculine acts performed on this feminine body recur across narratives as various in thematics and structure as *Troilus and Criseyde*, the *Legend of Good Women*, and the *Canterbury Tales*. Though not the only representation of literary activity in Chaucer, this image of the text as veiled woman focuses Chaucer's narrative and hermeneutic concerns with particular clarity and locates them within

large structures of social organization. It is to the literary development
of this image through the Middle Ages that I shall now turn.

3

Richard of Bury, bishop of Durham in the mid-fourteenth century,
makes the masculine structure of literary tradition exceptionally clear
in his *Philobiblon* (completed in 1345), and hence this work makes an
apt starting point for my investigation of the gender valence of medieval literary activity. Richard openly identifies the care and preservation of books with the care and preservation of the patriarchy.

The bishop of Durham wrote his treatise in defense of his vast and
costly collection of books: his detractors had accused him of lavishing
too much money and attention on them. (At the same time that he
was defending his library, he was defending his embattled northern
diocese against the Scots, and his king against the French.) Books,
both ancient and modern, Richard argues, contain the treasure of wisdom and thus must be preserved. He urgently exhorts men not to be
seduced (*subtrahit*) away from the "paternal care of books" (*paterna cultura librorum*) by the lures of "stomach, dress, or houses" (which are,
we note, the Wife of Bath's concerns).[37] Paternal care is necessary to
preserve the purity of the race of books against the loss of their ancient
nobility, against defilement by imposters pretending to be authors:
paternal care is necessary lest "the sons," as he puts it, be "robbed of
the names of their true fathers."[38] Indeed, the handing down or tran-
scribing of ancient books, Richard writes, "is, as it were, the begetting
of fresh sons, on whom the office of the father may devolve, lest it suffer detriment."[39] The ideas of passing on old books and of old books'
essential role in new learning were common enough in the Middle
Ages. No one, however, discloses the patriarchal investment in this
idea more forthrightly than Richard. In the act of preserving books,
Richard argues, one protects against violations of property, territory,
lineage, and family—against violations of the patriarchy.

Women's active participation in a literary culture characterized in
this way was obviously extremely limited. To be sure, some women in
the Middle Ages *did* own and compose texts—a few overcame institu-
tional obstacles and obtained the necessary education and leisure to
read and write.[40] And, by the late fourteenth century, they passed on
their books to their daughters as well as to their sons.[41] But women's
disenfranchisement within the literary sphere was certain, and medieval attitudes about women's expression preserved strong classical
and biblical prohibitions.[42] Juvenal writes, for example, in his *Sixth*

Satire, that virulently antifeminist diatribe whose influence extended to Walter Map, Jean de Meun, and Boccaccio: "Wives shouldn't try to be public speakers; they shouldn't use rhetorical devices; they shouldn't read all the classics—there ought to be some things women don't understand."[43] Aristotle's theory of social class structure in his *Politics* is based on the prohibition of women's expression:

> All classes must be deemed to have their special attributes; as the poet [Sophocles] says of women, "Silence is a woman's glory"; but this is not equally the glory of man.[44]

Aquinas, in his commentary on the *Politics,* repeats this formula—as does Averroës in his commentary on the Aristotelian text—and corroborates it with a biblical injunction, Saint Paul's prohibition (in 1 Cor. 14:34–35) of women's speaking in public: "Let women keep silence in the churches: for it is not permitted them to speak, but to be subject, as also the law saith. But if they would learn anything, let them ask their husbands at home" ("Mulieres in ecclesiis taceant, non enim permittitur eis loqui, sed subditas esse, sicut et lex dicit. Si quid autem volunt discere, domi viros suos interrogent"). Aquinas conflates the classical and biblical traditions and continues the discourse in his own works.[45] Significantly, Saint Paul's admonition to Timothy (in 1 Tim. 2:11–12) about women's speaking—"Let the women learn in silence, with all subjection. But I suffer not a woman to teach, nor to use authority over the man: but to be in silence" ("Mulier in silentio discat cum omni subiectione. Docere autem mulierem non permitto, neque dominari in virum: sed esse in silentio")—directly follows his admonitions (in 1 Tim. 2:9–10) about the adornment of women's bodies: such proscriptions as these on women's teaching, women's speaking, women's writing reflect intense and anxious responses to woman's physical being.[46]

A defining characteristic of the female, in both classical and Christian exegetical traditions, is her corporeality, her association with matter and the physical body as opposed to the male's association with form and soul.[47] Aristotle's political analysis of woman, mentioned above, is clearly related to his theory of the metaphysical female principle as *steresis,* the totally passive privation of the male principle, and is subtended by his association of her physical being with matter (as opposed to the male being, which is characterized by form, animation, and generation).[48] As Vern L. Bullough has suggested, assumptions about woman's body common in the ancient world were powerful determinants of the development of medieval law and doctrine regarding women: woman was seen in various classical medical and scientific writings as defective, deformed, or mutilated man; man turned inside out; a creature whose anatomy wouldn't stay still; a creature who needed to be kept under control.[49] Medieval limitations of woman's expression seem, in the final analysis, inseparable from the regulation of woman's body. The history, established recently, of the gynecological treatises by Trotula (who is included in Jankyn's "book of wikked wyves") is itself a neat testimony to the correlation between the masculine silencing of women's writing (and appropriation of women's voices) and the masculine control of their bodies: as John F. Benton has demonstrated, three treatises commonly attributed in the Middle Ages to Trotula were in fact written by men, whose control of medical theory and gynecological literature in the Middle Ages was complete.[50] The intense emotion—simultaneous fascination and repulsion—behind the connection of woman's body and woman's speech is expressed in Jean Gerson's almost obsessive comment about Saint Bridget: he speaks of her "insatiable itch to see and to speak, not to mention . . . the itch to touch."[51]

But clearly, if we return to consider Richard of Bury's genealogical allegory of literary tradition, we can see that a female is necessary to perpetuate the lineage, however passive her participation may be.[52] And thus it is *her* purity upon which the purity of the race depends.[53] This necessary protection of woman's purity associates her, allegorically, with the wisdom that must be protected, the truth contained in the old books to be preserved by the *paterna cultura*. Writing a few years after Richard of Bury, Boccaccio suggests an association of the female with the truth contained within books when, in his *Genealogia deorum gentilium*, he declares that the truth must be protected from the "gaze of the irreverent," so that "they cheapen not by too common familiarity."[54] And in this connection he points elsewhere in the *Genealogia* to the opening of Macrobius' commentary on the *Somnium Scipionis* (c. 400). At the beginning of that commentary, Macrobius presents a fully sexualized image of truths that must not be prostituted, must not be made into whores. He writes that the secrets of Nature that the text contains are wrapped in mysteries, veiled in the mysterious representations of fabulous narratives, so that the vulgar may not see and profane them. In an exemplum, Macrobius cites the brash Numenius, who expounded the sacred Eleusinian mysteries and thereby made prostitutes of them: the Eleusinian goddesses appeared to Numenius in a dream, wearing the garments of courtesans and standing by an open brothel.[55] The body of Nature, as Macrobius argues—or *nuda veritas*, as Richard of Bury refers to the hidden body—must be kept secret, clothed in the garments, veils, protective coverings of fiction, poetry, mystery.

This is, of course, the standard medieval analysis of the allegorical text: it contains truth veiled by obscurity. Augustine, Lactantius, Isidore of Seville, Vincent of Beauvais, Petrarch, Dante, Boccaccio use this figure of the veil to describe passages in both biblical and secular literature.[56] The figure is used in the service of quite different arguments, of course: Augustine identifies the veil of allegorical language in both biblical and pagan texts, delighting in the scriptural passages while condemning the pagan; Augustine's condemnation was mitigated through the period, as Lee Patterson remarks, until, at the end of the Middle Ages, Boccaccio argues for the licitness of the act of reading pagan fable.[57] Nonetheless, the structure of the allegorical text and the process of reading it remain the same from Augustine to Boccaccio: the spiritually healthy reader will discover the truth under the veil of fiction, under the covering of poetical words. As Boccaccio argues, fiction pleases even the unlearned by its surface blandishments, and it exercises the minds of the learned in the discovery of its beautiful, hidden truth (*Genealogia* 14.9).

So allegorical interpretation is, in this sense, undressing the text —unveiling the truth, revealing a body figuratively represented as female. This interpretive activity is only for initiates of the highest intelligence, Macrobius argues; only available to the learned, Boccaccio argues; and only for men, as the diction of heterosexual culture suggests. Richard of Bury, again, provides a clear example of this gendering of allegorical reading: in describing the difficult and tedious task of discovering the truth in a classical text, he uses the language of seduction: "The wisdom of the ancients devised a remedy by which to entice the wanton minds of men by a kind of pious fraud, the delicate Minerva secretly lurking beneath the image of pleasure."[58] The garments—that "image of pleasure"—seduce the reader to look further, to the body of Minerva. The image appeals to the "wanton minds of men" through the senses. It is the lying surface, the letter of the text, the *signifier*.

But according to Richard of Bury (and Augustine before him), the reader must pass beyond that pleasurable surface, the signifier, to the hidden truth beneath, the signified.[59] To stop at the image of pleasure is to succumb to the seductions directed at the reader's "wantonness." To stop at the signifier is to enjoy something that should be used, to put it in Augustine's terms in the *De doctrina christiana* (3.5.7). In Richard's statement, then, we have the suggestion of another discourse, one that *reverses* the valence of woman as truth of the text: it's the patristic association of the surface of the text (the letter) with carnality (the flesh, the body), and carnality with woman—an association I alluded to earlier in reference to "Adam Scriveyn." Taking pleasure of the text is analogous to taking carnal pleasure of a woman: "letter" and "bele chose" are the site of that illicit bliss. Woman, in this Pauline model of reading, is not the "hidden truth" but is dangerous cupidity: she is what must be passed through, gone beyond, left, discarded, to get to the truth, the spirit of the text. When Dante, in *Inferno* 9, admonishes his reader to "mark the doctrine under the veil of strange verses," he links that veil with the threat of feminine beauty posed by Medusa.[60]

Saint Paul associated the letter of the text with death—with everything old, sinful; with things of the flesh. The text, as Claudius of Turin (c. 800) suggested of Scripture, has a body and a soul; to read literally is to read carnally (*litteraliter vel carnaliter*).[61] Earlier, Origen was concerned that the spiritual meaning of the Song of Songs could be missed by the carnal man; he warns not only that the carnally minded reader should not read this text but that youths should not even hold it in their hands—as though it is itself a dangerously seductive body.[62] The further association of the body, the carnal, with woman is commonplace in exegetes throughout the Middle Ages, from the church fathers to Chaucer's Parson: in tropological accounts of the Fall (by Philo of Alexandria, Augustine, John Scottus Eriugena, and the Parson, to name a few), Eve is associated with the carnal appetite, Adam with higher intellectual faculties. I've already alluded to the fallenness of language, in reference to "Adam Scriveyn"—the letter's fragmented, transitory nature, its association with the postlapsarian, newly mortal body and with Eve. Boccaccio associates the letter with "the fruit of sin," as seductive and enticing as the temptation used on the first woman and by her on the first man.[63]

To follow out this Pauline model of reading would mean to discard altogether the model of woman as central, naked truth of the text, to rigorously pass through the text's female body on the way to its spirit —its male spirit, as Ambrose and others suggest.[64] Augustine dismissed pagan fable as worthless precisely because he considered it to have only false or empty "spirit" below its enticing letter.[65] But Jerome addresses the problem of reading classical fable using a subtler model —Jerome, author of the notoriously antifeminist *Adversus Jovinianum* (a text the Wife of Bath knows and abhors), and a reader who was plagued by the seductions of classical style.[66] He likens the classical text to the beautiful captive woman in Deuteronomy 21:10–13.[67] The biblical passage reads:

> Si egressus fueris ad pugnam contra inimicos tuos, et tradiderit eos
> Dominus Deus tuus in manu tua, captivosque duxeris, et videris in

numero captivorum mulierem pulchram, et adamaveris eam, volue-
risque habere uxorem, introduces eam in domum tuam: quae radet
caesariem, et circumcidet ungues, et deponet vestem, in qua capta
est: sedensque in domo tua, flebit patrem et matrem suam uno
mense: et postea intrabis ad eam, dormiesque cum illa, et erit uxor
tua.

[If thou go out to fight against thy enemies, and the Lord thy God
deliver them into thy hand, and thou lead them away captives, And
seest in the number of the captives a beautiful woman, and lovest
her and wilt have her to wife, Thou shalt bring her into thy house:
and she shall shave her hair, and pare her nails, And shall put off
the raiment, wherein she was taken: and shall remain in thy house,
and mourn for her father and mother one month: and after that thou
shalt go in unto her, and shalt sleep with her, and she shall be thy
wife.]

Jerome defends his reading of the pagan text on the basis of its carnal
attractiveness, the elegance of classical style: "Is it surprising that I,
too, admiring the fairness of her form and the grace of her eloquence,
desire to make that secular wisdom which is my captive and hand-
maid, a matron of the true Israel?" [68] He is attracted by its beauty, but,
finally, the way to read the pagan text properly is to *divest* it of its sinful seductions, its Pauline deadness: to strip it of its garments, shave
its hair, and pare its nails.

Nevertheless, the text, though stripped, doesn't stop being a
woman. The Pauline model *would* discard the female when the male
spirit has been uncovered. But Jerome's captive woman is instead betrothed and married (indeed, this is an enactment of the paradigm
of marriage as a trade of women between men at war that Lévi-
Strauss outlines); she begets servants for God, just like Richard of
Bury's "sons." The truth of the text is itself feminine and fertile. The
alien woman, of an enemy people, has been won by the triumphant
warrior; her pagan seductions have been removed, but her essential
beauties are nurtured by washing, shaving, and clothing and are now
put to Christian use. The text's wisdom and truth are the key to the
increase and multiplication of the faithful; the warrior takes the alien
from her people, has her unclothed and reclothed in a ritual prepa-
ration for the nuptials, and transforms her from alien seductress to
fecund wife.

Jerome thus represents the reading of the pagan text as a captive
woman's passage between men, her marriage, and her domestication.

The reader is drawn to the text by its attractive appearance; the text is then interpreted—stripped of its stylistic and fictional blandishments, revealing and preparing its wisdom for Christian use. Jerome stresses the harsh necessity of taking a sharp razor to the woman, of making her bald, of scrubbing her with niter, of getting rid of all her carnal attractions.[69] That harshness is an index of the urgency in early Christendom of putting behind the temptations of pagan literature. But the act of interpretation is itself pleasurable, as the metaphor of ritual purification and arraying for the bridal suggests.[70] The tradition of later exegetes who use this figure of the beautiful captive confirms this sense that both harshness and pleasure are intimated here: the commentators fall into two camps, "les accueillants et les sévères," according to de Lubac.[71] Augustine acknowledges this pleasure of interpretation—with a certain amount of wonder—in relation to the figurative surface of some scriptural passages, in his *De doctrina*:

> No one doubts that things are perceived more readily through similitudes and that what is sought with difficulty is discovered with more pleasure.[72]

There is pleasure in the very act of interpretation—in the discovering and converting the truth of the text under the figures and ornaments of its letter. Boccaccio quotes both Augustine and Petrarch (*Invectives*, bk. 3) on this "delightful task" (*Genealogia* 14.12).

In Jerome's example of the captive woman, the pleasure is one-way: the woman's desires are not consulted or recognized. Indeed, as she is passed between men, from alien camp to Israelite household, masculine desire is the only motivating force. Guillaume de St.-Thierry calls attention (albeit inadvertently) to this ignoring of the female's desire (continued by all the others who follow Jerome's use of the figure) when he unprecedentedly adapts the captive image to represent the human soul longing for Christ, the victorious warrior.[73] In other uses of the image, by Peter Damian and Gregory IX, for example, the woman is to be "enslaved" by the warrior. Gregory IX reduces the image rather severely in an early twelfth-century letter: the captive woman should be obedient and subject to the warrior, just as man should dominate woman and spirit should dominate flesh.[74] Any subtle attractions and interactions of bride and warrior, text and interpreter are eliminated by Gregory here, and one point is clear: no independent desire of woman is vouchsafed. The value of the feminine (and the letter) is thus shifting and contradictory in exegetical tradition, ranging from Jerome's apparent nurturing of the feminine to Gregory's drastic reduction. But the hermeneutic paradigm itself remains resolutely patriarchal.

4

Chaucer's use of this hermeneutic is subtle and nuanced, demonstrating both his investment in patriarchal discourse and his awareness of its limitations. Chaucerians have by now, in this post-Robertsonian age, recognized that the poet deeply and persistently engaged patristic and postpatristic thought in his major works, but I suggest here a new aspect of his use of it, and, further, I suggest that his relationship to that discourse is shifting and flexible. Chaucer attempts to discern the consequences for literature and literary tradition, and the effects on lived lives, of understanding literary endeavor as masculine acts performed on feminine bodies. As I shall suggest in the chapters to follow, in *Troilus and Criseyde* and the *Legend of Good Women* the narrator, emphatically masculine, engages with his pagan source texts as if they were women, treats them in ways analogous to the ways in which male lovers in the narratives treat their women. In the *Man of Law's Tale*, pale Constance is traded between pagan shores just as the tale itself (along with other merchandise) has been traded across the seas; she is a blank, an empty sign, exchanged between men in the linguistic and commercial transactions that constitute patriarchal social structure. In all three of these narratives, interpretive acts are performed on an ultimately powerless feminine corpus.

But the alien woman herself speaks, as it were, in the Wife of Bath's Prologue and *Tale* and the *Clerk's Tale*, and the social effects of such patriarchal and misogynistic models of literary production—the unhappy consequences of the occlusion of feminine desire—are given urgent expression by the voices of the Wife and Griselda. Through the Wife of Bath's performance Chaucer suggests the possibility of a renovated patriarchal hermeneutic that acknowledges, even solicits, feminine desire; but this essentially sympathetic acknowledgment of the value of the feminine, though necessary and just, is seen in the *Clerk's Tale* to be impossible within the confines of a gender-asymmetrical patriarchal hermeneutic.

It is finally the Pardoner, however, who provides the most radically denaturalizing perspective on the hermeneutic model of woman as text read by man. He is outside this patriarchal—and heterosexual—hermeneutic altogether: his body, unlike the beautiful and distinctly feminine body of truth in the Hieronymian model, instead defies distinct gender categories of masculine and feminine (the narrator of the

General Prologue, indeed, can't tell exactly *what* he is). The Pardoner destablizes this hermeneutic project with its clear and certain discovery procedures by confounding binary oppositions such as man/woman, surface/meaning, truth/falsehood. His use of language in his pardons, sermons, and *Tale*—acknowledging their falsity while accepting them as true—thoroughly problematizes any traditional hermeneutic model. Only a language of presence, suggested in Chaucer's *Retractions* in his invocation of the incarnate Word, can adequately counter the radical absence on which the Pardoner's poetics is founded.

This series of texts—*Troilus and Criseyde*, the *Legend of Good Women*, the *Man of Law's Tale*, the *Wife of Bath's Tale* and its Prologue, the *Clerk's Tale*, and the *Pardoner's Tale*—forms a coherent narrative sequence of its own as well as a textual group whose iconography and thematics are closely coordinated. Each text after *Troilus and Criseyde* contains at least one character who is figured as having read the previous work. We recall, of course, that the narrator of *Troilus and Criseyde* is reading and responding to "Lollius' " tale of the lovers. In the Prologue to the *Legend of Good Women*, the God of Love and Alceste have read *Troilus and Criseyde*; they demand an explanation for it and reparation for the damages it has wreaked on the reputation of women—and the *Legend* is the result. The Man of Law, in turn, has read the legends, and solemnly approves of them; he is so impressed by Chaucer's propriety in writing them that he sets out to emulate them in his own *Tale*. But after his *Tale*, at the prospect of more solemnity and "difficulte," the Wife of Bath bursts out with her Prologue and *Tale*. Her Prologue is soon interrupted by the Pardoner; and the Clerk, in turn, wittily refers to her at the end of his own *Tale*. [75] While considering this group of texts as thus linked, however, I don't intend to ignore their formal diversity. *Troilus and Criseyde* is obviously and importantly a different kind of narrative undertaking from the *Legend of Good Women* and from the *Canterbury Tales*. [76] I shall argue, indeed, that the structure of *Troilus and Criseyde* has itself a gendered valence, in its positioning of an explicitly masculine narrator who manipulates the feminine text; in contrast, the narrative structure of the *Tales*, the structure of impersonation, is informed by a double perspective that I identify, apropos of Griselda, as "reading like a woman."

I have spoken of several characters just now—the Pardoner, the Wife of Bath, Griselda—as embodiments or reifications of patristic images and hermeneutic ideas. I consider all of these characters to carry symbolic or allegorical significance; that is, I read them as educing a tradition of patristic figuration or as signifying typologically (as does Adam, in "Adam Scriveyn"). But I want to suggest that they have psychological dimensions as well: they have the capacity to make choices—I understand the Man of Law to have chosen not to talk about incest, for example—and they have a certain interiority—the Pardoner's behavior, for another example, is motivated by his own sense of lack. My approach can be further distinguished from conventional iconographical or allegorical readings in its proposal that a telling metacritical level can be discerned in the poetry: I shall suggest that Chaucer explores via the Wife of Bath and Griselda in particular the consequences of using these literary forms, representations, models in the definition of human lives.[77] Chaucer does not passively employ an image or reify a traditional idea; he finally insists on accounting for the exclusions and effects of just such a representation.

Chapter One

Reading Like a Man:
The Critics, the Narrator,
Troilus, and Pandarus

I want to begin this analysis of *Troilus and Criseyde* by considering two famous readings of the poem, famous in themselves and famously at odds with each other. These are the readings of E. Talbot Donaldson and D. W. Robertson, Jr., whose methods and conclusions have formed the poles of critical controversy over this poem and in medieval literary studies in general. The two critics base their readings on diametrically opposed theoretical principles: Donaldson eagerly participates in the emotional vicissitudes of the narrative, even implying that such response constitutes the emotionality of the text's characters, whereas Robertson urgently resists such subjectivity as he tries to escape solipsism—the blight of modernity, in his view—via medieval literature. But as the near interchangeability of their names felicitously suggests, these two "sons" are in fact in accord with one another in making the same critical moves: as I hope to demonstrate, they both impose firm control on the dangerously "slydynge"—women and texts—in constructing their readings of *Troilus and Criseyde.*

Such a general and fundamental agreement between critics who are explicitly and vociferously divided on theoretical issues is significant, I find, because it is symptomatic of a larger, more pervasive literary structure subtending and informing their contrasting literary projects —New Criticism and patristic exegesis, respectively. This structure is the patriarchal structure of literary activity; I am interested in analyzing each critic as he articulates patriarchal discourse in his critical practice, and, further, I am interested in detailing the culturally pervasive, gendered understanding of literary activity that motivates this critical practice. Each critic, I shall suggest, reads "like a man": each defines the disruptive Other in, and of, the text as feminine and limits it, turns away from it, in order to provide a single, univalent textual

28

meaning fixed in a hierarchical structure. Each shaping the course of Chaucer criticism, these major critical articulations by Robertson and Donaldson thus perform "masculine" readings (as Donaldson initially refers to his own) while each critic implies that his reading is finally neuter and normative—"humanistic" in Donaldson's case, "objective" in Robertson's.

It is crucial to understand that "reading like a man," as I analyze it here, is not necessarily the destiny of male anatomy. As we shall see, Donaldson himself suggests that not all male readers respond "like a man," and Criseyde forecasts that some female readers indeed will. I am interested in this kind of reading as a gendered response, socially constructed, and I want to focus on the fact of its construct-edness. Such a denaturalization of the masculine response constitutes the first step in any feminist analysis: it sees that the dominant per-spective isn't given, natural, or universal and that there can therefore be other perspectives. The first step toward the formulation of alter-natives to a monistic reading strategy is to recognize the existence of such a strategy; the first step toward a knowledge of what it might be to read like a woman—an idea Chaucer explores fully later, with the Wife of Bath and Griselda, and an issue of great moment in cur-rent feminist theory, concerned with whether there is an authentically female literary experience—is to understand that there is "reading like a man."

And, in fact, I suggest that Chaucer provides us with precisely such a denaturalizing perspective on the act of reading in *Troilus and Criseyde*, in the figures of readers in the narrative. The narrator, Pandarus, and Troilus are all characterized as readers of feminine texts. After looking at the two modern critical readers—Donaldson and Robert-son—I shall analyze these three male readers in Chaucer's text; all three, I suggest, turn away from the feminine in their final responses to the affair gone bad. But Pandarus, unlike the other two, is only act-ing—is thus reading precisely *like* a man—and thereby opens up the suggestion that there are other ways to read *as* a man.

This is an immensely liberating prospect, one, I think, that proved abundantly fruitful for Chaucer. *Troilus and Criseyde* only hints—through the reading actions of Criseyde—at alternatives to totalizing strategies; but the very denaturalization of the masculine perspective becomes something of a structural principle in Chaucer's later poetic projects. In the *Canterbury Tales*, as we shall see in later chapters, he speaks in the voices of others, in the voices of sometimes ostenta-tiously gendered characters, and, further, he shows the costs, the risks, the personal and political stakes involved in the deliberate assumption of a gendered voice. When he impersonates the Monk, "a manly man," he is a man who speaks like a man; speaking in the voice of the Wife of Bath, he is a man who speaks like a woman; indeed, as a man who speaks in the voice of the Pardoner, who himself plays at masculinity, he is, we might say, a man speaking like a man speaking like a man. Chaucer foregrounds gender in such impersonations and shows it to be, in actuality, a set of assumptions, a catalog of postures.

But to return to Robertson, Donaldson, and *Troilus and Criseyde:* it must be remarked here that each of these critics did much to advance the academic careers of women scholars.[1] My analysis is not meant even to insinuate otherwise. I am concerned with a cultural phenomenon, a general understanding of literary activity that is articulated through these two critics, as it were. But the discrepancy is itself significant and needs to be theorized. In the final part of this chapter, I shall suggest that Troilus is caught in an analogous position: as an individual man, he is deeply attached to, deeply believes in the uniqueness and singularity, the free and individual subjectivity, of a woman; but he is simultaneously implicated in, indeed complicit in, a larger societal attitude that sees women as mere counters in a power-asymmetrical patriarchal social structure. There is a difference, of course, between this fictional character's position and modern readers': whereas one is stuck forever, the others, along with society, can indeed change. This possibility is what Chaucer's critique of "reading like a man" can finally suggest to us.

1

Donaldson was in love with Criseyde. He had been for years, from his earliest declarations in the 1950s (in lectures later collected in *Speaking of Chaucer*) to his last avowal in *The Swan at the Well: Shakespeare Reading Chaucer* (1985).[2] "Enchanted" by Criseyde (p. 53), in his writings he offers a reading of the poem that is a "masculine response" to this "attractive" woman (p. 64); like Troilus and the narrator, he is one of "those who love Criseide." Indeed, he claims that "almost every male reader of the poem" (p. 9) falls in love with her, and he explicitly fashions his analysis as a reenactment of the stages of the narrator's falling in and out of love:

> In . . . this paper I shall be following the narrator in his endeavor to avoid [the "moralitee" of *Troilus*], and indeed shall be eagerly abetting him in trying to avoid it, and even pushing him away when he finally accepts it. (P. 92)

Focusing on the attractions, seductions, "deceptions" (p. 61), and "mystery" (p. 54) of women, he finds Criseyde "charming"; even her deceptiveness and "consciousness . . . of her own complicity" curiously endear her to him (*Chaucer's Poetry*, p. 968). But she is revealed, finally, to be a thing of this unstable world; just as she must remain a "charming enigma" (p. 75), so she cannot provide lasting fulfillment of desire. The stark "moralitee" of *Troilus*, writes Donaldson, is that "human love, and by a sorry corollary everything human, is unstable and illusory" (p. 92). It may be true that this hard moral is qualified and enriched by our love for Criseyde: the poem leads "towards heaven, indeed, but towards heaven through human experience" (p. 101); yet if we love Criseyde, Donaldson maintains, we must nevertheless remain detached from her, recognizing the unstable nature of worldly things and, in contrast, the only true stability in God.

Donaldson openly embraces his vicarious response to the poem. He exuberantly declares that his reading is subjective, an expression of his masculine desires. Amorous behavior provides metaphors for much of Donaldson's criticism and, indeed, for his conceptualization of the foundational enterprise in medieval literary studies, the editorial setting of texts: as I mentioned in the Introduction, he likens (in "The Psychology of Editors of Middle English Texts," printed in *Speaking of Chaucer*) the selection of one manuscript reading over another to the selection of a wife. The text is a woman—a bride, in fact; the editor, a restless husband; and textual editing, a metaphorical courtship and marriage, fraught with "powerful charms," allurements, and disenchantments (pp. 109, 112).

But such unabashed amorousness is the last thing that D. W. Robertson, Jr., would think appropriate to critical analyses of medieval literature. Whereas he has characterized modern literature as appealing to parts of us "below the belt," reading medieval literature, Robertson contends, is essentially an intellectual experience, and he denies that any merely emotional response forms a valid basis for a reading.[3] Following Augustine in *De doctrina christiana*, Robertson takes a certain pleasure in the text, in the decoding of its figurative language—in the challenge of passing through the *littera* of the text to the *sententia* (of *caritas*) beneath. But this "pleasure" Augustine finds quite inexplicable,[4] and Robertson insists that it is very limited—it is strictly an "intellectual" pleasure. Solving the puzzle of the *littera* inspires the mind with a love of the *sententia* found within—a love that itself originates in God, not in human feelings. The "emotional" or "subjective" are Romantic and post-Romantic literary preoccupations;

thus he bases his analyses on the gap between the modern sensibility and the medieval mind. We can read medieval literature properly only if we attempt to recover the language, beliefs, culture, and intellectual milieu of the Middle Ages. Medieval people were not like us, and we are mistaken to see ourselves in medieval literature, he maintains: "If we impose our own terms on it, we might as well be studying ourselves rather than the past" ("Method," p. 80). Robertson's Middle Ages of "quiet hierarchies" (*Preface*, p. 51) is founded on Augustine and Boethius, and his medieval aesthetic is derived essentially from *De doctrina christiana* and the Christian exegetical tradition.

Augustinianism thus dominates his discussion of *Troilus and Criseyde* in *A Preface to Chaucer*. To begin, Robertson points to the distinction between medieval and modern concepts of tragedy:

> Medieval tragedy is, of course, very different from modern tragedy, in which the suffering protagonist becomes an emblem of humanity crushed by the mysterious iniquities of a strangely recalcitrant world. But to the medieval mind, that hostile world of fortuitous events was an illusion generated by misdirected love. . . . To attribute a modern conception of tragedy to Chaucer would be to deny his faith in the Providential order and to make him, in his cultural environment, a shallow fool. (*Preface*, pp. 473–74)

Troilus is a medieval tragedy whose characters are motivated by *cupiditas*, misdirected love. Its "moralitee" is simple and absolute: love of earthly things for themselves (not in service of love for God) is sinful and destructive.[5]

The simplicity and absoluteness of this "moralitee" are a reflection of the simplicity and absoluteness of the Middle Ages as a cultural whole. In essay after essay, Robertson assiduously defends that cultural whole from the historical imperialism of modern readers:

> The integrity of past structures must be respected. . . . Above all, it seems obvious that we shall need to exhibit far greater reluctance than we have usually shown to impose our own formulations . . . as though they were universal truths. ("Method," p. 77)

But perhaps this protection of the past exceeds scholarly historical concern: the diction of his analysis of *Troilus*, as well as of his other analyses, suggests that the discrepancy he formulates between the modern period and the Middle Ages is invested with deep feeling, feeling which goes explicitly unacknowledged (see *Preface*, 3–51; esp.

30–33, 38–44, 51). As he puts it in the passages quoted above, the modern age deals in "mysterious iniquities," "strang[e] recalcitran[ce]," "crushed" humanity, "suffering"; in the Middle Ages, such a "hostile world of fortuitous events" is only, comfortingly, "an illusion." And if the modern age is not seen as mysteriously terrifying (the exaggerated diction here suggests parody, even cynicism), the suggestion is that it is silly—"shallow," foolish—in comparison to the Middle Ages. Most of all, the modern age is characterized by solipsism, Robertson insists time and time again; by looking at the literature of another age in its own terms, we might be able to extricate ourselves from "that rancid solipsistic pit into which the major tendencies of post-romantic thought have thrust us" ("Method," p. 82).

Striking, then, in his analysis of *Troilus* is his focus on Troilus as modern man: the suffering Troilus of book 5 becomes

> the "aimlessly drifting megalopolitan man" of the modern philosophers, the frustrated, neurotic, and maladjusted hero of modern fiction, an existentialist for whom Being itself, which he has concentrated in his own person, becomes dubious. (*Preface*, p. 497)

Troilus, whose mind is a "mirour" (1.365), whose love of Criseyde Robertson sees as only narcissistic, only solipsistic, becomes in effect a figure of the bad literary critic who reads his own modern attitudes into the medieval work—the critic who, as Robertson puts it at the beginning of his book, turns "history into a mirror which is of significance to us only insofar as we may perceive in it what appear to be foreshadowings of ourselves" (*Preface*, p. 3). Only after his death and ascension into the eighth sphere does Troilus attain a fuller view of earthly life and detachment from that solipsistic self—the same sort of "equanimity and detachment" that Robertson recommends to the literary critic ("Method," p. 84)—and laugh at "all those who take a sentimental attitude toward such love as that between Troilus and Criseyde" (*Preface*, p. 501). That is, Troilus, redeemed critic, laughs at *us*, modern readers culturally steeped in sentimentality.

So *Troilus and Criseyde* provides a corrective for the post-Romantic critical sensibility. Although this is in part merely to say that Robertson sees the function of the poem—and of medieval literature in general—as didactic, it might also serve to suggest that there is a good deal of self-loathing in his reading. Robertson would want to identify himself with Troilus the redeemed critic, of course, but he also must see himself as that condemned solipsistic figure; he is constantly working to get out of that "pit" in which he thinks we all live in the modern age. Such disgust with the modern self is registered most often in Robertson's writings as a disgust with sexuality. For, in Robertson's eyes, Chaucer's main literary preoccupation—his "o sentence"—is the analysis and condemnation of cupidity, most often bad love in amorous relationships; and of all the kinds of love the Middle Ages knew, we as moderns know only "that carnal impulse which, as Virgil says, we share with the animals" (*Preface*, p. 462). Chaucer's works would seem to exist to condemn the very urges that, according to Robertson, identify and define us as modern people.

Thus Troilus's erotic impulses—modern man that he is—are seen as entirely bestial; the Boethian hymn he sings at the end of book 3 is blasphemous. We know what Troilus really wants, and it's a "deed of darkness" (*Preface*, p. 492): when Troilus exclaims, "O paleys desolat, / O hous of houses whilom best ihight, / O paleys empty and disconsolat, / O thow lanterne of which queynt is the light" (5.540–43), Robertson suggests that "the ironic pun on 'queynt' is a bitter comment on what it is that Troilus actually misses" (*Preface*, p. 500). The bitterness of Robertson's own comment here suggests that his continual preoccupation with and condemnation of sexuality may be at bottom a recoil from the female body. It is telling that although both lovers come off badly in Robertson's view—both are cynical, nasty, and brutish—Troilus, I believe, is seen with the lesser compassion throughout the analysis. And, tellingly in Robertson's hierarchical scheme, Troilus is the one who resigns his princely status and enslaves himself to a demeaning passion for a woman. The unhinging, destabilizing effects of the woman—finally, of her "queynt"—on Troilus are what is to Robertson most abhorrent in the poem.

Troilus does finally achieve the properly hierarchical view of fleshly love, of course, and it's the desire for that "queynt" that must be put in its place. Chaucer's urgent admonition in the poem's Epilogue is, Robertson maintains, his "o sentence" in all the major poetry. Robertson concludes the analysis, and his book, by lamenting that

> In our own society, although a few poets like Mr. Eliot continue to emphasize the value of love in Christian terms, the urgent need for a love that is neither lust nor avarice has now become the affair of psychologists and sociologists. (*Preface*, p. 503)

Robertson's reading of the literature of the Middle Ages is informed by a nostalgia for a prior, perfect time—a time of orderly and rational love, a time when sexuality was fully governed by the reason, a prelapsarian time such as Augustine imagined Eden to be.[6] Robertson

flees from the unfulfilling, the disorderly, the unsettling in modern experience—excessive emotionality; irrational sentimentality; rampant
eros; and sexuality, especially of the female "queynt"—and embraces
totality. In a process which Lee Patterson calls "ruthless totalizing,"[7]
Robertson's construction of a monolithic intellectual structure that is
the literature of the Middle Ages recovers a unity lost circa 1400 and restores the sexuality of people to its fully human—not bestial—realm,
thus fulfilling the "urgent need for a love that is neither lust nor avarice."

While Donaldson gleefully announces his emotional entrance into
the text, then, Robertson does not.[8] One way of characterizing differences in the styles of these two critical approaches (picking up on
Robertson's expressions of distrust, his suspicions of modern critics'
"concealed self-study" ["Method," p. 82])[9] is to invoke Paul Ricoeur's
contrast between the "hermeneutic of suspicion" and the "hermeneutic of recovery." The hermeneutic of suspicion—reductive, demystify-
ing—reveals the essential "poverty" of our natures; the hermeneutic
of recovery discovers a "full[ness]" of meaning.[10] Robertson posits
and reads against a sense of modern spiritual emptiness and sheer
carnality; Donaldson discovers a rich complexity of lived experience.
"Willingness to suspect, willingness to listen; vow of rigor, vow of
obedience"—Ricoeur's aphorism[11] captures the feeling of the two critics at work: Robertson, vigorously demonstrating that the text—no
matter what it *says*—always carries the message of *caritas*; and Donaldson, patiently following, even imitating, the text. Like psychoanalytic
interpretations, from which Ricoeur derives the hermeneutic of suspicion, Robertson's readings aren't "falsifiable," as R. S. Crane has seen;
since the text can always mean something other than what it says, the
exegesis can't be proven wrong.[12] This exegesis that is always "right,"
that has all the answers, is very different from Donaldson's hesitancy
in front of the text:

> Things are difficult to see steadily for more than a short period, re-
> appear in changed shape, become illusory, vanish; as the poem pro-
> gresses one finds oneself groping more and more in a world where
> forms are indistinct but have infinite suggestiveness. (*Chaucer's
> Poetry*, p. 966)

Donaldson delights in the text's indistinctness, its "infinite suggestiveness." And Criseyde, ever fascinating, never completely understood (p. 83), focus of desire in the narrative, is for him the emblem of
that textual indeterminacy. But for all his delicate nurturing of poetic

complexity, for all his understanding of the erotic instabilities of the text and his alertness to critical involvement in those textual erotics, I finally sense a desire for order, a desire to control a threateningly uncontrollable libido, in Donaldson's analysis not entirely unlike that in Robertson's. Despite his claims of identification with the narrator and Troilus as lovers of Criseyde, Donaldson is not, as are they, betrayed by the lady. The critic can see farther than the limited narrator and Troilus, who learn the hard way that Criseyde is a thing of this unstable world. Indeed, this critical vision makes him as all-seeing as the poet himself, and we might suggest that Donaldson identifies most deeply with that omniscient poet whom he formalistically posits as locus of creative power and textual control. The critic's own plain speaking, his simple-but-elegant style, and his ability to work language on several different levels (all epitomized in the title of his collected essays, *Speaking of Chaucer*), are intimated in his description of the omniscient Chaucer: he speaks of

> Chaucer's ability to describe things simultaneously from several distinct points of view while seeming to see them from only one point of view, and thus to show in all honesty the complexity of things while preserving the appearance of that stylistic simplicity which we feel to be so honest and trustworthy. (P. 47)

This could be, as well, the lucid and honest Donaldson. (And we note in passing that, like the poet, he includes a "retraction" at the end of a new and risky work: concluding "Chaucer the Pilgrim," he remarks that "it is now necessary to retract" some earlier comments about the Prioress [p. 11].)

Donaldson is fascinated by Criseyde precisely because he sees her as the essential indeterminacy of the text. In this way he associates textual "slydynge" as well as erotic errancy with the feminine. But he has Criseyde's potentially disruptive "corage," and therefore the poem's "infinite suggestiveness," under control.[13] "Attractive women" such as Criseyde, he states, have the power to make fools of "us male critics," as do beautiful and difficult poems; some measure of "complexity," "ambiguity," "slydynge" is nice, but some control is also necessary to reduce the threat of real disruption that *unlimited* "slydynge" poses to the reader who values a New Critical poetic whole. It is Donaldson's formalism, in this sense functioning like Robertson's historicism, that provides the structure for this delimitation and control. Donaldson's is less obviously a totalizing enterprise than is the essentially positivistic historicism of Robertson; nevertheless, the totalizing is there:

Donaldson's criticism can entertain some ambiguity and indeterminacy because it has already, in an analytically prior move, posited an author to whom all signifying responsibility can be referred as "the origin, and the proprietor of [the text's] significance," as Patterson puts it.[14]

It may be, further, that such a concept of an omniscient poet can itself be seen as part of a patriarchal literary project: with its concern to authorize, legitimate, and, finally, delimit meanings, the concept of an author as all-controlling locus of meaning promotes patriarchal values of final authority, fidelity, and legitimacy.[15] Certainly, as Donaldson invokes it, the formalistic model of omniscient poet manipulating his characters not only establishes the poet as firm center of meaning in the poem but particularly emphasizes that poet's manipulation and control of the female character. He stresses that the omniscient poet undercuts the narrator's naive, blindly loving presentation of Criseyde: time and again, while the narrator is doting on Criseyde, the poet (and critic) are showing her to be suspect, unfaithful. And while he continually celebrates Criseyde as fascinating—the reader can never fully understand her, he maintains, but will keep trying—her "complexity," that irreducible charm and powerful magnetism, is boiled down to "the unpredictability, the instability, of even the most lovely of mortal women" (*Chaucer's Poetry*, p. 971), in order to complete a reading of the whole poem. "You can never understand a woman" is a way of understanding her. Criseyde becomes a sign of instability, compared to and subsumed by Heavenly stability, and the poem's totality is asserted and assured.

Donaldson began, we recall, by characterizing his response as a "masculine" one, and carefully stated that "*almost* every male reader" falls in love with the lady. This leads to intriguing questions: What about the female reader of this text? Will she love Criseyde, too? Or, as Criseyde herself fears, will women hate Criseyde most of all? What about that male reader who *doesn't* fall for her? Is he not sufficiently "masculine," or is he just a churl? It would have been interesting to hear Donaldson approach these questions, as aware as he was of the subjectivity of the critic and the importance of gender; but he seems in fact to have forgotten about the gender-specificity of his claims. By the end of his analysis he has universalized and naturalized *his* response so as to make it the basis of everyone's response, speaking of "human love, and by a sorry corollary everything human" (p. 92).

So Donaldson and Robertson, theoretically antagonistic, in practice make very similar critical moves: a vigorous limitation of the disturbing, a rigorous structure controlling the unstable and threateningly destabilizing, are the foundations of both approaches.[16] Robertson, loathing modern-day bestiality, appeals to a Chaucer who presents "with a peculiar luminosity" (*Preface*, p. 502) a vision of well-ordered love and cosmic hierarchy. Donaldson, delighting in a certain measure of uncertainty, never lets eros get out of hand; he imposes a critical structure that limits textual disorder and sexual waywardness and situates them within an orderly hierarchy presided over by Chaucer the poet, a minor version of the Omniscient. In both cases the delimitation of the text's meaning is achieved through a rejection or containment of what is constituted as feminine.

How are we to explain this phenomenon—the fact that the opposite sides of this critical dispute over reading the poem seem to converge, and that they do so around the issue of the feminine? A clue is perhaps found in Donaldson's explicitly fashioning his reading as a sort of reenactment of the narrator's response to the story of Troilus and Criseyde. For the narrator is a reader, too, a translator who reads, comments on, and questions "Lollius" and other "olde bokes." This is, as the narrator stresses, a Latin text, a pagan fable, written in a strange language and depicting the unfamiliar customs of the ancients. It is, in other words, that captive alien woman of Deuteronomy 21:10–13 who provides the model for Saint Jerome's Christian hermeneutics, as I discussed in the Introduction. Just as the alien woman must be stripped and prepared for the bridal, made ready to marry the triumphant Israelite warrior and become a matron of his household, so, says Jerome, must the classical text be stripped of its eloquent letter to reveal its naked truth, the wisdom that can be put to Christian use.

The Christian narrator of *Troilus and Criseyde* might be expected to strip this alien woman of her garments of captivity, to pare her nails, shave her head, and scrub her down with niter—that is, to remove the pagan fable, its eloquence and mores, and discover underneath the fecund body of truth. He does not, however; the narrator at the outset of the poem suggests instead that the Christian "charite" in which he lives can be itself enhanced by the telling of the pagan tale of Troilus' woe (1.49). But not having divested this text of its feminine seductiveness, he responds in his reading to its carnal delights, the delights represented in the love story as well as the delights of narrative description and pacing—all the pleasures of the letter. And not having been divested, she remains an alien woman; the narrator does not domesticate her and, consequently, finds that her seductive *littera* won't issue in any fruitful *sententia*. It is only then, at the very end of the poem, that he strips and reclothes the woman, marries and properly domesticates her, and addresses his future progeny. He derives the "moralitee" in a critical move that closely parallels the one both Robertson and Donaldson make, a rigorous control of the dangerous feminine. And as we'll see, this containment of or turning away from the feminine also describes Pandarus' verbal rejection of the female character in the "text" that he has created and that he "reads"—the "old romaunce" of Troilus and Criseyde.

By figuring the role of the reader in the narrative, Chaucer makes the act of critical reading a major preoccupation of the entire poem. *Troilus and Criseyde* in fact provides a powerful analysis of reading—of *masculine* reading—and I take the convergence of these two disparate but masculine critics, Robertson and Donaldson, to be a precise corroboration of this analysis. Masculine reading in *Troilus and Criseyde* is dominated at last by a desire to contain instability, carnal appetite—those things that, as I have suggested in the Introduction, medieval writers (and their descendants, modern critics) associate with *femina*. The narrator, Pandarus, and Troilus, too, *all* characterized as readers of feminine texts, turn away at last from the disruptive feminine toward orderly, hierarchical visions of divine love in which desire is finally put to rest. Such efforts at containment, Chaucer shows in the poem, are urgent emotional responses to the rough disillusionments of carnal involvement, of involvement with the feminine.

Seen from a larger perspective, however, these efforts are ironically unnecessary, even redundant. The "slydynge" of Criseyde's "corage," as we shall see, turns out to work in conformity to masculine structures of control, to work as a function of her structural role as woman in Troy's patriarchal society.[17] Feminine "slydynge," as we'll see, does not actually threaten the power structures in this narrative. Pandarus, alone of all our masculine readers, recognizes this, and thus his response to Criseyde, expedient and tactical as it is, provides a perspective within the poem on "reading like a man."

But let us turn first to the narrator, to trace the arc of his pleasure in the letter of his text, in the garb of that alien woman.

2

The narrator presents himself at the outset of the poem as the uninvolved translator of the old, approved story of Troilus and Criseyde. Far from the God of Love's help, "in derknesse" (1.18), the narrator is not a lover himself, and he only hopes, in the proem to book 1, that his book may avail lovers in their "causes" (1.20). He will derive some satisfaction from furthering others' love affairs (if this poem helps any lover in his audience, he states, "Have he my thonk, and myn be this travaille!" [1.21]), and his soul will perhaps be advanced by praying "for hem that Loves servauntz be" (1.48). But he ostensibly removes any immediate basis for personal interest in the tale itself, asserting that emotional distance removes him from his "matere."

Geographical and temporal distance as well separate the narrator from his matter, according to his proem to book 2. Again asserting his inexperience in love, he states that he is merely a transmitter ("For as myn auctour seyde, so sey I" [2.18]), and he defends the credibility of what his *auctor* has written. The actions, speech, and courtship behavior of the lovers may seem odd to his fourteenth-century audience, he admits, but this account is accurate; habits, customs, even language were different in ancient Troy. The narrator draws attention to this fact and emphasizes his retention of these alien details, his text's classical garb:

> Ye knowe ek that in forme of speche is chaunge
> Withinne a thousand yeer, and wordes tho
> That hadden pris, now wonder nyce and straunge
> Us thinketh hem, and yet thei spake hem so,
> And spedde as wel in love as men now do;
> Ek for to wynnen in sondry ages,
> In sondry londes, sondry ben usages.
>
> (2.22–28)

The narrator proposes, then, to read and retell this text faithfully, noting and preserving all its classical otherness. He duly, even ostentatiously, notes the Trojans' "olde usage" of worshipping Pallas Athene at the feast of the Palladion, for example (1.150–61). His stated intent is not to modernize (that is, to "medievalize") the story but to render it in its ancient detail.[18] As mere translator he must follow his *auctor*, and it goes without saying—although the narrator says it often enough—that what his *auctor* doesn't tell him, he can't tell us. Whether Criseyde has children, for example: "I rede it naught, therfore I late it goon" (1.133). Neither can he provide the text of a letter that Lollius only mentions:

> For ther was som epistel hem betwene,
> That wolde, as seyth myn autour, wel contene
> Neigh half this book, of which hym liste nought write.
> How sholde I thanne a lyne of it endite?
>
> (3.501–4)

The narrator will not invent or deviate from his source.

But the playful, cagey tone of these lines ("How sholde I thanne a lyne of it endite?") indicates something beyond strict fidelity to the author. The narrator's *own* action of relaying the auctorial message is signaled at such a moment, of course: our awareness is drawn to the narrator as he reads and retells. But further, he seems to take pleasure in what he doesn't read: with delight he draws attention to what his *auctor* doesn't say. The unknown detail is provocative, suggestive, perhaps even mildly titillating: the presence of the unknown—whether Criseyde has children or not, what exactly the lovers' letters say—is not disruptive of the incipient love affair or the narrative but is itself generative, exciting.

"The pleasure of the text," writes Roland Barthes, describing a model of reading more appropriate to the narrator's choices here than models of *stripping* the body of the text (in Macrobius, Jerome, Augustine, Richard of Bury), "is not the pleasure of the corporeal striptease or of narrative suspense," which would lead directly to full revelation. Rather, "it is the very rhythm of what is read and what is not read that creates the pleasure of the great narratives." Not totality but "intermittence" is the figure of pleasure in reading, as Barthes puts it:

> The intermittence of skin flashing between two articles of clothing (trousers and sweater), between two edges (the open-necked shirt, the glove and the sleeve); it is this flash itself which seduces, or rather: the staging of an appearance-as-disappearance.[19]

Immediate revelation of the whole body of wisdom is not what the Barthesian reader or the narrator of *Troilus and Criseyde* seeks. The garb itself—the unfolding narrative—is the site of bliss.

Thus the narrator's careful pacing of the love affair's unfolding reveals his progressively escalating personal interest, a growing emotional involvement. He skips over details, makes choices, and paces his reading, taking pleasure in the encounter with the very surface of the text. He pares down the details of the Trojan War that are extrinsic to the story of Troilus and Criseyde: if you want to know, he informs us, read them in "Omer, or in Dares, or in Dite." The details of all the "Troian gestes" (1.145–47) would digress from his "matere," and he wants to concentrate on "the warmer parts of the anecdote" (as Barthes puts it).[20] He stops the flow of the narrative of Troilus's initial infatuation in book 1 to repeat "every word right thus" of the *Canticus Troili*, a rich, leisurely expression of the lover's condition. And he hastens the progress of the courtship in book 2, telling not every word this time, but "th'effect, as fer as I kan understonde" (2.1220) of Criseyde's first letter to Troilus. These narrative moves suggest the narrator's incipient interest in the text's own surface eloquence.

So although the narrator's reading and retelling of Lollius purports to be a straightforward, uninvolved rendering of the Latin text into English, it turns out to be a record of the narrator's gradual seduction by the text's letter, by its feminine charms. His involvement with the carnality of this text is apparent not only in these rhythms of the disposition of the narrative, the text's eloquent surface; it is thematized as vicarious erotic response to the love story itself. Without a lover of his own, he takes pleasure in the reading and rendering of others' pleasures; he substitutes their pleasures for his own. Erotic substitution—vicariousness—indeed defines his whole poetic project in *Troilus and Criseyde* as he sets it out in the proem to book 1: he will take pleasure in the advancement of the "causes" of lovers in his audience; he substitutes their amorous successes for his lack of amorous action. Further, the act of translation is itself both the substitution of one language for another, and, in the terms of classical rhetoric, the substitution of an "improper" term in the place of a "proper" one.[21]

We can see that the narrator's act of translation is itself eroticized both as it engages the surface of the narrative and as it finds a locus in the fable for his substitute erotic identification—his vicarious pleasures. His protestations that he is making a faithful translation of his author, simply a straightforward substitution of English for Latin, serve in fact to cover up the deeper substitutions he has made. Such protestations are abundant in the first part of the poem: let us consider, for example, his remarks about his rendition of the *Canticus Troili:*

> And of his song naught only the sentence,
> As writ myn auctour called Lollius,
> But pleinly, save oure tonges difference,
> I dar wel seyn, in al that Troilus
> Seyde in his song, loo! every word right thus
> As I shal seyn; and whoso list it here,
> Loo, next this vers he may it fynden here.
>
> (1.393–99)

Lollius as source is mentioned for the first time in the poem here, and the narrator asserts that he is in accord with that source. In fact, he is *more* than absolutely faithful: the narrator gives the particular words of a song of which his *auctor* gives only the "sentence."[22] Where *did* the words of Troilus' song come from? The narrator suggests that he can know exactly what Troilus said *without a source:* Lollius is cited but at the same time seems to be unnecessary, superfluous. It seems that the narrator must have some channel of direct communication with Troilus: the parallel syntax brings the two characters into close relation: "al that Troilus seyde . . . I shal seyn." The narrator's claim of historically faithful, word-for-word translation here works as a cover for his deeper involvement, his deeper substitution: it masks his identification with the lover of the woman, Criseyde.

But even when the narrator claims that he can't follow his *auctor* strictly, word for word—can't "tellen al . . . of his excellence"—his act of *translatio* expresses his carnal delight in the text. While describing the scene of the consummation of Troilus and Criseyde's love, the narrator pauses to make his literary intentions explicit:

> But sooth is, though I kan nat tellen al,
> As kan myn auctour, of his excellence,
> Yet have I seyd, and God toforn, and shal
> In every thyng, al holly his sentence;
> And if that ich, at Loves reverence,
> Have any word in eched for the beste,
> Doth therwithal right as youreselven leste.
>
> (3.1324–30)

Translation, according to medieval translators, could proceed either by rendering "every word right thus," a process the narrator alludes to in his rendition of Troilus' song, or by rendering "al holly [the] sentence," as he states here. Jean de Meun, for example, makes this distinction in the preface to his translation of Boethius' *De consolatione;*[23] and Jean de Hareng, in the afterword to his *Rettorique de Marc Tulles Cyceron,* a translation of the anonymous *Rhetorica ad Herennium* and two books of the *De inventione,* states that sometimes he translates word for word, but more often he tries to achieve the "sentence." A word-for-word translation is not adequate for rendering obscure passages, he claims, and in translating these, he must "sozjoindre et acreistre"—just as the narrator, here in book 3, suggests that he has "in eched" (added in) a word or two "for the beste," in achieving his author's "sentence."[24]

Fidelity to the authorial sentence is typically emphasized in medieval discussions of translation.[25] But *this* protestation of fidelity is not only a conventional statement: the narrator's act of translation is an expression of his carnal love. Thus we see that his strategy of "eching in" is enunciated at the moment of the lovers' highest bliss. Just as the idea of word-for-word translation is used in the service of his own identification with Troilus as lover of a woman, the idea of relaying his author's sentence is expressed at the moment of his deepest vicarious response to the tale. Throughout book 3, as the affair hastens toward consummation, the narrator's vicarious participation is loud and clear: he imitates the emotions of the characters and echoes their exclamations and prayers.[26] But further, he draws attention to his *literary* activity as he narrates the lovers' *amatory* actions. Again enjoying the intermittence of his *auctor*, he comments that he can't say exactly why Criseyde didn't ask Troilus to rise from her bedside, but he *does* know ("But wel fynde I . . .") that she kissed him (3.967–73). Using fidelity as a translator to cover for his erotic engagement, he protests that, having told of the weary trials of the lovers, he must continue to follow his *auctor* in relating their joys (3.1191–97). And just after Criseyde cries to Troilus, "Welcome, my knyght, my pees, my suffisaunce!" and we are told that the lovers that night "felten in love the grete worthynesse," the narrator bursts out:

> O blisful nyght, of hem so longe isought,
> How blithe unto hem bothe two thow weere!
> Why nad I swich oon with my soule ybought,
> Ye, or the leeste joie that was theere?
>
> (3.1317–20)

Then follows, at this climactic time for the lovers, the stanza in which the narrator confesses that he *might* have "in eched" a word or two; and, following that, there is a *further* stanza yet about his act of translation ("For myn wordes, heere and every part, / I speke hem alle under correccioun" [3.1331–36]). The narrator's *translatio* is not merely flat fidelity to the sentence; it combines the textual eroticism of intermittence with vicarious pleasure in the love affair. The act of translation is *his* version of consummation. Reading and relaying the fable, adoring the seductively clad woman, is a substitute activity with a very real erotics of its own.

But the delights of intermittence, like the pleasures of Troilus and Criseyde's love, are short-lived. We note that the narrator's delight in what he does not read and in auctorial hints lessens as he comes to Criseyde's betrayal. As we have seen with the critics, particularly Donaldson, instability and uncertainty in the fable are centered in Criseyde; the necessary qualifications of the worth of the fable stem from dissatisfactions with the female character. The feminine, again, is the letter's uncontrollability—both its ambiguous or uncertain details and its final, unalterable outcome—especially as it is concentrated in Criseyde. The pleasurable rhythm—"I read on, I skip, I look up, I dip in again"²⁷—is replaced by strain and discomfort, aloofness, doubt, and disagreement with his "olde bokes." In fact, we see in the narrator's treatment of Criseyde throughout the narrative a tendency to fill in the blanks where she is concerned, a nervousness that tends to foreclose the pleasure that those seductive gaps might afford. We have seen that an uncertainty early on, in book 1, opens up regarding Criseyde's maternity and that it is left open, apparently unproblematic; indeed, not to know all is even tantalizing. But the narrator's interjection in book 2, his defense of Criseyde against potential detractors, functions to close gaps that haven't even opened: it is a massive explanatory effort, designed to answer questions before they have arisen (that is, questions that begin to nag the narrator himself): "Now *myghte* som envious jangle thus" (2.666; my emphasis). If some uncertainties are still pleasurable in book 3 (why Criseyde didn't ask Troilus to rise, for example), they become uncomfortable in book 4; and by book 5 these lacunae have become dark pools where doubts spawn. Vicarious participant in the affair, the narrator wants to believe in Criseyde; he tries rather desperately to control those gaping holes, rushing in with a "But trewely . . ." after nearly every ambiguous or difficult detail that occurs to him:

> . . . Tendre-herted, slydynge of corage;
> *But trewely,* I kan nat telle hire age.
> (5.825–26; my emphasis)

> Men seyn—I not—that she yaf hym hire herte.

> *But trewely,* the storie telleth us,
> Ther made nevere womman moore wo
> Than she, whan that she falsed Troilus.
> (5.1050–53; my emphasis)

Even as the narrator tries to interpret matters to Criseyde's benefit, however, new vagueness and uncertainties proliferate.

> "But al shal passe; and thus take I my leve."

> *But trewely,* how longe it was bytwene
> That she forsok hym for this Diomede,
> Ther is non auctour telleth it, I wene. . . .
> For though that he bigan to wowe hire soone,
> Er he hire wan, yet was ther more to doone.
> (5.1085–92; my emphasis)

Pleasurable intermittence is indeed long gone; suspicion and distrust instead govern his response. Far from taking pleasure in what his books don't mention, the narrator suggests that the *auctores* might be lying or suppressing information (4.15–21; 5.1089–90). He holds himself aloof from them as he writes: "Men seyn—I not." And when he has finally related Criseyde's betrayal, he asserts that he would still prefer to defy the tradition and excuse her "for routhe" (5.1099). But the lady and the fable have disappointed him; the feminine here proves out of his control.

It is at this point, the point at which the seemingly uncontrollable feminine threatens to destroy masculine lives and masculine projects (the female character threatens Troilus' sense of himself; the feminine letter threatens the possibility of deriving any moral worth from this), that the narrator strips off the fable, in the Epilogue, to reveal the poem's moral message. When the alien woman isn't stripped, the narrator falls for her carnal charms, but still she remains Other, alien; undomesticated, she will not become a matron of Israel. That is, the classical fable itself does not impart wisdom that can be appropriated for Christian purposes: it does not provide a strong secular model for imitation. Consequently, the narrator removes the covering, the veil, the tale itself, gradually but completely, at the end of the poem. He apologizes to women for having written this story at all; it is distasteful, and its intent isn't exactly clear ("N'y sey nat this al oonly for thise men, / But moost for wommen that bitraised be / Thorugh false folk" [5.1779–81]). He would rather, he claims, undertake to translate classical texts whose fables are themselves useful for Christian imitation, tales of Penelope and Alceste. And if the tragic has proved unsatisfying, he sends it off, hoping to write a comedy next; "som comedye" (5.1788), with its Dantean divine intimations, would be more useful for Christian readers. He then removes the action from the classical battlefield, elevates the "lighte goost" of Troilus into the heavens, changes the perspective (Troilus' "lokyng") to that of divine Providence, and has Troilus damn his own story—"al oure werk" (5.1823).[28] The fecund body is available only when the feminine seductiveness of the alien woman is distanced and finally removed, only when the narrator separates himself from the possibility of erotic involvement by getting rid of the tale.[29] It is then that the "moralitee" of the tale, as the narrator reads it, can emerge: all is "vanite / To respect of the pleyn felicite / That is in hevene above" (5.1817–19); the joys of the world are brittle, unstable, transitory. When the letter itself is done away with—when the classical "forme of olde clerkis speche" is cast aside—this proper Christian spirit is revealed.

> Lo here, of payens corsed olde rites!
> Lo here, what alle hire goddes may availle!
> Lo here, thise wrecched worldes appetites!
> Lo here, the fyn and guerdoun for travaille
> Of Jove, Appollo, of Mars, of swich rascaille!
> Lo here, the forme of olde clerkis speche
> In poetrie, if ye hire bokes seche.
>
> (5.1849–55)

The "moral" and "philosophical" spirit of the text is then offered to the correction of Gower and Strode. That spirit will be productive, as the letter has not been: the narrator addresses directly his progeny here. From the alien woman now domesticated by the narrator as reader will issue guidance for "yonge, fresshe folkes" (5.1835).

The spirit underneath the letter has nothing to do with "slydynge" earthly love "that passeth soone as floures faire" (5.1841); it is founded on an insistence on solidity, security, "circumscription" (5.1865). This is an unexceptional Christian "sentence," and its intention is to increase and multiply the faith in others. But the alternating vehemence and desperation, the emotional careening of the narrator in the last ten stanzas of the poem—listen to the vast tonal shifts (which Donaldson has ably noted [pp. 93–101]), from the narrative of Troilus' "lighte gooste" to the "Swich fyn!" stanza, the address to the "yonge, fresshe folkes," the "Lo here!" stanza, the address to the zealous Gower and Strode, and the final prayer to the Three-in-One— suggest that Chaucer means to represent this movement toward unity, solidity and closure as an intense, emotional urgency. As I shall suggest in a moment, *everyone* needs some such solidity and closure; but after the narrator's amatory participation in the preceding narrative, his concluding response can well be considered a markedly gendered one, a masculine response under the pressure of what he construes as feminine. Chaucer's critique reasons not the need but a misogynistic formulation and fulfillment of it.

3

If the narrator's act of encountering the letter is erotic, Pandarus' vicarious love act of bringing Troilus and Criseyde together is represented as literary. There are in fact many parallels between these two figures: both take vicarious pleasure in the lovers' pleasure, for example, as many critics have noted.[30] Most apposite to my purposes, both are characterized as readers. Pandarus' actions are in fact

thoroughly paralleled to the narrator's—climactically, likened to reading an old romance—and, as a consequence, reading as an activity
with a gendered valence is more fully developed in the poem. Looking at Pandarus will enable us to determine, finally, *why it matters* that
reading be understood in gender terms: the figure of Pandarus will
allow us to perceive this masculine activity in relation to the larger
social organization of patriarchy—of Troy or of any patriarchal society.
But let us first observe the extent of the parallels between the narrator
and Pandarus, and therefore the thoroughness with which Chaucer
associates reading in *Troilus and Criseyde* with masculine control of the
feminine.

The narrator is not the only excited onlooker in the consummation
scene in book 3: Pandarus, too, is loudly present. His presence is ob-
trusive, his vicarious enjoyment almost obscene. He has, of course,
contrived the entire event; throughout the first three books of the
poem, his self-interest and pleasure are clearly noticeable in his constant references to the affair that use the first person plural possessive
adjective: he speaks of "oure joie." And now, bustling around the
lovers in this climactic scene, as he has earlier shuttled to and fro
between the lovers, his energy is frenetic, sexual, as the language suggests: "But Pandarus, that so wel koude *feele* / In every thyng, to *pleye*
anon bigan" (3.960–61; emphasis mine). Pandarus arranges the scene:
he tells the lovers where to kneel and what to say; he even tosses the
faint Troilus into Criseyde's bed. Finally he takes his cue to leave the
bedside, but he apparently does not even leave the room. The narration of his lying down to sleep immediately follows upon Troilus'
taking Criseyde in his arms: the three of them are packed into the
stanza as they are into the chamber.[31]

Pandarus' activity, like the narrator's act of translation, provides
its own erotic satisfactions. It keeps him physically active, breathless,
and sweaty: he leaps, he perspires, he moves back and forth between
the two lovers (2.939; 2.1464). Both of these mediating acts, pandering
and translating, are substitutes for amorous action—Pandarus and
the narrator are both, by their own admission, unsuccessful in love—
and both activities yield vicarious pleasures. It's no coincidence that
the two characters should describe themselves in the same terms:
Pandarus likens himself, as unsuccessful lover advising a would-be
lover, to a whetstone: "A wheston is no kervyng *instrument*, / But yet
it maketh sharppe kervyng tolis" (1.631–32; my emphasis). The image
allies Pandarus' vicarious amorous role with the narrator's poetic role
—it is from Horace's *Ars poetica*, where Horace (ironically) describes

his vicarious role as teacher of the poetic art: "So I'll play a whetstone's part. . . . Though I write naught myself, I will teach the poet's office and duty."[32] And the narrator, in turn, sees himself as the "sorwful *instrument,* / That helpeth lovers, as I kan, to pleyne" (1.10–11; my emphasis).[33]

These lexical links make the amatory charge of literary activity in this poem all the clearer. "Matere," "purpos," and "werk" are used to describe the affair (in a figure taken from Geoffrey of Vinsauf's *Poetria nova*) *and* the poem (1.1062–71; 1.53; 1.5; 2.16). Critics have noted that Pandarus, in creating his "werk," is much like a poet creating a text, inventing scenes, planning dialogue, "shaping" (2.1363) the plot—a poet being a "shaper" (*scop*) in Old English. But what interests me most is that he reads a thoroughly eroticized text, just as the narrator does: at the consummation scene,

> with that word he drow hym to the feere,
> And took a light, and fond his contenaunce,
> As for to looke upon an old romaunce.
>
> (3.978–80)

Pandarus withdraws from the lovers, sits himself down near the fire, and reads the lovers' persons as characters in a script he has himself written—reads them as if *they* constituted "an old romaunce."

In the end, Pandarus responds to the apparent uncontrollability of his text much as the narrator does to his, by pushing away the feminine. Criseyde, unfaithful to Troilus, spoils Pandarus' "romaunce," turning it into tragedy. As Donaldson notes, Pandarus tries at first to create a new "romaunce" (offering to find Troilus other women) and then to prolong this one (trying to defend Criseyde's honesty against Troilus' understanding of his dream).[34] Eventually, however, he disowns the traitor and gives up on the affair. He has spent the last book halfheartedly encouraging Troilus, all the while certain himself of Criseyde's infidelity; but at the last he erupts in two stanzas (5.1731–43), declaring that he has done all he can for Troilus, that he hates Criseyde and will forever, and that, finally, he resigns himself to silence: "I kan namore seye."

Pandarus' response is, in fact, very similar to the narrator's in verbal form as well as in emotional dynamics.[35] The extravagance of the emotional expression is shared: Pandarus cries, "I hate, ywys, Criseyde; / And, God woot, I wol hate hire evermore!" (5.1732–33); the narrator's tone at points becomes heated, vehement, the syntax obsessive:

> Swich fyn hath, lo, this Troilus for love!
> Swich fyn hath al his grete worthynesse!
> Swich fyn hath his estat real above!
> Swich fyn his lust, swich fyn hath his noblesse!
> Swych fyn hath false worldes brotelnesse!
> And thus bigan his lovyng of Criseyde,
> As I have told, and in this wise he deyde.
>   (5.1828–34)

Both Pandarus and the narrator plead that they not be blamed for the treacherous feminine instability or its representation (5.1738–39; 5.1772–75). Pandarus states, "Right fayn I wolde amende it" (5.1741); the narrator would like to amend the effects of his tragedy by writing "som comedye" (5.1788). Pandarus prays to "almyghty God" that Criseyde will soon be delivered from this world, and then falls silent ("I kan namore seye"); the narrator utters a final prayer "to the Lord," invoking the love of the Virgin, and ends in silence. The one rejecting Criseyde, the other doing so and calling on the only unblemished earthly woman, both appeal ultimately to providential order in response to the destabilizations and dissatisfactions of involvement with the feminine—woman and the letter of the text.

There is, of course, another masculine reader of a feminine text in the poem: Troilus. We might see him as a gracious reader of Criseyde, taking the spirit *in bono* even when he cannot understand the letter. In book 3, for example, in his most explicit equation of woman and text, he suggests that though the "text" of mercy is not easy to read in Criseyde's eyes, it is that kind message that he knows is there and that he will persevere in seeking:

> This Troilus ful ofte hire eyen two
> Gan for to kisse, and seyde, "O eyen clere,
> It weren ye that wroughte me swich wo,
> Ye humble nettes of my lady deere!
> Though ther be mercy writen in youre cheere,
> God woot, the text ful hard is, soth, to fynde!
> How koude ye withouten bond me bynde?"
>   (3.1352–58)

Earlier, when he reads her first letter (the exchange of letters constitutes the lovers' intercourse at that point in the affair), he "took al for the beste" (2.1324–27). Even when he senses some "chaunge" in her

last letter—the letter being, again, a substitute for Criseyde's body
—"fynaly, he ful ne trowen myghte" (5.1632–35). He is unwilling to
draw conclusions until he sees the irrefutable ocular proof; and when
he does see it, he wails in anguish at the sight: "I ne kan nor may . . .
unloven yow a quarter of a day!" (5.1696–99). But as I shall suggest
more fully in a moment, we might rather see his readings as interpretations attending less to the words or signs and more to what he
wants to see—turning away from the difficult, the resistant, or the recalcitrant in making some sense of the text; and he, at last, turns away
from earthly woman's love from his vantage on high. Looking down at
this little spot of earth, he condemns "blynde lust, the which that may
nat laste" and appeals to the surpassing, ever-fixed love in Heaven. In
this totalizing impulse—the desire to eliminate instability, adjudicate
difficulties, secure a clear moral structure and enduring rest—enacted
as a turning away from a woman, Troilus is finally joining the others
in reading like a man.

The connection between closure and masculine reading thus comes
into clear focus in the Epilogue. To "read like a man" in this poem
is to impose a structure that resolves or occludes contradictions and
disorder, fulfills the need for wholeness. It is to constrain, control, or
eliminate outright the feminine—carnal love, the letter of the text—in
order to provide a single, solid, univalent meaning firmly fixed in a
hierarchical moral structure. Donaldson, Robertson, the narrator, Pandarus, Troilus all read like men: they invoke structures of authority in
order to order the disorder, to stop the restless desire represented in
and enacted by their texts, to find rest.

Everyone needs such rest, of course, not just men. The issue is
not whether a text should be left open or should be closed—indeed,
I turn away from complications and recalcitrant details in creating a
whole, unified reading of the poem—but how that rest is achieved,
whether the costs and sacrifices of closure are understood, acknowledged, problematized. Such rest and closure are what every ideology
provides; but the problem with "soothing and harmonious ideologies"
is that they achieve their vision of wholeness by unacknowledged exclusion, elimination, constraint.[36] And the problem with this particular
ideology, this masculine ideology activating "reading like a man," is
that it achieves its harmonious rest by constituting the feminine as
disruptive Other, constraining, and finally turning away from it.[37] This
is a high price to pay for order and stability, and the high cost is made
clear in the reductiveness of the Epilogue. The Epilogue takes back
the whole project, at last, of *Troilus and Criseyde,* as Waswo also sees:

That everything in human life is temporary does not mean that it
is valueless; the whole poem elicits pathos for the temporal loss of
something that was both real and valuable. But nothing would ever
be gained, even temporarily, if we were to act on the doctrine that
it's all false anyway. To practice this preachment would be paraly-
sis: we would do no business, have no love affairs, and write no
poems.[38]

To read like a man, to turn away from the feminine (the letter, the
woman) constituted as disruption, radically limits all human experience in the world.

4

But if that's "reading like a man," what might it be to "read like a
woman"? Is there any alternative to this masculine reading response
suggested in the poem? Is there such a thing in this work as a feminine response? To begin to answer these questions, we must turn now
to Criseyde, for she is not only a text read but is herself a reader.

At the beginning of this romance, in a city under siege, Criseyde
reads a romance about a city under siege—Thebes (2.78–84).[39] Thebes
was associated in the medieval imagination with an unending cycle
of violence and familial transgression. Likewise, romance narrative,
considered generically, itself proceeds by dilation, delay, incessant
deferral.[40] The very book, then, that she reads is one that in itself
problematizes closure. But further, the romance she's reading adumbrates the outcome of *her* romance: it tells the ancestry of her future
lover, Diomede. It tells her of the events that ultimately place him in
the Greek camp, available and eager to win her love. Diomede will
eventually in fact narrate these very events to her in book 5, as he con-
vinces her to forget Troilus and give her love to him. And Cassandra
(another woman reader) will narrate these very events to Troilus, who
will, at length, accept them, recognize Criseyde's betrayal, and seek
his own death.

That is, that romance *would* tell Criseyde of her own story if she
were allowed to finish it. It *would* then enact a kind of narrative impossibility: Criseyde would be reading her own narrative. But Pandarus
interrupts Criseyde's reading (alluding to the twelve books already
written on this matter) before she can ascertain *her* romance's origins
and begins to work on *his* "text"—a romance of his own creation,
which he will soon sit back and "read."[41] It is as if, in this inaugu-
ral moment in the affair of Troilus and Criseyde, Criseyde threatens

to know too much, to get ahead of the narrative, to read things impossible for her to read, things that must remain hidden from her. Cassandra (the other major female reader in the poem as I've just mentioned) not only threatens to but does indeed know too much. Troilus explicitly scorns her reading of his dream. We might suggest that, in this text, feminine reading seems to male readers to be excessive: it goes beyond licit or proper awareness; it is potentially disruptive of orderly, logical, linear narratives that have well-delimited boundaries; and it is therefore curtailed, kept in check.[42]

Criseyde herself seems to be aware of such constraints imposed upon her as reader. When Pandarus cuts off her reading, insisting instead that she get up and dance with him, "And lat us don to May som observaunce" (2.112), Criseyde refuses, in what sounds like mock shock:

> "I! God forbede!" quod she. "Be ye mad?
> Is that a widewes lif, so God yow save?
> By God, ye maken me ryght soore adrad!
> Ye ben so wylde, it semeth as ye rave.
> It satte me wel bet ay in a cave
> To bidde and rede on holy seyntes lyves;
> Lat maydens gon to daunce, and yonge wyves."
>
> (2.113–19)

She knows that she, as widow, as woman without a husband, should be reading saints' lives—uniform, unambiguous narratives based on the repetition of one life on earth.[43] Criseyde's tone suggests here that everyone knows the reading appropriate to a woman without a man is the reading of perfectly closed narratives whose letter is itself worthy of imitation. And if Criseyde feels the constraints on her own reading activity, she is also aware of herself as the future victim of masculine reading: she knows that her literary reputation as a traitor is in fact set, that she'll be interpreted only one way, by male *auctores* who write "thise bokes" and by "wommen" who will believe them:

> She seyde, "Allas, for now is clene ago
> My name of trouthe in love, for everemo!
> For I have falsed oon the gentileste
> That evere was, and oon the worthieste!
>
> "Allas, of me, unto the worldes ende,
> Shal neyther ben ywriten nor ysonge
> No good word, for thise bokes wol me shende.

O, rolled shal I ben on many a tonge!
Thorughout the world my belle shal be ronge!
And wommen moost wol haten me of alle.
Allas, that swich a cas me sholde falle!

"Thei wol seyn, in as muche as in me is,
I have hem don dishonour, weylaway!
Al be I nat the first that dide amys,
What helpeth that to don my blame awey?"

(5.1054–68)

It is in fact these "wommen" whose rancor Criseyde dreads most. Male *auctores*—this narrator included—who write "this bokes" present readers with final castigations of Criseyde: literary tradition represents Criseyde as a traitor to be turned away from;[44] and "wommen" have no access to her other than through this authoritative lens, as Criseyde well knows. Their view of Criseyde is thus "immasculated," to use Judith Fetterley's felicitous term, and such immasculation turns women away from women.[45] Or, in the terms of my analysis, they are reading like men. Rather than being sex-determined, masculine reading as the totalizing imposition of control is indeed constructed, a behavior rather than a "natural" biological destiny.

When Criseyde is left alone, though, or remains uninterrupted in the company of women, she performs acts of reading that suggest —just hint at—a positive alternative to constricting masculine reading. The problem with "reading like a man" is that it totalizes, that it not only insists on a unified reading but construes as feminine and consequently excludes whatever does not accord with that whole. In contradistinction, the emphasis in Criseyde's response to Antigone's song in book 2 is on her absorbing, taking in every word, without any excisions or occlusions. After she has talked with Pandarus at the beginning of book 2, she thinks about their conversation, then walks out into the garden with her three nieces and a "gret route" of her women; she hears Antigone's song and, in an attempt to interpret it, to "read" it, she inquires about the author and comments on the experience of "thise loveres" that might yield such "faire" verses.

But *every word* which that she of hire herde,
She gan to prenten in hire herte faste,
And ay gan love hire lasse for t'agaste
Than it dide erst, and synken in hire herte,
That she wex somwhat able to converte.

(2.899–903; my emphasis)

This passage describes her initial impression ("She gan to prenten in hire herte faste"); it doesn't describe her further process of interpretation, her choices and eventual exclusions. But I want to point to another instance of her reading in which the emphasis is again on this sense of the entire text, every word of it: when Pandarus boldly delivers Troilus' first letter (by shoving it down her front), she retires to her chamber, away from that uncle, "Ful pryvely this lettre for to rede"; she "Avysed word by word in every lyne, / And fond no lak" (2.1176–78). In contrast, in a passage I have already quoted above, Troilus reads Criseyde's first letter as allegorical and concludes with a general reading, without reference to the particulars:

> But finaly, he took al for the beste,
> That she hym wroot, for somwhat he byheld
> On which hym thoughte he myghte his herte reste,
> Al covered she tho wordes under sheld.
>
> (2.1324–27)

This contrast is based on slender evidence, admittedly, and is dependent on the unknowable words of each letter; but I want to pursue it, tentatively, a little further. Certainly, critics have noted time and again that Criseyde deliberates, ponders, carefully considers every word in her early encounters with Pandarus and Troilus (the narrator in fact is the first to make this kind of point [2.666–79]). This is again in contrast to Troilus, who falls in love in an instant; in private Criseyde "every word gan up and down to wynde / That he had seyd, as it com hire to mynde" (2.601–2) after her uncle has dropped the big news about the prince. Perhaps this slight emphasis in Criseyde's responses indicates not the mere scheming of a woman—a negative judgment that has been made often enough—but, rather, hints at a kind of (reading) response that keeps the whole in view—every word of it.

Considerable arguments might be mounted against Criseyde as reader, particularly in the latter books of the poem; she could easily be seen as preemptive and self-serving, for example, distorting the text and creating interpretations for her own benefit. But these early reading acts, foundational to her identity in the love affair, do contain a consistent, delicate emphasis and appear to suggest something of a contrast to the men reading in the narrative. I suggest that Criseyde's reading acts here adumbrate alternatives to misogynistic, totalizing reading, alternatives we'll see most fully developed by the Wife of Bath and the Clerk. But even in the well-controlled masculine representation of Alceste in the Prologue to the *Legend of Good Women*, as we'll see, there is an emphasis in her responses on inclusiveness, on hearing both sides of a question, on various possibilities of interpretation. Further on, the Wife of Bath suggests that the letter— "every word"—must be considered and valued, and she uses forms that upset linear narrative logic and closure. And the Clerk, identifying with Griselda and even described in feminine terms, suggests that any reading must keep in mind, must keep poignant and ever present, a paradoxical knowledge: an awareness of what that very reading excludes. Such strategies upsetting totalizing literary acts are associated, I suggest, with the feminine in Chaucer's texts, and this slight emphasis on "every word" in Criseyde's depiction as she reads alone or among women may in fact point to them.

If Criseyde leads us to a perspective on masculine reading, there is a further awareness yet in the poem of "reading like a man" in the figure of Pandarus—a man who reads like a man. Such an awareness is an especially powerful demonstration of the constructedness of the masculine response: if Criseyde suggests that women can and do read like men, Pandarus suggests that men don't have to read like men. To get to Pandarus, though, and his awareness of reading like a man, requires that we take a rather drastic turn in the analysis. It is a shift suggested directly, however, by Saint Jerome's image of reading as a masculine act performed on the feminine body. For that body of the text, we recall, is represented as the body of a woman exchanged between groups of men at war, taken as the spoils of battle by the triumphant Israelite. As we shall see, such an exchange, as analyzed by Lévi-Strauss, constitutes society as we know it. We turn now from consideration of individual men's relation to the feminine (Robertson's, Donaldson's, the narrator's, Troilus') to examination of the entire patriarchal social structure's relation to, or use of, the female character and female desire. We turn now to consider Criseyde not as reader but once again as read—for she is just such a body passed between groups of men at war. Her "slydynge," her autonomy and desire, found by individual men to be intolerable, proves in fact to be a capacity with a definite utility within patriarchal culture as a whole.

5

Let us look briefly, schematically, at the role of women in patriarchal social structure, in order to discern, finally, how Pandarus reads Criseyde—for Troy, viewed in the English Middle Ages and later as the mythic point of origin of lineality, associated with the orderly and legitimate *translatio* of rule, is represented in the poem, indeed, as a patriarchal social organization. I draw here on Gayle Rubin's brilliant and influential article, "The Traffic in Women: Notes on the 'Political Economy' of Sex."[46] Patriarchal society can be described, very simply, as men bonded together by women. It is, of course, gender-asymmetrical—that is, male-dominated with respect to descent, property, and public and private authority. Women are the conduit by which power is passed on; they bear sons. They are thus the means by which man is bonded to man. But further, as Marcel Mauss suggests, society is constituted by the exchange of gifts between groups of men. Mauss refers to primitive society in particular, but, as Rubin has discerned (p. 172), his claims are much more general: he argues in effect that the gift liberated culture itself.[47] Lévi-Strauss, in *The Elementary Structures of Kinship*, follows and extends Mauss's analysis: society depends not only on linguistic and commercial exchange but on the exchange of women. Women are the most precious of gifts —"the supreme gift": accordingly, the regulation of the exchange of women between families and groups is the very basis of social organization.[48] The rule of exogamy is "at the center of an agreement to control warfare among men"; rules governing the exchange of women are the "most basic peace treaty."[49] I shall critique Lévi-Strauss's analysis of the incest prohibition in detail in reference to the *Man of Law's Tale*; for now, what matters is the basic idea of women in patriarchal social structure as tokens of exchange, as gifts, peace offerings, as the means of establishing or maintaining peace between groups of men at war. Such "traffic in women" can be witnessed across societies and across centuries: Rubin notes that women

> are given in marriage, taken in battle, exchanged for favors, sent as tribute, traded, bought, sold. Far from being confined to the "primitive" world, these practices seem only to become more pronounced and commercialized in more "civilized" societies. (P. 175)

The relevance of this paradigm to *Troilus and Criseyde* will no doubt be clear. Troy is, of course, a city at war. Criseyde is a woman traded between groups of men at war. And when she chooses to shift her allegiance from Troilus to Diomede, she in fact acts in the best interests of Troy in the repair of its losses in battle and in the reestablishment of truce or temporary equilibrium of the siege. She acts, that is, in the best interests of patriarchal society itself. For, as Rubin drily remarks, it is in the interest of the smooth operation of the patriarchal exchange system that the woman "not have too many ideas of her own about whom she might want to sleep with": if patriarchy is to perpetuate

itself, the woman exchanged between men must adapt her desire to
the desire of the man who has received possession of her (p. 182).
The "slydynge" of Criseyde's "corage," then, her very ability to be
unfaithful, is thus capable of being used to further patriarchal social
organization: the autonomous sliding of her heart is exactly what fits
her for use as a thing passed between men.

Criseyde's role as that thing passed between men informs her deportment in fundamental ways. She is, of course, subject to and at
the mercy of men, always needing their protection: when her father
leaves Troy—leaves his furniture and Criseyde—she must plead to
Hector for security; she appeals to Pandarus as her rightful protector;
she refers to Troilus as her shield, her wall.[50] Her very characterization
—her "style," as Charles Muscatine has deftly analyzed it—consists
of the adoption of the styles of the men around her. She is stylisti-
cally, in her linguistic idiom, *between* Pandarus and Troilus. When she
is with Pandarus, she speaks the language of Pandarus—practical,
witty, wily, tactical; she speaks the language of Troilus—matches him
aube for *aube*—when she is around him. When Muscatine remarks that
Criseyde's "ambiguity is her meaning,"[51] he is exactly right: that sliding character functions in her position as that thing passed between
men. And when Donaldson, describing what he sees as Criseyde's
constitutive passivity, comments that she will "desire what most desires her," he is right, too: the conformity of her desire to the desire of
men around her is necessary to, and compelled by, patriarchal social
organization.[52] Her act of infidelity can thus be analyzed more in terms
of complicity in than disruption or betrayal of fundamental masculine
social control. What she betrays is not the power structure of masculine control; she betrays, in truth, only an illusion of reciprocity
between men and women, an illusion generated as a cover for the real
workings of traffic in women.

For trafficking in women is a fundamental activity in Troy, and the
real power relations are between men.[53] Pandarus is, of course, the
principal participant in this activity, and he is certainly conscious of
his status as "meene," as go-between. He bursts into Troilus' room
in book 1 eager to help him obtain his love, to get the woman, *whoever* she is (1.617–865). When consummation is in fact imminent, in
book 3, he urges Troilus to keep quiet about his actions as "meene,"
in a sort of *crise de conscience*: especially as Criseyde's "em," Pandarus
confesses, he should not be doing this (3.274–80). His perfect willingness to engage in this activity *and* his reluctance to have it known
suggest both that he views women as things to be traded and that this
is an operant truth that Trojans (especially those ostensibly courtly
lovers) would perhaps rather not acknowledge.

Pandarus has been compared to the lower-class waterfowls of *Parliament of Fowls*, to whom one girl-bird is interchangeable with another ("But she wol love hym, lat hym love another!" [567]). Indeed, his view of women as interchangeable, as commodities to be traded, clashes with Troilus' courtly view of the uniqueness of his love object and concurs more closely with the voice of the "peple" in Parliament who clearly view the woman as material to be traded between men at war, as spoils of battle (4.183–217). When Troilus and Pandarus learn that Criseyde will be traded, Pandarus offers to get Troilus another woman, since Troy is full of beauties, he alleges, twelve times prettier than Criseyde. Women are functionally interchangeable in Troy, Pandarus suggests here, and he tries to make Troilus acknowledge this:

> And over al this, as thow wel woost thiselve,
> This town is ful of ladys al aboute;
> And, to my doom, fairer than swiche twelve
> As evere she was, shal I fynde in som route—
> Yee, on or two, withouten any doute.
> Forthi be glad, myn owen deere brother!
> If she be lost, we shal recovere an other.
> (4.400–406)

Troilus is not cheered by this prospect. In fact, he accuses Pandarus of not abiding by his own stated beliefs:

> But tel me now, syn that the thynketh so light
> To changen so in love ay to and fro,
> Whi hastow nat don bisily thi myght
> To chaungen hire that doth the al thi wo?
> (4.484–87)

Pandarus may, of course, be speaking to Troilus in this way only "for the nones" (4.428). Muscatine suggests that Pandarus' sincerity as a courtly lover is not to be questioned, but this is a belief difficult to maintain; for, as Muscatine also points out, Pandarus owes much of his characterization to Amis, the friend of Amant in the *Roman de la rose*. Amis' view of the relations between the sexes is unremittingly cynical; he sees that the present-day relations were established in the sad moments when sovereignty of husband over wife was established and when, in a telling concurrence, possessions were made private (vv. 8355–8466, 9493–9665). I suggest that Pandarus' courtly love of "oon" to which Troilus refers here, always obscure and undefined in the narrative (1.666; 2.57–63; 2.98; 2.1105–7), is more a convenient fiction sustained for Troilus, and courtly Trojans, than a poignant reality for Pandarus himself.[54]

Contra Pandarus here, Troilus is indeed convinced that Criseyde is the only one for him. Pandarus asks the desperate Troilus, "Artow for hire and for noon other born? / Hath Kynde the wrought al only hire to plese?" (4.1095–96). And Troilus would reply, unhesitatingly, "Yes." He cries out to the absent Criseyde:

> I ne kan nor may,
> For al this world, withinne myn herte fynde
> To unloven yow a quarter of a day!
> In corsed tyme I born was, weilaway,
> That yow, that doon me al this wo endure,
> Yet love I best of any creature!
>   (5.1696–1701)

But Troilus has also said something to Pandarus that would seem to contradict this whole notion and acknowledge a more fundamental system of trade of women. It is a statement that has shocked readers by its incongruity with Troilus' professed belief about the uniqueness of women. No critic, to my knowledge, has been able to make adequate sense of this moment when the larger social reality of Troy suddenly erupts in the narrative, suddenly impinges upon the private world to which the narrative has heretofore been devoted. When Pandarus has his crisis of conscience, acknowledging that he is a pander, Troilus denies that Pandarus has done a "bauderye." Some distinctions are in order, he declares: call him who takes money for this kind of thing whatever you will; but what Pandarus does, call it "gentilesse, / Compassioun, and felawship, and trist" (3.402–3). He then volunteers his own pandering service to Pandarus, not only to prove that he doesn't disapprove but also as a repayment, *a thank-you gift*. After he has protested, "And that thow hast so muche ido for me / That I ne may it nevere more disserve," he makes his offer to Pandarus:

> And that thow knowe I thynke nought ne wene
> That this servise a shame be or jape,
> I have my faire suster Polixene,
> Cassandre, Eleyne, or any of the frape—
> Be she nevere so fair or wel yshape,
> Tel me which thow wilt of everychone,
> To han for thyn, and lat me thanne allone.
>   (3.407–13)

"Any of the frape": in the ease with which Troilus offers his "servise" —indeed, his *sister*—we sense that this view of women as gifts, tokens of exchange, is more basic to the relations between men in Troy than is the view of women as singular and unique.[55] Troilus enacts the split between an individual courtly response to the female character—he is fascinated with Criseyde and desires to hold on to her—and the larger societal attitude that mandates that her desire must be able to transfer itself from man to man. When Troilus finally turns away from instability in his turning away from earthly love (from the perspective of the eighth sphere), that patriarchal attitude that controls and directs woman's "slydynge" asserts itself at last.

But the "peple" of Troy are entirely disabused. They operate explicitly by the rule of exchange, insisting that Criseyde be traded (4.183–217). Later, the silly friends who visit Criseyde to console her, saying "wommanysshe thynges" (4.694), suggest the same thing: woman is a gift, a peace offering:

> Quod tho the thridde, "I hope, ywis, that she
> Shal bryngen us the pees on every syde,
> That, whan she goth, almyghty God hire gide!"
> (4.691–93)

When, then, Hector—Troilus' brother—protests in the Parliament, "We usen here no wommen for to selle" (4.182), he is referring to ideals—courtly ideals—that may be seen as a cover for the real workings of patriarchy. (Shakespeare, in his redaction of this tale, emphasizes the split between Hector's idealism and his patriarchal functionalism; see, for example, 2.2.164–94.) The Trojans may not approve of commercialized traffic in women—they don't approve of prostitution or procuring women for money—but they clearly understand that a woman is man's possession and can be traded. They are of course engaged in a war to defend the passage of a woman from one man to another—Helen, from Menelaus to Paris—and they will repair their losses in war by further traffic. Peace, as Criseyde herself suggests, will come when Helen is traded back to the Greeks (4.1345–48).[56]

Criseyde, then, "muwet, milde, and mansuete" (5.194) as she is ceremoniously led out of the Trojan camp by Troilus and handed over to Diomede, is in this way obedient, compliant, furthering the aims of Trojans at war. Her act of "slydynge," even as it may seem to be the most poignant disruption of the individual man's desires and control (being an expression of her autonomous desire), does not in fact threaten the operant structures of power. She knows this, I suggest, knows how constrained her subjectivity is (just as she is aware of

the constraints on her reading), and thus makes the best of it with
Diomede:

> But syn I se ther is no bettre way,
> And that to late is now for me to rewe,
> To Diomede algate I wol be trewe.
>
> (5.1069–71)

In some sense she *is* as "trewe" to Diomede as she was to Troilus. She,
as "slydynge" woman, that is, proves finally "trewe" to patriarchal
society.

Pandarus, from his perspective as trafficker in women, sees that
because women are treated as mere objects of trade in this society,
their hearts must by necessity be "slydynge." He knows Criseyde and
never thinks for a moment that she will return. He knows that heart,
that is, not only because he knows his close relative but because he is
a pander.

> "Ye, haselwode!" thoughte this Pandare,
> And to hymself ful softeliche he seyde,
> "God woot, refreyden may this hote fare,
> Er Calkas sende Troilus Criseyde!"
> But natheless, he japed thus, and pleyde,
> And swor, ywys, his herte hym wel bihighte
> She wolde come as soone as evere she myghte.
>
> (5.505–11)

This issue is less that Calkas won't let Criseyde go (5.508) than that
Criseyde herself won't come (5.511). Pandarus is aware that she will
never return, and he only keeps up appearances for Troilus' sake:

> Pandare answerde, "It may be, wel ynough,"
> And held with hym of al that evere he seyde.
> But in his herte he thoughte, and softe lough,
> And to hymself ful sobreliche he seyde,
> "From haselwode, there joly Robyn pleyde,
> Shal come al that that thow abidest heere.
> Ye, fare wel al the snow of ferne yere!"
>
> (5.1170–76)

Pandarus' final rejection of Criseyde in book 5—his reading her
like a man, turning away from the feminine—is an act performed

for the benefit of Troilus. These angry last words, furious, excessive, final, cannot really be an expression of his own disappointment or disillusionment. He is acting *like* a man—rejecting the feminine—and soon Troilus and the narrator will do the same. But from the fact of Pandarus' expedient behavior we can extrapolate an idea of considerable importance: reading *like* a man is a behavior that can be adopted in specific circumstances; there are thus other ways to read *as* a man. This is a principle with deep and broad implications: literary history, tradition, hermeneutics—although they are represented in male-dominated society as, and indeed proceed by, a containment or occlusion of the feminine—do not necessarily have to be structured according to this dynamic. The literary enterprise need not be constituted by opposition, by exclusion, by oppressive mastery and consequent constriction. The fiction of the *Legend of Good Women* picks up precisely this point: a tradition alternative to the one Criseyde is aware of, a tradition that does not proceed by constraining the feminine viewed as disruptive Other, is urgently needed.

There may not have appeared to be alternatives in the 1950s to Robertson's and Donaldson's assumptions about reading. But *Troilus and Criseyde* itself is a corrective to that apparent reality; it suggests that a first step toward finding alternatives in literary practice to containing and rejecting the feminine is an awareness that this "natural" literary practice is not natural, that it is, precisely, a fabricated strategy —that of reading like a man. Chaucer suggests just such a larger view through the characters of Criseyde and Pandarus. They are the characters who understand constrained necessity; and they are the characters with whom Chaucer, after all, had much in common. Chaucer, too, as a bourgeois in the aristocratic court, was constrained by dominant (masculine) power, as were aristocratic women. And Chaucer, like Pandarus, was responsible for its various traffics, as Waswo also observes: we recall that he served as messenger for Prince Lionel; as esquire, transacted Edward III's business; monitored commercial traffic in the Port of London as Controller of Customs; managed royal property as clerk of the works; even participated in negotiations regarding Richard II's marriage.[57] The connection between Chaucer and Pandarus seems to have been picked up, in fact, by Deschamps, in his famous lyric to Chaucer: a *crux* in his *ballade* (probably written in the 1390s) can be explicated in these terms. Calling England the "Kingdom of Aeneas," Deschamps lauds Chaucer as a translator, a linguistic go-between—as, precisely, "Pandras."[58]

It is evident that fourteenth-century readers, apparently women in particular, responded to the upsets, the disruptions, the discomforts of *Troilus and Criseyde* by wanting soothing, harmonious, unified narratives: it is no coincidence that the palinode for the poem, the *Legend of Good Women*, is written in the form of saints' lives, those rigorously controlled narratives such as Criseyde ought to be reading. But as we'll see, this response is again an "immasculated" one; it is gendered as masculine in the legends themselves. The very masculine narrator, increasingly restive, immobilizes female characters and keeps a tight grip on the letter of his pagan texts. And the consequences are drastic: the series breaks off mid-sentence. If the feminine is too rigorously constrained—if people keep reading *like* men—poems indeed stop.

Chapter Two

"The naked text in English to declare": The Legend of Good Women

Criseyde was right. Having transferred her "trouthe" from Troilus to Diomede, she predicted the outrage of "wommen" as they read and hear her story, the tale of the treacherous female who is "slydynge of corage." She knew that "thise bokes" would represent her only as unfaithful to the steadfast Troilus, would castigate or turn away from her in drawing their moral conclusions, and that "wommen" would be schooled by these books.[1] As we have seen, the narrator of *Troilus and Criseyde*—that "litel bok"—has dealt with her, finally, in just this manner: like the rest of the masculine readers in and of the poem, he finally rejects unsatisfying involvement with the female character and closes off the tale by getting rid of the troubling feminine.

Even the narrator himself recognizes, toward the end of his poem, that women in his audience might take offense at his choice to write of an unworthy, guilty woman. But this recognition does not mitigate his final antifeminist gesture; in fact, his apologetic lines reinscribe the authority and veracity of the essentially antifeminist tradition of representing Criseyde, as he beseeches

> every lady bright of hewe,
> And every gentil womman, what she be,
> That al be that Criseyde was untrewe,
> That for that gilt she be nat wroth with me.
> Ye may hire gilt in other bokes se;
> And gladlier I wol write, yif yow leste,
> Penolopeës trouthe and good Alceste.
>
> (5.1772–78)

The narrator maintains that he would rather write of Penelope and Alceste.[2] Of course he would; for this would give him the opportunity apparently to appease "every gentil womman" while still reading like a man.

In fact, if it is "ladies" (and their advocates) in the courtly audience who call out for stories of simply good women—who call out for an antidote to *Troilus and Criseyde* and the *Roman de la rose*—they, too, are reading like men. It is Criseyde who intimates a knowledge of such a phenomenon. She not only laments that "wommen" will hate her because they will have read authoritative (masculine) versions of her story (their view is thus immasculated, as we saw in the last chapter); she also implicitly acknowledges that what men would have her read is very different from what she does read. When Pandarus bursts into her parlor at the beginning of book 2, as we've seen, he interrupts her reading of a romance of Thebes in the company of several of her women; when he insists that she put that book away, she says that, as widow, she *should* be sitting in a cave, dutifully reading saints' lives. As opposed to the romance, a form associated with the feminine, saints' lives are uniform, unambiguous narratives—perfect for immasculated readers. A "Seintes Legende of Cupide" (as the Man of Law will later call it [*CT* 2:60–61]) is exactly what the narrator's audience of immasculated readers—represented in the Prologue to the *Legend of Good Women* by the God of Love and Alceste—demands: after the threat of disorder and unfulfillment that the feminine poses in *Troilus and Criseyde*, they want unproblematic fables of faithful women repeated over and over.

The narrator is indeed willing to comply. His self-defense in the Prologue is brief, and he expresses gratitude to Alceste for her intercession and imposition of the light penance of writing a legend of good women. After the disappointments of pagan letter and female character, he wants his females simple, stable, and orderly. He again narrates pagan fables and again positions himself as masculine lover, as we'll see; but this time he immediately strips and cleans up that alien woman, as he did only *after* being seduced by her in *Troilus and Criseyde*. This time he refuses to become vicariously, erotically involved in the act of *translatio;* this time he rigorously chastens the letter and controls the slippery feminine.

Chaucer thus continues in the *Legend of Good Women* to analyze readers' responses of flight into security and control in gendered terms, as, specifically, a masculine—or immasculated—flight from the threateningly mobile, "slydynge" feminine "corage." If, as seems likely, this palinode was indeed written in response to discussion at court of his works, Chaucer's analysis reveals the reductiveness and unhappy social implications not only of an abstract notion of totalizing reading and literary history but of the demands for simplicity and closure made by his own audience. As we'll see at last, the *Legend of Good Women* makes clear that it is not just the feminine "corage" —the fable, the female character—that suffers under such restraint. Constraining the feminine takes its toll on the *masculine* as well—on the moral "spirit" of the fables and on the male characters. Indeed, it stops literature itself.[3]

1

If *Troilus and Criseyde* is thoroughly but implicitly preoccupied with reading, the Prologue to the *Legend of Good Women* is directly and explicitly about readers' (and listeners') responses to Chaucer's works. Chaucer's later revisions of the F Prologue in the G Prologue (the version I shall focus on) make literary concerns even more central.[4] The Prologue stages a heated confrontation between the narrator—fictionalized image of the real poet—and his audience, disgruntled with his having translated *Troilus and Criseyde* and the *Roman de la rose*. Contemporary witnesses suggest that medieval readers were deeply unsettled by both the *Rose* and *Troilus and Criseyde*. Since response to the latter is my concern here, I'll not document the vast evidence of upset over the *Rose;* suffice it to note that the whole *querelle* (dating from 1399 to about 1402) evinces high-level agitation over the *Rose's* representation of women.[5] Several medieval responses to *Troilus and Criseyde* in fact reenact the masculine response as we have seen it represented in the poem itself: after reading the work Henryson felt the need to finish off the narrative by finishing off Criseyde, making his moral point loud and clear. And an anonymous fifteenth-century reader of the poem, a male cleric instructing women religious—a man teaching women, implicitly, how to read—felt a similar need for moral disambiguation and closure of the poem.[6] If, then, Queen Anne herself demanded a palinode for these poems (as an enduring but unlikely notion would have it), she was responding precisely as other readers in and of *Troilus and Criseyde* responded.[7] Alceste and the God of Love—fictional (and perhaps rather exaggerated) representations of Chaucer's real readers —articulate this immasculated courtly response; wanting to hear only of good women, simply refusing to hear of any other kind, they chide the narrator: "Why noldest thow han writen of Alceste, / And laten Criseide ben aslepe and reste?" asks the God of Love (G:530–31).

The narrator's unsettling confrontation with his public takes place in a dream vision. Chaucer's choice to return to the courtly dream-vision form after *Troilus and Criseyde* has puzzled critics, but it seems to me that this courtly form as Chaucer has developed it is well suited to a critique of masculine reading and literary history. The courtly genre alone serves him well: from what we saw of "courtly love" in *Troilus and Criseyde* (its use as a cover for the patriarchal exchange of women, which denies women independent desire) we can infer a fundamentally patriarchal intent under the courtly setting of this Prologue as well. Chaucer typically uses dream visions to explore the dreamer-narrator's imaginative response to a text that is narrated in the frame: in *Book of the Duchess* it is Ovid's tale of Ceyx and Alcione that appears in the frame; in *Parliament of Fowls* it is the *Somnium Scipionis*; and in *House of Fame* the *Aeneid* appears in the dream. In the Prologue to the *Legend of Good Women* Chaucer explores not only response to *Troilus and Criseyde* and the *Rose* in the dream but response to the whole authoritative, monolithic tradition of "olde bokes," introduced by the narrator in the frame's first twenty-eight lines. The problems of representation in *Troilus and Criseyde* and the *Rose* are problems in all "olde bokes"; the credibility of literary tradition and, indeed, the monumental structure of "authoritees" itself (83), so anxiously advanced by the narrator at the beginning of the poem (he haltingly explains why he even brought the subject up: "But wherfore that I spak, to yeve credence / To bokes olde and don hem reverence, / Is for men shulde autoritees beleve . . ." [81–83]), are implicated in the dream confrontation between the poet and his audience.

The dream-vision setting, further, encourages us to read these characters as parts of the narrator's own mind. Just as we can understand the Black Knight and the dreamer in the *Book of the Duchess* as figures who work through a grief like the narrator's own,[8] we can read the God of Love and Alceste as reifications of the narrator's uneasiness about the reception and understanding—the afterlife—of his works. They have value as figures both exterior and interior to the narrator's own psyche, and his interactions with them in the dream indicate the way the narrator will find resolution of the issues opened up by the end of *Troilus and Criseyde*. Cupid gives voice to the essential dilemma of the narrator after *Troilus and Criseyde*: if one begins to become aware, as he does via women in his audience, that authoritative tradition proceeds by defaming women, how would one be able to write a poem or construct a literary tradition that is *not* misogynistic in theme and/or structure? Alceste's representation in the Prologue suggests that the problem can be articulated; however, a positive solution is far from imminent.

The dream opens by figuring the narrator in an uneasy position.[9] He finds himself in a meadow straight out of the *Parliament of Fowls*—

apparently beautiful, but the scene of erotic dissension and problematic closure, deferred resolution. Although we are told that the birds choose their mates and consummate their desire in this lovely setting beyond compare, we are also told, as John Fyler notes, that the delightful meadow isn't always like this: the baleful season of winter has just departed.[10] The narrator listens to the sound of the birds and hears a lark proclaim the arrival of the God of Love, with Alceste, clothed "al in grene" (174), and a huge crowd of women: it is a sight that astonishes (164). After the women sing a *balade,* they arrange themselves perfectly in order and "nat a word was spoken in that place / The mountance of a furlong-wey of space" (232–33). A very long silence ensues. The narrator hides near a hillside, keeping "as stille as any ston" (236), only to be discovered and berated by the God of Love. On the basis of the narrator's literary endeavors, the God sets his worth at less than a worm's.

Cupid's objections are twofold: he claims that by translating the *Roman de la rose,* Guillaume de Lorris' and Jean de Meun's "heresye," the narrator has made "wise folk fro me withdrawe" (257) and that by writing *Troilus and Criseyde,* he has been intent on "shewynge how that wemen han don mis" (266). These objections are of course interrelated: by demonstrating in the *Rose* that "he nys but a verray propre fol / That loveth paramours to harde and hote" (259–60), the narrator has, in the God's opinion, turned readers' attention away from worthy women. It is upon this alleged defamation of women that the God focuses his remonstrations:

> Why noldest thow as wel [han] seyd goodnesse
> Of wemen, as thow hast seyd wikednesse?
> Was there no good matere in thy mynde,
> Ne in all thy bokes ne coudest thow nat fynde
> Som story of wemen that were goode and trewe?
> (268–72)

The narrator's mistake, according to Cupid, is in his ill-advised choice of bad "matere"; and the rectification of this mistake, Cupid advises, lies in the proper choice of stories of good, true women.[11] There is a long literary tradition, he claims, of just such stories of women true in love: "al the world of autours," including "Valerye, Titus[,] . . . Claudyan[,] . . . Jerome[,] . . . Ovyde[,] . . . Vincent" (280–310), write them. The fact that he can reasonably appeal to the notorious "Jerome" and "Valerye" here—they do contain images of women true in loving—is not merely "ironic"; it is a symptom of the antifeminism inherent in the act of totalizing, of the misogyny that closure enacts. The God of Love would turn away from the literature that threatens his order and embrace totality, would embrace the "world of autours" that celebrates a single, uncomplicated, unwavering image. He elides the "draf," the bad woman, and advances an ideal that immobilizes woman, effectively kills her off. And further, he makes that immobility her choice. As he tells the narrator,

> For to hyre love were they so trewe
> That, rathere than they wolde take a newe,
> They chose to be ded in sondry wyse,
> And deiden, as the story wol devyse.
>
> (288–91)

Shaking with masculine ire, Cupid claims that the narrator will repent the errors of his ways. At this moment Alceste intervenes— Alceste, who has been cited in desperation by Troilus as an exemplary true woman, Alceste, who is extolled by the narrator in this Prologue as "calandier" of "goodnesse . . . and . . . wifhod" (533–35). She urges the god to allow the narrator a chance to reply to these accusations, insisting that a good ruler should not be an overbearing "tyraunt" (357). In her insistence that both sides of the story be heard and in her advancing *various* hypotheses or possible answers to the god's objections, she may be said to be responding *not* like a man; and because she does this while interceding between two men at odds with one another—that is, she is at this moment in the paradigmatic position of woman in patriarchal social structure—we might suggest that this response is a response not just *like* but *as* a woman.

But the penance she orders the narrator to perform is in fact an entirely totalizing literary activity. She orders him to compose a series of legends that repeatedly represent women as nothing but steadfast in love and that consequently must represent men as fickle and faithless.

> Thow shalt, whil that thow livest, yer by yere,
> The moste partye of thy tyme spende
> In makynge of a gloryous legende
> Of goode women, maydenes and wyves,
> That were trewe in lovynge al here lyves;
> And telle of false men that hem betrayen,
> That al here lyf ne don nat but assayen
> How manye wemen they may don a shame;
> For in youre world that is now holden game.
>
> (471–79)

The legends in *Legend of Good Women,* as we have them in all their flatness and reductiveness, are indeed what Alceste ordered: "trewe" women, "false" men, and a "game" played over and over in which women are the inevitable losers. Compelled to right the balance of misogynist literary tradition, she commissions a very long work dedicated only to positive images of women; but her plan ensures a work peopled by caricatures. Her totalizing vision severely limits the feminine—the female character, the letter itself—and in so doing it finally and necessarily constrains the masculine—the male character, the moral spirit of these fables—as well.

The figure of Alceste seems itself a concentrated locus of the narrator's conflicting impulses. She is beautiful, full of grace, virtue, wisdom. But perhaps there's something slightly unsettling about this female, too. Her critical reputation might itself serve as a testament to a certain ambivalence in her representation. A long series of critics has seen Alceste as an unspotted, ideal lady whose poetic valence includes daisies, the Virgin Mary, the sun, the transcendent powers of the imagination, effective metaphoric language. Others, though, have pointed to inconsistencies in her representation that make her laughable, the butt of satire, or have characterized her behavior as aggressive and peremptory.[12] The narrator's representation of her is indeed double. He praises her in ways that recall the Blessed Virgin (wearing a crown of pearls, she acts as an intercessor for the poet). In her going down to Hell in an act of self-sacrifice, and in her association with the sun and resurrection, she is associated, further, with Christ himself. Moreover, she's wise: she instructs the God of Love in the duties and the merciful spirit of an earthly governor. She is acquainted with the narrator's whole oeuvre, from his earliest productions ("Orygenes upon the Maudeleyne") to his latest works, including even obscure and ephemeral ones: she recalls "al the love of Palamon and Arcite / Of Thebes, thogh the storye is knowen lite; / And many an ympne for your halydayes, / That highten balades, roundeles, vyrelayes" (408– 11). And she knows enough about the circumstances of courtly literary production to attempt a defense of him—enough, perhaps, even to make a little fun of him: in addition to the above virtues, perhaps she even has a sense of humor. In her lighthearted intercession, she is responding as a woman, breaking up, dispersing the lugubrious seriousness of masculine conflict and desire for closure.

But if she's not "slydynge of corage," she is nonetheless physically shifting and changeable, having been metamorphosed into flower and star. (Chaucer in fact created these myths of metamorphosis and stellification for her.) She knows *all* of the narrator's works, major and minor—more, perhaps, than are even in his own "remembraunce" (as Chaucer will express it later in the Retractions)—and she abruptly ends his self-defense (his "arguynge") even after she has pointedly instructed the God of Love to hear whether he can "replye / Ageyns these poynts" (319–20). One critic has shuddered at this "fierc[e] re-buk[e]."[13] The narrator himself praises her mercy, praises her generosity in imposing a light penance; but he does in fact have this disturbing female under control. In his dream he both represents the independent, forceful woman, so troubling in *Troilus and Criseyde*, and neutralizes her power. He has Alceste ask for simplistic stories of women constantly duped and betrayed. The narrator gets what he wants—a long series of passive women—and adds credibility to it by having a *woman* ask for it. In this masculine fantasy, woman herself authorizes the antifeminist work.[14] But antifeminism is not, finally, man's best friend: a totalizing vision such as Alceste's not only silences women and constrains the letter but makes every man in the text unspeakable and, at last, unspeaking.

2

Alceste orders the narrator to spend most of the rest of his life making a "gloryous legende / Of goode women, maydenes and wyves" (473–74). The penitential writing of such a "legende" is, as we've seen, exactly suited to the narrator's masculine desire. Fed up with the feminine in *Troilus and Criseyde,* wanting unproblematic tales and subdued, predictable female characters, he again takes up with an alien woman; but this time he shaves her head, pares her nails, strips off her garments of captivity. He edits his pagan tales—tales of "hethene" women, as Cupid says (299)—to conform to a single, closed, secure, and comforting narrative model. He pares down the tales so drastically, refusing to be engaged by the narratives, that no possible textual seduction can take place. And it is the form of hagiographic narrative, the saint's life, that allows the narrator to manipulate the feminine letter of the classical text and to enervate traditionally aggressive, passionate, even dangerous female characters like Cleopatra, Medea, Philomela, and Procne, and, equally unnerving, women capable of independent moral judgment and action, women like Lucrece, Hypsipyle, and Hypermnestra.

Let us consider the form of the saint's life for a moment, to see how it provides the narrator with so precise a narrative tool for control of the feminine. The similarity among saints' lives that so strikes modern readers is in fact a defining feature of the form.[15] Saints' lives not only *seem* all the same to readers, they very frequently *are* the same: the

Life of Saint Hubert, the *Life of Saint Arnold of Metz,* and the *Life of Saint Lambert,* for example, contain several parts in common; and the *Life of Saint Remaclus* is entirely an imitation of the *Life of Saint Lambert.*[16] A life is written to witness the sanctitude of its subject, and, to that end, particular details of everyday life are often pared out; hagiographic conventions and topoi are invoked; and heavy, often verbatim borrowing from other written lives is routine. Hagiographers considered it perfectly credible to attribute the same miracles to saints in entirely different centuries. A pattern with its themes and motifs is clearly followed in the process of saintly "mythmaking," as Weinstein and Bell put it.[17] The fact that individual saints' lives do differ in purpose from one another, having been written in various forms and for various audiences, should not obscure the theory of the genre: it is *based on* a principle of imitation.[18] Agnellus of Ravenna explains his practice of composing the history of the bishops of Ravenna, by remarking that when he could not find material about particular bishops, he *made up* lives for them, on the principle that all things are common in the communion of saints.

> Wherever I found material they [the brothers of the see] were sure about, I have presented it to you; and anything I have heard from the elderly graybeards, I have not withheld from you. Where I could not uncover a story or determine what kind of a life they led, either from the most aged or from inscriptions or from any other source, to avoid a blank space in my list of holy pontiffs in proper order according to their ordination to the see one after another, I have, with the assistance of God through your prayers, made up a life for them. And I believe no deception is involved, for they were chaste and almsgiving preachers and procurers of men's souls for God.[19]

This is an echo of Gregory of Tours' oft-cited conclusion that

> it is better to talk about the *life* of the fathers than the *lives,* because, though there may be some difference in their merits and virtues, yet the life of one body nourished them all in the world. (My emphasis)[20]

Differences in "merits and virtues" are minimized; references to particular times, dates, and places are systematically eliminated (as in Bede's *Life of Saint Cuthbert*); the conventional "One Life" of the saint emerges as definitive.

In the history of the legend of Saint Marciana we can in fact observe the emergence of just such a conventional hagiographic narrative. In a telling retelling of the *Acta* of the martyr, the author of a hymn in her honor turns a detail in the spare prose narrative into a wondrous sign of sanctitude. According to the prose *Acta*, a lion was released into an amphitheater in order to devour the Christian maiden (during the persecution of Diocletian and his successors), but after smelling her, did her no harm: "Martyris corpus odoratus eam ultra non contigit" ("Having smelled the body of the martyr, he bothered her no further"). The later author of the hymn undertakes to explain why the lion didn't harm her: exploiting, perhaps, the phonological similarity between *odoratus* and *adoratus*, he proclaims:

> Leo percurrit percitus
> Adoraturus veniens
> Non comesturus virginem.[21]

In the latter version the saint's body *odor* has thus been interpreted as miraculous and becomes the cause of a leonine act of *ador*ation—a convention in hagiographic narrative.

The Christian saint's life, of course, demands the recognition of the *constitutive* imperfection—the all-too-human odors—of the body. "When I am weak, then I am strong": Saint Antony's asceticism recognizes his own imperfection and leads him, paradoxically, to perfection.[22] On the level of narrative form, however, paradox or contradiction do not enter in. The soothing regularity and repetition of the canonical saints' lives is intended to bring about in the reader a recognition of—even a participation in—the unified community of the blessed.[23]

But the narrator of the *Legend of Good Women* uses the form defensively. To protect himself from complications—from the dissatisfactions of involvement with the feminine—he reduces or omits entirely details that would distress or vex his working definition of the "good woman." Having been seduced by the unfaithful, ultimately unfruitful feminine in *Troilus and Criseyde*, the narrator uses the form of hagiographic narrative like "niter" on the alien woman's body that Jerome speaks of (in letter 66), to eliminate any disturbing odors in the lives of his heroines—to eliminate anything in the narratives of these women that threatens to upset or undermine patriarchal order. But he so severely reduces the letter that he does not produce a text that invites the mimetic participation of the reader. Indeed, his strategy for controlling his material, as he cuts and pares and scrubs, is to make it downright boring.

3

Passive women, weak martyrs of love, thus populate the *Legend*, and we witness in these tales not only the suppression of female characters in the making of individual narratives but the appropriative and exclusionary processes of masculine literary tradition in its entirety. John Fyler and Elaine Hansen, in their excellent discussions, demonstrate the narrator's individual choices in detail: Cleopatra's infidelities, for example, are glossed over; Medea's grisly revenge is only vaguely mentioned; Phyllis' angry words of recrimination are softened.[24] Virtuous acts, strong expressions of will, are omitted as well: Dido's vow to be true to Sichaeus is not mentioned; Hypsipyle's helping her father escape the murderous Lemnian women is elided; and the uniqueness of Hypermnestra's refusal to murder her husband is not evident in the narrator's redaction. As the heroines lose their individuality in the series of legends, they come to seem increasingly passive, until we reach the final image in the series: Hypermnestra, in flight from her father, finally just *sits down* in abandonment and defeat (2720–22). Expressions of violence, recrimination, and revenge are softened or, more often, elided altogether; the ugly fates of many of the women are mollified; the violent rupture of death, the sudden shock of metamorphosis are lessened as Philomela and Procne are simply left sobbing in each other's arms, Hypsipyle pines away for Jason and finally expires, Medea merely fades from the picture.

These enervated, passive heroines, put into unfamiliar situations and strange places by men, don't have even basic motor control of their own bodies: they quake, shake, tremble for dread. Philomela "quok for fere, pale and pitously" (2317); Hypermnestra "quok as doth the lef of aspe grene. / Ded wex hire hew . . . / dredfully she quaketh" (2648–49, 2680). The narrator's version of the *Legend of Lucrece* indeed exaggerates her physical loss of control: it is the one of the few redactions in which she actually loses consciousness.[25] About to be raped by Tarquin, she

> loste bothe at ones wit and breth,
> And in a swogh she lay, and wex so ded
> Men myghte smyten of hire arm or hed.
> (1815–17)

Men literally do divide up women's bodies and separate their bodies from their spirits: Philomela's tongue, for example, is carved out of her mouth. The narrator revises a passage from Ovid's treatment of

Hypermnestra to emphasize her dissociation from her own body: Hypermnestra looks at her hands, which are forced by her father to carry a knife, and remarks on their incongruity with the rest of her being:

> Allas! and shal myne hondes blody be?
> I am a mayde, and, as by my nature,
> And bi my semblaunt and by my vesture,
> Myne handes ben nat shapen for a knyf.
>
> (2689–92)

The narrator, similarly, picks up and expresses Ovid's sense of the violated Lucrece as separated from herself: Lucrece, whose "contenaunce is to hire herte dygne, / For they acorde bothe in dede and sygne" (1738–39), is deprived by rape of that pure accord of body and heart; her "herte" is still "so wyfly and so trewe" (1843), but her bodily appearance is deathly (1829–34). Indeed, it is only in death that she is able to try to regain that accord:

> And as she fel adoun, she kaste hir lok,
> And of hir clothes yet she hede tok.
> For in hir fallynge yet she had a care,
> Lest that hir fet or suche thyng lay bare;
> So wel she loved clennesse and eke trouthe.
>
> (1856–60)

In the death of the female body, in its un-quickening, the narrator allows the woman to be significant, to signify. Good women gain their identity—become significant—only by dying; as the God of Love says, good women *are* good women because they "chose to be ded in sondry wyse" (290). In killing herself—an act regarded by Augustine[26] as in fact the sin of murder—the good woman takes her only strong action, *constitutes herself.* Thisbe, in her final words, explicitly offers her dead body as sign of woman's "trouthe":

> "But God forbede but a woman can
> Ben as trewe in lovynge as a man!
> And for my part, I shal anon it kythe."
> And with that word his swerd she tok as swythe,
> That warm was of hire loves blod, and hot,
> And to the herte she hireselven smot.
>
> (910–15)

Hypsipyle keeps herself chaste and joyless, and finally dies for love of the absent Jason, "as for his wif" (1577): she dies because, to be his good wife, she must. Phyllis tells Demophon that soon he will be able to see her floating in Athens' harbor, her body the ironic image of his own stony hardness:

> My body mote ye se withinne a while,
> Ryght in the haven of Athenes fletynge,
> Withoute sepulture and buryinge,
> Thogh ye ben harder than is any ston.
>
> (2551–54)

Lucrece, laid out on her bier, offers a publicly legible sign, in death, of woman's "trouthe": Brutus

> openly let cary her on a bere
> Thurgh al the toun, that men may see and here
> The horryble dede of hir oppressyoun.
>
> (1866–68)

It is, of course, an index of the patriarchal context of this text that the self-defining or self-signifying act—the only strong act of the heroines—is a sin, and is, furthermore, both overdetermined by men's actions and completely self-destructive. "The death of a beautiful woman is, unquestionably, the most poetical topic in the world," according to Edgar Allan Poe in *The Philosophy of Composition*, and to the narrator of the *Legend of Good Women* before him.[27] Criseyde's "corage" may threateningly "slyde," but the narrator fixes Lucrece firmly to her bier.

Even as Lucrece's body makes it known, Brutus openly tells her tale to the town of Rome. The female body as sign of "trouthe" is still supplemented, explained by a man, and it is perhaps this condition that allows Lucrece in particular to be canonized ("she was holden there / A seynt" [1870–71]). The idea of masculine appropriation of feminine story, or feminine wit and knowledge, comes up also in the legend of Medea, wherein Jason is "taught" by Medea how to win the fleece; he "gat hym a name ryght as a conqueror, / Ryght thourgh the sleyghte of hire enchauntement" (1649–50). Medea's magic arts may have been suspect as wisdom or truth, but they win Jason glory. Similarly, Phaedra, in the *Legend of Ariadne*, solves the puzzle of the labyrinth for Theseus. As the series of legends goes on, as the heroines get more passive and the narrator more restive, masculine appropriation of the feminine becomes more obvious, and processes of masculine literary tradition become more and more explicit. I want to focus now on the last four tales in the series of legends to see how they in fact reveal the workings of patriarchal literary history.

Such workings are delineated precisely in the *Legend of Ariadne*. Feminine knowledge, truth, wisdom are represented by the "clewe of twyn" Ariadne (prompted by Phaedra) gives to Theseus as a solution to the problem of the labyrinth. For this solution, Theseus promises that he will not "twynne" from her (2029–40). But he does, of course, and the *Legend of Ariadne* is yet another demonstration of masculine perfidy, made worse perhaps than others in the series because Theseus will father the faithless Demophon, "wiked fruit . . . of a wiked tre" (2395). But *Ariadne* is not only a paradigmatic legend of betrayed love; its central image, the labyrinth, is one associated by Chaucer and other medieval readers and writers with texts, and, I shall argue, with the female body. The *Legend of Ariadne* offers an image of gendered reading as well as of betrayed love.

A labyrinth was known in the Middle Ages as both a literal and a figurative maze. Isidore enumerates and describes the four classical labyrinths in his *Etymologies,* as do writers through the medieval period. Boethius exploits the figurative meaning: in Chaucer's translation, the prisoner addresses Lady Philosophy:

> "Scornestow me," quod I, "or elles, pleyestow or disseyvistow me, that hast so woven me with thi resouns the hous of Didalus, so entrelaced that it is unable to ben unlaced, thow that otherwhile entrist ther thow issist, and other while issist ther thow entrest?" (Bk. 3, pr. 12)

A labyrinth is an argument wherein one can get lost; in Trevisa's translation of Higden's *Polychronicon* it is the complex "matir" of the book; it is also the name of the mark made by a perplexed reader in the margin of a difficult text.[28] Chaucer himself makes the connection of labyrinth and text specific and constitutive in *House of Fame:* the narrator comments that the House of Rumour, where all literature originates, is even more intricately—"queyntelych"—wrought than is Daedalus' labyrinth (1918–23).[29]

That charged word, "queynte," reappears in *Ariadne* in Phaedra's description of the labyrinth:

> And for the hous is krynkeled to and fro,
> And hath so queynte weyes for to go—

> For it is shapen as the mase is wrought—
> Therto have I a remedye in my thought.
> (2012–15)

Sheila Delany has recently drawn attention to the obscene punning that pervades the *Legend of Good Women,* citing as one loaded locus Phaedra's long speech here ("Lat us wel taste hym at his herte-rote, / That if so be that he a wepen have / . . . / And we shul make hym balles ek also" [1993–94, 2003]).[30] The references to male sex organs are obvious; but I suggest that there is, in addition, in this legend a specific association of the labyrinth with female sexuality and the female body. This association (which Delany observes in passing) is dependent not only on the remark that Theseus will have room in the labyrinth "to welde an ax, or swerd, or staf, or knyf" (2000), this line running through the repertoire of euphemisms for penis. The description of the labyrinth, with its "krynkeled" walls (in Trevisa's translation of the *Polychronicon* it is "wrynkyngliche i-wroght")[31] housing a "monstre" (1991), a "fend" (1996), accords with the strident vocabulary of antifeminist literature's descriptions of women. To cite one example among many, Walter Map ("Valerius") tells "Rufinus" (in *De nugis curialium* 4.3) that woman is a monster, polluted and stinking.[32] The association of woman with the "fend" is well known and deployed, as we shall see, by Chaucer's Man of Law. Images of monstrous females —wrinkled, reeking, sagging, dripping—populate Le Jaloux's tirade in the *Roman de la rose.* Further on, sexual intercourse in the *Rose* is associated with seductive bypaths ("queynte weyes" of the labyrinth), turnings and twistings of the straight way. And such turnings and twistings are identified as "il laberinto d'Amore" in Boccaccio's late dream vision, *Il Corbaccio,* a treatise that seethes with images of monstrous females.[33]

Woman has the "clewe" to the labyrinth; she knows the secrets not only of her own body (which knowledge is a source of fury and suspicion to Le Jaloux) but also of the labyrinth that is a text. Woman's body is associated with the truth of the text here—an association also suggested by the image of the allegorical text as veiled female body in Macrobius, Jerome, Richard of Bury. But as is also suggested by that image—as I discussed it in the Introduction—*femina* is assimilated to the superfluous surface as well; and here, as labyrinth, she is something to be *passed through.* It is thus no coincidence that in the *Legend of Ariadne* her "remedye" becomes "*His* wepne, *his* clewe, *his* thyng" (2140), where "wepne" and "thyng" are established euphemisms for the penis and, between them, as Delany also suggests, "clewe" becomes one, too. The hermeneutic value of *femina* thus shifts from truth—from spirit—to carnal letter; the spirit of the text assumes a concomitant masculine value.

The "clewe of twyn," then, passes into masculine hands. Theseus, in return, promises never to "twynne" from Ariadne. "Twynnen" here means "to divide, to separate," but the Middle English verb can also mean "to multiply by two." "Twinning" is in fact an important function in *Ariadne* and in the patriarchal tradition that is demonstrated on a small scale by the *Legend of Good Women*. Multiplication occurs as good women are multiplied into what appears to be a potentially endless series (note that even within *Ariadne*, Nisus' daughter is made into another good woman, despite her treachery to father and country;[34] Phaedra's role is also enlarged from the sources). But division seems to be the dominant function. Women are divided from their men (Theseus does, after all, "twynne" from Ariadne, as do all the rest of the men from their women), and women are divided from one another as well: Theseus runs off with Ariadne's sister; Tereus, in another legend, imprisons Philomela, Procne's sister. This separation of women from women is necessary to the perpetuation of a misogynist literary tradition, and it is what Criseyde implicitly understands as the inevitable result of women's reading authoritative "bokes." Although there is filiation ("twyn") among the men in the *Legend of Good Women*—Tarquin and Tarquin, Jr.; Theseus and Demophon; Danao and Lyno—there is and must be no society of women in which women can teach one another.[35] Sisters are divided up, and any communication of ethics or mores is cut off by the narrator: Dido complains to "hire syster Anne," but the narrator, in a hurry to finish up the tale, hastily excuses himself, "I may nat wryte, / So gret a routhe I have it for t'endite" (1344–45). No wonder women in the *Legend of Good Women* are not trainable: the narrator may chide "sely wemen, ful of innocence" for their credulity ("Have ye swych routhe upon hyre feyned wo, / And han swich olde ensaumples yow beforn? / Se ye nat alle how they ben forsworn?" [1257–59]), but lack of their own tradition prevents women in the legends from seeing and learning. Divided from men, divided from women, divided from themselves (as the examples of Hypermnestra and Lucrece have shown), they can only try to regain themselves, paradoxically, in death or metamorphosis.

"Twyn" becomes "twynne"; Ariadne's "thred" (2018) becomes, in the next legend, Philomela's "cloth." The *Legend of Ariadne* parabolically articulates principles of a male-centered tradition as it shows the appropriation of the truth of the text and demonstrates the necessary separation of women from each other. The *Legend of Philomela* elaborates on these patriarchal literary techniques. Philomela is a prime example of a woman denied the "proper" means of making meaning, signifying: Ariadne wanders around the island, able only to produce an echo from the hollow rocks, but Philomela's very *glossa* is removed by Tereus. To make this woman's limitations in the signifying project of literary tradition even more obvious, the narrator specifies that "She coude eek rede and wel ynow endyte, / But with a *penne* coude she nat wryte" (2356–57; my emphasis). She can, however, weave letters, and she creates a *textus* whose motive and theme are the violation and silencing of a woman.[36] This is a story that doesn't get told by the tongue or pen; it is the story of the origin of the narrative tradition of which the *Legend of Good Women* is an exemplar. To know narrative origins is, as we've seen in the case of Criseyde at the beginning of book 2, denied the female because such knowledge is potentially disruptive of linear masculine order; in the *Legend of Philomela* the silenced woman's story remains between the two sisters, in prison, weeping in each other's arms.

We might pause for a moment here to recall that the Philomela legend figures in *Troilus and Criseyde* at several critical moments. At the beginning of book 2, at the moment when the love affair of Troilus and Criseyde is about to begin, the narrator alludes to the tale. Pandarus, having tossed and turned all night in the throes of unrequited love,[37] is roused by the song of a swallow:

> The swalowe Proigne, with a sorowful lay,
> Whan morwen com, gan make hire waymentynge
> Whi she forshapen was; and ever lay
> Pandare abedde, half in a slomberynge,
> Til she so neigh hym made hire cheterynge
> How Tereus gan forth hire suster take,
> That with the noyse of hire he gan awake.
>
> (2.64–70)

Awakened by the story of Tereus' rape of Philomela, Pandarus gets up and dressed, "Remembryng hym his erand was to doone / From Troilus, and ek his grete emprise" (72–73). In this narrative whose background is a war begun with a rape, Procne, the betrayed sister, sings a "lay" of rape that reminds Pandarus to begin the wooing of Criseyde. Pandarus, as we have seen in the previous chapter, is a character who understands most thoroughly the patriarchal necessity of the exchange of women—in Troy as in every patriarchal society—of which rape is but the most violent acting-out.[38]

The story of Philomela in fact haunts *Troilus and Criseyde:* after she has heard Pandarus' profession of Troilus' love and has heard Antigone's song of love, Criseyde is lulled to sleep by a bird's song:

> A nyghtyngale, upon a cedre grene,
> Under the chambre wal ther as she ley,
> Ful loude song ayein the moone shene,
> Peraunter in his briddes wise a lay
> Of love, that made hire herte fressh and gay.
>
> (2.918–22)

Criseyde falls asleep, only to dream that an eagle violently (though without pain to her) rips open her breast and exchanges her heart for his. When, in book 3, she herself "Opned hire herte" to Troilus, she is likened to a "newe abaysed nyghtyngale" (3.1233–39).

The story of Philomela is thus deeply implicated in the motive of this narrative: it appears, but only indirectly, at crucial moments of the affair's inception and consummation.[39] The wooing and winning of Criseyde is not a rape in any simple sense; Criseyde does not consistently resist, emotionally or physically, the development of the affair. She finally states the fact of her complicity baldly when Troilus orders her to yield: "Ne hadde I er now, my swete herte deere, / Ben yold, ywis, I were now nought heere!" (3.1210–11). But on another level, there's a rape going on: it's a figurative violation of Criseyde by literary tradition—a future violation, of which she herself is aware when, in book 5, she bewails her future literary reputation. Tradition will record *only* her infidelity. And if the exchange of women, always potentially a rape because it proceeds regardless of women's independent desires, structures the workings of Troy, as we've seen, it also describes the workings of literary history as they are alluded to at the end of *Troilus and Criseyde:* the feminine body of the text, enjoined to "kis the steppes" of the great male *auctores,* can itself be violated in the process of scribal transmission (5.1786–98). The careless scribe is, we recall in "Adam Scriveyn," blamed for his "rape" (7).

Some alternative to such a tradition of patriarchal literary history and representation is explicitly wished for in the *Legend of Phyllis,* following Philomela. *Phyllis* is, in plot outline, one of the sparest of the lot: Demophon arrives, weak and weary, on Phyllis' island; she nurses and weds him; he leaves and doesn't come back. Phyllis laments her loss, laments her beguilement ("How coude ye wepe so by craft?" she writes the absent Demophon), and prays to God that Demophon get no more glory than that of having betrayed a "sely mayde":

> And whan thyne olde auncestres peynted be,
> In which men may here worthynesse se,
> Thanne preye I God thow peynted be also
> That folk may rede forby as they go,
> "Lo! this is he, that with his flaterye
> Bytraised hath and don hire vilenye
> That was his trewe love in thought and dede!"
>
> (2536–42)

In such a depiction, she continues, the viewer would be able to discern Demophon's relation to Theseus, "For he begiled Adriane, ywis, / With swich an art and with swich subtilte / As thow thyselven hast begyled me" (2545–47). What Phyllis prays for here resembles the revision of patriarchal tradition the Wife of Bath calls out for, a reversal revealing *men's* "wikkednesse" and "vilenye":

> By God, if wommen hadde writen stories,
> As clerkes han withinne hire oratories,
> They wolde han writen of men moore wikkednesse
> Than al the mark of Adam may redresse.
>
> (3:693–96)

But women *didn't* write the "stories," and the narrator of the *Legend of Good Women* will report only what he considers well put by Phyllis in her letter to her false lover: "Here and ther in rym I have it layd, / There as me thoughte that she wel hath sayd" (2516–17). Both Phyllis' prayer and the Wife's exclamation remain in the conditional; the only means of Phyllis' entering into patriarchal signifying activity —let alone changing it—is through death: she warns Demophon that she will make of her dead body a sign of her "trouthe" to him (2551–53). Phyllis does kill herself, at last, but not by drowning; instead, a "corde" (like "twyn") cuts off her breath, stopping her *glossa* forever.

What follows *Phyllis* is in effect a tale that is not told. The *Legend of Hypermnestra* is not finished, but it is not simply because of its lack of explicit "conclusioun" (2723) that there is a story left untold. The tale of Hypermnestra and her no-good husband follows the profile of all the legends, and its unspoken conclusion need hardly be drawn for the reader to be able to formulate it. But the tale of Hypermnestra and her *father* remains unexplored, a tale of "abhomynacion" (to use the Man of Law's term) unspoken. Hypermnestra's victimization is double, but the narrator's narrative model doesn't allow him to acknowledge that, as Anne Middleton puts it, "incestuous rape, threatened if not performed, activates the plot."[40] Patriarchal ideology, the mechanism by which he manipulates his narratives, will not allow the explicit recognition of father-daughter incest, for incest, as we shall see in detail in the *Man of Law's Tale*, violates patriarchy's necessary structure of the circulation—the exchange—of women between men. But incest is certainly implicit here: Hypermnestra's father, on her wedding night, summons her, looking on her with "glad chere" and telling her, "So nygh myn herte nevere thyng ne com / As thow, myn Ypermystre, doughter dere" (2631–32). He orders her to obey his will, then whips out his "knyf, as rasour kene"—we recall all the euphemisms for Theseus' "wepen"—to force her to kill her new husband, whom her father has dreamt will be his "bane." Hypermnestra disobeys her father by warning her husband and trying to escape with him, but Lyno, in a hurry, leaves her in the dust to be caught and incarcerated. At this point the narrator breaks off the legend. Hypermnestra's victimization is in fact not double—by father and husband—but triple: having become bored with her, the narrator cuts off her story.

Terminally bored, the narrator finally quits. He is bored not just with the tale of Hypermnestra but with the whole series of legends of good women and false men. His weariness grows from legend to legend: he has registered masculine perfidy over and over. As he begins the tale of Tereus' outrage, for example, he plans "But shortly of this story for to passe, / For I am wery of hym for to telle" (2257–58). It's the same old story; there is little need to go into detail about Demophon, for another example, because the narrator has already in effect told the tale while speaking of Theseus:

> Me lyste nat vouche-sauf on hym to swynke,
> Ne spende on hym a penne ful of ynke,
> For fals in love was he, ryght as his syre.
>
> (2490–92)

The tale of the betrayed is, similarly, always the same: the narrator has told it again and again, and by the time he gets to Phyllis the redundancy is almost overwhelming:

> But, for I am agroted herebyforn
> To wryte of hem that ben in love forsworn,

> And ek to haste me in my legende,
> (Which to perform God me grace sende)
> Therfore I passe shortly in this wyse.
>
> (2454–58)

The women's words, in their letters to their false men, are always the same, and the narrator hints that they are not very interesting to begin with. I have already mentioned the narrator's editing Phyllis' letter, with his indirect suggestion that the whole is tedious stuff:

> Hire letter was ryght long and therto large.
> But here and ther in rym I have it layd,
> There as me thoughte that she wel hath sayd.
>
> (2515–17)

The other letters—by Dido, Hypsipyle, Medea, Ariadne—are mentioned only to be omitted: "It is so long, it were an hevy thyng" to report it (2219); it is "to longe to wryten and to sen" (1565); "as now to long for me to wryte" (1679); "Rede Ovyde, and in hym he shal it fynde" (1367).[41]

The narrator's weariness with the fables links him in fact to the betrayers who tire of and leave their women. The narrator has, of course, enlisted the trust of amorous ladies in his audience by alleging his faithfulness in love: "trusteth, as in love, no man but me" (2561).[42] Aeneas, in contrast, departs because he has wearied of Dido:

> This Eneas, that hath so depe yswore,
> Is wery of his craft withinne a throwe;
> The hote ernest is al overblowe.
>
> (1285–87)

Demophon, second-generation womanizer, arrives in Phyllis' land, tellingly "Wayk, and ek wery, and his folk forpyned / Of werynesse" (2427–29). Jason and his men, similarly, arrive at Lemnon, Hypsipyle's land, ready to "pleye" because they are "wery" of the sea-voyage (1492–96). Theseus even feigns weariness for his own erotic purposes: sailing from Crete with Ariadne and Phaedra, he stops along the way on an island, saying "that on the lond he moste hym reste" (2168). Ariadne falls asleep, with true "werynesse atake" (2182); Theseus' "werynesse," however, proves to have been a mere convenience: he energetically sails away with Phaedra while Ariadne slumbers. But as inevitably as do the lovers, the narrator wearies of his "craft": they abruptly leave their women, with little or no explanation, moving on to the next victim (Jason, for example, moves on to "yit the thridde wif anon" [1660]); the narrator passes "shortly" on to the next story, protesting that the rest is "to long" (1679), or is "no charge for to telle" (2383).

Stripped, clipped, and scrubbed, his pagan source texts are like female bodies in the narrator's masculine hands. As he promised, he indeed delivers the "naked text" (86) of the legends. His *translatio* this time is not the record of his seduction but is, rather, a record of his continual exercise of control over the feminine. He domesticates the alien woman—marries her, settles her down in his household; he produces a dull text and wearies of it. His weariness, unlike Ariadne's exhaustion, is powerful: it is a specifically masculine defense against the feminine.[43] The narrator's excising of the women's acts of honor and virtue, or recrimination and revenge—his rendering of all the fables as "the same old story"—constitutes this masculine narrative strategy of weariness: he makes his heroines and the fables boring because they would otherwise terrify. Philomela and Procne dully and passively dissolve in tears; better narrate this than recount the horrifying Bacchanalian revels, the killing and cooking of Itys, the thrusting of the son's bloody head in Tereus' face, the disorienting shock of metamorphosis. This is, again, an ideological strategy designed to provide comfort and rest, functioning the same way we have seen the Epilogue to *Troilus and Criseyde* functioning. There *is* something soothing and reassuring about the repetition of a single narrative pattern over and over, as the example of saints' lives demonstrates; but here, the specifically gendered defensive function of that reassurance and security is apparent in the masculine associations of the totalizing gesture. Woman's story—the letter—becomes dull, a formula. The female character is reduced to a never-varying caricature.

As is the male character. The men of the *Legend of Good Women* are as undifferentiated and unsavory in their villainy as the women are in their victimization. Men are, of course, the motivating agents of the narratives: every legend, with the exception of the *Legend of Thisbe*, as Peter L. Allen observes, begins with the introduction of a male character, usually with a vehement excoriation of his vile nature and acts.[44] The narrator at points even admits that he talks about women so that he can talk about men: he tells the tale of Ariadne "for to clepe ageyn unto memorye / Of Theseus the grete untrouthe of love" (1889–90), and, similarly, brings up Phyllis "for this ende . . . / To tellen yow of false Demophon" (2397–98). Simple statistics reveal the narrative dominance of men over women: men are named much more frequently than are women (for example, Jason is named thirty-five times, while Hypsipyle and Medea a total of seven times).[45] And the proportions of several of the legends betray the narrator's greater interest in sea battles (the *Legend of Cleopatra*) or the challenge of the Golden Fleece (the *Legend of Hypsipyle*) than in his heroines. Even as these women die, violated, betrayed, and abandoned, their men characteristically skip out, as Allen also remarks, escaping without harm. It can't be denied that the motive power of this series is masculine.

But the male characters are unvarying, nothing but opportunistic scoundrels in love, and the "moralitee" of each fable is a truism. The techniques of reading like a man—imposing a single pattern, insisting on reducing complexity to produce a whole, monolithic structure, thus constraining the feminine—are reductive of *all* human experience, just as we saw in *Troilus and Criseyde.* And although closure in the Epilogue to that poem proved satisfying to the narrator, in the *Legend of Good Women* reductiveness is, finally, shown to be profoundly narrow and unsatisfying. The narrator, defending himself against the mobile feminine, becomes himself bored, idle, torpid, *silent.* It's clear from the abandoned series of legends that reading like a man leads to no literary activity at all. If the Second Nun tells *her* legend of a saint—Cecilia—in order to stave off "ydelnesse"—purposeless talk or sterile silence—the narrator of the *Legend of Good Women* approaches, rather, the condition of the idle in the *Inferno,* who can't even speak whole words. You can't found a tradition on the constraining of the feminine, Chaucer suggests here, because it will eventually silence men, too. The Man of Law, who picks up directly where the narrator of *Hypermnestra* leaves off, finds plenty *not* to talk about.

Chapter Three

The Law of Man
and Its "Abhomynacions"

Reading the *Man of Law's Tale* can be a trial much like Constance's, as she floats on the sea, rudderless, for "yeres and dayes": the text is bewildering, disorienting, and seemingly endless. Numerous contradictions, gaps, visible seams in the narrative, and sudden shifts in tone punctuate the Man of Law's performance. He promises to tell a tale in prose, for example, but instead we get a poem in rime royal.[1] The "poverte" Prologue seems to have only the barest, most expedient relation to the *Tale* itself. The *Tale* is a mixture of hagiography, romance, and chronicle history, in which Constance plays roles of saint and romance heroine that ultimately prove contradictory in the narrative. The Man of Law's rhetorical interjections vary in tone from high moralism to something close to outright prurience. This list doesn't exhaust the available contradictions,[2] but perhaps most puzzling of them all is the Man of Law's specific insistence, on the one hand, that he will not tell a tale of incest, and his choice, on the other hand, of a narrative whose motivation in well-known analogues is, in fact, incest.[3] Despite his shrill claim that he will not mention "swiche unkynde abhomynacions" (2:88), his tale is shot through, as we shall see, with implications of just such unkindness.

A late-medieval audience may not, in fact, have felt as bewildered in reading this tale as we now feel, comfortably familiar as that audience was with just such episodic romances and hagiographies. But they had also presumably heard or read other *Canterbury Tales*—the tales of the first fragment in Ellesmere, for example, which directly precede the Man of Law's performance—which are much more tightly and logically put together; in this way they could have become sensitive to the ruptures and discontinuities in Fragment 2 that bother later readers. Many recent critics, indeed, have chosen not to read the *Man of Law's Tale* at all: their preferred solution to the problem of dealing with these contradictions has been to bypass the tale altogether, with its cruxes and incoherences, for the more refined pleasures of the *Clerk's Tale*. I have analyzed such avoidance or omission of complications as "reading like a man" in my discussions of *Troilus and Criseyde* and the *Legend of Good Women*. Reading like a man can end up to be, in fact, *not* reading, just as the masculine narration of the *Legend* ends up to be active *not* telling.[4] Just like a woman, then, I want to resist that masculine gesture of closure; in my reading I want in fact to focus on those contradictions and those problems.

Such an analysis could try to explain these problems as purely matters of circumstance (manifestations of the unfinished nature of the *Canterbury Tales*), or as aesthetic faults (evidence of Chaucer's own nodding, or, alternatively, of his subtle and sophisticated indictment of the Man of Law's literary taste). Perhaps there was some polemical occasion or subtext, now beyond modern reach, that would explain the irregularities of tone and reference. These explanations would account for specific contradictions or local incoherences, in what are perhaps individually satisfying ways.[5] But the very multiplicity of lapses in Fragment 2—they pervade the text, from its referential claims to its stylistic register to its main character—leads me to suggest a more general principle governing the Man of Law's performance.

We might recall that the narrator of the General Prologue refers to the "Sergeant of the Lawe"; it is only later, in Fragment 2, that the lawyer is addressed as "Man of Lawe." Manly castigates Chaucer for shifting to the general and "colorless" title here, not distinguishing the Sergeant of Law (of a high order of lawyer, one allowed to plead at the Court of Common Pleas and one from which justices of higher courts are selected) from any ordinary lawyer.[6] But I take this appellation, "Man of Law," to be itself significant. He is, indeed, a man of law—a man made up of law; he carries around in his head the whole of the common law: "In termes hadde he caas and doomes alle / That from the tyme of kyng William were falle. / . . . / And every statut koude he pleyn by rote" (General Prologue, 323–27). I suggest that the unresolved contradictions, sudden shifts, visible seams indicate the Man of Law's limitations not just as storyteller but *as a man of law:* they indicate the limits of the law that gives him his identity and constitutes his subjectivity.[7] The Man of Law not only tells his tale "like a man" but incarnates the very principle behind such narrating: he incarnates patriarchal ideology and its expressed system of law.

The common law prescribed and maintained the structure of medieval English society, a structure that was fundamentally patriarchal (gender asymmetrical, dominated by men). This law expresses patriarchal ideology, and the Man of Law is its embodiment. It is no surprise, then, that the Man of Law should tell a tale of a woman thoroughly subject to "mannes governance" and dependent upon patriarchal protection; we shall find, concomitantly, that the disjunctions in his performance occur at moments when women's role and identity in this structure emerge as problematic. I shall argue that these lapses reveal the limits, and thus the workings, of patriarchal ideology: those gaps and disjunctions reveal the energy of suppression and exclusion, and the efforts at reconciliation of contradictions, that are necessary to patriarchal ideology's construction of itself as a seemingly seamless, coherent, and natural whole.[8] As we shall see, the Man of Law has a profound stake in suppressing threats to the patriarchal order—in defining these threats as unnatural and outside the realm of humanity. They are the "unkynde abhomynacions" (medieval etymologies derived the word from *ab-hominibus*—"away from humankind"): "tyrannical" women and tales of incest.

1

Let us look for a moment first at the kind of Law he is Man of. Regardless of the shadiness of his personal dealings—from the General Prologue it could be inferred that his wealth is ill-gotten—he is committed to upholding the form of the law, as his pantomime of busyness (General Prologue, 321–22) makes clear.[9] The "caas and doomes" and statutes that he knows flawlessly—the common law of England —legislated land tenure, commercial relations and transactions, and the structure of the family: they regulated who owned and held the land; how money and goods changed hands; and what constituted the basic unit of social organization, the family. The Man of Law is professionally engaged in maintaining society as it is, in prescribing and reproducing its basic power structure.

His perfect knowledge of family law in particular makes this especially clear. Family law was concerned with the forms and customs of the marriage gift (*maritagium*), legitimacy of offspring, rules of descent, establishment of the household, and succession to property. It was (and is) most concerned with the reproduction of the family unit. According to the dictates of the common law, marriage was contracted in order to produce legitimate offspring. Laws of succession expressed the family in terms of property, as legal historian Theodore Plucknett writes, and "were points at which the family sought most eagerly to preserve its stability and safety."[10] And the inheritance system—transmission *mortis causa*—of any society, according to Jack Goody, is both "the means by which the reproduction of the social system is carried

out [and] the way in which interpersonal relations are structured. . . .
The manner of splitting property is a manner of splitting people": it
both creates and reflects a "constellation of ties and cleavages."[11] Rules
of property and succession are the means by which social power is
maintained and reproduced.

And that social power was masculine. Profoundly influenced by the
Church's insistence on exogamy and monogamy (in formulations after
A.D. 1000 in theology and canon law), the structure of the family legislated by medieval English common law was essentially patriarchal:
the father was established as head of the household (a position reproduced on the public level as well), and descent was reckoned through
the male line.[12] There were qualifications in the common law of this
patriarchal power: the Church's insistence that the verbal consent of
eligible partners alone constituted a valid marriage bond held sway in
the common law and thus undermined paternal authority in arrang-
ing marriages.[13] A woman—to cite another qualification of patriarchal
power—could hold land in dower for the term of her life, apparently with proprietary rights.[14] Females, further, were not absolutely
excluded from succession to property, as they were in Salic law (in
which females could never inherit ancestral land); they were merely
"postponed." But laws of inheritance very definitely favored the male
line; "the rule that males exclude females of equal degree" was old
and deeply rooted.[15] Understanding such qualifications—understanding that patriarchy was not by any means absolute in late medieval
England—I nonetheless find the term useful to indicate the structure
of the family, a structure that is gender asymmetrical: medieval English society was male-dominated with respect to descent, property,
and public and private authority. The common law regarding land
tenure and commercial usages reinforced this structure.

Engaging those "caas and doomes" he knows so thoroughly, the
Man of Law can "endite and make a thyng" (General Prologue, 325),
a legal document beyond cavil. The diction in the General Prologue
links the writs of law with literature; "endite" and "thyng" are used
throughout Chaucer's works to refer to literary output (note in particular that the *Melibee* is Chaucer's "litel thyng" [7:937]). For the Man
of Law, the act of tale-telling is all in a day's work. It not only takes
place in a group ruled by a man ("of manhod," enthuses the narrator
in the General Prologue about the Host, "hym lakkede right naught"
[1:756]), but it is subject to the strictures of law, and it serves as well
to further the interests of patriarchy, as we shall see. The language of
the Man of Law's Introduction continues to implicate tale-telling and
the law: asking him to tell a tale, the Host reminds the Man of Law

of his "forward," his promise "thurgh youre free assent, / To ston-
den in this cas at my juggement" (35–36). Harry's legalistic diction not
only shows off his vague but prized knowledge of the legal profession
but also situates tale-telling in the realm of contracts.[16] The Man of
Law's response carries further this legal contextualization: he readily
agrees to make good his promise ("For swich lawe as a man yeveth
another wight, / He sholde hymselven usen it, by right" [43–44]).
Even his hesitation—he knows of no "thrifty tale" that Chaucer hasn't
already told—extends the rule of law here: Middle English "thrifty"
denotes commercial profitability as well as moral profitability; in the
first stanza of the *Tale* itself, the Syrian merchants' "chaffare" will be
called "thrifty." As is the making of a commercial transaction, the telling of a tale is regulated by law, and tales themselves should be, like
merchandise, "so thrifty and so newe" (138).

   For the Man of Law, the two kinds of profit that tales and commodities offer—moral and monetary—are indissolubly linked. Drawing on
the paronomasia R. Howard Bloch has discussed in medieval French
literature, I would venture that the Man of Law is invested in the
propre—in moral propriety as well as in real property.[17] We recall that
in the General Prologue his land-holding is emphasized:

>   So greet a purchasour was nowher noon:
>   Al was fee symple to hym in effect;
>   His purchasyng myghte nat been infect.
>   (1:318–20)

And in the Introduction to his tale he rigorously stresses moral propriety: he commends Chaucer for writing the *Legend of Good Women*
and for *not* writing of incestuous relations. Moral propriety ensures
uncontested succession to property: the Church's commands regarding celibacy, monogamy, and exogamy, Jack Goody has suggested
recently, may have been themselves part of its own strategy for obtain-
ing real property, inalienable lands.[18] According to the Man of Law,
then, Chaucer's celebratory representation of true lovers furthers the
proper familial organization under patriarchy, which, in turn, ensures
orderly descent, unadulterated inheritance.

   Tale-telling, for the Man of Law, thus maintains and reproduces
social power through its implied participation in the law—in structures of contract, commerce, and family. The Man of Law's claim in
the Prologue that follows that his tale was told him by an old merchant
is consistent with this cultural function of tales: the story is delivered
directly from the world of commerce. The Man of Law bewails the

discomforts and evils of poverty and praises merchants; his praise is not just for their "wele" (122)—their possessions, their property—but for their nobility and prudence, their wisdom. As in the *Shipman's Tale*, wealth apparently guarantees wisdom: property guarantees propriety. Merchants, according to the Man of Law, are fit to be kings, for "ye knowen al th'estaat / Of regnes" (128–29); in addition they are "fadres of tidynges / And tales" (129–30). Tale-telling is thus an activity homologous to—even metaphorically equated with—paternity, kingship, and commerce.

Tales are firmly established in the Man of Law's Introduction and Prologue as part of patriarchal social organization, a large and well-coordinated structure of homological functions. But there are a few moments in the narrative thus far that disrupt a smooth, even progress and tone; they reveal that structure, from within which the Host and Man of Law are speaking, constructing itself. At the very outset of Fragment 2, the Host, urging the pilgrimage and the tale-telling game forward, calculates the time of day and admonishes the pilgrim company to avoid "ydelnesse" (hardly a necessary warning to the "bisy" Man of Law). In his characteristic style, Harry quotes an authority on the subject of lost time and cracks a dirty joke:

> Wel kan Senec and many a philosophre
> Biwaillen tyme moore than gold in cofre;
> For 'Los of catel may recovered be,
> But los of tyme shendeth us,' quod he.
> It wol nat come agayn, withouten drede,
> Namoore than wole Malkynes maydenhede,
> Whan she hath lost it in hir wantownesse.
>
> (25–31)

In the scheme of salvation, time is precious: life progresses toward death and urgently necessitates redemption through individual salvation. But as Jacques Le Goff suggests, the flight of time may have had a more immediate urgency in the late Middle Ages: as networks of commerce became organized and established across the West, time was closely and explicitly linked to monetary profit and consequently was more and more carefully regulated.[19] The Host's association here of time with fortune—"gold" and "catel"—thus has a specific late-medieval resonance, as does his association of the regulation of time with the regulation of the human body. The mechanical clock, an invention of the late Middle Ages, made possible the imposition of man-made measure onto nature.[20] Thus the comments of the Dominican Domenico Calva, who writes that the idler, the one who does not adequately regulate his time, is a beast.[21] We note that in the Host's joke the idler, the body that is unregulated, is the body of a wanton woman.[22]

The Host's shift in stylistic register and tone from his rather serious admonitions about time to a joke about "Malkynes maydenhede" should set us on the alert for a glimpse of ideology at work here. (In fact, since the audience may have come to expect such remarks from the Host by this time in the *Canterbury Tales*, I might suggest that his function as master of ceremonies may well be to register unacknowledged ideology in the *Tales* as a whole.) The loss of time is worse than the loss of fortune, according to the Host, because it can never be recovered; it's analogous to the loss of a woman's virginity.[23] This conjunction of time and female virginity suggests a similarity even beyond their shared quality of transience. Time is valuable in itself because it is pure potential; it is empty, blank, an expanse to be filled and made profitable. And a woman's "maydenhede," similarly, is a literal blank, an empty space, an "O" that is valued precisely in its being void of spot, of any mark.[24] But to be properly regulated, time should be filled, whereas maidenhead should be left intact. Woman's body should remain empty, blank; man-made measure would keep it so. "Malkynes maydenhede," according to the Host's casually ribald remark, has been lost already, through her own "wantownesse"; there's an inevitability to woman's desire and sexual activity here that supplies the comedy but might also express something darker. The unregulated body of woman—remember Calva's "beast"—is linked to the dissipation of time, to the unprofitable conduct of life. Woman's desire, her lasciviousness, it is suggested here, is deeply disruptive of the man-made order of things.

But the Host does not dwell on the loss of "Malkynes maydenhede." He turns to the Man of Law and addresses him in the language of law; narrative order is restored after the slight disruption and consequent ideological revelation the joke occasions. The Man of Law responds to the Host in kind, praising Chaucer's morally correct works and excluding tales of incest. But as he mentions these unacceptable tales, the pitch of his voice seems to rise; his syntax becomes a little choppy; his diction increases in its vehemence: "Of swiche cursed stories I sey fy!" he cries (80). His exclusion of tales that violate proper lineage is necessary if tale-telling is to advance the patriarchal order, as I've already suggested. But why does he go into detail about what tales Chaucer doesn't tell? Why does he mention incest, in particular, and not adultery or sodomy? At the very least, his comments introduce the subject of incest, and perhaps set his listeners thinking about it: might not it be more a part of his narrative than he allows here? The narrative disjunctions that follow—his claim that he will speak in "prose," leaving "rymes" to Chaucer, only to go on in rime royal; his sudden and illogical plunge into the harsh rhetoric of Innocent III— suggest that the Man of Law's relation to proper poetry (poetry that he perceives as advancing patriarchal values) is indeed uneasy. In his Introduction and Prologue, the Man of Law makes one ideological move explicit: if tale-telling is to serve patriarchy, tales of incest must be suppressed. But in the process, he unwittingly suggests a deeper one: even if patriarchy must suppress tales of incest to advance its own structures of power, this doesn't mean that such tales aren't there for the telling.

2

If tales and tale-telling are firmly established as part of patriarchal social organization, it is fitting indeed that Constance, when we are first introduced to her in the *Man of Law's Tale* itself, is a tale told by men. The Man of Law opens the narrative with Syrian merchants doing business in Rome. They hear stories about the Emperor's daughter; she is first introduced not in person but in—*as*—narrative: her "excellent renoun" is declaimed in "the commune voys of every man" (155). Constance exists as a tale of a virgin. When the merchants return to Syria, they narrate their "tidynges" to the Sultan, highlighting the story of Constance. And it is with this very story that the Sultan falls in love: he "hath caught so greet plesance / To han hir figure in his remembrance" (186–87) that he determines he must have her. Middle English "figure" denotes both "shape, form" and "figure of speech," of whom the merchants can be said to be "maistres" (141). This woman exists not only in but as narrative; she is both "real" character and linguistic form.

While the merchants are still in Rome, preparing to sail back to Syria, they meet Constance in person. But the parallel narration of loading their ships with merchandise and loading their eyes with Constance underscores her position as a thing—a tale, a commodity—that merchants trade:

> Thise marchantz han doon fraught hir shippes newe,
> And whan they han this blisful mayden sayn,
> Hoom to Surrye been they went ful fayn.
>
> (171–73)

Sent off by her father to marry the Sultan, traveling in a ship from Rome to Syria, she is very obviously not only like the tales but the "chaffare" of the merchants returning from Rome to Syria. The trade of the woman in marriage is homologous to the trade of goods and the trade of tales, of words. Such an understanding of trade as structuring the use of women and words is well attested in various late-medieval uses of the word "chaffare."[25] In Gower's *Confessio amantis*, for example, women are "that chaffare" that lovers "take a parte of." In *Piers Plowman*, it's tidings that are the merchandise: "Tythes of un-trewe thinge [are] ytilied or chaffared." And marriage itself, in *Hali Meidenhad*, is called "that chaffere"—that trade, that deal, that (bad) bargain.[26]

The marriage at the outset of the *Man of Law's Tale* is figured forth as the trade of a woman. Such an image turns out to be a precise literary representation of the anthropological analysis of marriage put forward by Lévi-Strauss, who claims that the exchange of women is the very mechanism of marriage and kinship systems. It is the mechanism, he finds, of all social organization. The plot thickens when we recall that his analysis was formulated in the study of *incest*—in an investigation of the universality of the incest prohibition. A look at Lévi-Strauss's *Elementary Structures of Kinship* turns out to be remarkably appropriate to a consideration of the Man of Law's performance: the book is not only an analysis of a power asymmetry between the sexes but an implicit defense of that asymmetry. It is, in other words, a patriarchal text itself, just as is the *Man of Law's Tale*; the workings of its ideology are visible through the same kinds of fissures that we've seen in the Man of Law's performance, lapses having to do with woman's place in a male-dominated structure. Lévi-Strauss belongs in a long ideological tradition of which the Man of Law is an early, card-carrying member; a look at *Elementary Structures of Kinship*, then, will suggest something of great Constancy.[27]

It could be asserted that trade or exchange (I shall use the two words interchangeably) indeed structures every society. As I remarked in Chapter One, Marcel Mauss has suggested that the exchange of gifts constitutes society; he refers to primitive society in particular, but, as Gayle Rubin—to whose article, "The Traffic in Women," I am again deeply indebted—has acutely discerned, his claims are much more general: he suggests indeed that the gift liberated culture itself.[28] It is evident that society depends on linguistic communication (the trade of words), and on some form of commerce (the trade of goods). But the trade of women? Following and extending Mauss's analysis, Lévi-Strauss suggests that women are the most precious of gifts—"the supreme gift" (*ES*, p. 65)—and that marriage should be seen as an exchange or trade of these valuables: marriage is "the archetype of exchange" (*ES*, p. 483). Georges Duby uses this analysis of marriage, we may note, in his study of medieval marriage.[29]

In the regulation of this exchange Lévi-Strauss in fact finds the very basis of social organization: to ensure that these most prized gifts will be circulated widely, distributed evenly, this exchange must be made *between* families and groups. "It will never be sufficiently emphasized," urges Lévi-Strauss, "that if social organization had a beginning, this could only have consisted in the incest prohibition."[30] The universal prohibition of incest, then, follows from the need for a wide circulation of women if social order is to be maintained. David Herlihy corroborates the applicability of Lévi-Strauss's analysis to the Western Middle Ages: the medieval Church's unusual preoccupation with the prohibition of incest (unprecedented in Roman or Mosaic law), he suggests, forced a "freer, wider circulation of women through society" and a "fairer distribution [of women] across social classes."[31]

So the Man of Law's puzzlingly specific and adamant remarks in his Introduction about tales of incest make immediate sense when considered via Lévi-Strauss's hypothesis of a connection between the exchange of women and the prohibition of incest. When we locate Constance within the clearly delineated structure of commerce in the world of his tale, the remark, in retrospect, gains a particular urgency. For the Man of Law has depicted a society in which women are exchanged, and the prohibition of incest is universal and necessary to that social organization. Further, the power asymmetry that Constance herself bewails as she is being shipped off to Syria ("Wommen are born to thraldom and penance, / And to been under mannes governance" [286–87]) is built into a society based on the exchange of women. Gayle Rubin observes that

> if it is women who are being transacted, then it is the men who give and take them who are linked, the woman being a conduit of a relationship rather than a partner to it.[32]

If, as Lévi-Strauss asserts, the exchange of women is behind the universal taboo, then the power asymmetry, too, between giver and gift, man and woman, is universal.

But it's precisely this issue of power asymmetry between the genders that leads Lévi-Strauss into unresolved contradiction at the end of *Elementary Structures of Kinship*, a contradiction that Rubin also notes. In remarks on method which close the work, Lévi-Strauss compares the work of the sociologist of the family and the linguist. In considering the incest prohibition and language, their respective objects of study, he suggests that both have fundamentally the same function: communication and integration (since "the relations between the sexes can be conceived as one of the modalities of a great 'communication function' which also includes language" [*ES*, p. 494]). Misuses of language and violations of the incest prohibition, therefore, can be grouped together and considered as identical situations. He then draws a conclusion from this conjuncture:

> What does this mean, except that women themselves are treated as signs, which are misused when not put to the use reserved to signs, which is to be communicated? (*ES*, p. 496)

This conclusion, however logically in keeping with the whole of his analysis of exchange as the basis of kinship relations, creates a contradiction with perceived reality: women are, after all, speakers as well as spoken, active generators of messages as well as passive constituents of them. This contradiction seems to provoke an uneasiness—one Lévi-Strauss exhibits again in "The Family"—with women readers' potential response to his analysis of their function as empty signs, mere counters in trade.[33] He hastens to add that women are not only spoken, but are speakers as well, and have their own individual "values"; they are not merely arbitrary significances assigned to empty signs:

> Woman could never become just a sign and nothing more, since even in a man's world she is still a person, and since in so far as she is defined as a sign she must be recognized as a generator of signs. In the matrimonial dialogue of men, woman is never purely what is spoken about; for if women in general represent a certain category of signs, destined to a certain kind of communication, *each woman preserves a particular value arising from her talent, before and after marriage, for taking her part in a duet.* In contrast to words, which have wholly become signs, *woman has remained at once a sign and a value.* This explains why the relations between the sexes have preserved that *affective richness, ardour and mystery* which doubtless originally permeated the entire universe of human communications. (*ES*, p. 496; my emphasis)

In this penultimate paragraph, Lévi-Strauss lapses into a romantic idiom foreign to the analytical discourse of the foregoing 495 pages.

That romantic diction, a break in the academic language, marks the effort of reconciliation: women are, according to his theory, homologous to empty signs; but according to patriarchal myth (or tale), which Lévi-Strauss seems eager to advance here against the exigencies of his own theory, each preserves a mysterious "particular value." The contradiction simply remains intact—"woman has remained at once a sign and a value"—and the diction is heightened to cover it over: "the relations between the sexes" are romanticized, mystified, and woman is seen as a kind of eternal paradox.

This break in tone at the end of *Elementary Structures* is a crack in the "monument" (as one reviewer, quoted on the back cover of the Beacon Press paperback, called the book)—a crack in this analysis of masculine prerogative as constituting culture—which reveals its ideological workings.[34] Lévi-Strauss's theory of exchange depends on woman's blankness and intrinsic valuelessness for it to work. The way of all ideology, to adopt Susan Griffin's phrase, is to differentiate the selfsame from the Other, to create a group in power and define all else as lack. Lévi-Strauss's analysis of marriage is fully appropriate to the analysis of the Man of Law's representation in his *Tale* because Lévi-Strauss participates in the same long tradition of thinking—the same patriarchal ideology—as the one that informs the Man of Law's performance. In this ideology it is "woman" who is indeed an empty "thing" (*ES*, p. 496), "a sign and nothing more," whose value is arbitrary and ascribed to her by men. Constance, floating rudderless and will-less in her boat for "yeres and dayes" (463), is not far behind.

3

A further ideological mystification can be seen in Lévi-Strauss's very focus on the *prohibition* of incest, and it is with this observation that I shall now turn my attention directly to the *Man of Law's Tale* for good. Women may be traded in marriage, but the goods may be spoiled; acts of incest do indeed occur, even if incestuous marriages are prohibited.[35] Incest, in Lévi-Strauss's analysis an act instigated and perpetrated by men, can be seen as in fact another—and more fundamental, because lawless—exertion of control over women. Men make the rules necessary for the establishment of culture and society, but men can break them, too—without, it is a tautology to add, violating masculine prerogative. Incest itself doesn't violate the general principle of masculine dominance, but *narratives* of incest threaten patriarchal social organization because they reveal its violations of its own laws. The Man of Law properly eschews tales of "swiche unkynde abhomynacions"—in such a move as Lévi-Strauss will later make in his focusing on the prohibition of incest—yet we find throughout his tale the charged presence of incestuous desires and potentially incestuous relationships. Further, what is absolutely disruptive of masculine prerogative, what the Man of Law mentions *first* as a tale not to be told, is the tale of *feminine* incestuous desire; it is *this* tale's uneasily suppressed presence within the *Man of Law's Tale* that I hope, finally, to demonstrate.

In a large number of its folktale sources and analogues, the narrative of Constance's adventures is motivated by incest. Margaret Schlauch has stated persuasively that Chaucer must have known versions of the Constance legend that begin with the exile of the heroine by a father who makes sexual demands. Schlauch argues that the lines in the Man of Law's Introduction regarding tales of incest are Chaucer's announcement of his choice of a version in which this "most unpleasing feature" has been removed.[36]

> But certeinly no word ne writeth he
> Of thilke wikke ensample of Canacee,
> That loved hir owene brother synfully—
> Of swiche cursed stories I sey fy!—
> Or ellis of Tyro Appollonius,
> How that the cursed kyng Antiochus
> Birafte his doghter of hir maydenhede,
> That is so horrible a tale for to rede,
> Whan he hir threw upon the pavement.
> And therfore he, of ful avysement,
> Nolde nevere write in none of his sermons
> Of swiche unkynde abhomynacions,
> Ne I wol noon reherce, if that I may.
>
>   (77–89)

We must attribute choice and revisions of sources, as well as any knowledge of analogues, to Chaucer rather than to the Man of Law himself, since the Man of Law appears to be unaware of his tale's narrative sources and analogues (whereas the narrator of *Troilus and Criseyde*, in contrast, is aware of and resistant to his sources). The Man of Law tells it, we must assume, as he has heard it from the old merchant. But the point is that Chaucer has characterized the Man of Law as reacting to tales of incest; in this way the subsequent *lack* of incest in his tale (even though Chaucer based the tale on a source that doesn't include the motif) serves to delineate the Man of Law's values.

The Man himself seems oblivious to the disparity between what he promises (a tale in which incest has been suppressed) and what he delivers (a narrative structured by incest). I see no indication (no consistent irony, for example) that he is conscious of the pervasive, informing pattern of incest in his tale. But this obliviousness does not serve to demonstrate that the Man of Law is merely dull-witted or perhaps sinful; as spokesman of patriarchal ideology, he does not even register the discord. As Macherey has stated, at the source of ideology we find a desire for reconciliation of opposites, resolution of contradictions.[37] Thus tales of incest are prohibited, and the incestuous potential of relationships in the *Tale* is interpreted by him in some way as legitimate or is not even recognized; actual occurrences found in the well-known analogues have been removed.

In the most popular versions of the Constance legend, the "accused queen" flees unwanted sexual advances of her father, and her adventures begin as she ends up on foreign shores.[38] But in the *Man of Law's Tale* the motive of the action is converted into the Sultan's desire to marry Constance: reassigned to another man, the desire is made legitimate. The narrative context is thus made fully patriarchal: proper marriage is arranged; dynasties are consolidated; heathens are converted.[39] There may be a trace of the incest motif yet in the *Tale*, Schlauch notes, in Constance's consistent refusal to identify herself throughout her travels: the woman pursued by a spurned lover who is her father and king would have good reason to want to conceal her identity. I shall suggest, later, another reading of Constance's behavior here; suffice it now to accept this as a trace of incest gaping through the patriarchal text.

Incestuous advances of father toward daughter are checked, then, at the outset of the tale, and the daughter's flight becomes a legitimate and celebrated betrothal, spanning East and West and absorbing barbarians into the fold. But this is not the end of intimacy between father and daughter, the Emperor and Constance; their highly charged, emotional reunion at the end of the tale effects the final closure of this narrative of potentially ceaseless wandering. The suggestions of incest at the close of the tale are subtle, but the presence of incest in its suppression at the beginning renders these suggestions compelling at the end. Recalling to the reader's mind the position of daughter vis-à-vis father in the Man of Law's description of incest in *Apollonius of Tyre* (Antiochus raped his daughter "whan he hir threw upon the pave-

ment" [85]),[40] Constance falls onto the street at her father's feet when
she sees him at last in Rome:

> And whan she saugh hir fader in the strete,
> She lighte doun, and falleth hym to feete.
> "Fader," quod she, "youre yonge child Custance
> Is now ful clene out of youre remembrance.
>
> "I am youre doghter Custance," quod she.
>
> (1103–7)

They embrace and are reconciled; Constance then leaves with Alla for
England. After Alla dies, Constance returns to Rome one final time,
to her father, and again sinks to the ground: "And whan that she
hir fader hath yfounde, / Doun on hir knees falleth she to grounde"
(1152–53). (That Constance's falling actions are voluntary only serves,
as will become clear later, to strengthen the implications of incest.)
Thus reunited, the two live together "Til deeth departeth hem" (1158),
the phrase echoing late-medieval marriage vows "to hold and to have,
at bed and at burd, for farer for lather, for better for wars, in sekenes
and in heil, *to dethe us depart."* [41]

The potential of father-daughter incest, announced *a contrario* in
the Introduction, thus lurks at both ends of the tale but is absorbed
into the proper scheme the Man of Law delineates at the outset. If
Constance's father in folktale analogues threatens to violate the rule
of reciprocity in trade of women by retaining possession of her, the
Man of Law's Tale corrects the threat by emphasizing the exchange:
it trades Constance with great pomp to the Syrians. The father's in-

Constance's relationship to her father, with its undertones of incest,
is able to close the tale—narrative closure depending on the *settle-
ment* of disruption—only because the Man of Law does not recognize
what it is. He narrates the final reunion as an example of the way
the world goes, makes it an exemplification of a platitude: there is, in
the sublunar world, joy after woe, just as there will follow woe after
gladness. Having spoken of the passing of joy at Alla's death, the
Man of Law narrates the final bliss of Constance and her father, then
hopes for similar "joye after wo" (1161) for the Canterbury pilgrims.
The conversion of this incestuous relation into a truism about the way
of the world—joy after woe, woe after gladness—shows us ideology
in action, naturalizing all events according to its values. Reconciliation of father and daughter and suppression of incest in the service
of patriarchal propriety stop the wandering progress of the romance,
and no discord is perceived or revealed.

cestuous desire is replaced by the Sultan's desire for Constance. But the threat of father-daughter incest does not violate the mechanism of the rule of exchange of women: father-daughter incest creates a trade imbalance, but it does not violate the power and prerogative of males to determine the destination of the female and, consequently, of feminine desire. This is a crucial point: in the economy of female exchange among men, woman's desire must "respon[d] to the desire of others"; woman, if the exchange is to be made expediently, will desire the man to whom another man has traded her.[42] But there is another kind of incest *in potentia* in the *Tale* that I want to uncover, one that does not operate within this structure of mimetic desire and that, therefore, poses a radical threat to masculine prerogative: it is the jealousy of the mothers-in-law, which I read as the potentially incestuous desires of mothers for their sons. These relations are not so easily ignored or absorbed into supports of the patriarchal structure. Schlauch in fact associates the hostility of mothers-in-law toward their sons' wives with matrilineage: the mother-in-law perceives that the wife threatens her dominance in domestic authority as well as in lines of inheritance.[43]

Clearly, the mothers-in-law in the *Tale* are fundamentally threatening to the Man of Law, voice of patriarchy: he expends great energy in excluding these women from society—from Christianity, from "femynynytee," from all of humankind. These mothers-in-law overtly desire power and control and have the capacity to seize and exercise them. Their abilities to manipulate language in cunning plots—the Sultaness demands a verbal act of fealty from her followers (344); Donegild exchanges written letters via messenger—appropriate power that is deemed properly patriarchal. Further, these women are responsible for mass butchery and heartless exile, and must, therefore, themselves be extinguished. Nothing less than the murder of the mothers will do: Alla, of course, is later penitent for the murder he commits, but no action other than Donegild's swift dispatch seems adequate at the time. The threat to patriarchy posed by the mother-in-law, I maintain, is radical: it involves not just the rule of the realm, or structures of descent and rules of succession (as Schlauch implies), or even the authority of language. There is the lingering sense, in Alla's penitential journey, that he must be cleansed of the taint of contact with this unnatural creature, this woman with an independent will.

It is in the context of such overtly threatening gestures that the indications of incest function—function perhaps even more powerfully for being so nervously suppressed. The motives of the murderous mothers-in-law are either *too* well accounted for or left entirely vague in the Man of Law's narrative. The Sultaness resents her son's decision to convert to Christianity and refuses to join him in the new religion: "The lyf shal rather out of my body sterte / Or Makometes lawe out of myn herte!" (335–36). Her violent refusal to accept a change of "creance" should be adequate to explain the desire to eliminate the Syrians who do renege their faith; granted, mass murder is an extreme reaction, but it is explicable nonetheless in these terms. But an additional explanation is later offered by the Man of Law after "this cursed dede": "She hirself wolde al the contree lede" (434). This, too, is a plausible motive, conjuring up the figure of the usurping female, the overweening mother; but the combination of the two explanations seems excessive, and casts her determining motive into doubt. Chaucer here seems to combine Trivet's account of the Sultaness' behavior with Gower's: Trivet explains that the Sultaness resists her son's change of religion, while Gower attributes her actions to envy: "Than have I lost my joies hiere, / For myn astat schal so be lassed."[44] Chaucer's splicing of these two versions creates a superfluity that requires explication.

Donegild's motivation is even less clear. Full of "tirannye," like the would-be usurper the Sultaness, Donegild agonizes over Alla's marriage:

> Hir thoughte hir cursed herte brast atwo.
> She wolde noght hir sone had do so;
> Hir thoughte a *despit* that he sholde take
> So strange a creature unto his make.
>   (697–700; my emphasis)

Alla's mother is undoubtedly not pleased at his conversion to Christianity; like the Sultaness, Donegild too might be understood to be motivated by religious fervor. But such spiritual ardor is not specified, as it is in the case of the Syrian; "strange creature" is the only suggestion. (Note that Gower gives no motive, either; Trivet gives "strangeness" of Constance's ancestry and religion, and envy for her popularity among the people).[45] Donegild's "despit" (699) is more convincingly identified with the angry "despit" (591) of the young knight in Northumbria whose sexual desire—"foul affeccioun"—for Constance is rejected. "Fy, mannysh, fy!" cries the Man of Law at Donegild; "o nay, by God, I lye— / Fy, feendlych spirit" (782–83). The thrice-uttered "Fy!" recalls his earlier imprecation apropos of the incestuous love of a woman for a man, Canacee for her brother: "Of swiche cursed stories I sey fy!" (80). It may be true that, as Drogon of Bergues remarked in his eleventh-century *vita* of Saint Gode-live, "Omnes socrus oderunt nurus" ("All mothers-in-law hate their daughters-in-law"). Drogon identifies this as a piece of popular wisdom, a commonplace saying; such animosity is certainly a widespread folk motif which Schlauch explains in terms of the transition from one phase of family organization to another, a shift from filial allegiance to marital allegiance.[46] I suggest that, whether or not the tale charts a historical shift from matrilineage to patrilineage, as Schlauch argues, the context suggests a quite specific emotional motive for this resentment of mother-in-law for daughter-in-law: incestuous desire of mother for son.

4

But how can these women be impelled by incestuous desires? Incest would seem to be, in Lévi-Strauss's view at least, an affair of male choice. Behind the taboo, as we have seen, is an economy of exchange which regards women as blank "things" to be traded. In accord with such patriarchal ideas, in the *Man of Law's Tale* these women with "unkynde" desires are represented as *not women at all*.[47] The Man of Law becomes rhetorically "hyperactive," to use Rodney Delasanta's term,[48] when faced with the difficult project of determining how it can be that a woman, the Sultaness, can be so evil; of women we have had so far only the example of the virtuous Constance. In two agitated stanzas he bursts out:

> O Sowdanesse, roote of iniquitee!
> Virago, thou Semyrame the secounde!
> O serpent under femynynytee,
> Lik to the serpent depe in helle ybounde!
> O feyned womman, al that may confounde
> Vertu and innocence, thurgh thy malice,
> Is bred in thee, as nest of every vice!
>
> O Sathan, envious syn thilke day
> That thou were chaced from oure heritage,
> Wel knowestow to wommen the olde way!
> Thou madest Eva brynge us in servage;
> Thou wolt fordoon this Cristen mariage.
> Thyn instrument so—weylawey the while!—
> Makestow of wommen, whan thou wolt bigile.
>
> (358–71)

In this Sultaness the Man of Law fixes the origin of all evil: she is "roote," "nest," "welle" of sin. We might hear this as a typical antifeminist diatribe, associating all women with Eve as The One Who Started It All. But as it turns out here, the Sultaness is a *"feyned* womman" (my emphasis), a "serpent under femynynytee," like the Serpent who snakes his way into real women ("Wel knowestow to wommen the olde way!"). Eve, the first of many, was made Satan's "instrument"; she was not herself vicious. The Sultaness, not a woman but a "serpent," later "this scorpioun" (404), and finally "this wikked goost" (404; removed from even the realm of the living), is truly malicious. "Femynynytee" itself is thus kept free of evil, free, in fact, of independent desire or action.

Similarly, Donegild is explicitly not feminine, not even human:

> O Donegild, I ne have noon Englissh digne
> Unto thy malice and thy tirannye!
> And therfore to the feend I thee resigne;
> Lat hym enditen of thy traitorie!
> Fy, mannysh, fy!—o nay, by God, I lye—
> Fy, feendlych spirit, for I dar wel telle,
> Thogh thou heere walke, thy spirit is in helle!
>
> (778–84)

Monstrosity, "venym" (891), devilishness, and death are associated with these creatures, and the urgent necessity of their absolute exclusion from "femynynytee" is audible in the Man of Law's overexcited syntax.

The Sultaness and Donegild are excluded from human society not, primarily, because they are heathens; other heathens (the constable, Hermengyld, Alla) are treated with respect in this narrative.[49] And neither are they excluded from "femynynytee" just because their desires are "unkynde"; they are excluded because they have independent desires at all. They are active women: they want to retain power over their sons; they want to rule the social order; and they have sexual desires independent of, and contrary to, the social order. These desires do not originate in the desires of others, as they must in society which is founded on the exchange of women.[50] Emily in the *Knight's Tale* provides perhaps the clearest example in Chaucer of the feminine desire that conveniently adapts itself to the desires of those who trade her. We recall that, Arcite having won her in battle,

> she agayn hym caste a freendlich ye
> (For wommen, as to speken in comune,

> Thei folwen alle the favour of Fortune)
> And was al his chiere, as in his herte.
>
> (1:2680–83)

Emily makes herself into what Arcite desires (2683), and turns an ami-
able eye toward him. (Note here that when the Knight tries to explain
this phenomenon of the ever-plastic feminine libido, his tone breaks in
the process: "as to speken in comune . . ." The break in tone indicates
the Knight's difficulty in explaining this patriarchal phenomenon; he
senses something remarkable in this idea of feminine adaptability,
and has to try to get outside his high-style aristocratic ideology—to
speak commonly—to explain it. The notion of courtliness as a cover
for the patriarchal exchange economy, as we've seen earlier in *Troilus and Criseyde*, is suggested here as well.) Later, Arcite dead, Emily
uncomplainingly, even blissfully, marries Palamon. For the smooth
operation of the system, women's desires must conform to the desires
of men.

The Man of Law, we might note, seems to be aware of this condition and the effects it might have on women. Early on in the narrative
he recognizes Constance's unhappy plight as a token of exchange
between men, but is unable, in the terms available to him under patriarchy, to explain why it must be this way:

> Allas, what wonder is it thogh she wepte,
> That shal be sent to strange nacioun
> Fro freendes that so tendrely hire kepte,
> And to be bounden under subjeccioun
> Of oon, she knoweth nat his condicioun?
> Housbondes been alle goode, and han ben yoore;
> That knowen wyves; I dar sey yow na moore.
>
> (267–73)

In a complete reversal of emotional logic in the last two lines that
alerts us to ideology reconciling itself to contradiction—ideology constructing itself—the Man of Law unironically gives the only possible
answer under patriarchy: husbands *must be* all good, because women
must be traded in marriage. He may be able to sense that something
is wrong in this gender asymmetry, but he has no way to think of
it outside of patriarchal categories. Thus his hasty retreat: "I dar sey
yow na moore."

The principle of mimetic desire enables the successful exchange of
women; women who independently desire, let alone mothers who
desire their sons, violate it. The seriousness of this disruption—the

anxiety it generates among men—can be discerned by the extreme pressure the Man of Law exerts in his exclusion of these creatures from human society: he uses images of scorpions, snakes, fiends in hell, death. But his trouble with feminine desire is not confined to the two mothers-in-law; it becomes explicit in reference to Constance herself. Female sexual behavior provokes a prurient remark and leads him into paradox when he undertakes to describe what happens on the wedding night of Constance and Alla. Even the mimetic desire of women —their imitative, passive responses—is problematic. He has just mentioned the lavishness of the nuptial feast and entertainments, having deployed *occupatio* to excuse himself from the task of describing them in detail. He could, of course, in the next stanza, use another *occupatio* to extricate himself from the difficulty of describing the saintly, virginal Constance's entrance into sexuality. But he instead brazens it out:

> They goon to bedde, as it was skile and right;
> For thogh that wyves be ful hooly thynges,
> They moste take in pacience at nyght
> Swiche manere necessaries as been plesynges
> To folk that han ywedded hem with rynges,
> And leye a lite hir hoolynesse aside,
> As for the tyme—it may no bet bitide.
>   (708–14)

The Man of Law suggests that just when Constance has become a wife, on her wedding night, she can't act like one, or can't be one: wives are holy things, but to be wedded means that wives must "as for the tyme" lay their holiness aside. Wives must stop being wives, as it were, if they want to be wives. The paradox of this wedding night is left intact and reveals a crucial patriarchal formation of woman. "Hoolynesse" cannot encompass female sexual behavior; what is revealed when wives lay their defining holiness aside is an effect of masculine desire. The Man of Law depicts a wife as something that, at least "for the tyme" (we recall time and maidenhead as blanknesses to be filled in by men), becomes an "embodimen[t] of men's projected needs" (husbands "take . . . / Swiche manere necessaries").[51]

It comes as no surprise, then, that any potential of incestuous relation of Constance to her son Mauricius is entirely absorbed into and made to further the patriarchal order. Active and independent drives are what characterize the mothers-in-law, but not this mother. The relationship between Constance and Mauricius is parallel, rather, to the relationship between the Virgin Mary and her Son. Mary's presence is constant throughout the narrative: Constance prays to her, calls on her for aid; and the Virgin, indeed, finally puts an end to Constance's perils. The parallels between the two women are clear: Constance's heart is a "chambre of hoolynesse" (167), resembling Mary herself, a closed chamber; [52] she acts as mediator in the salvation of the Northumbrians (684), just as Mary's role is mediatory (850); and Constance eventually attains the position of "queene" (693). The parallel relationships between the mothers and their sons are equally clear. Not only does Constance make the connection explicit, praying to the Virgin to pity Mauricius' plight because she has suffered the death of her own Son (848–54), but even the iconography matches: Constance lays her "coverchief" on Mauricius as she carries him to the boat of their exile from Northumbria (837), just as Mary covers Christ at his birth (and later at his death) with her kerchief. Constance at this point is "knelyng" on the shore, just as the Virgin is pictured kneeling at the Nativity. This position of mother kneeling before son Simone de Beauvoir calls "the supreme masculine victory," and, indeed, both maternal roles here subordinate mother to son.[53] The Virgin is hardly viewed as independent or self-determining before her Son; Mauricius, we note, eventually becomes emperor.

Thus, instead of being disrupted by an incestuous relationship between mother and son, the bond between father and son is powerfully established at the end of the *Tale*. During the feast at the Roman senator's house, Alla stares into the face of the unknown young boy as "The child stood, lookynge in the kynges face" (1015); Alla recognizes Constance's countenance in him, much to his amazement, and recognizes him as his son *because* he sees Constance's countenance therein. Speaking to Constance, Alla later refers to "Maurice my sone, so lyk youre face" (1063). The woman's image binds father and son, and, later, grandfather and son (1095–96) in what must be called the patriarchal gaze. It is the same gaze that with "sobre cheere" (97) sees incest between father and daughter but re-vises it as legitimate, the exemplification of a bland truism. And it is the same gaze that removes "tyrannical" women from its line of sight.

5

It seems finally that the operant distinction in the *Man of Law's Tale* is not between good women and bad women. The line between the good female figures and the bad ones in the tale, at first glance so sharp, becomes blurry on closer look.[54] The similarity of the names

"Hermengyld" and "Donegild" and the fact that Chaucer's treatment of his source enhances this nominal similarity suggest that there is in the narrative some essential resemblance between these figures. Donegild accuses Constance of being an "elf" who has given birth to a "feendly creature" (754, 751); she's lying, of course, but the association of Constance with otherworldly and hellish creatures—and, in turn, with the mothers—once made, comes to seem less and less inappropriate: note how many dead bodies Constance herself leaves behind her as she travels from country to country (the Christianized Syrians, the would-be lover in Northumbria, Hermengyld, two mothers-in-law, the would-be rapist on the unidentified shore, more Syrians in revenge).

The vital distinction is rather between all women and all men, or, more precisely, all not-men and all men. "Woman" in the ideology of the *Man of Law's Tale* is an essential blankness that will be inscribed by men and thus turned into a tale; she is a blank onto which men's desire will be projected; she is a no-thing in herself. The Man of Law's outburst at the Sultaness leaves "femynynytee" in itself free from sin; "wommen," he states, are vulnerable to becoming Satan's "instruments." This pure instrumentality of woman is, in fact, definitive of her. If "Eva" demonstrates that bad women are Satan's instruments, Constance demonstrates that saintly women are God's instruments: "God liste to shewe his wonderful myracle / In hire, for we sholde seen his myghty werkis" (477–78). Constance's defining characteristic, her virtuous suffering, is, indeed, not her own; it results from her father's "governance," his sending her off—despite her tears— to marry the Sultan in the first place.[55] And her most aggressive gesture, "hir struglyng wel and myghtily" against the thief who would rape her (921), is made possible only by the intervention of Mary (920) and Christ (924). The Man of Law's most memorable images of Constance serve to emphasize her no-thingness: she spends years floating at sea, without a rudder. Hers is the *pale* face in the crowd as she faces her accuser in Northumbria: "Have ye nat seyn somtyme a pale face . . . ?" (645). And "deedly pale" again, she walks toward her exile from Northumbria, followed by a crowd (822). In this context, Constance's association with death—all those corpses, mentioned earlier —takes on another valence: as Gilbert and Gubar tautly put it in *The Madwoman in the Attic*, "To be selfless is not only to be noble, it is to be dead."[56]

To point out only Constance's blankness and pure instrumentality is, however, to overlook aspects of the narrative that suggest she does have some sense of self-consciousness, indeed, some sense of the kind of "tale" she herself constitutes. The Man of Law works overtime in imposing biblical and hagiographic identities on Constance, but he is not the only one who is aware of her participation in a larger pattern; Constance is aware of herself in the community of saintly Christians, daughters of the Church (566–74). This fact makes her quite unlike the "good women" of the *Legend of Good Women*, cut off from the perception of themselves in any kind of community. Not only does the Man of Law use language that associates her with the Virgin Mary (she is a "queen," "unwemmed"); Constance herself prays to the Virgin, making her own recognition of saintly analogy clear:

> Thow sawe thy child yslayn bifore thyne yen,
> And yet now lyveth my litel child, parfay!
> Now, lady bright, to whom alle woful cryen,
>
> . . . .
> Rewe on my child.
>
> (848–52)

She makes her own Marian role explicit, just as, earlier, she understands that she and others work as daughters of the Church (566–74). She does have a sense of herself as a saint, as participant in a community whose exemplar is Christ: she senses that her own position under attack in Northumbria is like Susanna's; she may even, as Weissman suggests, enact a sacred parody of the Crucifixion scene as she leaves Northumbria.

Constance has, too, a definite ability to shape her life as a perfect romance, to write, in a sense, her own story. Early on, when she leaves her home for Syria, "She peyneth hire to make good contenance" (320), demonstrating that she has some awareness of shaping appearances. When she is found by the constable on the Northumbrian shore she tells a little tale about herself, concealing her true identity:

> She kneleth doun and thanketh Goddes sonde;
> But what she was she wolde no man seye,
> For foul ne fair, thogh that she sholde deye.
>
> She seyde she was so mazed in the see
> That she forgat hir mynde, by hir trouthe.
>
> (523–27)

She again withholds her identity when she is found on the open sea by the Roman senator. And she persuades Alla not to reveal it to her father in Rome when he invites the old man to dine with them. She thus contrives a denouement full of drama, reversal, and recognition, in which she utters her own name in the moment of reconciliation with her father: " 'I am youre doghter Custance,' quod she" (1107). Constance may be a tale told by men, but she seems to be given, by the Man of Law, a certain power of determining her own narrative kinesis.

But Constance's limited self-consciousness in fact serves patriarchy well (as do the romance hagiographies that provide the most immediate context for Constance's self-portrayal here).[57] The tale she tells in order to conceal her identity, after all, is that she "forgat hir mynde" (524). Dominant ideology (and its expressed system of laws) controls and manipulates the principle of similarity and difference, analogy and repetition; if Constance has access to these principles—is conscious that she is like others (saints, romance heroines, women)— that consciousness enables her only to suffer and to be constrained. Her self-perceived identity as saint enables her to do no more than endure injuries, as does her consciousness of her own womanhood ("I, wrecche womman, no fors though I spille! / Wommen are born to thraldom and penance, / And to been under mannes governance" [285–87]). And at the moment of her greatest self-consciousness, the moment in which she pronounces her own name, Constance plays a part in a larger system of patriarchal constraint that ends this romance narrative. Her happiness in reunion with her father—the "pitous joye" (1114), the "wepynge for tendrenesse in herte blithe" (1154)—is assimilated by the Man of Law into the pattern of joy after woe, woe after gladness that he identifies as the natural rhythm of earthly life.

It's an ending that appeals to the Host, who commends the tale at its conclusion as "a *thrifty* tale for the nones!" (1165; my emphasis). His enthusiastic response reinforces the smoothly running patriarchal system that trades women and tales, women as tales. Constance's minimal self-awareness allows her no more than passivity. But there's one woman on this pilgrimage who knows that she's merchandise and uses that knowledge of woman's commodification to her own advantage: "With daunger," she assures us, "oute we al oure chaffare" (3:521). She knows that "woman" has been written by clerks in their oratories. And she takes that "book of wikked wyves" and tosses it into the fire.

Chapter Four
"Glose/bele chose":
The Wife of Bath and Her Glossators

The Man of Law has just concluded his tale of Constance, reuniting father and daughter in one big ideological embrace, and it has pleased that manliest of men, Harry Bailly. The Host's delight in this tale, expressed in the Epilogue of the *Man of Law's Tale*, comes as no surprise: as we've seen, the Man of Law's *vita* of Constance—like Chaucer's "Seintes Legende of Cupide" that the Man of Law mentions in his Introduction—has represented its heroine as a will-less blank and has thus controlled the threat that an independent female "corage" would pose to patriarchy. Such control of the "sleightes and subtilitees" of women (as he will put it later, in response to the *Merchant's Tale* [4:2421]) is immensely appealing to the henpecked Harry; impressed by the Man of Law's performance, he stands up in his stirrups and calls out: "Goode men, herkeneth everych on!" He then asks another one of "ye lerned men in lore," the Parson, to tell a tale. But the prospect of a suffocating sermon, especially after the *Man* of Law's tale, is too much for the Wife of Bath. Out of this company of "goode men" the voice of the woman bursts: "Nay, by my fader soule, that schal he nat! . . . He schal no gospel glosen here ne teche." Instead, "My joly body schal a tale telle," a tale having nothing to do with "philosophie, / Ne phislyas, ne termes queinte of lawe."[1] The Wife opposes her tale to the "lerned men's" lore: it is her "joly body" against their oppressive teaching and glossing.

The Wife—a clothier, dealer in *textus*—continues in her Prologue to oppose herself to glosses. "Men may devyne and *glosen*, up and doun" (3:26; my emphasis) about how many men one may have in marriage, but the Wife knows that God bade us to increase and multiply: "That gentil *text* kan *I* wel understonde." In this endlink to the *Man of Law's Tale* and beginning of the Wife of Bath's Prologue, woman is associated with the body and the text—as in the Pauline exegetical assimilation of literality and carnality to femininity I discussed in the

Introduction—and is opposed to the gloss, written by men, learned, anti-pleasure, and anti-body.

Indeed, outfitted in her ostentatious garb—thick kerchiefs, fine stockings, new shoes, huge hat—and emphasizing that those "gaye scarlet gytes" are well used, the Wife of Bath herself is an embodiment of the letter of the text as Jerome has imaged it in his paradigm of proper reading: like the alien woman of Deuteronomy 21, she is a woman whose clothed appearance is centrally significant. But unlike that new bride, she retains her costume (which she intends, I argue, to be alluring, however overwhelming and repellent others might find it), revels in her seductive person and adornment: *her* hair isn't shaved, *her* nails aren't pared.[2] Unlike that silent bride—and unlike her virtually mute relations, the passive feminine bodies manipulated by the narrator of the *Legend of Good Women* and Constance in the *Man of Law's Tale*—the Wife speaks: whereas that alien captive is passed between men at war, her desire conforming to the desire of the men in possession of her, the Wife makes her autonomous desire the very motive and theme of her performance.[3] And if Jerome's paradigm—a forerunner of Lévi-Strauss's patriarchal paradigm, just as we have seen the *Man of Law's Tale* to be—runs on the assumption that all women are functionally interchangeable (an assumption on which Pandarus and Troilus operate as well), the Wife of Bath would seem to regard *men* as virtually interchangeable: "Yblessed be God that I have wedded fyve! / Welcome the sixte, whan that evere he shal," she declares (44–45), and elaborates:

> I ne loved nevere by no discrecioun,
> But evere folwede myn appetit,
> Al were he short, or long, or blak, or whit;
> I took no kep, so that he liked me,
> How poore he was, ne eek of what degree.
> (622–26)

The Wife of Bath, in fact, articulates, makes visible, exactly what that patriarchal hermeneutic necessarily excludes, necessarily keeps invisible. She represents what the ideology of that model—an ideology incarnated, as we've seen, by the Man of Law—can't say, can't acknowledge, or acknowledges only by devalorizing and stigmatizing as Other: she represents independent feminine will and desire, the literal body of the text that itself has signifying value and leads to the spirit without its necessarily being devalued or destroyed in the process.[4] The woman traded must be silent; the Wife talks. The woman's desire must be merely mimetic; the Wife chronicles her own busy "purveiance / Of mariage" (570–71). The gloss undertakes to speak (for) the text; the Wife maintains that the literal text—her body —can speak for itself. If the Man of Law must energetically suppress the feminine, the Wife vociferously speaks as that Other created and excluded by patriarchal ideology, and in this way she reveals the very workings of this ideology. Most penetratingly, as her *Tale* suggests in its narrative focus on a rapist, if the patriarchal economy of the trade of women proceeds without woman's necessary acquiescence, it is always potentially performing a rape. (The rape is, in fact, Chaucer's own innovation to the traditional stories that inform this tale, a deliberate alteration that argues for its significance in the whole of the Wife's performance.)[5]

We might say, then, that the Wife is everything the Man of Law can't say, everything Criseyde, everything Philomela might have said, given the chance. She makes audible precisely what patriarchal discourse would keep silent, reveals the exclusion and devalorization that patriarchal discourse performs. Speaking as the excluded Other, she explicitly and affirmatively assumes the place that patriarchal discourse accords the feminine. Far from being trapped within the "prison house" of antifeminist discourse, the Wife of Bath, I argue, "convert[s] a form of subordination into an affirmation," to adapt Luce Irigaray's words here; she *mimics* the operations of patriarchal discourse. As Irigaray has characterized it, such mimesis functions to reveal those operations, to begin to make a place for the feminine:

> There is, in an initial phase, perhaps only one "path," the one historically assigned to the feminine: that of *mimicry*. One must assume the feminine role deliberately. Which means already to convert a form of subordination into an affirmation, and thus to begin to thwart it. . . . To play with mimesis is thus, for a woman, to try to recover the place of her exploitation by discourse, without allowing herself to be simply reduced to it. It means to resubmit herself— inasmuch as she is on the side of the "perceptible," of "matter"—to "ideas," in particular to ideas about herself, that are elaborated in/by a masculine logic, but so as to make "visible," by an effect of playful repetition, what was supposed to remain invisible: the cover-up of a possible operation of the feminine in language.[6]

Irigaray's own project of mimesis is immense—it intends the thwarting of all patriarchal discourse—and I cannot engage here the complex context in which she develops the idea. Such a concept of mimesis is in itself, however, very powerful: it seems to me strikingly useful to the analysis of the Wife of Bath's performance, a performance that is at once enormously affirmative and adversative. But the Wife is also crucially unlike the woman Irigaray describes here; she "plays with mimesis," mimics patriarchal discourse ("Myn entente nys but for to pleye," she maintains [192]), not in order to "thwart" it altogether, to subvert it entirely, but to *reform* it, to keep it in place while making it accommodate feminine desire. What the Wife imagines in her Prologue and *Tale* is a way in which such patriarchal hermeneutics as imagined by Jerome, Macrobius, and Richard of Bury can be deployed to the satisfaction of everyone under patriarchy, according a place of active signification to both masculine and feminine: clerk and wife, gloss and text, spirit and letter, "matter" and "ideas" (Irigaray mentions the Aristotelian terms I've discussed in my Introduction). What would be necessary to the satisfying formulation of sexualized hermeneutics is, in fact, inherent in that Hieronymian image itself, an understanding of the feminine not as only the distracting veil but the fecund body, not as merely something to be turned away from, gotten rid of, passed through, but as something that is, in itself, at once a locus of pleasure *and* a locus of valuable signification. The Wife thus articulates the happy possibility of reforming the patriarchal and fundamentally misogynistic hermeneutic based on the economy of possession, of traffic in texts-as-women, to make it accommodate the feminine—woman's independent will and the signifying value of the letter.

The Wife of Bath, in fact, would seem to be Chaucer's favorite character, and the reasons for this become clearer and clearer. As Robert A. Pratt has put it in his analysis of Chaucer's evolving idea of the Wife, from her early characterization as teller of the *Shipman's Tale* to her fully fleshed-out form as we know it now,

> She appears to have interested Chaucer more, to have stimulated his imagination and creative power more fully and over a longer period, than any other of his characters.[7]

She pops up again and again: apparently irrepressible, she bursts out of even the confines of her "fictive universe," the *Canterbury Tales*—where she provokes the excited interjections of Pardoner and Friar and is deferred to as a certain kind of authority by both Clerk and Merchant—to be cited in Chaucer's own voice in "Lenvoy de Chaucer a Bukton."[8] The Wife is a source of delight for this male author precisely because through her he is able to reform and still to participate in patriarchal discourse; he recuperates the feminine *within* the solid structure of that discourse.

This is a male fantasy, of course. And when we consider that such desire for the reform—not the overturning—of patriarchy is represented as a woman's desire, it is even more apparent that this is a masculine dream. Granted that it is indeed such a fantasy, we might remark that it is not a bad one, after all; it is not exploitative of the feminine for purely masculine gratification. Through the Wife, Chaucer imagines the possibility of a masculine reading that is not antifeminist, that does acknowledge, in good faith, feminine desire; and further, he represents the struggle and violence to the feminine that accompany the articulation of this fantasy. Through the Wife, then, Chaucer recuperates the sexualized hermeneutic that he recognizes as both pervasive in the medieval literary imagination and manifestly flawed. He has shown its limits in *Troilus and Criseyde*, the *Legend of Good Women*, and the *Man of Law's Tale*, has shown the toll thereby taken on the feminine; he continues, in the Wife of Bath's Prologue and *Tale*, to register the toll taken on the feminine corpus in even the imagining of patriarchy's reform. The Wife expresses a dream of masculine reading that is not antifeminist and a feminine relation to the condition of being read that is not antimasculinist—but she does so after having been bruised and battered, permanently injured by that clerk Jankyn, in their concussive renovation of patriarchal discourse.

1

Crucial to the smooth passage of the alien woman between men at war, as we've seen time and again, is the exclusion of her independent desire. Criseyde is rejected by immasculated readers of her because she seems to them to be gratifying her own fickle desire; the women of the *Legend of Good Women* are featureless, enervated creatures, kept that way by the misogynistic plan of the narrator, the God of Love, and Alceste; pale Constance is assigned value by the men who trade her, and her sexuality, even as passive and mimetic as it is, is still a discomfort and confusion to the Man of Law. He denies that the mothers-in-law, with their transgressive desires, are even females of the species. The Wife of Bath, on the Other hand, actively and vociferously seeks her own sexual satisfaction. She spends the first 162 lines of her Prologue energetically defending a theology that acknowledges sexual activity, even sexual desire: our "membres," she maintains, are not only for "purgacioun / Of uryne" and for the differentiation of the sexes; they are also for "ese"—"Of engendrure," she adds, after a significant pause (115–28). Her desire for the frequent use of her "instrument" motivates this opening exegetical discourse; and in the account of her five marriages that follows, she continues to explicate her preferences and active choices. She wore out the first three old husbands "pitously a-nyght" (202), she tells us, though she makes it clear that "in bacon hadde I nevere delit" (418); she wanted to be the only source of "delit" for her adulterous fourth husband (482); and she loved her fifth the best not only because of his great legs but because "in oure bed he was so fressh and gay" (508).

The Wife's loud and happy occupation of a position that is denied by patriarchal ideology is witnessed in her full embrace of her own commodification. Lévi-Strauss attempts to cover up the implications of the commodification of women that is essential to his paradigm, as we've seen in the previous chapter; Hector in *Troilus and Criseyde* does something similar when he insists to the Trojan parliament that "We usen here no wommen for to selle" (4.182). But woman is indeed treated as a possession to be traded, "chaffare," merchandise —we think again of Criseyde as "moeble" (4.1380); of Constance, packed off as a load in a boat—and the Wife makes this explicit, assumes her position as female in the marketplace. She thus reveals the essential commodification of woman in patriarchy when she speaks the language of sexual economics.[9] Unlike Hector, the Wife clearly acknowledges that *"al* is for to selle" (414; my emphasis). She'll work the market, "make me a feyned appetit" when there's "wynnyng" to be had (416–17), withhold her sex when there's a "raunson" to be paid (409–12):

> With daunger oute we al oure chaffare;
> Greet prees at market maketh deere ware,
> And to greet cheep is holde at litel prys:
> This knoweth every womman that is wys.
>
> (521–24)

If Lévi-Strauss suggests that the law of supply and demand must regulate the masculine trade of women (scarcity of desirable women maintains the structure of exchange, as he points out in *Elementary Structures of Kinship*),[10] "wommen," the Wife contends, speaking as the excluded condition, have a "queynte fantasye" of their own: the "daungerous," withholding, scarce man generates their own desire.

Critics often argue that the Wife in her Prologue is but enacting an antifeminist stereotype of the greedy, insatiable, domineering wife —to put it in the terms of my analysis, critics argue that rather than embodying what patriarchal discourse *can't* say, she is enacting precisely what patriarchal discourse *does* say, and says endlessly (in the univocal chant of Theophrastus, Jerome, Walter Map, Andreas Capellanus, Jean de Meun, Matheolus, Gautier le Leu, Deschamps, and others such as are contained in Jankyn's book).[11] But this is another part of her process of mimicry: she not only uncovers what is hidden in the workings of patriarchal ideology but simultaneously appropriates the place of the Other that ideology openly creates; she assumes the place of the feminine (the stereotype) to which patriarchy explicitly relegates her. When the Wife rehearses to the pilgrim audience her diatribe against her three old husbands, she is repeating the very words antifeminist writers have given the out-of-control wife. Jerome, for example, quotes Theophrastus in *Adversus Jovinianum:*

> Then come curtain-lectures the live-long night: she complains that one lady goes out better dressed than she: that another is looked up to by all: "I am a poor despised nobody at the ladies' assemblies." "Why did you ogle that creature next door?" "Why were you talking to the maid?" [12]

The Wife of Bath harangues her husbands:

> Sire olde kaynard, is this thyn array?
> Why is my neighebores wyf so gay?
> She is honoured overal ther she gooth;
> I sitte at hoom; I have no thrifty clooth.
> What dostow at my neighebores hous?
> Is she so fair? Artow so amorous?
> What rowne ye with oure mayde? Benedicite!
> Sire olde lecchour, lat thy japes be!
>
> (235–42)

La Vieille, in the *Roman de la rose,* advises Bel Acueil on how a lover should play the game of love:

> He should swear that if he had wanted to allow his rose, which was in great demand, to be taken by another, he would have been weighed down with gold and jewels. But, he should go on, his pure heart was so loyal that no man would ever stretch out his hand for it except that man alone who was offering his hand at that moment.[13]

The Wife of Bath appeases her husbands just so:

> What eyleth yow to grucche thus and grone?
> Is it for ye wolde have my queynte allone?

> Wy, taak it al! Lo, have it every deel!
> Peter! I shrewe yow, but ye love it weel;
> For if I wolde selle my *bele chose*,
> I koude walke as fressh as is a rose;
> But I wol kepe it for youre owene tooth.
>
> (443–49)

Indeed, her words are the antifeminists' words; but she assertively, knowingly appropriates them and the position to which antifeminist writers have relegated wives ("sith a man is moore resonable / Than womman is, ye moste been suffrable [441–42]; "Deceite, wepyng, spynnyng God hath yive / To wommen kyndely" [401–2]), and she thus rehearses this discourse with a difference. She herself remains elsewhere, with a body, a will, a desire beyond that which she is accorded by patriarchal discourse—this is "the persistence of 'matter,'" as Irigaray puts it:

> If women are such good mimics, it is because they are not simply resorbed in this function. *They also remain elsewhere:* another case of the persistence of "matter," but also of "sexual pleasure." [14]

It is the Wife of Bath as incarnation of the devalorized feminine letter in the discourse of patriarchal hermeneutics that interests me most in this consideration of the Wife and mimesis. The Wife has been dealt with by critics time and again as a more or less psychologically rounded character, expressing feminine desire and Chaucer's desire for feminine desire; but her centrality to Chaucer's poetics, it seems to me, is due less to her significance as dramatic invention than to her value as a representation of the letter, the body of the text. I read her Prologue and *Tale* as most significant in their allegorical representation of the act of reading. The Wife speaks as the literal text, insisting on the positive, significant value of the carnal letter as opposed to the spiritual gloss; moreover, in doing so she appropriates the methods of the masculine, clerkly *glossatores* themselves, thus exposing techniques that they would rather keep invisible. I want now to focus specifically on the relationship of the Wife, as literal text, to the gloss and clerkly glossators; for it is through her mimicking patriarchal hermeneutics—incarnating the excluded letter and repeating the masculine hermeneutic moves—that Chaucer suggests a revision of the paradigm of reading as a masculine activity that would acknowledge, even solicit, feminine desire. First, though, a glance at the bibliographical history of the scriptural gloss and its relationship to the biblical text is in order; glossing's totalizing function vis-à-vis the text will become apparent, and we shall be able to see the energetic proliferation of glosses themselves—although they ostensibly undertake to limit proliferation—and the self-interest of clerkly glossators, which will in fact become the Wife of Bath's theme.[15]

"Gloss" comes from the Greek *glossa* ("tongue, language"). As Francis E. Gigot notes, in early usage, Greek grammarians used the term to refer to words of Greek texts that required some exposition; later, the term came to refer to the explanation itself. Early Christian writers, commenting on Scripture, adopted the word to refer to an explanation of obscure verbal usage in the text—of foreign, dialectal, and obsolete words in particular—as opposed to an explanation of theological or doctrinal difficulties. Such glosses would be single words, written interlinearly or in the margins of the manuscript. But the word *glossa* was soon used to indicate more elaborate expositions of Scripture: from individual words to explanatory sentences to running commentaries on entire books. These longer commentaries as well would be written interlinearly and in the margins. The twelfth-century *Glossa ordinaria* ("The Gloss") sought to compile all glosses on the Bible, which themselves often consisted of layers upon layers of glosses. There were, in addition, glosses of the *Glossa*. In fact, Robert of Melun, in the mid-twelfth century (the height of glossomania) complained that the masters were reading the text only because of the gloss.[16]

But glossing activity continued, apparently unabated: notes and commentaries—*sententiae, postillae, distinctiones*—were produced vigorously. Marginal and interlinear glosses of Scripture became so elaborate, crowding the text off the page, that Sixtus V determined in 1588, on publication of his authoritative version of the Vulgate, that there would be no glosses in future copies of it—no marginal annotations of variant readings. There are words in the text of scripture as we know it now that were originally marginal or interlinear glosses— brief comments or explanations of a word—but were subsequently inserted into the text itself by scribes or owners of manuscripts. The gloss crowds out the text, the gloss becomes the text. And the gloss preserves the text from oblivion: to take a secular example, the only reason Chaucer knew a fragment of book 6 of Cicero's *Republic* is that Macrobius wrote a commentary on it, about sixteen times the length of the Ciceronian piece itself. What is supplementary, what is marginal, becomes the very condition of the primary text's existence, and itself proliferates. We might observe, too, with Graham D. Caie, that the glosses on Chaucer's own text in the Ellesmere manuscript

> are written in as large and as careful a hand as the actual text, which
> is placed off-centre to make room for the glosses, each of which

begins with an illuminated capital in the same colours as those of
the text itself. In a sense it is a misnomer to call them "marginalia"
at all, and one might confidently assume that the Ellesmere scribe
considered the glosses to be an important part of the work as a
whole.[17]

At the same time—the twelfth century—that scriptural glossing is
at its most fervent, and that Robert of Melun is complaining that the
gloss is more important than the text, the word "gloss" acquires pejorative connotations. *Gloser* in French, "glosen" in English, meant
"to explicate, interpret" but also "to give a false interpretation, flatter,
deceive"—thus, as we say, "to gloss over." Amant, in the *Roman de
la rose,* insists that Raison provide a courteous gloss for some nasty
words that she uses. If she *must* talk about "testicles" ("coilles"), he
maintains, she ought at least to disguise her subject with a gloss. And
in the *Summoner's Tale* (following the Wife of Bath's and Friar's performances) the hypocritical and avaricious friar rejoices, "Glosynge is
a glorious thyng, certeyn, / For lettre sleeth, so as we clerkes seyn"
(3:1793–94). He can make the text of Holy Writ do whatever he wants
via the gloss. I shall find it "in a maner glose," he states (1920), even
though his meaning isn't in the letter. (And it is the very carnal fart
of the enraged Thomas that puts an end to this phony spiritualizing
glossing.)

This pejoration makes explicit, makes part of the very definition of
the word, the self-interestedness that is always potential in the act of
glossing. Glossing is a gesture of appropriation; the *glossa* undertakes
to speak the text, to assert authority over it, to provide an interpretation, finally to limit or close it to the possibility of heterodox or
unlimited significance. Attracted by the beauties and difficulties of
the letter, the glossator opens, reveals and makes useful the text's
hidden truth, recloaking the text with his own interpretation. Glossing thus registers the literal attractions of the text and the delight of
understanding its spirit, but it can overwhelm the text as well. Robert
of Melun complains of the aggression with which masters defended
their glosses as having authority; he suggests that they were in fact
ready to fight to a bloody finish for their glosses. And not only Robert
charges glossators with doing violence to the literal text; Christine de
Pizan's reference to an aphorism about glossing makes it clear that the
view of its appropriative and totalizing nature was commonplace: in
her letter to Pierre Col (about what she saw as antifeminism in the
Rose) she remarks, "Surely, this is like the common proverb about the
glosses of Orleans which destroyed the text."[18]

The Wife suggests that the appropriative nature of glossing has a particularly masculine valence. In her so-called *sermon joyeux*, the first 162 lines of her Prologue, the Wife as "noble prechour" (165) categorically opposes the text to the gloss. As I mentioned above, she has already countered the "glossing and teaching" of "lerned men" with her "joly body" in the Man of Law's Epilogue: glossing has a totalizing function much like that of masculine reading in *Troilus and Criseyde* and the *Legend*, working to turn away from the feminine body —woman and literal text. Glossing seeks to find one answer, impose one interpretation on the meaning of Christ's words to the Samaritan woman, for example:

> What that he mente therby, I kan nat seyn;
> But that I axe, why that the fifthe man
> Was noon housbonde to the Samaritan?
> How manye myghte she have in mariage?
> Yet herde I nevere tellen in myn age
> Upon this nombre diffinicioun.
> Men may devyne and glosen, up and doun . . .
>
> (20–26)

When she says "Men" in line 26, she undoubtedly means *men*. Glossing seeks to deny the functions of the body (115–24), and in particular to limit the Wife's uninhibited use of her "instrument." But the letter, she contends, authorizes her to use that "instrument / As frely as my Makere hath it sent" (149–50), even though clerks would insist that she keep her body chaste. The Wife's reliance on the letter, her heartily espousing the literal text in her justification of the fulfillment of feminine desire, is a commonplace among critics.[19] She points to a passage in Genesis when arguing against glosses on the wedding at Cana and on the Samaritan woman; she asserts that no biblical text mentions a specific number of marriages; she adduces scriptural precedents for multiple wives; appeals to the Pauline text that it is better to marry than to burn; reminds her audience that the apostle only counsels virginity and does not command it; refers to Christ's admonition that those who would live perfectly should sell all they have and give to the poor (and "that am nat I" [112]); repeats Paul's statement that the wife has power over her husband and that husbands should love their wives.

Of course, the Wife may oppose herself to them, but she is arguing here precisely like a glossator herself.[20] She poses *quaestiones*, like the twelfth- and thirteenth-century glossators. "If ther were no seed

ysowe, / Virginitee, thanne wherof sholde it growe?" (71–72); "Telle
me also, to what conclusion / Were membres maad of generacion?"
(115–16). She works through this question logically (prompting the
Friar to label her narrative "scole-matere" [1272])—the "membres of
generacion" were made not only for "purgation of urine" and "to
know a female from a male"; they are also for the purpose of procre-
ation:

> Why sholde men elles in hir bookes sette
> That man shal yelde to his wyf hire dette?
> Now wherwith sholde he make his paiement,
> If he ne used his sely instrument?
>
> (129–32)

Her argumentation in these early lines of her Prologue repeats the
points of the heretical Jovinian, as has often been observed, in Jerome's
Adversus Jovinianum, but it as well mimes Jerome's own pseudologi-
cal moves in that treatise. If the Wife of Bath's reasoning is slippery,
prompting critics to castigate her, it is because Jerome's itself is: commenting on Saint Paul's statement that it is good for a man to be un-
married, for example, Jerome contends, "If it is good for a man to be
so, then it is bad for a man not to be so." [21] And if the Wife amputates
biblical passages to fit her scheme (forgetting, for example, the second half of Paul's exhortation when she blithely declares: "I have the
power durynge al my lyf / Upon his propre body, and noght he. / Right
thus the Apostel tolde it unto me" [158–60]), she is but mimicking the
methods of those late glossators whom Henri de Lubac describes as
"pulverizing" the text (suppressing parts of passages, distorting and
rearranging texts) to fit their schemes. [22] In this active mimicking, the
Wife reveals most powerfully that these glossators' concerns are indeed carnal: she has made her own self-interest explicit, and her act of
appropriating their methods for openly carnal purposes indicts their
motivations as similarly carnal. She indeed affirms this outright a little
later:

> The clerk, whan he is oold, and may noght do
> Of Venus werkes worth his olde sho,
> Thanne sit he doun, and writ in his dotage
> That wommen kan nat kepe hir mariage!
>
> (707–10)

It is the bad-faith glosses written by men in order to limit and control the feminine body that the Wife exposes, rips up, and has burned.

But, curiously, it is the openly pejorated, carnal, ostentatiously masculine glossing by the clerk Jankyn that the Wife—the body of the text
—finds so appealing, so effective, so irresistible:

> . . . in oure bed he was so fressh and gay,
> And therwithal so wel koude he me glose,
> Whan that he wolde han my *bele chose;*
> That thogh he hadde me bete on every bon,
> He koude wynne agayn my love anon.
>
> (508–12)

Flattery and blandishments cajole the Wife into bed so that Jankyn
may take his pleasure of her *"bele chose"* (a foreign term in need of
exposition; see also her *"quoniam"* [608]). Glossing here is unmistak-
ably carnal, a masculine act performed on the feminine body, and it
leads to pleasure for both husband and wife, both clerk and text. This
glossing wipes out the Wife's immediate pain in her bones—inflicted
by Jankyn, we must remember—and it does so because it satisfies the
Wife's own desires even as it seeks to fulfill his. The Wife is left, of
course, with bruises on her body: as she explains her love of Jankyn,
she remarks,

> And yet was he to me the mooste shrewe;
> That feele I on my ribbes al by rewe,
> And evere shal unto myn endyng day.
>
> (505–7)

But of all her men he is her favorite nonetheless, precisely because he
—unlike Jerome's warrior—acknowledges and knows how to arouse
feminine desire: "I trowe I loved hym best, for that he / Was of his
love daungerous to me" (513–14).

The Wife thus describes a marriage relationship—and, allegorically,
a relationship between text and glossator—that would acknowledge
the desires of both sides and would yield satisfaction to both. The
conclusion of her Prologue strongly suggests that what she wants is
reciprocity, despite her talk of "maistrie"; she most wants mutual recognition and satisfaction of desires. Once Jankyn apologizes to her
and burns the book that has caused her so much "wo" and "pyne"
(787), she becomes kind and true to him. She gains the "soverayne-
tee" but doesn't want to exercise it, as Donald Howard has suggested;
she seeks rather to be "acorded by us selven two" (812).[23] Whether
she actually has attained such complete mutuality is, despite her positive assertion of the fact, made doubtful by the language in which she

expresses it: it is the language of fairy tale, rendered ironic by what has gone before (after the exposition of tricks and lies wives use, how "trewe" is "any wyf from Denmark unto Ynde"? [824]). But in the Wife's dreams, at least—in the male author's dreams that she dreams —there is full understanding between husband and wife, between clerk and text. Having married a clerk, having married him "for love" (526), she is a literal text that *wants* to disclose its hidden meaning, its truth. Her fairy-tale conclusion hints at a hermeneutic that respects the integrity and value of the literal text—Jankyn burns the book of glosses, they never have any further "debaat"—*and* that will arrive pleasurably at the spirit, the "truth" ("I was to hym . . . kynde / . . . And also trewe" [823–25]). This is a dream of a resolutely masculine reading of the feminine text—a dream of a man's reading *as* a man— that does not sacrifice the feminine in getting to the spirit but sees, in fact, that the text, stripped, reclothed, glossed, is still and ever feminine.

2

The Wife of Bath's Prologue thus renovates the patriarchal hermeneutic to accommodate the feminine, and her *Tale* continues to reveal and recover those things necessarily excluded by patriarchal discourse. She begins by immediately and forthrightly deploying the romance genre, a form relegated to women (as is clear from book 2 of *Troilus and Criseyde*, when Criseyde, reading a "romaunce," is cut off in her narration by Pandarus' allusion to Statius' "bookes twelve"), against the world of masculine authority represented by the Friar.[24] Friars gloss, as the Summoner makes clear in his tale, and the Wife uses the feminine romance against precisely such glossators—"hooly freres"— revealing, in fact, their engagement in carnal pursuits in the bushes.

Digression, dilation, delay of closure are features of this narrative form, as we've suggested in relation to Criseyde, and are in marked contrast to masculine totalizing. The Wife indeed digresses, and she does so into a classical text. Her Ovidian digression, which Lee Patterson has brilliantly analyzed, mimics such misogynistic use of the classical text as is made by the narrator of the *Legend of Good Women;* she alters the pagan text for an ostensibly antifeminist purpose: women, her fable says, can't keep secrets. But, as Patterson suggests, the Wife's use of the pagan text ends up problematizing most deeply not women's irrepressible speaking but men's listening. Midas, after all, has ass's ears; the Wife challenges male readers to resist the "immediate self–gratifications of antifeminism" in order to gain "self-knowledge."[25] The Wife manipulates the classical letter, the body, but does so to suggest something about just such a misogynistic strategy: it deprives not only the female of her significance but the male of self-understanding.

The particular narrative the Wife sets out to tell, the tale of the knight and loathly lady, makes visible and explicitly seeks to adjust the crucial structural workings of the patriarchal exchange of women. As in the Prologue, the Wife here does not seek to overthrow patriarchal power structures; the tale begins with a rape, always potential in the exchange structure that doesn't acknowledge feminine desire, and makes its central narrative problematic the correction of the rapist. The rapist, and the patriarchal power structure of possession that he enacts, must learn "what thyng is it that wommen moost desiren" (905)—must acknowledge the integrity of the feminine body and act in reference to feminine desire. That much of the energy of the first part of the narrative is devoted to enumerating the many things that women desire—"Somme seyde . . . Somme seyde . . . Somme seyde . . . Somme . . . somme . . ." (925–27)—attests to the notion that it's more important to acknowledge *that* women desire than to specify *what* it is that pleases them most. After the knight's year-long quest, the court is packed with women—"Ful many a noble wyf, and many a mayde, / And many a wydwe" (1026–27)—waiting to hear him declare, "with manly voys" (1036), what they presumably already know —waiting, that is, for the moment in which feminine desire will be acknowledged, publicly, by a man.

It is again, as in the Prologue, the Wife's allegorical working-out of the relationship between glossator and text that interests me here. As we've seen in "Adam Scriveyn," "rape" connotes not only sexual but textual violation; in *Troilus and Criseyde* and the *Legend of Philomela*, rape—the violation of the feminine—is the way misogynistic literary history is inaugurated and proceeds. In the rape and subsequent education of the rapist, the Wife of Bath works out the ideal of a hermeneutic that submits to the letter of the text and that will, as a consequence, arrive at its beautiful truth.

An act of violence is perpetrated by "a lusty bacheler" (883) on the corpus of a woman at the outset of the *Tale*. Riding out, a knight sees a "mayde" walking along, "Of which mayde anon, maugree hir heed, / By verray force, he rafte hire maydenhed" (887–88). The knight has stripped her of her protective garments and takes "hire maydenhed," the truth secreted within. He makes a whore out of her, as Macrobius would say, by exposing and soiling the pure body, a body he does not understand as anything but naked flesh. He is a brash reader, an intruder, tearing the garments, gaping at truths, violating and manhandling secrets more properly left veiled—because incomprehensible—to him.

This patently self-interested and abusive glossator's punishment is to discover "What thyng is it that wommen moost desiren" (905). How *should* he treat the body of the text? Must all glossing be violent, an unwelcome deformation of the letter? Is the alluring letter itself to be enjoyed? What is the relationship between the seductive outer garments and the wisdom underneath? Are both to be respected, are both properly sites of pleasure? The knight's quest does not, in fact, seem to promise a positive answer to questions of pleasure. For on his last day, when he approaches the dance of the four-and-twenty ladies in the forest, they vanish; and of the seductions of the letter the untutored knight, in his wantonness, is left with an ugly hag, pure wisdom with no bodily attractions to lure him toward her: "Agayn the knyght this olde wyf gan ryse" (1000), not vice versa. The old hag is the opposite of the troublesomely alluring text that torments Jerome in letter 22, to Eustochium. She is not just a text that is pure wisdom, pure spirit, with no appeal to wantonness (a *Parson's Tale,* for example); she's a literally repulsive text whose appalling letter challenges the reader to endure for the sake of its perfect spirit.

The knight is not up to the challenge of this text, even after his year-long tutelage in feminine desire. Like many men, as Patterson observes in reference to the Midas exemplum, he has to be taught, it seems, yet again: on the night of their mirthless wedding, the loathly bride lectures her groom on the advantages of her lowly birth, poverty, old age, and ugliness, quoting texts of Cicero, Juvenal, Seneca, Dante (in an act, it seems, of exemplary glossing of herself). But when at last the chastened knight acknowledges her wisdom ("I put me in youre wise governance" [1231]) and her desire—and even suggests in a crucial reversal that *his* desire will conform to *hers* ("Cheseth youreself which may be moost plesance / And moost honour to yow and me also . . . / For as yow liketh, it suffiseth me" [1232–35])—she invites him to unveil her: "Cast up the curtyn, looke how that it is" (1249). The text's truth is revealed when *she* wants it to be. Here is an ideal vision of perfect reading, the ideal relation between text and glossator: the veil is respectfully, even joyfully lifted by the reader at the text's invitation, and there is full disclosure of the *nuda veritas.*

What is revealed is precisely the beautiful truth Macrobius and Richard of Bury talk about: the hidden body of woman, wise and fecund. Here is Jerome's alien woman, now arrayed for the bridal: this is, of course, the wedding night of the knight and lady.

> And whan the knyght saugh verraily al this,
> That she so fair was, and so yong therto,
> For joye he hente hire in his armes two.
> His herte bathed in a bath of blisse.
>
> (1250–53)

This is the Wife's fantasy of the perfect marriage, not unlike her fairy-tale version of her marriage to the clerk; the knight and lady live "in parfit joye" for the rest of their lives. It is a representation, further, of a specifically gendered literary act that succeeds in respecting both reader and text—both the masculine reader and the feminine read. The hag has, after all, conformed herself—her whole body—to his desire: after she lectures him on her inner goodness, after she undoes all patriarchal ideas of lineage (she argues that true "gentillesse" comes from God alone), possession (she contends that poverty is a blessed state) and feminine beauty (she maintains that her "filthe and eelde" [1215] are safeguards of chastity), she concedes, "But nathelees, syn I knowe youre delit, / I shal fulfille youre worldly appetit" (1217–18). And ever after she conforms her desires to his: the last lines of the Wife's narrative avow that "she obeyed hym in every thyng / That myghte doon hym plesance or likyng" (1255–56). The patriarchal paradigm is still in place; the trade of the captive woman, the stripping and reclothing goes on, and, as before, the Wife exploits the commodification of woman's sex that is the basis of that paradigm. She concludes her performance with a strong wish for husbands who have money and who will use it; "And olde and angry nygardes of dispence, / God sende hem soone verray pestilence!" (1263–64). But, crucially, feminine signifying value, integrity, and desire have been recognized, have been acknowledged, and the Wife celebrates "Housbondes meeke, yonge, and fressh abedde" (1259) in this last passage. Her final call for wifely governance and longevity functions, I think, *within* the renovated patriarchal scheme; her final repetition of the language of mastery reveals and indicts its power of exclusion. Men's desire is still in control, as her tale shows, but feminine desire must continue to be acknowledged.

Chaucer thus responds to the imperatives raised by his representation of masculine narrators' misogynistic literary acts in *Troilus and Criseyde*, the *Legend of Good Women*, and the *Man of Law's Tale* by creating the Wife of Bath, who speaks as the excluded feminine. Her *Tale*'s final vision of the joyous and mutually satisfying unveiling of the feminine is, of course, deeply gratifying to the male reader and author—one who, as we have seen, has worried about the vulnerability, even the potentially wayward afterlife of his little books (and one who, moreover, was apparently himself threatened with an accusation of rape). But Chaucer was not *only* fulfilling his masculine authorial dreams in creating the Wife. He has imagined patriarchy from the Other's point of view and has duly reckoned the costs of clerkly discourse in terms of the feminine body. The first thing we hear about the Wife is that she is permanently injured: "A good WIF was ther OF biside BATHE, / But she was somdel deef, and that was scathe" (1:445–46). The story of that injury perpetrated by a clerk motivates the narrative of the Prologue ("But now to purpos, why I tolde thee / That I was beten for a book, pardee!" [711–12]). She is deafened, and she will feel Jankyn's blows in her bones forevermore (505–7); clerks cause her emotional and physical "wo . . . and pyne" (787) for writing of women as they do.[26] That a woman would respond to patriarchal discourse in precisely these terms is dramatically affirmed by Christine de Pizan, who describes a scene that powerfully recalls the book-inspired violence of the Wife's Prologue. Christine's specific point here, one among many in her long letter to Pierre Col about the deleterious effects of the *Rose,* is that women suffer physically on account of clerkly antifeminist writing:

> Not long ago, I heard one of your familiar companions and colleagues, a man of authority, say that he knew a married man who believed in the *Roman de la Rose* as in the gospel. This was an extremely jealous man, who, whenever in the grip of passion, would go and find the book and read it to his wife; then he would become violent and strike her and say such horrible things as, "These are the kinds of tricks you pull on me. This good, wise man Master Jean de Meun knew well what women are capable of." And at every word he finds appropriate, he gives her a couple of kicks or slaps. Thus it seems clear to me that whatever other people think of this book, this poor woman pays too high a price for it.[27]

Chaucer revises and keeps the patriarchal ideology behind the image of the captive woman, but he recognizes that the achievement of respectful relationships of husband and wife, reader and text—the acknowledgement of the value of the feminine, both woman and letter—is accomplished at a dear cost and that it is still only a fantasy —the Wife's, in the fictionalized happily-ever-after of her Prologue and *Tale,* and his own fantasy, dreamed through her. In the real relations between husband and wife, clerk and text, as he makes clear, masculine glossing does not come without violence to the feminine corpus. It remains for another clerk, the pilgrim traveling on the way to Canterbury and listening to the Wife of Bath, to elaborate on the lived bodily effects of literary acts—the bodily effects on women, and the bodily effects of making literary images at all. The affinity of *this* Oxford clerk, we find unexpectedly, is with the Wife of Bath, with Griselda in his tale, with the feminine. Chaucer has not done with the Wife of Bath and "al hire secte" by any means. In her Prologue and *Tale* he represents the woman as assertively mimicking masculine discourse; the *Clerk's Tale* turns out to be a reflection on what it means for a male author to be a female impersonator.

Chapter Five
Griselda Translated

The story of Griselda in the fourteenth century is a story of translation. Boccaccio's version of the folktale, the last tale in his *Decameron*, was translated by Petrarch into Latin (*Seniles* 17.3) and adapted by Sercambi in his *Novella*. Petrarch's version, in turn, was translated into French by Philippe de Mézières, whose version was then adapted by the author of *Le Ménagier de Paris* and by the author of a play in verse, *L'Estoire de la Marquise de Saluce*. Petrarch's Latin prose was also the basis of a Latin verse adaptation by Peter de Hailles. Chaucer's English verse translation works from both Petrarch's Latin and an anonymous French prose translation of Petrarch, *Le Livre Griseldis*.[1]

One might well ask why the history of Griselda was so popular, so apparently compelling, in the second half of the fourteenth century. The particular narrative outline of the tale, we might observe, seems well suited to the specific literary preoccupations of the late fourteenth century in England and on the continent.[2] The tale's clear, almost schematic outline of the relationship between husband and wife rendered it useful as an exemplum (the French versions); its potential for pathos suggested both dramatic treatment (*L'Estoire*) and an upward shift in level of style, rendering it an occasion for affective response (Petrarch); and the moral issue of the truth-value of fictional discourse itself could be thrown into relief by the tale's inclusion in collections of narratives (Boccaccio, Sercambi, Chaucer), where the meaning or value of the tale could be debated.

But these features of the narrative do not, I think, constitute the whole of its attractiveness, either to the fourteenth century or to later generations of redactors. Many late-medieval readers seem in fact to have found the story of Walter's treatment of his wife repugnant: Dioneo, who narrates the tale in the *Decameron*, was not alone in deeming Walter's trial of Griselda a needless outrage.[3] How *can* the "difficult" relationship—to use one critic's delicate euphemism—between Walter and Griselda be explained?[4] The tale's appeal, I suggest, lies precisely in its posing of this interpretive problem; for each translation—each literary treatment—provides an interpretation, implicit or explicit, of that question.

If the tale's attractiveness does indeed lie in its hermeneutic difficulty, the treatment of a woman, a wife, is the focus of this interpretive interest. What concerns me here is not the suggestion that relations between men and women are always in need of exegesis. This may in fact be true, but I am more interested in the very conjunction of the problem of the treatment of a wife with the problem of the interpretation of a text—the intersection of hermeneutics with the question of the feminine. In this literary history of the Griselda tale we see that once again woman is associated with a text to be read and interpreted by men (and to be read, as well, by women who are being trained by men to be wives). Petrarch's own approach to the text itself clearly points up this association: as he documents it in *Seniles* 17.3, the occasion of translating this tale of the proving of a wife becomes an occasion for his proving the affective value of the literary text itself.[5] Implicitly, Petrarch takes the thematic, domestic issue of the proper function of a wife and links it with a literary issue, the proper function of a text. And it is this link, I suggest, that interested Chaucer's Clerk, surely the most literate storyteller among the Canterbury pilgrims, and a reader who, as we shall see, is profoundly concerned with the social effects of literary activity. If this preoccupation seems unlikely for the unworldly Clerk—the one who keeps twenty volumes of Aristotle at his bed's head—we might remember that he not only learns but teaches; the Clerk's world is not only one of books but of books as they become part of the social fabric.

For it is not only, in the *Clerk's Tale,* the tale of Griselda that is translated. Griselda *herself* is "translated . . . in swich richesse" (385).[6] Translation takes place on a feminine body, as it does as well in *Troilus and Criseyde;* like "glossing" in the Wife of Bath's Prologue and *Tale,* it is a masculine hermeneutic gesture performed on the woman, on the text. Walter "translates" Griselda: he sees her and recognizes her natural beauty and virtues even in her impoverished condition, under her ragged clothes; he chooses her for his bride, takes her from her father, orders her to be stripped and reclothed in finery, and makes her wife and mistress of his household. The Hieronymian image of the classical text as alien woman to be passed between men, stripped, and reclothed for the bridal—the representation of allegorical reading as a trade, reclothing, marriage, and domestication of a woman—that we have been following throughout Chaucer's works is very useful in discussing Walter's acts of translation: the allegorical reading Jerome describes is, as we shall see, fundamentally an act of translation, an act of discovering, interpreting, and carrying over wisdom from one social group to another (from pagans to Christians). Walter's "translating" Griselda closely enacts this Hieronymian hermeneutic parable; the Clerk's narrative attention to the passage of Griselda between men (from Janicula to Walter, back to Janicula, and finally back to Walter) and his attention to Griselda's clothes in this tale gain hermeneutic significance when we read the tale in reference to the image of the alien woman. These narrative preoccupations gain even greater hermeneutic dimensionality when viewed in relation to the Wife of Bath, that vociferous incarnation of the ostentatiously garbed alien herself, for whom the "Envoy" to the *Clerk's Tale* is sung. I shall argue, in fact, that the Clerk's performance is a further expression of the Wife of Bath's point that there are real and poignant consequences for women of conceiving of literary activity as a masculine enterprise that is dependent on the occlusion of feminine desire.

Among the Canterbury pilgrims, the highly educated Clerk is the one who can most easily be imagined actually to know this image of the allegorical text as veiled captive woman passed between men. But whether or not he does, his focus on specific narrative details, particularly clothing, suggests a connection to the issues of interpretation that are his explicit concern as he tells of Walter's behavior. This notion of such a connection is supported by the fact that Chaucer has heightened and pointed the clothing imagery of the Griselda tale in creating the Clerk's version, as Severs notes.[7] If the assertively clothed Wife of Bath is an embodiment of the captive woman who hasn't been stripped, whose head isn't shaved, nails aren't pared—an incarnation of the *letter* of the text—Griselda, despoiled of her old, ragged clothes and reclothed for her marriage to Walter, is, I suggest, the truth or *spirit* of the text that has been discovered and put to Christian use.

But like "glossing" in the Wife's Prologue and *Tale*, translation in the *Clerk's Tale* has a double valence. *Translatio*, as we'll see in medieval writings, has the potential for revealing the truth and wholeness, the plenitude of the female body, but it also has a potential for turning away from, obliterating, that body; for dissembling and substituting; for estranging truth and fragmenting that wholeness. Walter's actions throughout the narrative realize both potentials of *translatio:* if he discovers the virtue, the "trouthe" of the woman, he also, subsequently, doubts that "corage"—he lies, dissembles, separates her from her offspring, and finally acts out the precise reverse of the Hieronymian warrior's action of marriage by pretending to divorce Griselda. And as in the *Legend of Hypermnestra* and the *Man of Law's Tale*, the patriarchal model's breakdown is associated with the violation of patriarchy's laws regulating its exchange of women: Walter stages a marriage to a woman who is in fact his own daughter.

As he narrates the tale, the Clerk is outraged by Walter's actions, his "nedelees" testing of the perfectly steadfast Griselda. But we must remember, of course, that the Clerk is himself a translator, like Walter, and is thus implicated in this double-valenced activity: he is translating the tale from Petrarch, that other "worthy clerk." That text, "the body of his tale" (42), is taken by one man from another in the Clerk's own act of *translatio*. Indeed, as a student at Oxford, "unto logyk . . . longe ygo," the Clerk is associated with *translatio* in various ways: he studies the translations of Aristotle that came to the Latin-speaking world through Boethius (and, later, through the Arabic); he thereby observes, in his studies, the *translatio studii* from Greece to Rome. An elaborate myth of *translatio studii* was cultivated in reference to Oxford University itself: the legend begins with the institution's foundation by King Mempric, a contemporary of David, and traces its *translatio* by Greek professors who allegedly came over to England with Brutus after the fall of Troy; they established a school in Wiltshire, which was later transferred to Oxford.[8] And as one who himself teaches, the Clerk participates further in this *translatio studii*, this transfer of knowledge.

But despite this parallel with Walter as translator, the Clerk sympathizes, in the telling of his tale, not with the translator but with the translated, not with Walter but with Griselda, not with the man but with the woman. Throughout his performance he condemns Walter's actions with unequivocal statements and indignant outbursts, and advances three different explanations for his extraordinary behavior (each more severe than the last, his final suggestion being that Walter is a compulsive maniac: "ther been folk of swich condicion . . ." [701–7]). Explicitly opposing himself to other clerks, he celebrates what he identifies as Griselda's specifically womanly strength and humility (932–38); and in his "thredbare" (1:290) cloak and poor-scholar aspect, he even looks a bit like Griselda, that "povre creature" (232), in her old, threadbare garments—a similarity that, given the sartorial preoccupations of the tale, is significant. Even before the Clerk speaks, the Host picks up this something about him, this resemblance to or sympathy with the female, so that Harry identifies him proleptically with the newly betrothed heroine of his tale—" 'Sire Clerk of Oxenford,' oure Hooste sayde, / 'Ye ryde as coy and stille as dooth a mayde / Were newe spoused . . .' " (1–3)—and not with translators or *glossatores:* "This day ne herde I of youre *tonge* a word" (4; my emphasis). The Clerk responds to the Host by putting himself under the

Host's "yerde": "Ye han of us as now the governance, / And therfore wol I do yow obeisance" (23–24), that "obeisance" echoing Griselda's "obeisance" to Walter (cf., e.g., 502).

The Clerk is in a Griselda-like position not only vis-à-vis the burly Host (a would-be Walter, perhaps: he wishes his wife had heard this tale; it is, he comments, "a gentil tale for the nones / As to my purpos" [1212e–f]). He is also in such a position in relation to another figure of authority: the *auctor* Petrarch, "lauriat poete" (31). Walter and Petrarch, of course, are both translators, translators into the "richesse" of the "heigh stile." The Clerk's identification with Griselda suggests a relationship to the translator Petrarch similar to that between Griselda and the translator in the narrative, Walter (that is, the Clerk is to Petrarch as Griselda is to Walter). Both Griselda and the Clerk are in lowly positions in relation to the others: Griselda is elevated by Walter, completely dependent upon him for her noble status; the Clerk comes after Petrarch, derives his narrative material from the Italian, and praises the great poet for his "rethorike sweete" (31–32). But there is a level of aggression, too, that both Griselda and the Clerk demonstrate against the others; albeit quiet, it is deep. As Judith Ferster has observed, Griselda responds to Walter's initial marriage demands with a promise of even more than he asks, as if rising to a perceived challenge or proving that she is in fact stronger than even he requires: she promises never to disobey him "In werk ne thoght" (363), although he has asked only that she not "grucche" or contradict him "Neither by word ne frownyng contenance" (356); although he does not ask her to, she swears "For to be deed" (364).[9] When he orders her to return to her father's house, she demands a smock in return for her lost virginity, with words that are assertive, even vaguely threatening. Finally she warns him forthrightly not to "prikke with no tormentynge" (1038) his new wife as he did her. The Clerk, similarly, displays some aggression toward Petrarch: the great poet is not only dead but "nayled in his cheste" (29), and the Clerk dwells a moment too long to be innocent on the power and inevitability of death. He dismisses Petrarch's "prohemye" (unique in all the fourteenth-century versions and distinctly characteristic of Petrarch's rhetorical style) as "a thyng impertinent"; he eschews Petrarch's "heigh stile," choosing instead to render the tale in the vernacular; and by the end of his performance, as we shall see, he has demonstrated that Petrarch's allegorical interpretation— part and parcel of his "heigh stile"—is radically inadequate.[10]

The relationships among the translators and the translated, then, are not simple in the Clerk's performance. *Translatio* always involves a relation to a previous authority or figure of the proper. Whether considered as the basis of a theory of history (*translatio imperii*) or literature (*translatio studii*), or as a general rhetorical term that encompasses all kinds of tropes (figurative language, in which there is a substitution of one term for another), *translatio* articulates a movement away from the authoritative, the proper, and an establishment of another authority or propriety.[11] Taking a cue from the etymology of *translatio*, we might call this structure of identifications (Clerk/Griselda, Petrarch/Walter) loosely transferential, drawing upon the psychological implications of the term.[12] The aspect of psychoanalytic transference relevant to our purposes here is simply its structure: the relationship to a previous authority is played out in the structure of a present or current relationship. The Clerk's identification against Walter can be read as his critique of Petrarch's *translatio* and a working-out of a new kind of literary authority. I shall argue that Chaucer, through the Clerk, suggests a revision of the model of patriarchal hermeneutics more radical than the one he has developed through the Wife of Bath: the Clerk not only has the woman speak, as we shall see, and has her point out that the patriarchal model occludes feminine desire, feminine experience; he also breaks up the bonding between men that structures that patriarchal hermeneutic (and is its goal), identifying himself *against* Petrarch. As we shall see, a new hermeneutic—a way of reading, indeed, like a woman—proceeds from the Clerk's identification with the female.

Let us begin the analysis of the Clerk's performance, then, by considering two contrasting values attached to *translatio* in the Middle Ages. We have already considered translation briefly in *Troilus and Criseyde*, focusing on the act as an expression of the narrator's emotional response to the seductive letter of his text. Now I want to shift that focus to the interpretive function of the act, to argue that throughout the Middle Ages *translatio* is seen to have a dangerously double hermeneutic potential.

1

Jerome, "patron saint of translators," as Valery Larbaud has called him, uses the image of the clothed body to describe not only the classical text to be interpreted allegorically, for Christian use, but also the text translated from one language to another.[13] In the preface to his translation of Eusebius' *Chronicle*, for example, he comments that some readers of translations of the Scriptures "superficiem, non medullam inspiciunt, ante quasi vestem orationis sordidam perhorrescant, quam pulchrum intrinsecus rerum corpus inveniant" ("looking at the surface, not at the substance, shudder at the squalid dress before they discover the fair body which the language clothes").[14] And the image of the captive occurs not only in his description of the Christian interpretation of the classical text but in his famous letter 57, to Pammachius, on the best method of translation from one language to another: he commends Hilarius the confessor, who "quasi captiuos sensus in suam linguam uictoris iure transposuit" ("like a conqueror . . . has led away captive into his own tongue the meaning of his originals").[15]

As the fact that this imagery is used in descriptions of both interpretation and translation suggests, the structure of the two activities is the same: both involve the substitution of one signified for another, the transfer of meaning into a new context. *Translatio* is in fact an inclusive rhetorical term that encompasses not only what we identify as the usual act of translation (from one language into another—"interlingual translation," in Roman Jakobson's useful terminology) but also the making of a trope (all figurative language in general, in which there is a substitution of an "improper" term for a "proper" one) and the act of interpretation, since all interpretation, substituting as it does one signified for another, is essentially figurative.[16] The terms *interpretatio* and *translatio* were apparently synonymous and current during the Middle Ages, *translatio* becoming more prominent toward the end of the period. Jerome certainly uses the two interchangeably; Augustine, as Eugene Vance observes, in *De doctrina christiana* uses *interpretatio* to denote both the written *translatio* of Scripture and the understanding of figurative meanings (*translationes*). And interlingual translation in the Middle Ages had a pronounced hermeneutic function, one, as Rita Copeland demonstrates, of the discovery (*inventio*) and subsequent appropriation of meaning.[17]

Interlingual translation and interpretation, for Jerome, were not only contiguous activities; they constituted one integral project. Of his translation of Eusebius' *Onomasticon*, for example, he comments that he is at once "translator and founder of a new work" ("Semel enim et in temporum libro praefatus sum, me vel interpretem esse vel novi operis conditorem").[18] He has corrected, interpreted, and completed the Eusebius text. He wrote his scriptural commentaries at the same time that he was translating the Hebrew Bible, but he clearly engaged in translating *as* interpretation. Translation is indeed a philological project undertaken as exegesis: even though he claimed otherwise in the case of Scripture, in all his translations he rendered not the letter, not word for word, but the sense, the spirit. He expressed this most succinctly in his letter 57, to Pammachius, in which he claims that his intention was "non uerbum e uerbo, sed sensum exprimere de sensu" ("to render not word for word, but sense for sense"), but he adumbrates this intention in many comments on translation.[19]

Jerome clearly believed that in the act of translation he could discover and restore the original *sensus* of the Scriptures. He was compelled to return to the "Hebrew verity," first to write his *Hebraicae quaestiones* and *Liber interpretationis hebraicorum nominum*, then to produce his own Latin version of the Hebrew Bible and his commentaries on the texts, because he felt the Septuagint and other translations of the original language had dispersed, mistaken, confused its original authority.[20] As a return to Hebrew, the language thought to be the original language of humankind, Jerome's translation, I might suggest, even rediscovers the original oneness of all languages, a unity nostalgically yearned for throughout the Middle Ages.[21]

Translatio viewed in its aspect as trope can be seen, similarly, to have a creative, revelatory, interpretive potential. Augustine, in the *De doctrina*, remarks with wonder that figurative language in Scripture is more pleasing than literal statement; later, and in a secular context, Geoffrey of Vinsauf delights in the pleasures of metaphor (*transferatio*, under the category of *transsumptio*) which, he writes, transforms old clothes into something new.[22] The revelatory power of metaphor was celebrated most exuberantly by twelfth- and thirteenth-century writers: Chartrians laud poetry (of which *translatio* was the most important constituent) along with music as expressions of divine creativity.[23] *Translatio* has the capacity to make the reader (or hearer) see something in a new way. As Margaret Nims writes, it finds similarity in dissimilarity, gives mental perceptions verbal form, makes them available "in a new way to human sense and imagination" (Aristotle describes the experience of metaphor in the *Rhetoric:* "How true that is, and I had missed it!").[24] Nims, to whose discussion of *translatio* I am indebted here, explains this power in reference to Bede's description of metaphor in his *De schematibus et tropis:*

> Something qualitative happens to *king*, for instance, when he is called 'lion' or 'pelican' or 'sun,' and something happens also to the things signified by the nouns *lion, pelican, sun*. The word is receptive of metaphor, but words are signs of things, and things are themselves receptive of metaphorical meaning in so far as they have sign potential.[25]

The idea of the creative and interpretive power of *translatio* is sustained and extended, Nims suggests, by viewing Christ himself as "the supreme instance of a *verbum translatum*," a Word given form and made available to human sensibility.[26] We were created through God's utterance of this Word; poetic figure imitates the original Creation, in which God uttered the first *translatio*, and we were created.[27] Alain de Lille in fact characterizes the Incarnation as "nova translatio": translation is the mechanism of both the Creation and the Redemption. In Alain's fascinating *Rithmus de incarnatione Domini*, the personified Rhetorica rejoices in the Incarnation:

> Peregrinat a natura
> Nominis positio,
> Cum in Dei transit iura
> Hominis conditio;
> Novus tropus in figura,
> Nova fit constructio;
> Novus color in iunctura,
> Nova fit translatio.
> In hac Verbi copula
> Stupet omnis regula.[28]

On the other hand, just as we have noted the pejorative connotations of glossing in relation to the Wife of Bath, we note that *translatio* has a subversive potential. Like glossing, *translatio* can be undertaken for merely worldly ends, for selfish, cupidinous purposes. Jerome at times clearly engaged in *translatio* as polemic: in his acrimonious vendetta against Ambrose, as J. N. D. Kelly observes, he openly states that he has undertaken the translation of Didymus' treatise on the Holy Spirit to contrast himself to an incompetent plagiarist writing on the same subject, and he translates Origen's homilies on Luke, further, to show up the same sort of plagiarism in another commentary on that gospel. Ambrose is the accused in both cases.[29] Augustine, too, was aware of the practical consequences, the schisms, that could be provoked by translation, his concern proceeding from an acute perception of radical social disjunction of which differences among languages are a symptom: in letter 104 (Jerome's correspondence), he warns Jerome that his rendering the Scriptures from the Hebrew might cause a rift between Eastern and Western Christendom, because the Septuagint would still be used by Greek-speaking Christians.[30]

Similarly, *translatio* as trope involves a breaking apart of the "proper" relation between word and thing, and the possibilities it offers for out-and-out deceit are obvious. As the substitution of an improper term for a proper one (thus Donatus: "tropus est dictio translata a propria significatione ad non propriam similitudinem" ["a trope is a word or phrase transferred from its proper signification to a similitude which is not proper"]),[31] it effects a turning away from straight signification. The common description of the trope of allegory—found, for example, in Isidore of Seville's *Etymologies* (1.36.22) —can be used to describe all tropes, all translations: it is *alieniloquium*, other speech, saying one thing to mean another. (We might note that Puttenham, in his *Arte of English Poesie* [1589], calls the trope of allegory "False Semblant," alluding to the arch-hypocrite of the *Roman de la rose*, who threatens to disrupt entirely the possibility of determinate meaning in that narrative.)[32] Shifting from place to place— *translatio* is a transfer of one word into another place, into the place of another, into an alien place—can be viewed *in malo*, as undermining the fixity of meaning.[33] A trope disrupts logical propriety, as Aristotle (*Rhetoric* 1410b, 1412a), Geoffrey of Vinsauf (*Poetria nova* 883–85), and Peter Helias (commenting on Priscian) saw; one can concentrate on the imaginative potential of trope as discovery and expression of the essential accord of word and meaning below the surface, or one can concentrate on that potential for violation, that threat of disruptiveness.[34]

Walter's acts of *translatio*, in fact, vividly realize both of these potentials: he engages in both joyous discovery and heinous dissimulation. We return, then, to the *Clerk's Tale*, to consider Walter's treatment of his wife. He uncovers and puts to use the truth of that text, as we shall see, and he subsequently distorts, harms, and nearly obliterates that truth.

2

Walter's initial act of translating Griselda, his betrothed, "in swich richesse," and accepting her into his household as wife and mother, can be read positively, *in bono*, as a hermeneutic act very much like the triumphant warrior's reclothing of that alien woman for marriage and maternity in an Israelite household. Whereas Jerome's warrior is attracted to the captive because of her beauty, her bodily charms, however, the Clerk's Walter is pointedly *not* drawn by carnal delights: if the Israelite is seduced by the elegance and gorgeousness of the alien woman's appearance, Walter recognizes that "under low degree / Was ofte vertu hid" (425–26). He perceives Griselda's inner beauties, looks through her "wrecched clothes" to the "rype and sad corage . . . in the brest of hire virginitee" (220). In an action that is the reverse of the warrior's action, Walter orders her stripped of her plain garments —garb so rude that his refined ladies can hardly stand to touch it—

and reclothed in beautiful, rich apparel. But the hermeneutic value of his action is the same as the warrior's: he perceives the virtue and wisdom of this text, and, "translating" it (385), puts it to proper use. A good matron, Griselda runs Walter's household prudently (she "koude al the feet of wyfly hoomlinesse" [429]), ever increases in manners and gentility (407–13), and (recalling, to my mind, Richard of Bury's "sons" that make up the "race" of books) begets children: "she nys nat bareyne" (448).

In its deployment of the traditional image of the veiled woman as allegorical text, Jerome's hermeneutic parable focuses on woman's body underneath the clothes—the wisdom, the truth of the text under the letter—as the means of the increase and multiplication of the faithful. The Wife of Bath's performance has emphasized that the letter, the clothing, has an integrity and value in and of itself, but in the *Clerk's Tale* the body of Griselda is what matters; her value and significance are not in the least tied to or dependent on her clothing. Griselda increases "in swich excellence / Of thewes goode" in Walter's court, but the Clerk stresses that she remains "evere vertuous" (407). However clothed, or, more to the point, unclothed, she is absolutely true: when she strips herself at Walter's command and returns to her paternal domain "naked" (871), her purity and constancy, her "trouthe," are what are revealed. Jankyn's proverb, ruefully quoted by the Wife of Bath ("'A womman cast hir shame away, / Whan she cast of hir smok'" [3:782–83]), is thus poignantly corrected.

> Biforn the folk hirselven strepeth she,
> And in hir smok, with heed and foot al bare,
> Toward hir fadre hous forth is she fare.
>
> The folk hire folwe, wepynge in hir weye,
> And Fortune ay they cursen as they goon;
> But she fro wepyng kepte hire eyen dreye,
> Ne in this tyme word ne spak she noon.
>   (894–900)

Covered with "hire olde coote" once again, the cloth even older and rougher than it was when she was married, she is the same Griselda, "evere" and "ay." In these threadbare garments she returns to Walter's court to prepare for his second wedding; throughout she is patient, humble, "ay sad and constant as a wal" (1047). Walter calls attention to her tattered clothes (965), as does the courtly crowd (1020), but Griselda is conspicuously "noght . . . abayst of hire clothyng" (1011). When she is divested, for the last time, of "hire rude array" (1116) and draped in finery, it is the clothes that finally, properly, conform to her "naked" beauty and virtue:

> in a clooth of gold that brighte shoon,
> With a coroune of many a riche stoon
> Upon hire heed, they into halle hire broghte,
> And ther she was honured as hire oghte.
>
> (1117–20)

If we read this *translatio* as realizing the positive hermeneutic potential of translation, then, Walter's subsequent urge to test his wife's "trouthe," "stedefastnesse," and "constance" realizes the negative. Walter, the translator, is the one who with "insight / In vertu" (242–43) has discerned and revealed, made public and useful, the text's wisdom and truth. But this good *translatio* goes bad; Walter dissembles, saying one thing but meaning another; he moves about, separates people from one another, substitutes one woman for another. And he runs the risk of forever losing or damaging his wife, who, characterized by her unmoving "corage" (Griselda's is anything but "slydynge": once it is in place, nothing, she says, will "chaunge my corage to another place" [511]), would seem to promise the possibility of full disclosure of meaning, of truth.

Contrasted to Griselda's unchanging "corage" and her "contenance" (708) expressive of her "hool entente" (861; cf. 973), Walter, in fact—to shift the terms of my analysis for a moment—seems himself an embodiment of trope, of *translatio* itself:

> And whan this markys say
> The constance of his wyf, he caste adoun
> His eyen two, and wondreth that she may
> In pacience suffre al this array;
> And forth he goth with drery countenance,
> But to his herte it was ful greet plesance.
>
> (667–72)

This passage is a considerable expansion of the cursory Latin ("Admirans femine constanciam, turbato vultu abijt").[35] In an emotional tropism, he turns away "his eyen two"; his "drery contenance" says one thing, but his "herte" feels another; and he takes care to hide his real "entente" (e.g., 587). He not only feigns looks of displeasure (512–13, e.g.), but feigned documents enter the narrative, too, as he has fake bulls made for him (743). His appearance is divided from his intent, and he causes further division in the narrative, the violent separation of the mother from her children. This division is rendered vividly, almost melodramatically, by the Clerk: the cruel sergeant, made crueler in this redaction than in Petrarch's, grabs Griselda's daughter: he "spak namoore, but out the child . . . hente / Despitously" (534–35), and later he pitilessly seizes her son.[36]

If *translatio* proceeds by substitution, Walter's substituting one woman for another precisely acts out this process. As he orders Griselda to "voyde anon hir place," we recall Geoffrey of Vinsauf's description of the way to make a trope: "Noli semper concedere verbo / In proprio residere loco" ("Don't let a word always stay in its own place" [*Poetria nova* 758–59]). "I wol gladly yelden hire my place" (843), replies Griselda, a locus that will be filled by another woman who does not properly belong there: Walter's daughter is, in her turn, translated by him from Bologne to Saluzzo, to a *locus in quo propria non est.*[37] As we have seen, women are interchangeable in the paradigm of translation as a passage of a woman between men, and Walter's ostentatious staging of his remarriage proceeds according to this understanding.

Women are also functionally mute in this paradigm; the recognition of their desires is not material to the operation of the system of exchange. But Griselda *speaks*—less vociferously, certainly, than the Wife of Bath, but no less deliberately or significantly. She not only endures Walter's translations but reacts to and interprets these actions out loud. I want to turn my attention now from the translator to the translated, to the clothed and reclothed Griselda; I want to focus on the apparel itself and what various characters make of her costume changes. As we shall see, it is in fact Griselda's own response to her stripping that points to a powerful critique of patriarchal *translatio.*

3

Chaucer selects details from *Le Livre Griseldis* to supplement Petrarch's text, and frequently adds his own comments to highlight acts of clothing and reclothing in the *Clerk's Tale*. The extent to which attire is thematized within the narrative, as a result, is remarkable: the Clerk is made to fashion his narrative around Griselda's changes of clothes. We see that his eye is constantly on the "array" of those around her as well—on the rich garb of Walter, for example, and of her estranged children. In fact, not only the Clerk, as narrator, but everyone in the narrative is acutely clothes-conscious.[38]

The "peple" constantly respond to clothed appearances. We learn, for example, in a detail that Chaucer added from his French source, that Walter's retinue, his "ladyes," dispoiling the impoverished Griselda, "were nat right glad / To handle hir clothes" (375–76). Seeing Griselda in her new "bright" clothes and gems, the "peple" scarcely recognize her as the villager they knew, so dazzled are they by her unaccustomed "fairnesse." When Walter later stages his second marriage, the people see her children and respond to "the sighte / Of hire array, so richely biseye" (983–84). And they wonder who the badly dressed creature is who so graciously attends at the wedding feast.

Walter, too, is certainly attentive to attire; the diction describing his sartorial preoccupations is specific, detailed, tactile. Preparing to espouse Griselda, he orders clothing and adornments fit for a marquise to be made for her: "And of hir clothyng took he the mesure / By a mayde lyk to hire stature" (256–57). He then has her robed in them, "for that no thyng of hir olde geere / She sholde brynge into his hous" (372–73). Later, as he asks her to clean and prepare his chambers for his pretended wedding, he draws attention—gratuitously, it would seem—to her ragged old clothes: "Thogh thyn array be badde and yvel biseye, / Do thou thy devoir at the leeste weye" (965–66). But Walter also understands a symbolic import of Griselda's clothes. This is perhaps suggested by the gratuitousness of the remark just quoted, but it is already clear earlier in the narrative (in a passage that Chaucer has expanded and pointed toward the sartorial), when Walter first begins to torment his wife:

> "Grisilde," quod he, "that day
> That I yow took out of youre povere array,
> And putte yow in estaat of heigh noblesse—
> Ye have nat that forgeten, as I gesse?"
> (466–69)

"Array" and "estaat" are interchangeable here; Walter refers by "array" not only to Griselda's clothes but to her whole station in life.[39] (The narrator of the General Prologue to the *Canterbury Tales* similarly correlates "condicioun," "degree," and "array" as he sets out to describe the pilgrims [1:37–41].)

It is Griselda, however, who understands most fully the import of her own clothes. She's the one who offers an explicitly allegorical reading of her being dispoiled and reclothed, a reading that is more specific here than in any of Chaucer's sources:

> "For as I lefte at hoom al my clothyng,
> Whan I first cam to yow, right so," quod she,

"Lefte I my wyl and al my libertee,
And took youre clothyng; wherfore I yow preye,
Dooth youre plesaunce; I wol youre lust obeye."
(654–58)

Griselda here allegorically explicates her disrobing as a voluntary,
eager submission to Walter; she leaves her own will and liberty at
home and takes on his will symbolized by the new clothes on her
back.[40] She likewise assigns a figurative value to her own nakedness
when she recounts the same scene later:

My lord, ye woot that in my fadres place
Ye dide me streepe out of my povre weede,
And richely me cladden, of youre grace.
To yow broghte I noght elles, out of drede,
But feith, and nakednesse, and maydenhede.
(862–66)

The last line—augmented by Chaucer to include her virginity—suggests a figurative equation between her faith and her naked, inviolate body—precisely the metaphoric valence assigned to the woman's
body in Jerome's figure. Indeed, we can read Griselda's words here
as the words of the captive woman herself, talking about her experience of being stripped and reclothed. Griselda reads her clothes and
her body symbolically. *She* exploits the symbolic power of the biblical
echoes in her next comment: " 'Naked out of my fadres hous,' quod
she, / 'I cam, and naked moot I turne agayn' " (871–72), associating
her trials with those of Job, the paradigmatic Christian "preved" by
God. Not only the Clerk adumbrates the symbolic value of Griselda's
experience in his narrative, explicitly mentioning Job, for example,
and creating a delicate and complex religious tenor with references to
a "welle," "thresshfold," "water pot," and "oxes stalle" (276, 290–91);
Griselda reads *herself* symbolically.[41]

But she also forces us to recognize the stark materiality of her
clothes (those "wrecched clothes, nothyng faire"), the vulnerability
of her body, and the loss of her virginity.[42] When she asks that Walter provide her with a smock so that her "wombe"—her fertile body
—will be hidden from the people, we hear the voice of Macrobius'
veiled woman, whose fertile body must be hidden from casual view.
Again we hear the woman speaking from inside the allegorical image,
as it were. But this time she reveals the sense of having been used.
Griselda's demand that she not go smockless ("Ye koude nat doon

so dishonest a thyng" [876]) is aggressive—very different from her accommodating tone in Petrarch and the *Livre*—her language vivid and biting ("Lat me nat lyk a worm go by the weye"), her tone even vaguely threatening ("Remembre yow, myn owene lord so deere, / I was youre wyf . . ."). Griselda reads herself as allegorical image and thereby "authorizes" us to read her allegorically, but at the same time she gives us a sense of what it feels like to be made into a figure of speech, what is left out when she is read *translative*. She reads herself as religious symbol, moral allegorical image. We read her, in addition, as an allegorical image of a text, or as providing an homologous relation to a text. But both *translationes* eliminate the particularity of Griselda's experience—her bodily pain, suffered because her wifeliness is being tested—and her acerbic words to Walter make this clear and poignant.[43] As Ruggiers notes (without irony), "allegorical equations . . . tend to redeem much that is difficult in the rare relationship of Griselda and Walter."[44]

In the *Clerk's Tale translatio* is represented as an act performed on the female body, but woman's experience does not enter into the conceptualization of the act. It thus does not enter into the understanding, formulation, or description of literary language (trope) or interpretation. Despite the centrality of woman's body in the model of translated (interpreted) text as unveiled woman, that model is based on man's experience, as we've seen time and time again. The narrative of the *Clerk's Tale* confirms this: *translatio* effects indeed a "turning"—a turning away from the female and her experience (when Walter turns from her, and separates her from her children; when she interprets herself as a symbol; even when Walter undresses her and dresses her again). And Griselda makes this known when she not only translates but speaks as the woman translated, the woman who would be translated away.

We read Griselda, then, both literally and figuratively—that is, when we read her *translative*, we retain the sharp awareness of what that method of reading excludes. When, in fact, Griselda mentions her "wrecched clothes"—in a confusing reference that makes sense if the clothes are figurative (or if she is somehow forgetting what happened when Walter took her from her village, which she recounts correctly two stanzas later)—she voices her literal pain.[45] Her deportment, otherwise "constant as a wal," cracks, and she utters for the first time words of surprise, bitter hurt, and heavy regret:

> But ther as ye me profre swich dowaire
> As I first broghte, it is wel in my mynde

> It were my wrecched clothes, nothyng faire,
> The whiche to me were hard now for to fynde.
> O goode God! How gentil and how kynde
> Ye semed by youre speche and youre visage
> The day that maked was oure mariage!
>
> (848–54)

It is hard to determine what Griselda means by this reference to her clothes; even if she is not reading them figuratively but is only confused, it strikes me as significant that her only moment of befuddlement in the poem should concern her clothing. (We might note that Chaucer's handling of his sources here produces this effect of confusion; both Petrarch and the *Livre* are quite straightforward and contain no expression of regret on Griselda's part.) Her uncertainty about her own coverings brings a recognition of Walter's duplicitous troping, an understanding of the discord between his intention and his "speche and visage." This recognition is registered in words that echo Walter's own words to her earlier, as he would discount her discomfort by turning her, *translative*, into an exemplum, as it were, an allegorical image of "pacience":

> Shewe now youre pacience in youre werkyng,
> That ye me highte and swore in youre village
> *That day that maked was oure mariage.*
>
> (495–97; my emphasis)

In the narrative representation of the *Clerk's Tale, translatio*—interpretation, all figuration itself—is a turning away from female experience. The implications are broad indeed: Griselda's double reading of her clothes suggests that the nature of poetic figure itself—the very basis of literary activity—excludes woman's experience from its purview.

4

The Clerk's performance invites us to extend beyond the narrative this observation of a real, felt effect of literary acts and literary formulations on women: he creates a parallel between the two translators, Walter and Petrarch—Walter, who translates Griselda "in swich richesse," and Petrarch, specialist in "rethorike," who translates the tale into "heigh stile." Let us return to Petrarch now, to consider his well-documented project of translating the Griselda tale. For, as his project will demonstrate, the ways in which literary activity—*translatio*, interpretation, allegorization, figuration—is conceived and represented have real social correlations and consequences.

Petrarch's *translatio*, like Walter's in the tale, realizes both positive and negative potentials of translation that I outlined earlier. Translation into Latin, as a humanist project, aims at discovering and restoring the glory of the classical past that has departed through *translatio imperii*, through the fall and translation of empires. Petrarch suggests, moreover, in his letter to Boccaccio, that vulgar tongues fragment and isolate speakers from one another; he undertakes to translate Boccaccio's tale into Latin, attempting to create a unified (if not universal) community of readers. Petrarch's *translatio* is in fact twofold, for he performs an allegorical reading—a reading *translative*—of the tale he has translated from Latin. Through this translation, he discovers Christian wisdom in the text: Griselda's relationship to Walter, as he reads it, is most usefully seen as every human being's relationship to God.[46] In *Seniles* 17.3, he explains to Boccaccio:

> Hanc historiam stilo nunc alio retexere visum fuit, non tam ideo, ut matronas nostri temporis ad imitandam huius uxoris pacienciam, que michi vix imitabilis videtur, quam ut legentes ad imitandam saltem femine constanciam excitarem, ut quod hec viro suo prestitit, hoc prestare Deo nostro audeant.

> [My object in thus re-writing your tale was not to induce the women of our time to imitate the patience of this wife, which seems almost beyond imitation, but to lead my readers to emulate the example of feminine constancy, and to submit themselves to God with the same courage as did this woman to her husband.][47]

But his translation is associated with disjunction and disruption, too, suggesting *translatio*'s negative potential. Petrarch creates a unified literary community, but it is one that excludes all but those who can negotiate Latin "heigh stile." Evident in his letter to Boccaccio is a sharp sense of exclusivity: he writes to Boccaccio as a fellow poet and stresses the mutuality of their friends, Petrarch's *legentes;* indeed, he insists that "all is common between us." His *translatio* may unite readers but it creates, all the same, an elite and homogeneous community. Dante, in his *De vulgari eloquentia*, associates the vernacular with mothers and nurses, and it is precisely this vulgar language—"babytalk," as Robert Hollander has called it, or "woman talk," which amounts to the same thing—that Petrarch turns away from.[48]

What is most striking to me, in fact, in Petrarch's explanation is his distinct and deliberate redefinition of the literary community, from *matronas nostri temporis* (for whom, as Boccaccio happily declares, the *Decameron* was written) to *legentes*, readers of Latin, a brotherhood of literate men of all times and all places. As Anne Middleton puts it, "This *stilo alio* is not, like Boccaccio's, for gentlewomen, but for those who possess the language of the ancients and of high written eloquence."[49] The tale is no longer intended for—or available to —women. And it is not *about* them, in particular, either: the suffering of Griselda, the "tormentynge" practiced on the wife, becomes the suffering of everyone in relation to God (or, rather, the trials of Petrarch's own readers, literate, leisured men). This allegorization, in fact, precisely thematizes what Petrarch's *translatio* in general does: as interlingual substitution, it excludes women from the audience of the tale; as trope here, it eliminates the particular concerns of women and subsumes them into a larger vision of *man*kind. There is here an actual social corroboration of the representation of trope in the tale: *translatio*, in the narrative of the *Clerk's Tale*, is enacted on the feminine body; it is, and effects, a turning away from the woman— and Petrarch's *translatio* does just that. To represent literary activity as gendered—as a masculine activity that is performed on a feminine body, as in Jerome's parable and Richard of Bury's metaphor—is not, I suggest, mere metaphoric caprice. The context of Petrarch's *translatio* allows us, even forces us, to reread and reevaluate the images that are used in the representation of literary activity—to recognize their real bases and consequences, their power in creating and reinforcing social relationships. In this crucial sense, "the body of his tale" (42) is not metaphoric.

That the Clerk is alert to the implications of Petrarch's *translatio* is evident in his treatment of Petrarch's allegorization and his juxtaposition of it with his final comments and song for the Wife of Bath. He recounts "this auctour's" allegorical identification of Walter and Griselda with God and "every wight," and elaborates the justification for this reading in three stanzas at the close of his narrative.

> This storie is seyd nat for that wyves sholde
> Folwen Grisilde as in humylitee,
> For it were inportable, though they wolde,
> But for that every wight, in his degree,
> Sholde be constant in adversitee
> As was Grisilde; therfore Petrak writeth
> This storie, which with heigh stile he enditeth.

> For sith a womman was so pacient
> Unto a mortal man, wel moore us oghte
> Receyven al in gree that God us sent;
> For greet skile is he preeve that he wroghte.
> But he ne tempteth no man that he boghte,
> As seith Seint Jame, if ye his pistel rede;
> He preeveth folk al day, it is no drede,
>
> And suffreth us, as for oure excercise,
> With sharpe scourges of adversitee
> Ful ofte to be bete in sondry wise;
> Nat for to knowe oure wyl, for certes he,
> Er we were born, knew al oure freletee;
> And for oure beste is al his governaunce.
> Lat us thanne lyve in vertuous suffraunce.
>
> (1142–62)

As other critics have noted, the second sentence in the second stanza, extending into the third stanza ("But he ne tempteth no man . . . / He preeveth folk al day . . . / And suffreth us . . . / Nat for to knowe oure wyl . . . / And for oure beste is al his governaunce" [1153–61]), seems curiously incomplete.[50] Petrarch writes:

> Probat tamen et sepe nos multis ac gravibus flagellis exerceri sinit, non ut animum nostrum sciat, quem scivit ante quam crearemur, sed ut nobis nostra fragilitas notis ac domesticis indicijs innotescat.
>
> [He still may prove us, and often permits us to be beset with many and grievous trials, not that he may know our character, which he knew before we were created, but in order that our weakness should be made plain to ourselves by obvious and familiar proofs.][51]

"Non ut . . . sed ut"; in the Clerk's version, though, the "Nat for" in line 1159 goes begging for a "But" (cf. 1142–45), and we're left feeling that the reasoning behind Petrarch's allegorization, the reasoning behind God's proving us, and Walter's proving of Griselda, is not fully understood, or is not compelling. The Clerk rounds off the stanza with a couplet assuring us that God's governance is best and admonishing us, therefore, to suffer virtuously. But the justification is completed, as it were, in the next stanza: the "But" comes when the Clerk appends "o word," relocating us in the present and regendering Griselda. A brisk direct address to the audience breaks up the Latinate sonority of "governaunce / vertuous suffraunce," as Elizabeth Salter comments:[52]

> But o word, lordynges, herkneth er I go:
> It were ful hard to fynde now-a-dayes
> In al a toun Grisildis thre or two.
>
> (1163–65)

And since no Griseldas can be found in the modern world, he turns
to what can be: "archewyves," both "strong" and "sklendre." He thus
leaves us mindful of female bodies—uncomfortably so, perhaps—as
he sings a song for that most incarnate of women, the Wife of Bath.
The Clerk restores to our attention what has been translated out by
Petrarch. He addresses himself, finally, not to another man—he does
not pass his text on from clerk to clerk—but to women; he thus—
crucially, it seems to me—breaks that man-to-man structure of clerkly
translatio with his "But" turned toward women.

The value of these ending maneuvers, however, is very hard
to determine with any finality; Petrarch's allegorization, the Clerk's
added "o word," and the song to the Wife of Bath form a sequence that
is shiftily contradictory. In his recapitulation of Petrarch, the Clerk
claims he has not told the tale in order that wives should emulate
Griselda; but in his "o word" that follows immediately, he suggests
that the tale is in fact just such an exemplum:

> But o word, lordynges, herkneth er I go;
> It were ful hard to fynde now-a-dayes
> In al a toun Grisildis thre or two;
> For if that they were put to swiche assayes,
> The gold of hem hath now so badde alayes
> With bras, that thogh the coyne be fair at ye,
> It wolde rather breste a-two than plye.
>
> (1163–69)

For all his sympathy with the trials of the female, these lines suggest
that such trials, however rigorous, can be endured—Griselda endured
them, and women today should be able to endure them as well. The
Clerk notes here that the trials are played out on bodies, but his primary point is not sympathetic: modern-day wives would fail the test,
their bodies breaking instead of just bending.[53]

The song for the Wife of Bath that follows suggests that the tale is
no exemplum: wives should not emulate Griselda. Griselda does not
and *should not* exist now. Wives, the Clerk ostensibly suggests in this
song, should not take such treatment from husbands: "Ne suffreth nat
that men yow doon offense" (1197). The burden of this song—taken

straight, not ironically—would seem to be consonant with the Clerk's continual criticism of Walter throughout the tale.[54]

But the triumphant females whom the Clerk thus celebrates are derived directly from the clerkly antifeminist literature he has disavowed earlier (932–38), and the song, as Salter and many others have seen, paints a grotesque picture of wives and marriage. "Strong as is a greet camaille" (1196), "egre as is a tygre yond in Ynde" (1199), armed with the "arwes of thy crabbed eloquence" (1203), and ever clapping "as a mille" (1200), these wives are parodies, stock figures of the wife out of control. As products of intentionally repellent antifeminist satire, these women are hard to embrace as preferable to Griselda; it could be argued that such unappealing female bodies *should* be erased from view. What can we make of this Envoy and its juxtaposition to what has gone before? Perhaps the contrast to Griselda that these wives provide in fact renders the Griselda ideal palatable, even appealing, if also impossible; perhaps it emphasizes the purity of that ideal as against their adulterated, fallen mores. These wives would then send us right back to Griselda with an appreciation for her "relentless submissiveness."[55] Or perhaps the Clerk is conceding the "reality" of the Wife of Bath even as he holds high the "ideal" of Griselda.[56] Or maybe the Clerk is just allowing his audience comic relief here, stinting "ernestful matere" with this song "to glade yow." But what kind of relief is afforded here? Relief that we don't have to be Griseldas, or don't have to deal with Griseldas nowadays, or don't have to figure out what to make of her? And what kind of "gladness" will be conferred? We should think twice about that word "glad"; it doesn't denote pure selflessness, by any means: the Clerk's and Griselda's "gladness" seems indeed alloyed with self-assertiveness and aggression.[57]

It is important, I think, to hold the contradictions in suspension, not to rest on any single point. As has often been done, we could connect the Clerk's moves with a "dialectical spirit" derived from his university training.[58] But I am not suggesting a dialectic here between Griselda and the Wife of Bath, between some "ideal" and the "real." I am suggesting, rather, that there is something paradoxical at the heart of the Clerk's poetic method, his practice of *translatio*, a paradox that derives from the representation of Griselda. The Clerk restores what has been eliminated from the tale by *translatio*—he restores gender, the here and now, and a consideration of woman's point of view— *even as* his language, the language of antifeminist satire, would deny or preclude such a consideration or restoration. Griselda, as I have attempted to show, is a character both figurative and not figurative; that is, authorized by her reading of herself, we read her as an allegorical image while retaining, at the same time and at her insistence in the narrative, a trenchant awareness of what that *translatio* is not saying. The Clerk extends this kind of double reading to his whole conclusion: he offers three different *translationes*, each of which narrows the significance of the tale and clearly excludes something that is considered significant in the tale. Petrarch makes it an exemplum for all, thus allegorizing away Griselda's cares as wife; the Clerk restores Griselda as exemplum for wives now, thereby denying his earlier contentions that the hardships are needless; the song to the Wife of Bath reduces the tale to an entirely literal contest between husband and wife, ignoring the religious suggestions of the tale. The point is not that the Clerk offers a happy pluralism at the end, throwing open the tale to various possibilities of interpretation; the point is close to the opposite: instead of concentrating on the polyvalence of tropes, the Clerk shows that *translatio* can indeed function to exclude, to turn away from something. The Clerk's identification or sympathy with the female—one who is fundamentally left out of patriarchal society—allows him to understand translation in this way, allows him to read with an eye to what is left out of the very reading he is performing—allows him to read, that is, like a woman.[59]

It is significant, I think, that this final "Envoy" is "de Chaucer." This scribal heading might be a mere textual coincidence of the unfinished nature of the *Canterbury Tales,* but if it is, it is nonetheless a revealing one. The voices of the Clerk and Chaucer are formally conflated in this scribal heading; the *Clerk's Tale,* I suggest, articulates a double reading, a double perspective associated with the feminine, that describes larger Chaucerian poetic concerns as well. Such a double perspective —the awareness of what is left out by the literary act even as that act is being performed—is the product of the structure of impersonation. It describes the effect, that is, of the narrative structure of the entire *Canterbury Tales.* Impersonation depends on both the imagined presence and the simultaneously perceived absence of the character impersonated.[60] When that character is usually silenced, is excluded from or marginalized within society—when that character is, for example, a woman—impersonation thus enacts—gives visible and formal expression to—this social condition. Impersonation can thus be deployed as a "feminine" poetic strategy—as it is, I suggest, in the *Canterbury Tales* —making clear who is *not* speaking in the very act of speaking.

Further, it is this double perspective that constitutes that famous "Chaucerian irony": Chaucerian irony is not simply saying one thing while meaning another, but saying one thing with a clear sense of and vivid interest in what is left out of that saying (and who it is who is not saying anything). These basic and notoriously "Chaucerian" poetic strategies must be understood in their social dimensions; Chaucer's sexual poetics always engages the play between what is said and what is consequently not said, what is brought into being and what is thereby eliminated, who is talking and who is not talking, who or what is allowed to signify and who or what is not allowed to signify.

That literary acts—the making of impersonations, tropes, interpretations—have social implications is made manifest in Chaucer's repeated use of the image of the text as feminine, acted on by distinctly masculine readers, narrators, interpreters, glossators, translators. I have focused on these explicitly heterosexual hermeneutic acts in *Troilus and Criseyde*, the *Legend of Good Women*, and the *Man of Law's Tale*, the *Wife of Bath's Tale*, and the *Clerk's Tale*. But what about literary acts that are outside the bounds of this patriarchal, heterosexual paradigm? Can they mean anything? Do they have a hermeneutic of their own? There is no better place to begin to consider these questions than the *Pardoner's Tale*. For if Chaucer's sexual poetics can be described, at least in part, as engaging a simultaneous perception of speaking and silence, presence and absence, then there is no more apt illustration of this poetics than the person of the Pardoner—figuratively, if not literally as well, a eunuch; for he is perhaps the most compelling storyteller on the pilgrimage, and the one who is most obsessed with, the one who speaks from the authority of, what is patently *not there*.

Chapter Six
Eunuch Hermeneutics

Very early in her Prologue, just as she is warming to her theme, the Wife of Bath is interrupted by the Pardoner. He initially bristles at her images of "tribulacion in mariage" (3:173), but after she orders him to hear her out, he in fact urges her to teach him the tricks of her trade. It might seem that there couldn't be a more unlikely pair: the Wife, flamboyantly arrayed and ostentatiously heterosexual, "carping" and in good fellowship with the company, and the Pardoner, that defective man, who makes the "gentils" cry out even before he begins his tale. But characters are never only coincidentally brought together in Chaucer's works, and similarities between these two become apparent even on the surface level of apparel: once again, we find that clothing is an important index of broader significance in Chaucer's poetics. The Pardoner is as clothes-conscious as is the Wife of Bath in her intentionally alluring "hosen . . . of fyn scarlet reed" (1:456): wearing no hood, with only a cap, "Hym thoughte he rood al of the newe jet" (1:682). If, as I have suggested, the Wife of Bath is an incarnation of the seductive letter of the text, we might ask what hermeneutic significance this Pardoner, styled *à la mode,* carries. What would we find if those clothes were stripped?

Not a female body, beautiful and fertile, needing protection from the gaze of the uninitiated, as in the traditional image of the allegorical text we've seen in writers from Macrobius to Richard of Bury. But underneath those clothes we might not find a whole male body either. The narrator of the General Prologue apparently does not know *what* the Pardoner is: "I trowe he were a geldyng or a mare" (1:691) is his notorious speculation.[1] Clear and straightforward gender categories of masculine and feminine—categories, as I have suggested throughout this book, fundamental to the social discourse of the Canterbury pilgrimage—apparently do not apply.

The patriarchal hermeneutic I have been describing—the passage of a woman between men and her stripping, reclothing, marriage, and domestication—is a *heterosexual* hermeneutic as well; it has as a goal the increase and multiplication of a univocal truth.[2] But the Pardoner, that sexually peculiar figure, problematizes all these terms and procedures. For one thing, he does not allow himself to be stripped and revealed, as it were: he won't allow himself to be known, won't reveal his intentions, his meaning, his truth. He expends much energy on keeping a veil on, on keeping himself screened from the gaze of others. He attempts to create a screen, first of all, via the self-conscious style of his clothes, a screening the narrator senses. The Pardoner is the only pilgrim in the General Prologue whose own sartorial intentions—his will to dress—are reported by the narrator: "Hym thoughte he rood al of the newe jet." Some critics have suggested, further, that the Pardoner's insistent profession of his own avarice works to screen a sin or condition judged to be more heinous. Robert Burlin, for example, supposes that the Pardoner obscures his sexual peculiarity from his audience's view with his "cynical revelations" of greed, while Lee Patterson suggests that "the very excess of the Pardoner's revelations" itself hides him from his hearers.[3] In that busy process of screening, the Pardoner might be seen to pick up roles offered by others around him, as critics have pointed out again and again: he seems in fact to play at homosexual display as the Summoner joins him in his love song, "Com hider, love, to me" (1:672); he plays at heterosexuality, imagining stepping into the place the Wife of Bath delineates for husbands; he advertises the kind of corruption the "gentils" seem to expect from pardoners, boasting of loose tricks with "wenches" in every town *after* those "gentils" have insisted they won't listen to any "ribaudye" (6:324).

By keeping that veil on, the Pardoner generates the desire to know —"I trowe . . . ," imagines the narrator—and then plays off it, indeed appearing to satisfy it excessively.[4] But no one really knows what the Pardoner is, neither the narrator nor later interpreters of his performance; his clothes do not necessarily promise a beautiful, fecund, normal, or even identifiable body beneath.[5] Put in hermeneutic terms, the Pardoner's clothed body suggests that the existence of the letter of the text does not at all ensure the existence of a spirit, a truth beneath it. In fact, the Pardoner opens out another—unnerving—possible hermeneutic significance of the image of the body swaddled in veils: there is perhaps *nothing* underneath those cloaks of representation. There might be nothing but veils and letters covering a fundamental absence, a radical lack of meaning or truth.[6]

The Pardoner is, after all, a "geldyng or a mare"; he is identified, that is, in terms of an absence of something: either male sexual organs (he is a gelding, a castrated horse) or masculine gender identification

(he is a mare, a female horse).[7] The context rendering this identification significant is, of course, patriarchal, heterosexual, fundamentally
androcentric; the Pardoner can be distinctly identified in terms of such
lack because masculinity—located in these attributes—defines identity and power in the culture. As we've seen in the *Man of Law's Tale*,
the crucial distinction in patriarchal culture between man and woman
is really between man and not-man; if the Pardoner is a eunuch, as
the widely accepted critical gloss of "geldyng" goes, he is a man who,
significantly, is not a man (he is a not-man); but if he is an effeminate
male, as a gloss of "mare" has it, he is womanish but not a woman (a
not-woman or, better, a not-not-man).[8] If he is neither man nor not-
man, his identity is constituted by a negation of, or alienation from,
the Same *and* the Other in androcentric culture.

Further, if the Pardoner is taken to be an effeminate homosexual, as
another gloss of "mare" goes, he is, in the normative terms of patriarchal, heterosexual culture, a man who puts himself in the "feminine"
position in homosexual intercourse.[9] He would thus bodily enact what
I have suggested (in Chapter 5) the Clerk and Chaucer imaginatively
do: as men who put themselves in the woman's place, they see things
from the woman's point of view. For those male figures, such a "feminine" position yields opportunity, a valorization of what is devalued
in patriarchal culture, a speaking of and for what is silenced; but for
the Pardoner, such a position yields not opportunity but torment. In
his lacking being he reifies the disturbing suggestion that there is no
guarantee of meaning, realizes the unsettling possibility that there is
no fullness and plenitude of signification underneath the wraps of
the letter. If, as we've seen in the *Clerk's Tale*, a "feminine" poetic
strategy provides a positive, fruitful alternative to oppressive, power-
asymmetrical patriarchal discourse, the Pardoner's strategy, I suggest,
would threaten an end to reading and telling tales altogether.

The Pardoner is defined by absence—he's a not-man or not even
that—and it is in this fundamental sense that I shall take him to be a
eunuch, a figurative one if not in fact a literal one as well. His sense of
his own lack informs his social behavior, his interactions with others;
his incompleteness, moreover, informs the very thematics and narrative strategies of his *Tale*. Most tellingly, it represents his view of
the nature of language itself. As we shall see, it is not only modern
theorists who analyze language as radically fragmentary: medieval
thinkers too were preoccupied with a sense of the fundamental incompleteness of human language. The Pardoner enunciates a strategy of
using language in a postlapsarian world, cut off from primary wholeness and unity: he acts according to what I call a hermeneutics of the

partial, or, for short, eunuch hermeneutics.[10] The hermeneutic I have identified as heterosexual discards the surface of the text, the letter and its wanton seductions, for the uncovered truth, but the eunuch suggests that the passage between the letter and any sentence within is not so smooth, is not guaranteed. Indeed, the Pardoner disrupts altogether the hierarchy of values placed on the letter and the spirit. His hermeneutic is motivated in fact by a fundamental *refusal* to know; it is informed, I shall suggest, by a logic of fetishism.

As we shall see, the Pardoner surrounds himself with objects—relics; sealed documents; even words, regarded as objects—which he substitutes for his own lacking wholeness. But these objects, used thus as fetishes, are themselves fragments and can't properly fill the lack that hollows the Pardoner's being. Robert P. Miller has demonstrated that eunuchry was used in the Christian exegetical tradition as a powerful figure for the spiritual condition of radical wanting, radical desire, that is *cupiditas*. I propose to analyze eunuchry as a figure as well but shall concentrate on its psychological valence: the substitute objects the Pardoner adopts can't convert his bottomless *cupiditas* into *caritas*, a state of oneness, plenitude, fullness.[11] Nevertheless, even though the Pardoner *knows* that his relics, documents, words are defective substitutes—they are fakes, and he tells us so—he holds on to the fetishistic belief that they can make him whole, part of the body of pilgrims, and of the larger body of Christians. If we express this in terms of the problematics of interpretation, we can say that the eunuch's hermeneutics proceeds by double affirmations, double truths, the incompatible positions of recognition and disavowal, knowledge and belief.

Chaucer's initial juxtaposition of the Pardoner with the Wife of Bath in the interruption in her Prologue introduces a perspective utterly outside patriarchal discourse and suggests a potential unsettling of its hermeneutic enterprise altogether. The Pardoner's Prologue and *Tale* further problematize the assumptions and procedures of that patriarchal project. As we've seen, the relative stability, significance, and value of the letter and the spirit, on the one hand, and the culture's construction of gender, its establishment of unambiguous gender distinctions and hierarchy, and its prohibition of transgressive sexual relations, on the other, are interdependent. The Wife of Bath, speaking as an incarnation of literality, carnality, and femininity from within a patriarchal paradigm, dreams of a renovation of oppressive patriarchal discourse: she dreams of an ideal relationship between wife and husband, text and gloss, letter and spirit. But that dream of recuperation, as she and the Clerk show, is idealistic indeed; the discourse, as they know it, depends on a turning away from the body and experience of woman, and thus the Wife's dream remains a dream. The Pardoner in his person deepens this critique of patriarchal, androcentric discourse; he in fact shows the inadequacy of the very categories—masculine/feminine, letter/spirit, literal/figurative—by which it proceeds. He confounds the idea of an easy passage between clothes and the body, the surface and the meaning, the letter and the spirit, and deconstructs the neat, reassuring discovery procedures of interpretation we have seen figured among the Canterbury pilgrims. He is a paradoxical figure of wily cynicism and plangent desire, as we'll see, and his performance threatens to derail (so to speak) this pilgrimage to Truth, "compounding" as it does verity with falsehood, "fals" with "soth" (*House of Fame*, 1029).

But the Pardoner does not, in fact, end the pilgrimage. Instead, his performance urges his audience to think further, in ways entirely outside established social categories. I shall suggest at last that Chaucer, through the Pardoner—that figure utterly different from the other men and women, that figure entirely out of their bounds, that figure of fundamental, radical absence—leads his listeners to contemplate another being entirely out of their bounds: this one, however, of absolute Presence.

1

Richard of Bury provides an image for the heterosexual reading act, but he nonetheless associates reading with eunuchs as well. As I've said, he images reading as a *seduction* by the wanton letter of the text, a penetration to the naked body of woman. But he also—and somewhat contradictorily—emphasizes, with Saint Paul, that the reader must leave behind the carnality of the text to get to its spirit; thus he suggests elsewhere in the *Philobiblon* that the end of reading is, finally, beyond the sexual. He commends Origen as an exemplary reader, one who was not distracted by any improper lusts of the flesh; and he cites the eunuch mentioned by Saint Paul in the Acts as an example to all those who would learn to read properly: reading the Scriptures without understanding, the eunuch asked Philip to guide him; Philip "preached unto him Jesus" (Acts 8:35), and the eunuch was baptized.[12] To pursue this association of eunuchry with spiritual understanding beyond these citations in Richard of Bury, we need only think of Abelard, perhaps the most famous of medieval castrati. Abelard built his career as a Christian philosopher upon his castration. He writes in the *Historia calamitatum* that in order to gain spiritual understanding—to read properly—it was necessary that he not only cease reading as he had been with Heloise (a literally heterosexual use of reading); more important, it was necessary that he be castrated—although he admits that this was not among the *remedia amoris* he would have chosen—so that he would be freed for the work of the true philosopher.[13] From this point of view, the eunuch—untempted by, and discontinuous in, the flesh—is the perfect reader.[14]

But Chaucer's Pardoner—a eunuch figuratively, if not literally too—is hardly the perfect, "spiritual" reader. He is preoccupied by, chained to the flesh, never rising out of it to reach the spirit. It is no coincidence that the Pardoner follows the Physician in telling his tale; the Physician is the pilgrim most concerned with the body—he is professionally dependent upon it. The tale the Physician tells, the story of Appius and Virginia, is taken from the *Roman de la rose,* and its narrative position there is significant: the story is told by Raison after her account of Saturn's castration. Raison's point is that justice was lost when Jupiter castrated his father; castration, in the *Rose,* marks the loss of the Golden Age, the loss of an ideal.[15] And it does, I argue, in fragment 6 of the *Canterbury Tales* as well (and in the modern psychoanalytic version of the myth of loss and wished-for reconciliation, as we shall see). The Pardoner follows the Physician's redaction of this tale as if to explain the sordid world of the *Physician's Tale:* it's an unjust world, a world cut off from natural justice, natural love—a castrated world.

Harry Bailly's significantly garbled oath in calling for a tale to follow the Physician's ("By corpus bones!" [6:314]) is a response to both the Physician's occupation and the sense of the corporal that surrounds the Pardoner. That sense of the corporal is reflected in the focus on the body in the Pardoner's portrait, Prologue, and *Tale*—a focus that might more properly be said to be a focus on *fragments* of the body. If the narrator's first guess of "geldyng" is indeed literally correct, the Pardoner's body is itself the first on the list of these fragments. The pieces of information the narrator gives in the General Prologue—thin hair, glaring eyes, high voice, beardlessness—suggest a medieval stereotype of the eunuch, either congenital or castrated. But as Monica McAlpine argues, the category of eunuchry was conflated or confused sometimes in medieval representations with other categories of effeminacy and homosexuality,[16] which could be themselves associated with genital defects as well: there is an Aristotelian tradition of viewing homosexuality, for example, as the result of a natural defect. As John Boswell has suggested, the *Physical Problems,* attributed to Aristotle, speculated on the cause of "passive" male sexual behavior as a congenital defect, a genital blockage, found in the case of eunuchs too; Aquinas, significantly following Aristotelian thinking about the conception of females, considered homosexuality to result from "a defect in nature" in a man.[17] The narrator's latter guess of "mare" could itself thus indicate a physically fragmented, defective body; in a remarkable treatise that discusses gender confusion by using an example of horses and mules, the great eleventh-century Arabic medical writer Rhazes (ar-Rāzī) suggests that homosexuality, the "hidden illness," was produced by a predominance of female sperm over male sperm in conception and resulted in effeminacy and paltry genitals. Avicenna differed—Gerard of Cremona translated the comprehensive works of both Rhazes and Avicenna—but Rhazes' older Christian contemporary, Qustā ibn-Lūgā, agreed.[18] The point, I think, is that such sex and gender associations seem fluid and variable in a variety of related and influential traditions in the later Middle Ages. And what is clear and crucial for the Pardoner is the perception that *something* is missing: as I see it, an enormous lack—an unquenchable *cupiditas*, repeatedly expressed in the Prologue as "I wol . . . I wol . . . I wol" and as a disjunct sexual identity—constitutes the Pardoner's being as essentially defective, lacking, fragmented.

Such a fragmented being, suggests Jacques Lacan, the modern theorist of the *corps morcelé*, "usually manifests itself in [images] when . . . analysis encounters a certain level of aggressive disintegration in the individual. It then appears in the form of disjointed limbs."[19] Indeed, body parts move grotesquely, almost surrealistically, through the Prologue and *Tale*. "Myne *handes* and my *tonge* goon so yerne / That it is joye to se my bisynesse" (398–99; my emphasis); "Thanne peyne I me to strecche forth the *nekke*" (395; my emphasis). "The shorte throte, the tendre mouth" (517) are the loci of gluttony; the "womb, belly, stinking cod" are sites of sin. "Oure blissed Lordes" body (474) is torn, by swearing, into "herte," "nayles," "blood," and "armes" (651–54). Tongues, noses, gullets freely animate the Pardoner's sermon. The Old Man in the exemplum wails that he is nothing but "flessh, and blood, and skyn" (732); his "bones" await their final rest.

But relics are perhaps the things that we remember the best about the Pardoner—even though, as Kellogg has shown, they are not conventional characteristics of abusive pardoners.[20] Relics are holy fragments—scraps and chips of saints—and it is wholly appropriate that the Pardoner claims to have many. He has "a gobet of the seyl / That Seint Peter hadde" (1:696–97), a jar of "pigges bones," a "sholderboon / Which that was of an hooly Jewes sheep" (6:350–51), a "miteyn" (in the shape of a hand), and a "pilwe-beer" (supposed to be Our

Lady's veil). I want to consider the nature of relics—those sacred fragments—for a moment here.[21] The Pardoner's relics are not the most
fragmentary of medieval relics on record: the relics that would seem
to be paradigms of the fragmentary are *splinters* of the True Cross
("the croys which that Seint Eleyne fond" [951], by which the Host
swears in response to the Pardoner). Pilgrims, according to several
sources from the early and the high Middle Ages, kissed the Cross
and surreptitiously carried the splinters away in their teeth.[22] Other
holy monuments, such as tombs and gilded shrines, were broken into
bits by pilgrims eager to bring back tokens. Body parts, however, were
the medieval relics valued most highly: heads, arms, fingers of saints
were severed and boxed in jeweled reliquaries. The efficacy of the
whole body of the saint was powerful in these parts, these fragments:
synecdochically, "in the divided body grace survives undivided."[23]
Interestingly, partition—dismemberment—of saints' bodies was not
allowed originally by the early Church, but the great demand for relics
made more relics necessary: by the eighth century, relics had come to
be regarded as requirements for the consecration of a church; and private collectors, from the very early years of Christianity, were greedy
for them. In the face of this demand, dismemberment was eventually
allowed. (Fortunately, the saints themselves approved of dismemberment, as the story of Saint Mammas attests: a finger of that saint
detached itself of its own accord when a priest came to the body to
collect relics.)[24]

But it was the very practice of fragmentation that led to widespread
frauds. Once the bodies were divided into pieces and translated from
one church to another, it was *impossible* to verify their authenticity.[25]
And the fragments proliferated: if all claims were to be believed, there
were, by the twelfth century, at least three heads of John the Baptist,
innumerable arms and fingers of various saints, five or six foreskins
of Christ.[26] Despite growing concern in the late Middle Ages about
"multiple" relics—Guibert of Nogent's arguments about the absurdity
of some claims to authenticity, very unusual in the twelfth century,
began to be echoed by fifteenth-century pilgrims—the cult of relics in
itself was not questioned. In *Mandeville's Travels* (c. 1357), for example,
the history of John the Baptist's head is carefully recounted (the head
was first enclosed in a wall of a church in Sebaste, then translated to
Constantinople, where the "hynder partye" remains; the "forpartie"
is in Rome, the jaws and platter in Genoa) but then called into question by the claim that the whole head might in fact be at Amiens.
But the hesitancy this competing claim provokes is overwhelmed by
devotion:

> And summen seyn that the heed of seynt John is at Amyas in
> Picardye And other men seyn that it is the heed of seynt John the
> bysshop; I wot nere, but god knoweth. But in what wyse that men
> worschipen it the blessed seynt John holt him apayd.[27]

Indeed, there is more than a suggestion that competing claims to the
same body part could be believed. A plurality of bodies seems to have
been not only plausible but preferable to a single one in the case of
the Blessed Virgin: Our Lady of Coutances was a different entity from
Our Lady of Bayeux; some worshippers preferred the former, some
the latter.[28] And in the case of Christ's foreskins, the multiplicity was
perhaps even cultivated, as an index of virility, "humanation," as Leo
Steinberg would call it.[29]

But the Pardoner's scraps and chips of saints substitute for his *lack*
of virility. As free-floating body parts, they are both reifications of his
own fragmentariness and substitutes for his own masculine lack. He
doesn't increase and multiply literally or spiritually, as R. P. Miller
stresses. But he uses the proliferating relics as the means by which he
causes unnatural increase and multiplication: his relics, he claims, will
make grain and cattle multiply; he increases the number of believers
(even though "that is nat my principal entente" [432]); and he makes
his income grow outrageously.

His other artifacts, those sealed documents from Rome, are just as
closely associated with his own masculine lack. I will get to the pardons' more complicated psychological value later; but already we can
see the substitution he has made. We are told in the General Prologue
that he carries his pardons in his lap: "His walet, biforn hym in his
lappe, / Bretful of pardoun comen from Rome al hoot" (1:686–87). As
rolled-up parchments with seals dangling from them, the Pardoner's
documents and bulls, placed conspicuously in his bulging "male"
(6:920), present an iconographic substitute for his own lacking masculinity. He emphatically declares that these bulls validate his body,
make it legitimate and unquestionable. Exhibitionistically he brags:

> my bulles shewe I, alle and some.
> Oure lige lordes seel on my patente,
> That shewe I first, my body to warente.
>   (336–38)

Written documents and relics *both* function as masculine substitutes
for the Pardoner. And historically, they were sometimes assimilated
to one another: in the early Middle Ages, a book such as the Lindis-
farne Gospels was considered a relic and a shrine, because of its asso-

ciation with Saint Cuthbert. Documents were kept along with relics in early treasure stores, and relics, to insure their authenticity, were sometimes sealed with bulls.[30]

Fragmentary and partial themselves, relics and documents also function for the Pardoner as "partial objects," to adapt a psychoanalytic idea to my purposes here. A "partial object" is an object used by the subject in the attempt to fill the lack brought into being by the loss of an original ideal, an original wholeness and plenitude.[31] In the psychoanalytic story—a reworking of a myth of original loss and the desire for restitution, a myth that informs the Christian analysis of human history as well—the loss of an ideal, a loss of fullness, plenitude, is always associated with castration: the original fullness of continuity with the mother is lost as the child, first perceiving physical differentiation from the mother, fears for the integrity of its own body. With the father's interruption of the mother-child union (his interdiction of incest), the child perceives sexual difference and, specifically, the mother's lack of a penis. According to the Freudian story of the male castration complex, when the boy perceives the mother's lack— and the lacks of other females around him—he fears his own castration. "If a woman ha[s] been castrated, then his own possession of a penis [is] in danger": this threat of castration puts an end to the boy's Oedipus complex, as he (ideally) detaches himself from the mother and submits to the father.[32] Lacan, reinterpreting Freud, argues that the child not only *fears* his own castration upon recognition of physical differentiation; he *is* castrated, at this moment, precisely because he is cut off from primary nondifferentiation, primary identification with the mother. This castration—the father's interdiction and the imposition of the law—through a kind of deferred action gives meaning to all prior divisions, in particular the *méconnaissance* that according to Lacan constitutes subjectivity in the mirror stage. In this sense, everyone is castrated, male and female alike; everyone is separated from the realm of primary union and continuity and is subjectively constituted by division. "It is, therefore, the assumption of castration which creates the lack through which desire is instituted": law and language, symbolic forms associated with the father, are imposed in the castrated realm of difference; the distance opened up by the entrance of the father creates the distinction between subjects and objects, signifiers and signifieds, and creates as well the possibility of gender distinction.[33] And, as Anthony Wilden explains, "The partial object conveys the lack which created the desire for unity from which the movement toward identification springs—since identification is itself dependent upon the discovery of *difference*, itself a kind of absence."[34]

Such a definition of the subject and its relation to symbolic forms and cultural institutions is androcentric, as many commentators and critics acknowledge.[35] The mother is understood to be lacking, to be incomplete; as Sarah Kofman reads Freud, his vision "endows woman with an incomplete sexuality and . . . overwhelms her power in favor of the man."[36] And even more clearly in Lacan, the absence of the mother, opening "the lack through which desire is instituted," is made culturally crucial: it constitutes subjectivity and conditions the subject's access to law and language. Moreover, the putative experience of the male child is universalized into a normative description of human development. Lacan maintains that "it is in the mother— for both girls and boys—that what is called the castration complex is instituted."[37] "What marks the father is his possession of the phallus," which becomes "the mark of sexual difference, that is, difference from the mother," as Margaret Homans summarizes Lacan. Yet, Homans continues,

> it is only for the son, and not for the daughter, that the entry of the phallus marks a difference between the mother and the self.

Homans points, further, to Lacan's "disingenuous confusion of trope and material condition," a confusion of the phallus as trope and as biological condition, and concludes that his psycholinguistic theory of development "depends on the literal difference between sex organs." Thus

> while Lacanian language assumes the lack of the phallus, it is only those who can lack it—those who might once have had it, as sons believe their fathers have—who are privileged to substitute for it symbolic language; daughters lack this lack.[38]

Even as Lacan insists that the entry into the Symbolic entails equally an exposure of the phallus as fraud, he is "implicated in the phallocentrism he describe[s]," as Jacqueline Rose acknowledges.[39]

But such a myth of development is not only a difficult one for women, as feminist theorists have thus argued; it is a difficult view of all human experience. Time and again Lacan's commentators stress "the difficulty inherent in subjectivity itself," the high cost of having the phallus, the painful fact of being itself as an effect of division. Kristeva, for example, remarks that

> the sadness of young children just prior to their acquisition of language has often been observed; this is when they must renounce for-

ever the maternal paradise in which every demand is immediately gratified. The child must abandon its mother and be abandoned by her in order to be accepted by the father and begin talking.[40]

I suggest that the lacking Pardoner demonstrates the pain that must attend the subject's development when it is seen to proceed along these lines, when it is seen to depend on a necessary absence—the necessary loss of plenitude initially associated with the mother's body and a definition of the woman as lack. To quote Eagleton's simple articulation of Lacanian life: "We are severed from the mother's body: after the Oedipus crisis, we will never again be able to attain this precious object, even though we will spend all of our lives hunting for it."[41] Although such a description of castrated existence is not universal or natural, it does accurately account for the cultural construction of gender and the gendering of culture in Western patriarchal society. This renders it useful in describing the Pardoner; and the Pardoner, in turn, helps us to interpret and, finally, suggest a revision of this cultural myth.

In this view, then, an ideal plenitude is lost, and because of the loss of that ideal, the castrated subject forever seeks reunion, forever seeks the realm of original fullness. The Pardoner's being is hollowed by desire; cut off, he obsessively desires wholeness, and wholeness is what he repeatedly claims his relics will deliver: he promises his rustic audiences again and again that their cows, calves, sheep will be made "hool" (357, 359) and that they themselves, through his pardons, will remain a part of the body of Christians. He comments to the pilgrims that "Paraventure ther may fallen oon or two / Doun of his hors and breke his nekke atwo" (935–36), but, he claims, he is "suffisant" to the task of making that broken body whole again. But the castrated subject, in this view, must be content with substitutes only partially sufficient. The Pardoner's relics cannot really produce that desired integrity, and he knows it. Written documents, as partial objects, fill the Pardoner's "male" (1:694; 6:920), though deceiving no one: the narrator remarks that something vital is lacking. The fundamental insufficiency of the Pardoner's partial objects is violently exposed by the Host's outburst at the end, as we shall see in a moment. These substitutes by their very nature *signify* the loss of an ideal, in fact, and therefore signify castration, even as they are—*because* they are—accepted as substitutes for lost wholeness. Every time the Pardoner attempts to repair his lack—with relics or documents or words—he points to it. This is the crucial paradox of the Pardoner's partial objects: they both represent lack and substitute for wholeness; they signify absence even as they suggest presence. The Pardoner is a figure of paradox, both a wily deconstructor of binary oppositions (such as gender and hermeneutics are built on) and a figure of plaintive desire; and as we'll see in more detail later, these two notions of the Pardoner derive from the uncanny nature of his substitutions.

That these relics carry gender value is fully apparent to Harry Bailly, who wishes, at the end of the tale, that he could make the ultimate relic for the Pardoner's collection out of the Pardoner's "coillons" ("balls"). The Host recognizes, that is, the substitutions the Pardoner has made:

> I wolde I hadde thy coillons in myn hond
> In stide of relikes or of seintuarie.
> Lat kutte hem of, I wol thee helpe hem carie;
> They shul be shryned in an hogges toord!
>
> (952–55)

But the Host seems himself caught up by the paradox of the Pardoner's partial objects. Does the Pardoner indeed *have* the "coillons" to be cut off? The Host may not know, any better than the others do, whether the relics, as it were, signify castration or suggest plenitude. "I wolde I hadde" suggests primarily that the Host doesn't have the balls in hand but wishes he did, but secondarily it suggests that he doesn't because he *can't*: they don't exist.

Harry's response to the Pardoner's invitation to "kiss the relikes everychon" is startling in its vehemence. That final moment between the two pilgrims—the one lacking "naught" of "manhod" (1:756), the other having "lytill of manhode" (as the Middle English *Secreta Secretorum* says of eunuchs)—is highly charged with sexual repugnance.[42] Perhaps, sensing something of the Pardoner's lack, the Host fears for his own manhood.[43] But whether or not this moment specifically enacts a Freudian scene, Harry's response powerfully corroborates the associations I have been pointing to here. In its association of relics and balls, it refers to another medieval discussion wherein relics, balls, and writing are all brought together in a discussion of castration. In the *Roman de la rose*—the text commonly acknowledged to contain, in Faus Semblant, a central source for the characterization of the Pardoner—relics, testicles, and language are brought together in a vivid treatment of the myth of the loss of an ideal as castration. How testicles, relics, and language are particularly implicated in this loss in the *Rose*, and how they gain their gender significance in the *translatio* from the *Rose* into the *Canterbury Tales*, shall now be my concern.

2

In the *Roman de la rose,* Raison's narration of the story of Saturn's castration—the event she identifies as the moment at which the Golden
Age, the original ideal community, was lost—has led to a discussion
of her use of language.[44] Amant quibbles with Raison's free naming of
"coilles" in her narration. "Balls are not of good repute in the mouth
of a courteous lady," he protests, perhaps referring to dirty sex as
well as to dirty language.[45] Her language goes against Amors' "clean
speech commandment," as John Fleming has put it.[46] If such things as
balls must be mentioned, Amant insists, Raison should at least use a
gloss. The word is dirty, he clearly implies, because the thing is dirty.

Raison counters by protesting that neither word nor thing is dirty.
Both word and thing are good, and she can name a thing which is
good—made by God—openly and by its own name. Her words are
the proper names of things; they are perfectly adequate to, share in,
the *propre* of, the things they name. Amant protests further that even
if God made the things, he still didn't make the words, which are
unspeakably nasty. But Raison goes on to declare that God could have
made the words at the time of Creation; instead, he deputized her to
do it at her leisure. Her comments trace language to the time before
the Fall and assert the widespread view (which I have discussed in
relation to "Adam Scriveyn" and the *Clerk's Tale*) that in the original
language spoken by Adam words partake of, share in, the nature of
the things they signify.

Raison then goes on to say that if she had called "reliques" "coilles"
and "coilles" "reliques," Amant would've objected that "reliques" is
a base word. Clearly, she implies, "reliques" is a good word because
"reliques" are holy things. But even in Raison's suggestion that she
could have named "reliques" "coilles" and vice versa, there is an implication of the arbitrariness of signs: the original relation between word
and thing, between *signans* and *signatum,* was, in fact, arbitrary. She
could have named the things anything. And her comments on "custom" that follow ("Acoutumance est trop poissanz" [*Rose,* v. 7107])
support this point: names are set by custom, by convention.

I have discussed the Christian story of the Fall in relation to the fall
of language and to "Adam Scriveyn," and have there suggested gender values and associations; here I want to discuss medieval theories
of language for a moment in terms not of a single myth of the Fall
but of two distinct and contradictory positions concerning language
(assumed to be postlapsarian): the one naturalistic, the other con-

ventional. The issue of the naturalness or conventionality of the relationship between word and thing—signifier and signified—had been
debated since Plato's *Cratylus,* and *both* positions are found in medieval writers on language. Medieval writers explicitly adopted Her-
mogenes' position, asserting that the sign's relation to the signified is
determined by convention, but at the same time, their linguistic and
analytical habits imply a belief in the natural fitness of signs to things.
Socrates, too, of course, had it both ways: he judged that there is a
natural resemblance between word and thing, but he acknowledged
the conventional establishment of meaning as well. This dichotomous
or ambivalent position, R. Howard Bloch has suggested, can be seen
in writers from the late Latin grammarians (Varro, Priscian) to writers
of the high Middle Ages (Abelard, John of Salisbury).[47] Such ambivalence may be very clearly seen in Augustine, whose discussions of
sign theory proved fundamental throughout the entire Middle Ages
and whose thought informs this passage in the *Roman de la rose.* [48]

Augustine accepts the anti-Cratylistic notion that the relation between *signans* and *signatum* is conventionally established. Very clearly
(even simplistically, as some critics have suggested)[49] in the *De doctrina*
he explains:

> the single sign *beta* means a letter among the Greeks but a vegetable
> among the Latins. When I say *lege,* a Greek understands one thing
> by these two syllables, a Latin understands another. Therefore just
> as all of these significations move men's minds in accordance with
> the consent of their societies, and because their consent varies, they
> move them differently, nor do men agree upon them because of an
> innate value, but they have a value because they are agreed upon.[50]

Verbal signs do not have innate referential values. Augustine suggests
to Adeodatus in *De magistro* that one can't even know that a word
is a sign until one knows what it means:[51] the decision to attend to
it as a sign is set by convention, as is its meaning. Language is a
social phenomenon and there cannot be, according to this position,
any constitutive similarity between thing and sign.

Nevertheless, there is in Augustine's writing a deep strain of belief in the natural relation of words and their referents. *De dialectica*
includes a chapter on the origins of words: Augustine argues there
against the Stoics' claim that *all* words can be traced to their natural
origins, but he endorses and practices etymological analysis of many
words, tracing them back to find an essential, constitutive similarity
between sound and thing.[52] Origins of words are essential to his argu-

mentation in *De civitate Dei:* the names of the founders of the two cities express the whole plan of human history.[53] His fascination with the infant's process of learning language in the *Confessiones* (1:6,8) suggests a profound desire for verbal signs rooted in the physical, in the body, a language understood by all humans (and associated most closely with babies and women, as I mentioned in Chapter 5, in reference to Dante's *De vulgari eloquentia*). Even though he is always careful to distinguish natural signs from conventional signs and to put language in the latter category, he expresses a definite linguistic nostalgia, a desire for a language in which word and thing are one again.

This nostalgia is a symptom of his desire to escape from the problems that the conventionality of language poses—the problems of language's unreliability, what we have seen, from another point of view, to be language's fallenness, its "femininity," its slippery and mediate nature. Language, established by convention, is radically inadequate. Augustine's *De magistro* is an extended treatise on the limitations of verbal signs. The conventions that link *signans* to *signatum* can be changed, disregarded, broken. Words are capable only of reminding, not teaching, says Augustine to Adeodatus; they are able to point to the truth but do not possess it. And consequently, all kinds of slips are possible between the speaker, his language, and his audience.[54]

Theologically speaking, the problem of language's defectiveness was solved by the Incarnation. As God took on humanity in a Word made flesh, so can human language express divinity; language is redeemed.[55] The Incarnation restores humankind to God, the word to the Word: the continuity of language and being, disrupted at the Fall, is reestablished. Nevertheless, the problem of language's defectiveness, exemplified most profoundly by its inability to express the divine, remained. We have already seen incorrigible, wayward language in particular in "Adam Scriveyn" and *Troilus and Criseyde* and have discussed the problematics of recuperative yet disseminative *translatio* in the *Clerk's Tale*. Augustine begins the *Confessiones* by lamenting the poverty of language and asserting the ultimate ineffability of God, and he ends the *De trinitate* similarly—even though it is in this latter treatise that he delineates the mimetic relation of the inner word of the mind to the Word.[56]

So human language was seen, by many medieval thinkers, to be *essentially* partial. This is why Raison's narration of castration leads to a discussion of language and relics: "coilles," "reliques," "paroles," they're *all* fragments. A sign itself, Augustine sees, is accurate but is by definition only a partial representation of the thing it signifies. The word we speak is only a fragment of what we think (*De magi-*

stro 14.46). And that inner word is only a partial representation of the Word (*De trinitate* 15.10–11). Words are, physically, fragments, one giving way to another in the construction of a whole message (*Confessiones* 4.11). And there is always something left over, unexpressed: language always lags behind the mind (*De catechizandis rudibus* 2.3).[57] Augustine's awareness of linguistic inadequacy, even as he formulated the idea of a redeemed rhetoric, reflects, as Bloch puts it, an "anguished ambiguity provoked by a deep split between what medieval writers knew about verbal signs and what they desired to believe about them."[58]

Many late-medieval fears about language's instability and unreliability centered on the use of language by self-seeking preachers, especially friars. Faus Semblant, false preacher and sometime friar of the *Rose*, gathers under his cloak of hypocrisy contradictory theories and anxieties about the use and misuse of language and is the focus of hermeneutic disruption in the poem, as I shall argue in a moment. The Pardoner, with his "hauteyn speche" (330), literally or figuratively missing "coillons," and fake relics, inherits the place of disruptive possibility from his literary forebear; he, too, is a false preacher.

Thirteenth- and fourteenth-century treatises on preaching emphasize, on the one hand, that preaching is mandated by Christ: it is both necessary and possible with a "redeemed rhetoric" such as Augustine describes, a rhetoric based on the "unity of substance" in the Word, as Robert of Basevorn puts it in his *Forma praedicandi* (1322). Christ preached and ordered his followers to preach; indeed, in so doing, he was following a tradition of preaching that dated from the Creation, when, as Robert writes, God first preached to Adam. Preaching is thus linked to unfallen language.[59] Humbert of Romans, in his mid-thirteenth-century treatise on preaching, also uses images that associate preaching with Creation.[60]

But on the other hand, language was understood to be partial and fragmentary; abuses of language in preaching were perceived as not only possible but rampant. The widespread uneasiness about false preaching had as its ultimate preoccupation the defective, shifting relationship of the spoken word to the Word. The *Rose* is deeply concerned with the antimendicant controversy (in which a major issue was the friars' assumption of the duty of preaching), as is Rutebeuf, from whose "Complaint de Guillaume" Jean de Meun derived the name for his hypocritical friar.[61] Wycliffe, a century later, charged again and again that false preachers—abusive friars—had obfuscated the true Word.[62] Wycliffe's literalism was extreme and unorthodox, but protests against friars who "redefined" or altogether discarded the Word to serve their own ends in sermons were rife: Chaucer's Summoner paints a perfect portrait of the "glosying" friar; Richard FitzRalph, archbishop of Armagh in the mid-fourteenth century, exclaims against friars who complain of his insistence on textual proof.[63] Such charges against preaching friars as hypocrites point directly to a deep split between the speaker's intention, his spoken word, and the Word.[64]

False preachers thus represent not just a threat to language; they represent what such medieval thinkers saw as a truth about language —in fact, language's "double truth." Language was understood to be at best a fragment, and—like "coilles" and "reliques"—could be cut off altogether from the Significator. Yet people necessarily believed in it with a faith that partook of nostalgia; they affirmed by speaking and listening that the spoken word could adequately express the inner word, and the inner word, the Word. Faus Semblant, false preacher, focuses linguistic and hermeneutic uneasiness in the *Roman de la rose*, and is the means, I suggest, by which it gains the particular gender value it has in the Pardoner's performance.

Faus Semblant is generally thought to be one of the most significant sources for Chaucer's characterization of his Pardoner. Critics cite the use of public confession as the crucial similarity between the two; the sins Faus Semblant reveals, "hypocrisy and self-interest," according to Germaine Dempster, are "exactly those of the Pardoner." Echoes of particular lines can be heard in the latter's speech, as Dean S. Fansler demonstrates; and the movement from Faus Semblant to the Pardoner is seen by P. M. Kean to proceed by an increase in naturalistic representation.[65] But what I think centrally important to the determination of the Pardoner's significance is Faus Semblant's peculiar embodiment of a particular threat to language and all hermeneutic enterprises—an embodiment that is variably gendered and variously clothed.

At all points Faus Semblant claims that he is a hypocrite, a fraud. All anyone can know for certain about him is that he is not what he seems:

> Mes en quel que leu que je viegne
> ne conment que je m'i contiegne,
> nule riens fors barat n'i chaz;
> ne plus que dam Tiberz li chaz
> n'entent qu'a soriz et a raz,
> n'entent je a riens fors a baraz.
> Ne ja certes par mon habit
> ne savrez o quex genz j'abit;

> non ferez vos voir aus paroles,
> ja tant n'ierent simples ne moles.
>   (*Rose*, vv. 11035–44)

>   But what herberwe that ever I take,
>   Or what semblant that evere I make,
>   I mene but gile, and folowe that;
>   For right no mo than Gibbe oure cat,
>
>   . . . .
>
>   Ne entende I but to bigilyng.
>   Ne no wight may by my clothing
>   Wite with what folk is my dwellyng,
>   Ne by my wordis yit, parde,
>   So softe and so plesaunt they be.
>   (*Romaunt*, C:6201–10)

He is one of the Antichrist's gang, as he baldly puts it, and there is no correspondence between their garments and their true selves:

>   il font un argument au monde
>   ou conclusion a honteuse:
>   cist a robe religieuse,
>   donques est il religieus.
>   Cist argumenz est touz fieus,
>   il ne vaut pas un coustel troine:
>   la robe ne fet pas le moine.
>   (*Rose*, vv. 11022–28)

>   They make the world an argument
>   That [hath] a foul conclusioun.
>   "I have a robe of religioun,
>   Thanne am I all religious."
>   This argument is all roignous;
>   It is not worth a croked brere.
>   Abit ne makith neithir monk ne frere.
>   (*Romaunt*, C:6186–92)

In fact, he makes many changes of clothes; he dresses in the habit of a knight, monk, prelate, canon, clerk, priest, disciple, master, lord of the manor, forester, prince or page (*Rose*, vv. 11157–68; *Romaunt*, C:6327–34)—yet none gives a clue as to what is underneath. Like the Pardoner, he is never stripped bare, and he incarnates the uneasy possibility that interpretation is impossible. It is not simply that allegorical reading *in malo* of Faus Semblant's surface might always be necessary (he is "blanche dehors, dedenz nercie" [*Rose,* v. 11983]; "Ryght blak withynne and whit withoute" [*Romaunt,* C:7333]); more fundamentally, the only constant about him is that he is not what he seems. It may be, then, that, as I've already suggested in regard to the Pardoner, there is *no* relation between surface and body, letter and spirit. "Mes de religion sanz faille / j'en lés le grain et pregn la paille. / . . . je n'en quier sanz plus que l'abit" (*Rose,* vv. 11185–88) ("But to what ordre that I am sworn, / I take the strawe, and lete the corn. / . . . / I axe nomore but her abit" [*Romaunt,* C:6353–56]): Faus Semblant in fact suggests here that there is nothing underneath those clothes but a consuming fraud; like the Pardoner, he is constituted by an absence within.

And, like the Pardoner, Faus Semblant has an essentially uncertain gender—sometimes he's a man, sometimes a woman:

> Autre eure vest robe de fame,
> or sui damoisele, or sui dame;
> autre eure sui religieuse,
> or sui rendue, or sui prieuse,
> or sui nonnain, or abbeesse.
>   (*Rose,* vv. 11177–81)

> Somtyme a wommans cloth take I;
> Now am I a mayde, now lady.
> Somtyme I am religious;
> Now lyk an anker in an hous.
> Somtyme am I prioresse,
> And now a nonne, and now abbesse.
>   (*Romaunt,* C:6345–50)

The principles of fraud and hermeneutic breakdown that Faus Semblant personifies are significantly multi-gendered, significantly sexually indeterminate. If one medieval idea of language—the sense of the signifier's oneness with its signified—associates it with prelapsarian times, a time of mythically perfect (hetero)sexual relations, gendered and uncorrupted, the other idea—referring to its arbitrariness, fragmentariness, and consequent potential for disruption—cuts it off from such perfect sexuality or even clearly defined gender. The breakdown of interpretive stability and determinate gender are of a piece, as it were; and the Pardoner, false preacher, of an unidentifiable sexuality, is Faus Semblant's descendant in every way.

3

The Pardoner both exposes and is caught in this apparent double truth of language. He uses language as he does his relics and his documents, as a partial object, as a substitute for his literally or figuratively absent genitals and for what that absence represents: a lost Golden Age, a lost realm in which there is no differentiation between self and other, signifier and signified—the realm of the Word. His partial objects are flawed; they are inadequate substitutes, and this is apparent to all, including himself. He does not try to hide this, either: in fact, he tells the pilgrims again and again that his relics are fakes; he insists that his words and his intentions are discrepant; he admits that Christ's, not his, pardon "is best." Yet he adopts these partial objects in the knowledge of their flawedness, in the knowledge of their insufficiency. The psycho-logic of knowingly accepting such faulty substitutes is succinctly expressed by Octave Mannoni: "Je sais bien, mais quand même . . ." ("I *know*, but *even so* . . ."). This is the logic of the eunuch—a radical unknowing—informing the hermeneutics of the partial.[66]

Mannoni, following Freud, is here discussing the fetish. Freud writes that the fetish "is a substitute for the woman's (the mother's) penis that the little boy once believed in, and . . . does not want to give up."[67] The fetish allows the child to retain the idea of the maternal phallus even after he has perceived sexual difference; it allows him to believe he remains in the realm of nondifferentiation and plenitude (his mother and he are not separate) even after he knows that she doesn't have an organ like his, even after mother and child are cut off from each other by the interruption of the father. But it is clear that such a substitute is inevitably inadequate; the child *knows* the mother is separate and other, and anxiously tries to fill that unfillable emptiness. The fetish is precisely what I've been calling a partial object: it admits the fact of castration even as it refuses to admit it. Thus the fetish is constituted of contrary ideas, of "two mutually incompatible assertions": the mother has her penis *and* she has been castrated; the child is united with the mother *and* is cut off from her.[68] The fetish thus confounds simple reading, univalent meaning: hardly a simple substitute—neither *Ersatz* nor *non Ersatz*, as Derrida in *Glas* shows —the object is a sign of absence and a suggestion of presence.[69] As such, it deconstructs hermeneutic gestures such as I've been describing throughout this book. The eunuch's hermeneutics paradoxically consists of a denial of knowledge: the fetishist maintains a "conceptual fiction," a fiction of nondifferentiation and plenitude, in the face of "perceptual knowledge."[70] "I *know*, but *even so* . . .": the fetish is the first model of *all* repudiations of reality.[71] Thus the medieval theorists of language *know,* but hold on to the belief otherwise, about the inadequacy of language. Just as the fetishist *knows* that a foot is just a foot—but even so . . .

From the fetishist's point of view, moreover, that foot—even as it is disavowed—is an embodiment of lost wholeness. From an analytical perspective, the fetish is a figure, a trope, something that *represents* what has been lost—the organ, plenitude—even as it represents lack itself. The fetishist, from this latter point of view, has an inadequately figurative understanding: he refuses to recognize that he is dealing with a trope, a figure; he takes it literally, as that lost body part that completes, guarantees wholeness. We have seen literal reading to be linked in the Pauline tradition to the carnal and the feminine and to be devalued in relation to the figurative; in the psychoanalytic scheme it is also linked to the body and the feminine (although the terms have different meanings in this instance), and, importantly, it is also devalued: inadequately figurative reading is a delusion.

The Pardoner, using his partial objects as substitute masculinity, is a fetishist; both conflicted disavowal and misreading of the literal for the figurative are evident in his performance. There is unfillable absence within him, and he uses his verbal arts, documents, relics as substitutes: they are admissions, signs of his lack even as they guard against his acknowledgment of it. He *knows* that they're only partial, that they're fakes, frauds, but *even so* he uses them—aggressively, desperately—in the belief that they can make him whole, somehow part of the body of pilgrims. This conflicted psyche can be seen represented in the narrative of his tale, a sample sermon. The world of the *Tale,* as we shall see, is an Old Testament one, punitive and unredeemed; the "riotoures thre" are dispatched by "Deeth" in a terrifyingly immediate judgment of their sin. Yet the "olde man," embodying mutually incompatible assertions, has—along with a knowledge of this implacable "Deeth"—a belief in redemption, "even so." But if the riotors fetishistically fail to distinguish figurative language—the result of that failure being lethal—the old man's ability to read allegory leaves him, as well, without access to fullness.[72]

The tavern world of the rioters is the world of the Law. Most of the Pardoner's exempla are drawn from the Old Testament, and he seems in fact to prefer the Old Testament to the New in setting the scene: "Witnesse on Mathew; but in special / Of sweryng seith the hooly Jeremye" (634–35). Christ's Redemption is duly acknowledged, but humankind's original corruption and consequent damnation—imposed by an angry God the Father at the Fall—vividly endure in the Pardoner's rhetoric:

> O glotonye, ful of cursednesse!
> O cause first of oure confusioun!
> O original of oure dampnacioun,
> Til Crist hadde boght us with his blood agayn!
> Lo, how deere, shortly for to sayn,
> Aboght was thilke cursed vileynye!
> Corrupt was al this world for glotonye.
>
> (498–504)

"Heighe Goddes heestes" (640), the tables of the Law, govern, and sin is inexorably punished: its wages is death. "Deeth," in fact, presides over "this contree"; he has slain "al the peple" (676) and will inevitably prevail over those who seek to slay him. In the emotional economy of the tale, this ineluctable Death is the same force as the Father, "verray God, that is omnipotent." When, then, the Pardoner assigns the three rioters—three stumbling, swearing drunks—to overcome Death, it becomes clear that, to his mind, redemption from the Law, from this forbidding "verray God," is impossible. "Deeth shal be deed!" the rioters yell, "al dronken in this rage" (710, 705): the three inebriated ruffians are incapable—obviously, lugubriously—of this salvific mission.

Indulging in all the sins of which the Pardoner says he is himself guilty, the three rioters are a representation of the Pardoner's belief in the impossibility of redemption and atonement. The deadly consequences of their literal-mindedness represent one part of the eunuch's logic, the Pardoner's knowledge that a foot is just a foot, so to speak —his knowledge that the fetish cannot bring atonement. Misreading or bad reading in fact is the motivation of the *Tale*'s plot. The rioters' informant at the tavern, the "boy" who is dropped from the tale once he has served his narrative function, speaks allegorically of the demise of the rioters' "old felawe" (672). He creates a spear-wielding personification of death itself:

> Ther cam a privee theef men clepeth Deeth,
> That in this contree al the peple sleeth,
> And with his spere he smoot his herte atwo,
> And wente his wey withouten wordes mo.
>
> .   .   .   .
>
> Me thynketh that it were necessarie
> For to be war of swich an adversarie.
>
> (675–82)

The tavern keeper concurs, speculating about "his habitacioun" in a "greet village" (687–89). The three, of course, take this talk literally and set out to find and do away with the thief Death. Their failure to recognize figurative discourse is the narrative equivalent of the fetishist's failure to acknowledge that the fetish is a figure. And this failure proves terminal: they are annihilated as a result of it. When directed to and presented with their death in the form of florins, they can't read it right; and they don't suspect that the *radix* on which the bushel sits might be *cupiditas*, either.

But if the Pardoner figures his knowledge ("I know") of the futility of the fetish in the three rioters, he figures a more complex self-understanding in the "olde man" whom they accost in the search for Death. He is, first of all, an incarnation of the Pardoner's anguished knowledge of his fragmentariness: "Lo how I vanysshe, flessh, and blood, and skyn!" (732). The old man wails for some redemption from his defective and dying corpse; and he expresses this desire not in terms of atonement with the Father but of reunion with his "leeve mooder":[73]

> Thus walke I, lyk a restelees kaityf,
> And on the ground, which is my moodres gate,
> I knokke with my staf, bothe erly and late,
> And seye "Leeve mooder, leet me in!"
>
> (728–31)

Between the old man and his "leeve mooder," that lost ideal realm of unity and plenitude, stands "Goddes wille." To be "at reste" in the "ground" with his mother would provide a return to nondifferentiation, a reunion of subject and object, a redemption from the torments of age and separation. Even though he knows of Christ's atonement for the loss of original plenitude—he tells the rioters of it—he remains unredeemed by him "that boghte agayn mankynde" (766): he walks continually "lyk a restelees kaityf" (728). The old man has an image and a belief in fullness and plenitude—"Deeth" to him is reunion, not separation, and he states that he has not been reunited with his mother "*yet*"—but the way to this plenitude is not through the Father: "Goddes wille" blocks it.

The "olde man" can certainly understand allegory; he replies immediately and knowingly to the rioters, interpreting their query about "thilke traytour Deeth" by sending them along to find "hym" under a tree. But such hermeneutic ability gets the old man no closer to achieving his own desperately articulated goal of reunion in death: "Deeth, allas, ne wol nat han my lyf" (727). He recognizes the allegorical as allegorical—he recognizes, in the terms of my analysis, the figurativity of the fetish—but is left without any access to fullness and plenitude, separated from his "leeve mooder." Instead he wanders, neither dead nor really living. Neither literal nor figurative has, finally, any redeeming value.

The characters thus enact the Pardoner's own understanding of the fetishist, stuck between knowledge and desire for wholeness. The form of the *Pardoner's Tale* itself—a sermon with narrative exemplum—further demonstrates the psychological stagnation of the fetishist, caught between incompatible affirmations.[74] The exemplum is unnecessary to the logical argument of the sermon; it doesn't develop or complicate a point but merely demonstrates it. *Radix malorum est cupiditas:* the three rioters are greedy and unscrupulous, and evil befalls them. The wages of sin is death: they set out to find death, and they find it. The plot is nothing but the rigorous working out of what is announced at the outset: *how* the rioters find death remains to be seen, but that they *will* find it is certain.[75] The tale itself is, from this standpoint, superfluous—we already know the outcome—and thus it is no coincidence that "superfluytee abhomynable"—drinking, gambling, cursing—(471; cf. 528) motivates the whole sermon. Yet despite the tale's excessive status there is nothing left over, nothing left behind. The clever reification of the *radix malorum* into "under a tree" is a function of the tale's essentially resolved form: everyone and everything is consumed in the turns of the narrative, either dying or fading out, going "thider as I have to go" (749), as the old man says.

So the Pardoner believes in plenitude as fact while knowing it is a fiction, and he successfully plays on that belief held by the members of his audiences as well. Cynical fraud and true believer at once, the Pardoner is a great success as a swindler—his promises of wholeness make him richer by far than any parish priest—precisely because he truly believes in his own false relics.[76] And he knows the pilgrims desire wholeness: when he interrupts the Wife of Bath to claim that he was about to wed a wife, when he later proclaims in his Prologue that he wants a jolly wench in every town, he is not simply trying to enter into the heterosexual world of the pilgrims; he is cannily playing on their desire to believe in integrity of the body—their desire to believe in the integrity of *his* body and the integrity of their own pilgrim body. He's exploiting their fetishistic ability to admit his oddity even while they refuse the practical consequences of their admission. They *know* (that he's sexually weird), but *even so* (even so, they demand a "moral thyng" from him). Their desire for an edifying tale is well described by this fetishistic logic: even out of the mouth of a ribald figure they insist that it will be a "moral thyng."

Fetishism is, finally, a conservative behavior: it allows one to maintain a conviction of plenitude even in the face of loss and dislocation. The Pardoner is fixed between knowledge of his fragmentation and belief that he can be made whole; knowledge of Death, God's Law, and judgment, and belief in the possibility of reunion and redemption; knowledge that his pardons are fraudulent and belief that they can restore him to an original unity. In its "stuck" quality, this mechanism of disavowal is similar to the cyclical mechanism, as Augustine analyzes it, of sinning that leads to despair that leads to further sinning.[77] Despair is finally cataclysmically destructive, however, while the Pardoner will continue to "go . . . as I have to go," neither destroying himself nor finding redemption.

The Pardoner's coup de grace—or, better, *coupure de grâce*—at the end of the tale is the final gesture of the fetishist among his peers: "I have relikes and pardoun in my male / As faire as any man in Engelond" (920–21), he boasts to the pilgrims. In other words: "I *know* that they're phony substitutes (but even so, I believe they're 'as fair' as any other man's). And *you know* that they're frauds (but even so, you want to believe in the grace of absolution). So step right up and kiss them." The Host's reaction to this offer—the expression of his desire to castrate the Pardoner—is fierce; he catches the fetishist in the act: "I wolde I hadde thy coillons in myn hond / In stide of relikes or of seintuarie" (952–53). And if that reaction is undermined by uncertainty, as I suggested above, the kiss of peace and reconciliation that follows, itself a loaded gesture in this overheated context, is also characteristically undecidable. It is hardly a clear restoration of the idea of community and friendship that has been devastated in the narrative of the three rioters. Who is reconciled to whom or what? Is the Pardoner, not-man, not-woman, welcomed into the "brotherhood" of the laughing pilgrims, as has been suggested by critics? Or is the Host, apparently all-man, no-woman, reconciled instead to his own castration, to the reality of life according to the Pardoner?[78] The Knight's intervention, cutting off this fetishistic performance, returns the company to the beginning: "And, as we diden, lat us laughe and pleye," he exhorts them. As before in fragment 1 (856), they again "ryden forth hir weye."

4

The Pardoner is stuck, his fetishes keeping him fixed in place, and it seems he has led the pilgrimage nowhere. But after the Pardoner's performance nothing on this pilgrimage, I would argue, can be quite the same again. The performance has poignantly and furiously exposed the cost of patriarchal discourse. I have argued throughout this book that Chaucer suggests androcentrism takes its toll on men as well as on women, limits the idea of the "masculine" as well as of the "feminine." As I suggested in reference to the Wife of Bath in particular, misogyny—the constraint of women's subjectivity, autonomous desire, signifying power—finally deprives men of their own self-understanding too. Turning away from woman limits all human experience, and, in particular, limits that subset of experience that has concerned me most in this book, literary activity. The Pardoner's conflicted performance demonstrates the pain for all humans that results from the essential move underwriting patriarchal discourse as I've analyzed it, the move to define woman as lacking, as incomplete, as a no-thing, and to make (her) absence the necessary condition of language and culture.

The Pardoner lays bare the presuppositions of patriarchal discourse: he exposes not only the asymmetry of its binary oppositions—he is identified in terms of a lack of masculinity, which determines his position as at best marginal—but he provides as well a perspective on the logic of the Same on which that discourse operates. He is neither the Same nor the Other, neither man nor not-man; that ideological structure is not universal or natural, as it strives to appear—his partial objects don't obey that binary and exclusive logic either.

The Pardoner thus destabilizes the project, calls into question the possibility of making morally redeeming tales or interpreting tales in Christian, spiritual terms. If "fables and swich wrecchednesse," to quote another critic of fiction-making, depend on a clear distinction between what is literally true and what is false, what could have happened and what could not have happened, if fables depend on a hermeneutic structure of binary oppositions (surface and nucleus, letter and spirit, clothes and body) that is homologous to the structure of gender oppositions, then the eunuch, outside these structures, suggests that some other literary activity with some other foundation is necessary. The Pardoner suggests the necessity of something beyond a model of interpretation that depends on a binary turning away from the literal, the carnal, the feminine and toward the figurative, the spirit, the masculine. He suggests the necessity of moving beyond a model of hermeneutics that proceeds by the anxious covering, uncovering, and recovering of the body of meaning—anxious in its desire to prove that there is a body underneath, that there is a meaning of all those words; anxious in its desire to domesticate that body, to legitimate that meaning. With his unclassifiable body beyond gender as we know it in androcentric culture, he suggests the possibility of a poetics based not on such mediations as gender and language but, perhaps, on something unmediated. And that, for Chaucer, would be a poetics based on the incarnate Word, on the body of Christ, which is itself an embodied word; it would be a poetics founded on the body of Christ who is God, in whom there is no lack, no division, no separation, no difference. This would be a poetics of presence, not absence, in which, finally, all difference would be obviated.

This is perhaps the direction in which Chaucer's poetics finally turned, away from a poetics that engages with the fallible, mediate letter of human language and the gendered human body. The other preacher on the road to Canterbury, the Parson, in a gesture that closes the narrative, rejects the whole tale-telling project and all the categories by which it proceeds: he eschews all engagement with the letter for its own sake—all fable, all rhythm and rhyme ("I kan nat geeste 'rum, ram, ruf,' by lettre, / Ne, God woot, rym holde I but litel bettre" [10:43–44])—and he will not "glose," either (10:45). He cares only to deliver a full sentence; his goal is "Jerusalem celestial," and the proper poetics on the "viage"—the literary approach that will show the way—proceeds by an unequivocal acceptance of the flawlessly incarnate Christ and a belief in His ability to guarantee the expression of "moralitee and vertuous mateere" (10:51, 49, 38). This is a negating, totalizing stroke, to be sure, as is the gesture of retraction that follows the Parson in almost all the manuscripts that contain the complete *Parson's Tale*. I take the voice of the *Retractions*, the voice of "the makere of this book," to be Chaucer's, without deliberate impersonation, and I take it to enunciate a final literary intention. But even as the Parson and Chaucer reject and attempt to take back what is problematic—and what has proved to be most enduring—in Chaucer's texts, these last gestures can be read as not only attempting a total closure (such as we have seen to be associated with the masculine) but as opening out an alternative possibility, too (something associated with the feminine in Chaucer's texts). As I read them, they open out a profound linguistic and literary possibility, even a challenge: to make and increase and multiply in a language guaranteed by the "precious blood" (10:1090) of a body constituted by no division, no lack.[79]

The *Retractions* appear to have preceded the final silence of the poet; this language of presence—the language of the divine—is not, after all, a language of this world.[80] But the Pardoner urges his audience to think about the possibility of linguistic presence even as the pilgrimage wends forth its way on earth. Constituted by absence, he sets his listeners to thinking about absolute Presence, about radical Being in which there is no lack and in which all difference and division are

obviated. So completely unlike the others around him, so far outside
the categories by which they operate that he isn't even their Other,
the Pardoner, not-man, not-woman, is the unlikely but best pilgrim
for this task on the road to Canterbury; for in the ideal Christian society too, according to Saint Paul, "non est masculus neque femina"
(Galatians 3:28).

Abbreviations
Notes
Bibliography
Index

Abbreviations

CC	Corpus christianorum, series latina
CFMA	Les Classiques français du moyen âge
ChauR	*Chaucer Review*
CSEL	Corpus scriptorum ecclesiasticorum latinorum
EETS	Early English Text Society
ELH	*English Literary History*
JEGP	*Journal of English and Germanic Philology*
JMRS	*Journal of Medieval and Renaissance Studies*
MGH	Monumenta Germaniae historica
MLQ	*Modern Language Quarterly*
PMLA	*Publications of the Modern Language Association*
PL	*Patrologiae cursus completus, series latina,* ed. J.-P. Migne (cited by volume and column)
SAC	*Studies in the Age of Chaucer*
SP	*Studies in Philology*
YFS	*Yale French Studies*

Notes

INTRODUCTION. *Chaucer's Sexual Poetics*

1 Geoffrey Chaucer, "Chaucers Wordes unto Adam, His Owne Scriveyn," in *The Riverside Chaucer,* gen. ed. Larry D. Benson, 3d ed. (Boston: Houghton Mifflin, 1987). All further quotations of Chaucer's works are from this edition, hereafter cited by line number (or by book or fragment and line number).

2 A contemporary exception is Russell A. Peck, who briefly suggests a figurative association with the first Adam (as does R. E. Kaske and as I shall do below, pp. 5–7) in "Public Dreams and Private Myths: Perspective in Middle English Literature," *PMLA* 90 (1975): 467. F. N. Robinson summarizes early conjectures: "Adam" might have been Adam Chaucer, who held a lease in Smithfield and might have been a relative of the poet (Aage Brusendorff's idea); he might have been Adam Lachares (Eleanor Hammond); Adam Stedeman, law scrivener (Ramona Bressie); Adam Acton, limner (John Mathews Manly); or Adam Pinckhurst, member of the Brotherhood of Writers of the Court Letter in London between 1392 and 1404 (B. M. Wagner) (*The Works of Geoffrey Chaucer,* ed. F. N. Robinson, 2d ed. [Boston: Houghton Mifflin, 1957], p. 859). It is symptomatic of current trends in Chaucer criticism that these speculations are not detailed in the notes by Laila Z. Gross in *The Riverside Chaucer.*

3 Biblical translations are from the Douay Version. All other translations, unless otherwise noted, are my own.

4 Philo of Alexandria, *On the Cherubim* 17, ed. F. H. Colson and G. H. Whitaker, Loeb Classical Library (Cambridge, Mass.: Harvard Univ. Press, 1929), p. 43. Cited in R. Howard Bloch, *Etymologies and Genealogies: A Literary Anthropology of the French Middle Ages* (Chicago: Univ. of Chicago Press, 1983), p. 39. See Bloch's excellent discussion of the original human language in early medieval thought, pp. 30–63.

5 Dante Alighieri, *De vulgari eloquentia* 1.4.4, ed. Aristide Marigo, 3d ed. (Florence: Felice le Mounier, 1957).

6 In his brief article, " 'Clericus Adam' and Chaucer's 'Adam Scriveyn' " (in *Chaucerian Problems and Perspectives: Essays Presented to Paul E. Beich-*

ner, C.S.C., ed. E. Vasta and Z. P. Thundy [Notre Dame, Ind.: Univ. of Notre Dame Press, 1979]), pp. 114–18, R. E. Kaske cites a thirteenth-century Saxon chronicle by Eike von Repgow as a witness to the tradition of Adam as inventor of letters: "Adam underdachte boch-stave allererst" (in a later Latin translation: "Adam primus adinuenit literas"). See Gesellschaft für ältere deutsche Geschichtskunde, ed., *Sächsische Weltchronik*, in *Deutsche Chroniken und andere Geschichtsbücher des Mittelalters*, MGH, Scriptores qui vernacula lingua usi sunt, 2 (Hannover: Hahn, 1877), 2:69; and H. F. Massmann, ed., *Das Zeitbuch des Eike von Repgow in ursprünglich niederdeutscher Sprache und in früher lateinischer Übersetzung*, Bibliothek des Litterarischen Vereins in Stuttgart, 42 (Stuttgart: Litterarische Verein, 1857), p. 15. It is interesting to note, with Kathleen Walkup ("By Sovereign Maidens' Might: Notes on Women in Printing," *Fine Print* 11, no. 2 [April 1985]: 100–104), that this chronicle was issued by Anna Rugerin in 1484 from her press at Augsburg, the first European press "solely owned and operated by a woman" (p. 100). For a statement of the traditional view that Moses invented letters, see Robert Hollander, "Babytalk in Dante's *Commedia*," *Mosaic* 8 (1975): 76–77, n. 10.

7 Cf. Petrarch, *De remediis utriusque fortunae* 1.43 ("De librorum copia"), on scribes:

> Nunc confusis exemplaribus et exemplis unum scribere polliciti, sic aliud scribunt, ut quod ipse dictaveris non agnoscas.
>
> [Now, with their confused copies and drafts, they promise to write one thing but write another, so that you do not recognize what you yourself dictated.]
>
> (*Petrarch: Four Dialogues for Scholars*, ed. and trans. Conrad H. Rawski [Cleveland: Western Reserve University, 1967], pp. 36–37)

8   [Beneath a certain tree Adam the clerk wrote
Of how the first Adam sinned by means of a certain tree.
Woman conquered, man was conquered by means of a certain
     tree;
Woman easily trusted the serpent, who was speaking
     about profound matters.
Woman made deceived fools out of wise men;
Woman overcame you, David, and you, Solomon;
Woman beguiled you, Samson, and on you, Job,
Woman did the same job; she conquered just as Genesis says.
Woman . . .
Woman . . .
Woman . . .]

For the full text, see S. G. Owen, "A Medieval Latin Poem," *English Historical Review* 2 (1887): 525–26; and Carlo Pascal, *Letteratura Latina Medievale: Nuovi Saggi e Note Critiche* (Catania: Francesco Battiato, 1909), pp. 107–15. Kaske's article, cited in n. 6, pointed me to this poem; I have adopted his translation of the first two lines.

9 Eue helde longe tale wiþ þe neddre in paradys and tolde hym al þe lesson þat god hadd forboden hem forto eten of þe Appel. And so þe neddre vnderstoode þorouȝ her woordes onon riȝth her feblesse. and her brotylnesse of fallynge. And fonde way þorouȝ her mychel speche hou he schulde brynge hire to forlernesse.

(*Ancrene Riwle*, Magdalene College, Cambridge, MS. Pepys 2498 [ed. A. Zettersten, EETS 274 (London: Oxford Univ. Press, 1976), p. 25])

Cited in Deborah Ellis's lively and perceptive article, "The Merchant's Wife's Tale: Language, Sex, and Commerce in Margery Kempe and in Chaucer," *Exemplaria* (October 1989).

10 In the *De planctu*, writing and sexual intercourse are figuratively equated; concomitantly, the laws of grammar are identified metaphorically with the laws of Nature. Dame Nature herself comments on her appointment of Venus to build a progeny on earth: Nature says she gave Venus "two approved hammers" and workshops with anvils in which the Fates might be defeated, and she ordered that the hammers should not on any account stray from the anvils. Similarly,

Ad officium etiam scripture calamum prepotentem eidem fueram elargita, ut in competentibus cedulis eiusdem calami scripturam poscentibus quarum mee largitionis beneficio fuerat conpotita iuxta mee orthographie normulam rerum genera figuraret, ne a proprie descriptionis semita in falsigraphie deuia eumdem deuagari minime sustineret.

[I had also bestowed on her an unusually powerful writing-pen for her work so that she might trace the classes of things, according to the rules of my orthography, on suitable pages which called for writing by this same pen and which through my kind gift she had in her possession, so that she might not suffer the same pen to wander in the smallest degree from the path of proper delineation into the byways of pseudography.]

(Alanus de Insulis, *De planctu naturae* 10.30–34 [ed. Nikolaus Häring, *Studi medievali*, 3d ser., 19 (1978): 845–46; trans. James J. Sheridan, under the title *The Plaint of Nature* [Toronto: Pontifical Institute of Mediaeval Studies, 1980], p. 156)

11 Genius threatens to excommunicate those who refuse to procreate:

>Mes cil qui des greffes n'escrivent,
>par cui li mortel tourjorz vivent,
>es beles tables precieuses
>que Nature por estre oiseuses
>ne leur avoit pas aprestees,
>ainz leur avoit por ce prestees
>que tuit i fussent escrivain,
>con tuit et toutes an vivain . . .
>o tout l'esconmeniemant
>qui touz les mete a dampnemant,
>puis que la se veulent aherdre,
>ainz qu'il muirent, puissent il perdre
>et l'aumosniere et les estalles
>don il ont signe d'estre malles!
>Perte leur viegne des pandanz
>a quoi l'aumosniere est pandanz!
>Les marteaus dedanz estachiez
>puissent il avoir arrachiez!
>Li greffe leur saient tolu,
>quant escrivre n'an ont volu
>dedanz les precieuses tables
>qui leur estoient convenables!

[But those who do not write with their styluses, by which mortals live forever, on the beautiful precious tablets that Nature did not prepare for them to leave idle, but instead loaned them in order that everyone might be a writer and that we all, men and women, might live . . . may they, in addition to the excommunication that sends them all to damnation, suffer, before their death, the loss of their purse and testicles, the signs that they are male! May they lose the pendants on which the purse hangs! May they have the hammers that are attached within torn out! May their styluses be taken away from them when they have not wished to write within the precious tablets that were suitable for them!]

(Félix Lecoy, ed., *Le Roman de la rose* vv. 19599–646 [CFMA (Paris: Honoré Champion, 1976); trans., Charles Dahlberg, under the title *The Romance of the Rose* (Princeton, N.J.: Princeton Univ. Press, 1971), pp. 323–24])

12 Note the significant change in *The Riverside Chaucer* from Robinson's second edition of *The Works of Geoffrey Chaucer*, which follows Root in printing another version of the line—"It is no shame unto yow ne no vice"—but notes the "rape" reading in the list of significant variants. For more on the textual history of this line, see R. K. Root, *The Tex-*

tual Tradition of Chaucer's "Troilus," Chaucer Society, 1st ser., no. 99 (London: Kegan Paul, 1916 for 1912), p. 201; and *The Manuscripts of Chaucer's "Troilus,"* Chaucer Society, 1st ser., no. 98 (London: Kegan Paul, 1914 for 1911), pp. 13, 33, 35.

13 Another example of Chaucer's attention to words' participating in the process of social change is "fre" in the final question posed by the Franklin in his tale (see 5:1622). In reference to "rape" here, it might be useful to recall in addition that Chaucer was fluent in French and Latin and could very well have added Latinate connotations to the Germanic word.

14 I want to distinguish my discussion here and throughout this book from the notion, current in some Chaucer criticism, of Chaucer's "androgyny." Donald Howard gives voice to much liberal critical sentiment when he writes of Chaucer's "androgynous personality":

> Chaucer was what may be called an androgynous personality. He lived in a man's world, achieved eminence as a public figure and a writer in a man's world, yet he had no difficulty at all seeing the world through women's eyes. "Androgynous" in this sense does not suggest any physical anomaly or any characterological limitation. It is simply the ability to see things from the viewpoint of either sex; Coleridge said that a great mind must be androgynous.
> (*Chaucer: His Life, His Works, His World* [New York: Dutton, 1987], p. 97)

However, as I shall attempt to demonstrate throughout this book, Chaucer has a deep and acute sense of the differences between the genders in Western patriarchal culture, the mutually exclusive relations between "masculine" and "feminine," and the personal and political stakes any individual may have in identifying with or taking up a particular gender position. The concept of "androgyny," it seems to me, elides or at the least blurs these considerations in its idea of the naturalness and ease of cross-gender or double-gender identification.

15 For texts of the documents and for summary bibliography of the scholarly discussion, see *Chaucer Life-Records*, ed. Martin M. Crow and Clair C. Olson (Oxford: Clarendon Press, 1966). See also P. R. Watts, "The Strange Case of Geoffrey Chaucer and Cecilia Chaumpaigne," *Law Quarterly Review* 63 (1947): 491–515.

16 Sheila Delany, in her provocative and speculative essay on the *Manciple's Tale*, is an exception here; see her *Writing Woman: Women Writers and Women in Literature, Medieval to Modern* (New York: Schocken, 1983), pp. 47–75.

17 Robinson, ed., *The Works of Geoffrey Chaucer*, xxiii.

18 See Theodore F. T. Plucknett, "Chaucer's Escapade," *Law Quarterly*

Review 64 (1948): 33–36. J. B. Post's essay, "Ravishment of Women and the Statutes of Westminster" (in *Legal Records and the Historian*, ed. J. H. Baker [London: Royal Historical Society, 1978], pp. 150–64), provides discussion and texts of the 1275 and 1285 Statutes; the statutes effectively blurred the distinctions between elopement, abduction, and sexual violation. For canon law's earlier blurring of these distinctions, see James A. Brundage, *Law, Sex, and Christian Society in Medieval Europe* (Chicago: Univ. of Chicago Press, 1987), p. 209.

19 Martin M. Crow and Virginia E. Leland, "Chaucer's Life," in *The Riverside Chaucer*, pp. xxi–xxii.

20 See Plucknett, "Chaucer's Escapade," pp. 33–36; and Haldeen Braddy, "Chaucer, Alice Perrers, and Cecily Chaumpaigne," *Speculum* 52 (1977): 906–11. Braddy identifies Cecilia as Alice Perrers's stepdaughter, a discovery that Donald Howard uses in his speculations about Cecilia's motives in *Chaucer*, pp. 317–20.

21 Lee Patterson makes a related point when, in his critique of New Historicism, he states that analyzing all historical actions as symbols reduces or obviates their practical impact or possibility:

> It is true that the literary historian must perforce operate within the closed world of textuality, and that he must not hypostasize a part of his evidence as the historically real. But our experience also teaches us that the historically real—as economic, political, social, and material reality—does indeed exist, and that action in the world has a presence and consequentiality that cannot be evaded.
>
> (*Negotiating the Past: The Historical Understanding of Medieval Literature* [Madison: Univ. of Wisconsin Press, 1987], pp. 62–63)

22 This is a crucial distinction several critics have begun to consider in relation to medieval texts: see, for example, Sheila Delany, "Rewriting Woman Good: Gender and the Anxiety of Influence in Two Late-Medieval Texts," in *Chaucer in the Eighties*, ed. Julian N. Wasserman and Robert J. Blanch (Syracuse, N.Y.: Syracuse University Press, 1986), pp. 75–92; and Susan Schibanoff, "Taking the Gold Out of Egypt: The Art of Reading as a Woman," in *Gender and Reading*, ed. Elizabeth A. Flynn and Patrocinio P. Schweikart (Baltimore: Johns Hopkins University Press, 1986), pp. 83–106.

23 For varied and nuanced perspectives on the problematic relationship between sex and gender, see *Men in Feminism*, ed. Alice Jardine and Paul Smith (New York: Methuen, 1987). Stephen Heath's "Male Feminism" (pp. 1–32) is especially clear and cogent in its articulation of the issues.

24 Petrarch wrote to Boccaccio in 1366 in praise of his young copyist:

although the letters of other scribes are sumptuous but ill defined,
those of his copyist are clear, neat, and chaste:

> Quas tu olim illius manu scriptas, prestante Deo, aspicies, non
> vaga quidem ac luxurianti litera . . . sed alia quadam castigata et
> clara seque ultro oculis ingerente.

> [God willing, you will see them [Petrarch's *Familiar Letters*] some-
> time, written in his hand, not with that pompous and fancy let-
> tering . . . but in neat and clear lettering, affecting more than just
> the eyes.]
> (*Le Familiari* 23.19, ed. Umberto Bosco [Florence: Sansoni, 1942],
> 4:205; trans. Aldo S. Bernardo, under the title *Letters on Familiar
> Matters* [Baltimore: Johns Hopkins Univ. Press, 1985], 3:301).

In *Seniles* 5.1, a letter to Boccaccio actually written at about this time,
Petrarch writes of the priest whom he has employed: "Whether he
will, as a priest, perform his duty conscientiously, or, as a copyist, be
ready to deceive, I cannot yet say" (trans. James Harvey Robinson and
Henry Winchester Rolfe, in *Petrarch: The First Modern Scholar and Man
of Letters*, 2d ed. [New York and London: Putnam's Sons, 1914], pp.
27–28).

25 Eugène Vinaver, "Principles of Textual Emendation," in *Studies in
French Language and Medieval Literature Presented to Mildred K. Pope*
(Manchester: Manchester Univ. Press, 1939), pp. 351–69. See B. A.
Windeatt's comments on the moralizing diction of textual criticism:
"The technical vocabulary of editing expresses itself through metaphors of moral degradation from purity of text" ("The Scribes as
Chaucer's Early Critics," *SAC* 1 [1979]:119). Windeatt's edition of *Troilus and Criseyde* (London and New York: Longman, 1984), attempts
to correct this moralistic view of scribal contamination by speaking
of scribal variants and interpretations. (For an example of the traditional textual criticism of Chaucer to which Windeatt is reacting, see
R. K. Root, *The Textual Tradition of Chaucer's "Troilus"* and *The Manuscripts of Chaucer's "Troilus."* A history of textual criticism of Chaucer
can be found in Paul G. Ruggiers, ed., *Editing Chaucer: The Great Tradition* [Norman, Okla.: Pilgrim Books, 1984].) For similar reflections
on scribal contamination, see Derek Pearsall, "Editing Medieval Texts:
Some Developments and Some Problems," in *Textual Criticism and Literary Interpretation*, ed. Jerome J. McGann (Chicago: Univ. of Chicago
Press, 1985), pp. 92–106; and Anne Hudson, "Middle English," in *Editing Medieval Texts*, ed. A. G. Rigg (New York: Garland, 1977), pp.
34–57.
26 See the invigorating analysis of textual editing, on which I have drawn

here, by Lee Patterson: "The Logic of Textual Criticism and the Way of Genius: The Kane-Donaldson *Piers Plowman* in Historical Perspective," in *Textual Criticism and Literary Interpretation*, pp. 55–91, esp. p. 59.

27 E. Talbot Donaldson, *Speaking of Chaucer* (London: Athlone Press, 1970), p. 103.

28 Ibid., p. 105.

29 See Peter L. Allen, "*Ars Amandi, Ars Legendi*: Love Poetry and Literary Theory in Ovid, Andreas Capellanus, and Jean de Meun," *Exemplaria* 1 (1989):181–207.

30 See Eugene Vance, "The Differing Seed: Dante's Brunetto Latini," in his *Mervelous Signals: Poetics and Sign Theory in the Middle Ages* (Lincoln: Univ. of Nebraska Press, 1986), pp. 230–55.

31 On the Redemption as an "admirable commerce," see R. A. Shoaf, *The Poem as Green Girdle: "Commercium" in "Sir Gawain and the Green Knight,"* University of Florida Monographs, Humanities no. 55 (Gainesville: Univ. Presses of Florida, 1984), pp. 15–30.

32 For a concise statement of the "substantial comparability" between women and signs, see Claude Lévi-Strauss, *Structural Anthropology*, trans. Claire Jacobson and Brooke Grundfest Schoepf (New York: Basic Books, 1963), pp. 61–62. See also his *Elementary Structures of Kinship*, trans. J. H. Bell, J. R. von Sturmer, and R. Needham, rev. ed. (Boston: Beacon Press, 1969). For Gayle Rubin's analysis of the impact of Lévi-Strauss's formulations on women, see her acute article, "The Traffic in Women: Notes on the 'Political Economy' of Sex," in *Toward an Anthropology of Women*, ed. R. R. Reiter (New York: Monthly Review Press, 1975), pp. 157–210.

33 See Jacques Lacan, "The mirror stage as formative of the function of the I as revealed in psychoanalytic experience" and "The Signification of the Phallus," in *Ecrits: A Selection*, trans. Alan Sheridan (New York: Norton, 1977), pp. 1–7 and 281–91; and his essays collected in *Feminine Sexuality: Jacques Lacan and the école freudienne*, ed. Juliet Mitchell and Jacqueline Rose, trans. Jacqueline Rose (New York: Norton, 1982). For the problematization of the place of the woman in Lacan's myth of language acquisition, see Margaret Homans, "Representation, Reproduction, and Women's Place in Language," chapter 1 of her *Bearing the Word: Language and Female Experience in Nineteenth-Century Women's Writing* (Chicago: Univ. of Chicago Press, 1986), pp. 1–39.

34 For the interrelations between structural anthropology and psychoanalytic theory, I have found Anthony Wilden very helpful: see his essay, "Lacan and the Discourse of the Other," included in *Speech and Language in Psychoanalysis*, by Jacques Lacan, trans. Anthony Wilden (Baltimore: Johns Hopkins Univ. Press, 1981), pp. 159–311.

35 See Jacques Lacan, "The Agency of the Letter in the Unconscious

or Reason since Freud," in *Ecrits: A Selection:* "Cf. the *De Magistro* of St Augustine, especially the chapter 'De significatione locutionis,' which I analysed in my seminar of 23 June, 1954" (p. 176 n. 10). For a suggestion of the deconstructive implications of Augustinian language theory, see Margaret W. Ferguson, "Saint Augustine's Region of Unlikeness: The Crossing of Exile and Language," *Georgia Review* 29 (1975): 842–64. Tracing the Platonic roots of Augustine's use of the figure of exile in *Confessions* 7, Ferguson analyzes Augustine's view of flawed, fallen human language as "exiled" into a region of dissimilitude, a region of figuration.

36 See, for example, Susan Gubar's article, "'The Blank Page' and the Issues of Female Creativity" (in *Writing and Sexual Difference*, ed. Elizabeth Abel [Chicago: University of Chicago Press, 1982], pp. 73–93), which articulates the idea, long implicit in French feminist thinking, of the text as woman's body.

37 Sed proh dolor! tam hos quam alios istorum sectantes effigiem a paterna cultura librorum et studio subtrahit triplex cura superflua, ventris videlicet, vestium et domorum.

[But alas! a threefold care of superfluities, viz., of the stomach, of dress, and of houses, has seduced these men and others following their example from the paternal care of books, and from their study.]

(*The Philobiblon of Richard of Bury* [ed. and trans. Ernest C. Thomas (London: Kegan Paul, Trench, and Co., 1887)], ch. 6, sec. 87)

38 Generositati nostrae omni die detrahitur, dum per pravos compilatores, translatores et transformatores nova nobis auctorum nomina imponuntur et, antiqua nobilitate mutata, regeneratione multiplici renascentes degeneramus omnino. Sicque vilium vitricorum nobis nolentibus affiguntur vocabula et verorum patrum nomina filiis subducuntur.

[Our purity of race is diminished every day, while new authors' names are imposed on us by worthless compilers, translators, and transformers, and losing our ancient nobility, while we are re-born in successive generations, we become wholly degenerate; and thus against our will the name of some wretched step-father is affixed to us, and the sons are robbed of the names of their true fathers.]

(Ibid., ch. 4, sec. 68)

39 "Sunt igitur transcriptiones veterum quasi quaedam propagationes recentium filiorum, ad quos paternum devolvatur officium, ne librorum municipium minuatur" (Ibid., ch. 16, sec. 207).

40 These women are, of course, the exceptions; their own discourse

and that of those around them make their exceptional status clear. Christine de Pizan's extended treatise on social obstacles to women's achievements, *Le Livre de la cité des dames*, may be taken as an epitome here. See Susan Schibanoff's recent analysis of Christine's attempt to read as a woman (to read, that is, according to her own experiences and knowledge), "Taking the Gold Out of Egypt: The Art of Reading as a Woman," in *Gender and Reading*, ed. Elizabeth A. Flynn and Patrocinio P. Schweikart (Baltimore: Johns Hopkins Univ. Press, 1986), pp. 83–106. Among the many recent discussions of medieval women's literary achievements, see Kathleen Walkup's brief comments in "By Sovereign Maidens' Might: Notes on Women in Printing" (see n. 6 above), pp. 100–104; Peter Dronke, *Women Writers of the Middle Ages: A Critical Study of Texts from Perpetua to Marguerite Porete* (Cambridge: Cambridge Univ. Press, 1984); Katharina M. Wilson, ed., *Medieval Women Writers* (Athens: Univ. of Georgia Press, 1984); and Joan M. Ferrante, "The Education of Women in the Middle Ages in Theory, Fact, and Fantasy," in *Beyond Their Sex: Learned Women of the European Past*, ed. Patricia H. Labalme (New York: New York Univ. Press, 1980), pp. 9–42.

41 Lady Alice West, Hampshire, for example, in a will proved in 1395, leaves to her son "a peyre Matins bookis," among other items, but to his wife she leaves "a masse book, and alle the bokes that I have of latyn, englisch, and frensch" (see *Fifty Earliest English Wills in the Court of Probate, London, A.D. 1387–1439*, ed. Frederick J. Furnivall, EETS o.s. 78 [London: Trübner, 1882], p. 5).

42 "Disenfranchisement" is R. Howard Bloch's term in his comments on woman's place in social history in "Medieval Misogyny," *Representations* 20 (1987): 1–24. That social structure did not accommodate literary women is suggested by the thirteenth-century author of *Urbain le Courtois*, who advises "mon filz chier" against choosing a bride who can read:

> Si femme volez esposer,
> Pensez de tei, mon filz chier,
> Pernez nule por sa beauté
> Ne nule ke soit en livre lettrié [sic],
> Car sovent sunt decevables
> Et relement sunt estables;
> Mès pernez une que soit sage,
> Ke vous ne i poise sa mariage.
>
> [If you want to take a wife,
> Think of yourself, my dear son,
> Take no woman for her beauty,

> Nor any who is skilled at reading,
> For often they are deceivers
> And rarely are they faithful;
> Instead, take one who is wise,
> Who will not trouble your marriage.]

(*Urbain le Courtois*, ed. Paul Meyer, *Romania* 32 [1903]: 72, ll. 57–64.)

I was pointed to this text by John F. Benton, "Clio and Venus: An Historical View of Medieval Love," in *The Meaning of Courtly Love*, ed. F. X. Newman (Albany: State Univ. of New York Press, 1968), pp. 19–42.

43   non habeat matrona, tibi quae iuncta récumbit,
        dicendi genus aut curvum sermone rotato
        torqueat enthymema, nec historias sciat omnes,
        sed quaedam ex libris et non intellegat.

(Juvenal, *Satires* 6.448–51, ed. G. G. Ramsay, Loeb Classical Library [Cambridge, Mass.: Harvard Univ. Press, 1940], p. 120; trans. Roger Killian et al., in Sarah Pomeroy, *Goddesses, Whores, Wives, and Slaves: Women in Classical Antiquity* [New York: Schocken, 1975], p. 172)

This passage is quoted by Lee Patterson, in his " 'For the Wyves love of Bathe': Feminine Rhetoric and Poetic Resolution in the *Roman de la Rose* and the *Canterbury Tales*," *Speculum* 58 (1983): 656.

44 Aristotle, *Politics* 1260a28–31 (trans. Benjamin Jowett, in *The Complete Works of Aristotle*, ed. Jonathan Barnes [Princeton, N.J.: Princeton Univ. Press, 1984], 2: 2000). Cited in Prudence Allen, R.S.M., *The Concept of Woman: The Aristotelian Revolution, 750 B.C. to A.D. 1250* (Montreal: Eden Press, 1985), p. 110. This encyclopedic volume contains thorough examination and documentation of classical traditions of thinking about "woman" and their continuation into the Christian era.

45   Ad mulieris enim ornatum vel honestatem pertinet quod sit taciturna, hoc enim ex verecundia provenit quae mulieribus debetur: sed hoc ad ornatum viri non pertinet, sed magis quod sicut decet loquatur. Unde et Apostolus monet quod mulieres in ecclesiis taceant, et si quid dicere volunt, domi viros suos interrogent (I *Cor.*, XIV, 34).

[For what is appropriate for the decorum of a woman or her integrity—that she be silent—comes from the modesty that is appropriate to women, but this does not pertain to the decorum of a man; rather, he should speak as is fitting. Therefore the Apostle warns, Let women keep silent in the churches and if they wish to learn anything, let them ask their husbands at home (I *Cor.* 14:34).]

(Aquinas, *In octo libros Politicorum Aristotelis expositio* 1.10, ed. Raymundi M. Spiazzi [Taurini: Marietti, 1966], p. 50)

Cited in Allen, *The Concept of Woman,* p. 400; I have altered her translation here.

46 Cf. R. Howard Bloch, who argues in "Medieval Misogyny" (*Representations* 20 [Fall 1987]:1–24) that masculine proscriptions on adornment are directed at its "perverse secondariness" and are not proscriptions of the flesh per se. Such secondariness, he argues, is a condition of the female at the Creation, a condition of ornament, and indeed a condition of all figuration or representation. As I shall develop more fully below, it seems to me that the exegetical assimilation of literality and carnality to femininity is more thorough and profound than the assimilation of the loss of the literal to femininity that Bloch suggests.

47 For the exegetical tradition, see below in this section. For the classical tradition, examples of the association of the female with matter abound: see Aristotle, *Generation of Animals* 738b20–25, trans. A. L. Peck, Loeb Classical Library (Cambridge, Mass.: Harvard Univ. Press, 1953), p. 12; and Pliny the Elder, *Natural History* 7.15, ed. H. Rackham, Loeb Classical Library (Cambridge, Mass.: Harvard Univ. Press, 1942), p. 549. This association was steadily carried through to the end of the Middle Ages by Averroës, *Colliget* 2.10, supp. 1 (*Aristotelis opera cum Averrois commentariis* [Frankfurt am Main: Minerva Verlag, 1962], p. 23); Albertus Magnus, *Quaestiones super De animalibus* 5.4 ("Utrum maior sit delectatio in viris quam in mulieribus in coitu"), ed. Ephrem Filthaut, vol. 12, *Opera omnia* (Monasterii Westfalorum in Aedibus Aschendorff, 1955), pp. 155–56; and Aquinas, *Summa theologica* 1a.92.1 ("Utrum mulier debuerit produci in prima rerum productione") and 3a.32.4 ("Utrum B. Virgo aliquid active egerit in conceptione corporis Christi") (*Opera omnia* [Parma, 1852–73; rpt. New York: Musurgia, 1948]).

48 Aristotle rejected any idea of an active contribution of seed or formative matter by the mother. The seed was a male product only, and existed "by potentiality, and we know what is the relation of potentiality to actuality," he argues in *Parts of Animals* 641b25–642a2 (trans. A. L. Peck, Loeb Classical Library [Cambridge, Mass.: Harvard Univ. Press, 1937], pp. 73–75). If the male seed is potentiality, therefore, the female matter is actuality. See Allen, *The Concept of Woman,* pp. 90–91, 95–103.

49 For discussion of the development of medieval ideas of women out of classical scientific and medical treatises, see Vern L. Bullough, "Medi-

eval Medical and Scientific Views of Women," *Viator: Medieval and Renaissance Studies* 4 (1973): 485–501. For woman as defective man, see Aristotle, *Generation of Animals* 728a13–27 (Loeb ed., p. 103); and Galen, *On the Usefulness of the Parts of the Body* 14.5–6, (trans. Margaret Tallmadge May [Ithaca, N.Y.: Cornell Univ. Press, 1968], 2:627–28. For woman as deformed man, see Aristotle, *Generation of Animals* 737a26–30, 775a12–16 (Loeb ed., pp. 175, 459–61). For woman as man turned inside out, see Galen, *Usefulness* 14.6 (trans. May, 2:628–30). Christian writers retained the classical notion of woman as imperfect; they adapted it to the notion that God's creation of male and female was flawless by distinguishing between *universal* nature and *particular* nature: the generation of men and women on the level of universal nature was willed by God, although the generation of individual women is a defect in the order of nature. See Allen, *The Concept of Woman*, p. 393. For the distinction between the individual and the species of humans, see Albertus Magnus, *Quaestiones super De animalibus* 15.2 ("Utrum generatio feminae intendatur a natura"); and Aquinas, *Summa theologica* 1a.75.4. On the creation of the female, see Aquinas, *Summa theologica* 1a.92.1. For discussion of the synthesis of Aristotle, Genesis, and New Testament discourse on the female, see Patricia Parker, *Literary Fat Ladies* (London: Methuen, 1987), pp. 178–85.

50 John F. Benton, "Trotula, Women's Problems, and the Professionalization of Medicine in the Middle Ages," *Bulletin of the History of Medicine* 59 (1985): 30–53. For the distinctive roles of *medicus* (male doctor) and *obstetrix* (female midwife)—theory and practice—see the brief comments in Helen Rodnite Lemay, "William of Saliceto on Human Sexuality," *Viator* 12 (1981): 180–81.

51 "Habet insatiabilem videndi loquendique, ut interim de tactu silentium sit, pruriginem" (Jean Gerson, *De probatione spirituum* 11 [(1415), in *Oeuvres complètes*, ed. P. Glorieux (Paris: Desclée, 1960–73), 9:184]). The treatise, prompted by Bridget's canonization, concerns false inspiration and attempts to provide some criteria for detecting it. Clearly, gender is at issue in this treatise; Gerson warns theologians of religious fervor in young people and in women, claiming that more is at stake than mere waste of time. For brief discussion of Gerson's treatise, see Barbara Obrist, "The Swedish Visionary: Saint Bridget," in *Medieval Women Writers*, ed. Katharina M. Wilson (Athens: Univ. of Georgia Press, 1984), pp. 227–39; the translation appears on p. 236.

52 Aristotle emphasizes the active role of the male in reproduction over the purely passive role of the female:

Thus, if the male is the active partner, the one who originates the

movement, and the female *qua* female is the passive one, surely
what the female contributes to the semen of the male will not be
semen but material [for the semen to work upon].
(*Generation of Animals* 729a25–30 [Loeb ed., p. 103])

Aristotle's rejection of the female seed or any female formative material was a clear break with earlier writers on generation (Parmenides,
Empedocles, Democritus, Anaxagoras, the Hippocratic writings) and
was not followed by Galen or, later, Averroës or Albertus Magnus.
All agreed, however, that passivity was the key to the female role in
reproduction: Aquinas, for example, wrote that the female was necessary but passive in reproduction (see *Summa theologica* 3a.32.4 ["Utrum
B. Virgo aliquid active egerit in conceptione corporis Christi"], also
1a.98.2 ["Utrum in statu innocentiae fuisset generatio per coitum"],
and 1a.118.1 ["Utrum anima sensitiva traducatur cum semine"]; *De
anima* 11.5 [*Opera omnia*, 8:500]; and *Summa contra gentiles* 4.11.1 [*Opera
omnia*, 5:307–8]). The male seed was understood to have primary importance. See the summary discussion in John T. Noonan, Jr., *Contraception: A History of Its Treatment by the Catholic Theologians and Canonists*
(Cambridge, Mass.: Harvard Univ. Press, 1966), pp. 88–91, and Allen,
The Concept of Woman, esp. p. 97.

53   See Aquinas' comments on monogamy in *Summa contra gentiles* 3.123:
monogamy is natural to the human species because there is in men
(*hominibus*) a certain natural solicitude to be certain of their offspring:

> Quaecumque igitur certitudinem prolis impediunt sunt contra
> naturalem instinctum humanae speciei. Si autem vir posset mulie-
> rem dimittere vel mulier virum et alteri copulari, impediretur cer-
> titudo prolis, dum mulier a primo cognita postmodum a secundo
> cognosceretur. Est igitur contra naturalem instinctum speciei hu-
> manae quod mulier a viro separetur.

> [So, whenever there are obstacles to the ascertaining of offspring
> they are opposed to the natural instinct of the human species.
> But, if a husband could put away his wife, or a wife her hus-
> band, and have sexual relations with another person, certitude
> as to offspring would be precluded, for the wife would be united
> first with one man and later with another. So, it is contrary to the
> natural instinct of the human species for a wife to be separated
> from her husband.]
> (*Opera omnia* 5:260; trans. Vernon J. Bourke, *Summa contra gentiles*
> [Notre Dame; Ind.: Univ. of Notre Dame Press, 1975], vol. 3, pt. 2,
> p. 148)

54   cum inter alia poete officia sit non eviscerare fictionibus palliata,
quin imo, si in propatulo posita sint memoratu et veneratione

digna, ne vilescant familiaritate nimia, quanta possunt industria, tegere et ab oculis torpentium auferre.

[Surely it is not one of the poet's various functions to rip up and lay bare the meaning which lies hidden in his inventions. Rather where matters truly solemn and memorable are too much exposed, it is his office by every effort to protect as well as he can and remove them from the gaze of the irreverent, that they cheapen not by too common familiarity.]

(Boccaccio, *Genealogia deorum gentilium* 14.13, ed. Vincenzo Romano [Bari: Laterza, 1951], 2:715; trans. Charles G. Osgood, under the title *Boccaccio on Poetry* [Indianapolis: Bobbs-Merrill, 1956], pp. 59–60)

55   Numenio denique inter philosophos occultorum curiosiori offensam numinum, quod Eleusinia sacra interpretando vulgaverit, somnia prodiderunt, viso sibi ipsas Eleusinias deas habitu meretricio ante apertum lupanar videre prostantes, admirantique et causas non convenientis numinibus turpitudinis consulenti respondisse iratas ab ipso se de adyto pudicitiae suae vi abstractas et passim adeuntibus prostitutas.

[Indeed, Numenius, a philosopher with a curiosity for occult things, had revealed to him in a dream the outrage he had committed against the gods by proclaiming his interpretation of the Eleusinian mysteries. The Eleusinian goddesses themselves, dressed in the garments of courtesans, appeared to him standing before an open brothel, and when in his astonishment he asked the reason for this shocking conduct, they angrily replied that he had driven them from their sanctuary of modesty and had prostituted them to every passer-by.]

(Macrobius, *Commentarii in Somnium Scipionis* 1.2.19 [ed. J. Willis (Leipzig: Teubner, 1963), pp. 7–8; trans. William Harris Stahl, *Commentary on the Dream of Scipio* (New York: Columbia Univ. Press, 1952), pp. 86–87])

56   For a short bibliography of medieval uses of this figure of the veiled text, see *Boccaccio on Poetry* (see n. 54 above), p. 157 n. 8.

57   On the relation of Augustine and Boccaccio here, see Lee W. Patterson, "Ambiguity and Interpretation: A Fifteenth-Century Reading of *Troilus and Criseyde*," *Speculum* 54 (1979): 327–29.

58   "Idcirco prudentia veterum adinvenit remedium, quo lascivium humanum caperetur ingenium quodammodo pio dolo, dum sub voluptatis iconio delicata Minerva delitesceret in occulto" (Richard of Bury, *Philobiblon*, ch. 13, sec. 180). I have altered Thomas' translation slightly.

59   This is where Boccaccio's project diverges from the strictly moral Au-

gustinian one echoed by Richard of Bury: Boccaccio suggests a relaxation in regard to pleasure in the letter—if the reader himself is armed by faith, a certain delectation of the letter might be allowable (*Genealogia* 14.18). See Patterson, "Ambiguity and Interpretation," pp. 327–29.

60 "Mirate la dottrina che s'asconde / sotto 'l velame de li versi strani." *Inferno* 9.62–63, in *The Divine Comedy: Inferno*, ed. and trans. Charles S. Singleton (Princeton, N.J.: Princeton Univ. Press, 1970), 1: 92–3. See John Freccero, "Medusa: The Letter and the Spirit," in his *Dante: The Poetics of Conversion*, ed. Rachel Jacoff (Cambridge, Mass.: Harvard Univ. Press, 1986), pp. 119–35.

61 In *The Study of the Bible in the Middle Ages*, 3d ed., rev. (Oxford: Basil Blackwell, 1983), Beryl Smalley begins her chapter "The Fathers" by quoting Claudius, *In libros informationum litterae et spiritus super Leviticum praefatio*, and suggesting that he "sums up the patristic tradition as it had reached the scholars of Charlemagne's day" (p. 1).

62 Origen, *The Song of Songs: Commentary and Homilies*, trans. and ed. R. P. Lawson (Westminster, Md.: Newman Press, 1957), pp. 22–23.

63 See Philo of Alexandria: "The serpent is a symbol of desire[,] . . . and woman is a symbol of sense, and man, of mind" (*Questions and Answers on Genesis* 1.47, trans. Ralph Marcus, Loeb Classical Library [Cambridge, Mass.: Harvard Univ. Press, 1953], supp. 1, p. 27); Philo: "The mind in us—call it Adam—having met with outward sense, called Eve . . ." (*On the Cherubim* 17–19 [Loeb ed., p. 43]); Augustine, *De civitate Dei* 14.10–26, CC 47 (Turnhout: Brepols, 1955), pp. 430–50); Augustine, *De trinitate* 12.12, ed. W. J. Mountain, CC 50 (Turnhout: Brepols, 1968), pp. 371–73; Augustine, *De sermone Domini in monte* 1.12.36, ed. A. Mutzenbecher, CC 35 [Turnhout: Brepols, 1967], p. 39); and John Scottus Eriugena, *De divisione naturae* 4.16 (*PL* 122:814B–29B). For a discussion of this tradition of tropological analysis of the Fall, see D. W. Robertson, Jr., *A Preface to Chaucer* (Princeton, N.J.: Princeton Univ. Press, 1962), pp. 69–75. See also Albertus Magnus: "Unde, ut breviter dicam, ab omni muliere est cavendum tamquam a serpente venenoso et diabolo cornuto" ("Briefly, therefore, everyone is to be warned away from every woman as from a poisonous serpent or a horned devil") (*Quaestiones super De animalibus* 15.11 ["Utrum mas habilior sit ad mores quam femina"]). Boccaccio's association of the letter of the text with the fruit of sin (*mala frux*) appears in *Genealogia* 14.15.

64 It is tempting, in fact, to develop a theory of the transsexual text, based on the metaphor of transsexuality used by Ambrose and by Jerome. Bullough quotes and translates both church fathers: Ambrose writes

Quae non credit, mulier est, et adhuc corporei sexus appellatione signatur; nam quae credit, occurrit in virum perfectum, in mensuram aetatis plenitudinis Christi.

[She who does not believe is a woman and should be designated by the name of her bodily sex, whereas she who believes progresses to complete manhood, to the measure of the adulthood of Christ.]

(*Expositio evangeliis secundum Lucam* [*PL* 15: 1844]; quoted in Bullough, "Medieval Medical and Scientific Views of Women" [see n. 49 above], p. 499)

And Jerome states:

Quamdiu mulier partui servit et liberis, hanc habet ad virum differentiam, quam corpus ad animam. Sin autem Christo magis voluerit servire quam saeculo, mulier esse cessabit, et dicetur vir.

[As long as woman is for birth and children, she is different from man as body is from soul. But if she wishes to serve Christ more than the world, then she will cease to be a woman and will be called man.]

(*Commentariorum in Epistolam ad Ephesios libri* 3 [*PL* 26:533]; quoted in Bullough, "Medieval Medical and Scientific Views," p. 499)

But in other—and more characteristic—places in the fathers, following Paul in 1 Timothy 2:15, woman's redeeming characteristic is her childbearing function, an idea that is carried into the metaphorics of discourse on the letter, as we shall see.

65 Augustine, *De doctrina christiana* 3.7 (ed. J. Martin, CC 32 [Turnhout: Brepols, 1962], pp. 84–85). Secular works, such as those of the Platonists, can be read, according to Augustine, if their occasional, useful precepts or truths are taken for better use by Christians. He likens these truths stolen from the pagan texts to gold taken from Egyptians by the Israelites (*De doctrina* 2.40 [pp. 73–75]).

66 Augustine is concerned with the truths of pagan philosophers—specifically, Neoplatonists—but Jerome, when discussing the virtues of classical texts, alludes more to Terence and Virgil than to Plato, as Henri de Lubac notes in "La belle captive," ch. 4, pt. 5, of *Exégèse médiévale* (Paris: Aubier, 1959), vol. 1, pt. 1, p. 293.

67 Henri de Lubac points out that Jerome got this image from Origen (in a homily on Leviticus), who likens the captive woman to the pagan text but associates her beauties with the rational wisdom the Christian might find there—not, as does Jerome, with the elegances of classical rhetoric and language (*Exégèse médiévale*, vol. 1, pt. 1, pp. 291–92).

68 "Quid ergo mirum, si et ego sapientiam saecularem propter eloquii uenustatem et membrorum pulchritudinem de ancilla atque captiua

Israhelitin facere cupio?" (Jerome, *Epistulae*, letter 70 (to Magnus), ed.
I. Hilberg, CSEL 54 (Vienna: F. Tempsky, 1910), 1:702; trans. W. H. Fre-
mantle, *A Select Library of Nicene and Post-Nicene Fathers of the Christian
Church* [1892; rpt. Grand Rapids, Mich.: Eerdmans, n.d.], 6: 149.)

69 See Jerome, *Epistulae*, letter 66 (to Pammachius) (1:658).

70 Jerome returns to this metaphor at two other important interpretive
   moments: letter 21 (to Damasus), and letter 66 (to Pammachius). As
   Laura Kendrick has recently suggested, interpretive pleasure lies not
   solely in the transformation of the carnal text into a spiritual one
   but also "in preserving, by such legitimization, the arousing, carnal
   images of the original text" (*Chaucerian Play: Comedy and Control in
   the "Canterbury Tales"* [Berkeley and Los Angeles: Univ. of California
   Press, 1988], p. 28). Her original and provocative argument concerns
   interpretation as more a veiling—a cover-up—than a stripping, but
   her comments on serious exegesis as "feed[ing] on the arousing aspects of the text" while taming and transforming them are appropriate
   to my discussion here.

71 Henri de Lubac, *Exégèse médiévale*, vol. 1, pt. 1, p. 300.

72 "Nunc tamen nemo ambigit et per similitudines libentius quaeque
   cognosci et cum aliqua difficultate quaesita multo gratius inueniri"
   (Augustine, *De doctrina* 2.6.8; trans. Robertson, in *Preface to Chaucer*,
   p. 38). It is significant that both Augustine and Jerome quote the *Can-
   ticles* in this connection: that text is an intensely erotic one whose
   female object is transformed from secular bride to the Church, in a
   pleasurable application of the cloak of interpretation.

73 Guillaume de St.-Thierry, *Expositio super Cantica canticorum* 4 (*PL* 180:
   473–546; quoted in de Lubac, *Exégèse médiévale*, vol. 1, pt. 1, pp. 301–2).
   De Lubac also implicitly acknowledges this ignoring of female desire
   when he comments that Peter the Venerable could hardly use the
   image in his correspondence with Heloise and so uses Augustine's
   Egyptian gold image (p. 298).

74 Gregory IX to the masters of theology at Paris, 7 July 1228; cited by de
   Lubac, *Exégèse médiévale*, vol. 1, pt. 1, p. 300.

75 This "narrative sequence" of texts does not depend on or presuppose
   a tidy chronology of Chaucer's works. Dating the canon is of course
   a vexed issue, and tentativeness must be the rule. The Prologue to
   the *Legend of Good Women*, for example, seems to have been revised
   well after various *Canterbury Tales* were written—in about 1394–96. It
   does make sense, however, to treat the *Legend of Good Women* as a
   palinode to *Troilus and Criseyde*—for that's what even the revised Prologue says it is—and to hold discussion of the *Man of Law's Tale* until
   after treatment of the *Legend*, because the Man of Law explicitly refers

to the *Legends* as if he has read them. For a good summary discussion, see Larry D. Benson, "The Canon and Chronology of Chaucer's Works," in *The Riverside Chaucer*, pp. xxvi–xxix. And on the ordering of the *Tales*, see E. Talbot Donaldson defending the Ellesmere order as "almost" entirely satisfactory, in "The Ordering of the *Canterbury Tales*," in *Medieval Literature and Folklore: Essays in Honor of Francis Lee Utley*, ed. Jerome Mandel and Bruce A. Rosenberg (New Brunswick, N.J.: Rutgers Univ. Press, 1970), pp. 193–204.

76 Winthrop Wetherbee, in *Chaucer and the Poets: An Essay on "Troilus and Criseyde"* (Ithaca, N.Y.: Cornell Univ. Press, 1984), has recently emphasized the classical and Dantean aspirations of *Troilus and Criseyde*, in clear contradistinction to the story collections, the *Legend of Good Women* and the *Canterbury Tales*.

77 H. Marshall Leicester, Jr., makes similar claims in his article, " 'Synne Horrible': The Pardoner's Exegesis of His Tale, and Chaucer's," in *Acts of Interpretation*, ed. Mary J. Carruthers and Elizabeth D. Kirk (Norman, Okla.: Pilgrim Books, 1982), pp. 25–50. From a different (Gadamerian) perspective, Judith Ferster explores the power of interpretive models in the perception of the world, in her *Chaucer on Interpretation* (Cambridge: Cambridge Univ. Press, 1985).

CHAPTER ONE. *Reading Like a Man*

1 The *Festschrift* for Donaldson includes a section of remembrances, "Speaking of Donaldson," in which his particular efforts to encourage and further women's academic pursuits are recognized: one comment, for example, notes a significant rise in the percentage of women graduate students admitted to the Department of English at Yale University while he was director. See *Acts of Interpretation: The Text in Its Contexts, 700–1600*, ed. Mary J. Carruthers and Elizabeth D. Kirk (Norman, Okla.: Pilgrim Books, 1982), pp. 365–73.

2 E. Talbot Donaldson, "The Masculine Narrator and Four Women of Style," "Criseide and Her Narrator," and "The Ending of 'Troilus,' " in *Speaking of Chaucer* (London: Athlone Press, 1970), hereafter cited by page number in the text; "Criseyde Becoming Cressida: *Troilus and Criseyde* and *Troilus and Cressida*," in *The Swan at the Well: Shakespeare Reading Chaucer* (New Haven, Conn.: Yale Univ. Press, 1985). See also his "Cressid False, Criseyde Untrue: An Ambiguity Revisited," in *Poetic Traditions of the English Renaissance*, ed. Maynard Mack and George deForest Lord (New Haven, Conn.: Yale Univ. Press, 1982), pp. 67–83; "Briseis, Briseida, Criseyde, Cresseid, Cressid: Progress of a Heroine," in *Chaucerian Problems and Perspectives*, ed. Edward Vasta and Z. P.

Thundy (Notre Dame, Ind.: Univ. of Notre Dame Press, 1970), pp. 1–
12; and *Chaucer's Poetry: An Anthology for the Modern Reader* (New York:
Ronald Press, 1958).

3 Robertson often made comments about modern literature's appeal
"below the belt" in his lectures and seminars at Princeton University. His major statement of his critical method is *A Preface to Chaucer*
(Princeton, N.J.: Princeton Univ. Press, 1962); hereafter cited, as *Preface,* in the text. See, further, his "Historical Criticism" (1950), "Some
Observations on Method in Literary Studies" (1969; hereafter cited,
as "Method," in the text), and "The Allegorist and the Aesthetician"
(1967), all reprinted in his collection *Essays in Medieval Culture* (Princeton, N.J.: Princeton Univ. Press, 1980), for briefer, specific statements
of method.

There have been many critiques of Robertson's method, in various forms (lectures, book reviews, introductory chapters of critical
studies); I do not attempt a full critique here. For a few of the most
cogent, see Donaldson, "Patristic Exegesis in the Criticism of Medieval
Literature: The Opposition," in *Critical Approaches to Medieval Litera-
ture: Selected Papers from the English Institute, 1958–1959,* ed. Dorothy
Bethurum (New York: Columbia University Press, 1960), pp. 1–26;
R. S. Crane, "On Hypotheses in 'Historical Criticism': Apropos of
Certain Contemporary Medievalists," in his *Idea of the Humanities and
Other Essays Critical and Historical,* 2 vols. (Chicago: University of Chi-
cago Press, 1967), 2:236–60; Donald R. Howard, review of *Fruyt and
Chaf,* by Robertson and B. F. Huppé, *Speculum* 39 (1964): 537–41; David
Aers, *Piers Plowman and Christian Allegory* (London: Arnold, 1975); Paul
Theiner, "Robertsonianism and the Idea of Literary History," *Studies
in Medieval Culture* 6/7 (1976): 195–204; and, most recently, Lee Patterson, "Historical Criticism and the Development of Chaucer Studies,"
in *Negotiating the Past: The Historical Understanding of Medieval Literature*
(Madison: Univ. of Wisconsin Press, 1987), pp. 3–39. Patterson's essay
contrasts and compares exegesis and New Criticism, as I do here, and
makes many related points.

4 See Augustine, *De doctrina christiana* 2.6.7–8 (ed. J. Martin, CC 32
[Turnhout: Brepols, 1962], pp. 35–36).

5 For the latest extended statement of this position, see Chauncey Wood,
The Elements of Chaucer's "Troilus" (Durham, N.C.: Duke Univ. Press,
1984).

6 Augustine discusses prelapsarian sexuality fully in *De civitate Dei*
14.10–26, CC 47 (Turnhout: Brepols, 1955), pp. 430–50. For similar
observations about Robertson's "nostalgia," and how that nostalgia is
expressed—indeed, at times cultivated—in the works of his students,

see Roy Reid Barkley, "A Study of the Historical Method of D. W. Robertson, Jr." (Ph.D. diss., University of Texas at Austin, 1974), pp. 23, 126–27.

7 Lee Patterson, *Negotiating the Past*, p. 34.

8 Robertson does acknowledge the scholar's inevitable subjectivity, but that acknowledgment is itself rendered ironic by its placement in a footnote: "The fact that empirical attitudes, for all their vaunted objectivity, imply the reality of the nervous system of the observer rather than that of anything observed is more often felt than faced squarely" ("Method," p. 82 n.16).

9 In "The Allegorist and the Aesthetician," Robertson links post-Romantic aestheticism with Mussolini, Hitler, and Stalin (see p. 101).

10 Paul Ricoeur, *Freud and Philosophy: An Essay on Interpretation*, trans. Denis Savage (New Haven, Conn.: Yale University Press, 1970), p. 27.

11 Ibid.

12 Crane, "On Hypotheses in 'Historical Criticism,'" esp. pp. 254–58.

13 For a major study of the poem in which similar moves to control the female character are made, see Winthrop Wetherbee, *Chaucer and the Poets: An Essay on "Troilus and Criseyde"* (Ithaca, N.Y.: Cornell Univ. Press, 1984). But Wetherbee is, significantly, aware that his focus on Troilus must inevitably lead him to read Criseyde *in malo;* see chapter 6, "Character and Action: Criseyde and the Narrator." McAlpine, *The Genre of "Troilus and Criseyde,"* pp. 230–33, also analyzes critical control of Criseyde.

14 Patterson, *Negotiating the Past*, p. 24, writing specifically about Charles Muscatine's criticism. Such a concept of omniscient author was important to the New Critics, who posited an author who "is perfectly aware" of what he is doing (Cleanth Brooks [writing about Keats], *The Well Wrought Urn: Studies in the Structure of Poetry* [New York: Reynald and Hitchcock, 1947], pp. 146–47). See Jonathan Culler's incisive analysis of Brooks in Culler's *On Deconstruction: Theory and Criticism after Structuralism* (Ithaca, N.Y.: Cornell Univ. Press, 1982), pp. 180–225, esp. 200–218. Michel Foucault, in "What Is an Author?" (in his *Language, Counter-Memory, Practice: Selected Essays and Interviews*, ed. Donald F. Bouchard, trans. Donald F. Bouchard and Sherry Simon [Ithaca, N.Y.: Cornell Univ. Press, 1979]), provides a succinct analysis of the function of the concept of the author as limiting and controlling meaning. On the "reduction terms" of the New Criticism, see R. S. Crane, *The Languages of Criticism and the Structure of Poetry* (Toronto: Univ. of Toronto Press, 1953), pp. 123–24, cited by Patterson (p. 19). As Patterson puts it, "New Criticism offers its adherents an interpretation kit that includes both interpretive techniques and the prescribed result

—i.e., a reading contributing to the reign of humanism" (*Negotiating the Past,* p. 37), and, he goes on, "so does Exegetics on its side."

15 Some recent feminist literary theory, especially French feminist theory, has focused on critical categories such as unity, realism, filiation, authorial omniscience, and critical mastery of the text, as loci of patriarchal criticism. A few particular examples include Shoshana Felman, "Women and Madness: The Critical Phallacy," *Diacritics* 5, no. 4 (1975): 2–10, for a critique of realism and unity; Barbara Johnson, "Teaching Ignorance: *L'Ecole des femmes,*" *YFS* 63 (1982): 165–82, on pedagogical mastery, which can be extended to the "single authoritative teacher" (p. 182) that is the omniscient poet of the New Critics; Hélène Cixous and Catherine Clément, *The Newly Born Woman,* trans. Betsy Wing (Minneapolis: Univ. of Minnesota Press, 1986), especially "A Woman Mistress," concerning mastery in the transmission of knowledge; and Luce Irigaray, *This Sex Which Is Not One,* trans. Catherine Porter (Ithaca, N.Y.: Cornell Univ. Press, 1985), indicting the logic of discourse and attempting to discover how to speak a language of the female body, undoing representation altogether. For more on writing the body, see below, Chapter 6, note 72.

For brief overviews of feminist literary criticism, I have found two sources especially useful: Toril Moi, *Sexual/Textual Politics: Feminist Literary Theory* (London: Methuen, 1985); and Jonathan Culler's chapter on feminist criticism in his *On Deconstruction: Theory and Criticism after Structuralism* (Ithaca, N.Y.: Cornell University Press, 1982), pp. 43–64. See, further, two critiques of Culler's chapter, one by Elaine Showalter and one by Robert Scholes, in *Men in Feminism,* ed. Alice Jardine and Paul Smith (New York: Methuen, 1987), pp. 123–27 and 204–18, respectively.

16 Richard Waswo, in "The Narrator of *Troilus and Criseyde*" (*ELH* 50 [1983]: 1–25), in a keen argument about irony and the Epilogue to the poem, demonstrates that critics who ostensibly oppose Robertson's reading nonetheless agree with and proceed according to his basic contention that the Epilogue is a seamless part of the whole poem, and that there are no essential contradictions in the poem.

17 For an analysis of the poem that reads Criseyde in relation to the exigencies of Trojan society, see David Aers, "Chaucer's Criseyde: Woman in Society, Woman in Love," in *Chaucer, Langland, and the Creative Imagination* (London: Routledge and Kegan Paul, 1980), ch. 5. Aers notes that Criseyde's "bad faith was almost impossible to avoid, encouraged and prepared for by the habits and practices of the very society which would, of course, condemn such a betrayal with righteous moral indignation" (p. 135). Aers sees Criseyde's betrayal as a "complicity" with established social practices, as do I, but con-

tinues to read Troilus as oblivious to these patriarchal social practices. Here I differ from Aers, as I do from his overarching emphasis on a "social psychology," evoked by the poem, "which grasped complex interactions between individual consciousness, action, conflicting ideologies, and social organization" (p. 138). Aers argues throughout his book against readings that would de-psychologize Criseyde; I set Criseyde's subjectivity in the larger frame of her structural function within patriarchy, which itself de-emphasizes her psychological value.

18 Chaucer may have indeed deliberately pointed up the "classical" details of Boccaccio's fable, as critics have argued *pace* C. S. Lewis (see Lewis's famous essay, "What Chaucer Really Did to *Il Filostrato,*" *Essays and Studies* 17 [1932]: 56–75). See, further, Waswo's suggestion, in effect countering arguments both for Chaucer's medievalization of the tale and for his classicization, that Chaucer "Petrarchized" Boccaccio ("The Narrator of *Troilus and Criseyde,*" p. 23). For a statement of Chaucer's "historical" outlook, see Morton Bloomfield, "Chaucer's Sense of History," *JEGP* 51 (1952): 301–13, and "Distance and Predestination in *Troilus and Criseyde,*" *PMLA* 72 (1957): 14–26.

19 Roland Barthes, *The Pleasure of the Text,* trans. Richard Miller (New York: Hill and Wang, 1975), p. 10. Barthes here talks about the reader's choosing and skipping parts of a complete narrative and does not explicitly address the reader's experience of the author's leaving something out. But the effect is the same, as I see it; both experiences are of a nontotalizing reading act. Laura Kendrick mentions Barthes's notion of the pleasure of the text in her claim that criticism (reading) is "likely to be a cover-up designed to partially censor and at the same time to enable the appreciation of the forbidden pleasures of the text" (*Chaucerian Play: Comedy and Control in the "Canterbury Tales"* [Berkeley and Los Angeles: Univ. of California Press, 1988], p. 30). The body of the text here in Barthes is not explicitly gendered—the reading act is not explicitly and only a masculine one—and this is one reason the Barthesian model has been taken as sympathetic to feminist analysis. However, for a suggestion that Barthes participates in a masculine discourse of sexuality, see Naomi Schor's discussion of Barthes in "Dreaming Dissymmetry: Barthes, Foucault, and Sexual Difference," in *Men in Feminism,* pp. 98–110. Donald Howard hints at an idea of "intermittence" in his discussion of the erotic rhythms of these authorial interruptions: he finds that the interruptions create in the reader an "oscillation between interest and detachment which parallels the ebb and flow of passion during protracted lovemaking" ("Literature and Sexuality: Book III of Chaucer's *Troilus,*" *Massachusetts Review* 8 [1967]:448).

20 Barthes, *The Pleasure of the Text,* p. 11.

21 *Translatio*, according to Quintilian and Donatus, denoted trope or figure of thought in general, as well as allegory, metaphor, metonymy,
and other tropes in particular. That substitution is the mechanism of
translatio is apparent in Quintilian:

> Est igitur tropos sermo a naturali et principali significatione trans-
> latus ad aliam ornandae orationis gratia, vel, ut plerique gramma-
> tici finiunt, dictio ab eo loco, in quo propria est, translata in eum,
> in quo propria non est. . . . Quare in tropis ponuntur verba alia
> pro aliis.
>
> [The name of *trope* is applied to the transference of expressions
> from their natural and principal signification to another, with a
> view to the embellishment of style or, as the majority of gram-
> marians define it, the transference of words and phrases from
> the place which is strictly theirs to another to which they do not
> properly belong. . . . Therefore the substitution of one word for
> another is placed among *tropes*.]
>
> (*Institutio oratoria* 9.1.4–5, ed. and trans. H. E. Butler, Loeb Clas-
> sical Library [Cambridge, Mass.: Harvard Univ. Press, 1969],
> pp. 348–51)

See also Donatus, *Ars grammatica* 3.6, ed. Henricus Keil (Hildesheim:
Georg Olms, 1961), 4:399. Geoffrey of Vinsauf's discussion of *ornatus
difficilis* also makes it clear that poetic trope depends on the substitution of one signifier's attributes for another (*Poetria nova* ll.765–67a [in
E. Faral, ed., *Les Arts poétiques du XIIe et du XIIIe siècle* (Paris: Honoré
Champion, 1958), p. 221]. See Eugene Vance, "Chaucer, Spenser, and
the Ideology of Translation," *Canadian Review of Comparative Literature* 8
(1981): 217–38, later expanded in his *Mervelous Signals: Poetics and Sign
Theory in the Middle Ages* (Lincoln: Univ. of Nebraska Press, 1986), pp.
311–51. I shall discuss *translatio* in its various functions (as interlingual
substitution, as trope, and as interpretation) in more detail in reference
to the *Clerk's Tale*; here I am mainly concerned with its affective value
for the narrator. Vance provides a different view of the value of translation in *Troilus and Criseyde*: he stresses that Chaucer viewed such acts
of substitution of "improper" for "proper" terms as immoral: "While
rhetoricians could see figurative speech . . . as a source of esthetic delight, Chaucer saw the cult of *translatio* as an antisocial and subversive
tendency," finally (at the end of the poem) censuring poetry itself as a
rhetorical act (p. 228).

22 I follow the punctuation of this stanza in Robinson, *Works of Geoffrey
Chaucer*, 2nd ed. Ida L. Gordon reads this particular stanza as a joke,
"a mockery of the narrator's attitude to his 'auctour'. . . . To give

'every word right thus' of a song (presumably composed by Troilo) of which his 'auctour' gives only the 'sentence' is a feat indeed on the narrator's part" (*The Double Sorrow of Troilus: A Study of Ambiguities in "Troilus and Criseyde"* [Oxford: Clarendon Press, 1970], p. 78). H. Marshall Leicester, Jr., similarly stresses the uncertainty in this stanza, in "Oure Tonges *Différance:* Textuality and Deconstruction in Chaucer," in *Medieval Texts and Contemporary Readers,* ed. Laurie A. Finke and Martin B. Shichtman (Ithaca, N.Y.: Cornell Univ. Press, 1987), pp. 15–26 (an article which was originally presented as a paper at the 1981 MLA Convention in New York). Compare Waswo, who mentions this way of reading the passage and suggests that another reading is also possible: Lollius is taken to give "not only" the gist "but . . . every word." Nevertheless, "the intromission of three clauses along with the narrative 'I' itself between the 'but' and the 'every' sufficiently weakens the formula to create considerable uncertainty about who is giving what" ("The Narrator of *Troilus and Criseyde,*" p. 17).

23 Jean de Meun writes in his preface that he took as a commandment Philip IV's suggestion that he express "la sentence" of the author without following too closely "les paroles du latin." He explains that a word-for-word rendering of the Latin into French would still have been too obscure to those readers who do not know Latin well. See "Boethius' *De consolatione* by Jean de Meun," ed. V. L. Dedeck-Héry, *Mediaeval Studies* 14 (1952): 168.

24 Jean de Hareng shows himself to be very sensitive to the particular character of each language (Latin and French), and his sense of the difficulty of translation comes through in his afterword. As closely as he can, he states, he follows the author's manner of treatment of the subject, but it is not possible to follow it absolutely, since properties of diction and syntax vary from language to language. Consequently, the translator must know the peculiarities of each language, writes Jean, and he will find that sometimes it is appropriate to translate "parole por parole," more often "sentence por sentence," and sometimes, because of the obscurity of the "sentence," it is appropriate to add and subtract. See Jean's afterword in "Notice sur la *Rhétorique de Cicéron,* traduite par Maître Jean D'Antioche, ms. 590 de Musée Condé," by Leopold Delisle, in *Notices et extraits* (Paris: Klincksieck, 1899), vol. 36, p. 261; and in "Humanisme et traductions au Moyen Age," by Jacques Monfrin, *Journal des savants* [1963]: 169.

25 On the model of *translatio studii,* medieval translation was seen as the handing down of authoritative sentence from past to present: the received idea was transferred to a contemporary context, historical differences unnoticed in the service of sentence. See Douglas Kelly,

"Translatio Studii: Translation, Adaptation, and Allegory in Medieval French Literature," *Philological Quarterly* 57 (1978): 291, for a discussion of *translatio* as a literary method of transferring received ideas. For a development of translation as literary appropriation and for a good bibliography of translation in the Middle Ages, see John Duane Longo, "Literary Appropriation as *Translatio* in Chaucer and the *Roman de la Rose*" (Ph.D. diss., Princeton University, 1982). See also Stephen G. Nichols, Jr., *Romanesque Signs: Early Medieval Narrative and Iconography* (New Haven, Conn.: Yale Univ. Press, 1983), on *translatio* as an important device in historical narrative of the early Middle Ages.

26 As Donald W. Rowe has pointed out, the narrator ends his description of the coming day with an *"aube"* ("But cruel day—so wailaway the stounde!" [3.1695]), just as the lovers end their nights with *aubes* bewailing the coming of the day (*O Love, O Charite! Contraries Harmonized in Chaucer's "Troilus"* [Carbondale: Southern Illinois Univ. Press, 1976], p. 160). And the narrator echoes Troilus' understanding of love as a cosmic force: both utter prayers to Love that are adapted from Boethius (bk. 2, meter 8).

27 Barthes, *The Pleasure of the Text*, p. 12.

28 As Wetherbee observes (*Chaucer and the Poets*, pp. 236–37), the syntax of the stanza renders unclear who, exactly, is speaking line 1825: it could be the completion of Troilus' thoughts or of the narrator's own, effectively damning his own poetic project:

> And in hymself he lough right at the wo
> Of hem that wepten for his deth so faste,
> And dampned al oure werk that foloweth so
> The blynde lust, the which that may nat laste,
> And sholden al oure herte on heven caste.
>
> (5.1821–25)

29 Wetherbee emphasizes the narrator's final "liberation" from his emotional attachment to the love story, suggesting that it is only with this release in the Epilogue that he is able to realize the transcendent spiritual value of poetry. See "The Ending of the *Troilus*," in *Chaucer and the Poets*, pp. 224–243.

30 Various parallels between the narrator and Pandarus have been noticed by critics: see, for example, Waswo, "The Narrator of *Troilus and Criseyde*"; Nevill Coghill, *The Poet Chaucer* (1949; rpt. London: Oxford Univ. Press, 1950), pp. 75–76; Donaldson, "Criseide and Her Narrator" and "The Ending of 'Troilus' "; Donald Rowe, *O Love! O Charite!*; and Evan Carton, "Complicity and Responsibility in Pandarus' Bed and Chaucer's Art," *PMLA* 94 (1979): 47–61. And several critics have specifically focused on Pandarus's function as "makere," among them,

Donaldson, "Chaucer's Three 'P's': Pandarus, Pardoner, and Poet," *Michigan Quarterly Review* 14 (1975): 282–301; Thomas A. Van, "Chaucer's Pandarus as an Earthly Maker," *Southern Humanities Review* 12 (1978): 89–97; and Rose A. Zimbardo, "Creator and Created: The Generic Perspective of Chaucer's *Troilus and Criseyde*," *ChauR* 11 (1977): 283–98. My reading of Pandarus owes much to Charles Muscatine, *Chaucer and the French Tradition: A Study in Style and Meaning* (Berkeley and Los Angeles: Univ. of California Press, 1957), pp. 137–53.

31 And on the morning after, if Pandarus does not actually enjoy Criseyde firsthand he certainly replays a *version* of Troilus' enjoyment of her the night before: Troilus "sodeynly" takes her in his arms (3.1186), and Pandarus "sodeynly" thrusts his arm under her neck (3.1574) as he jokes, pokes, and finally kisses her.

32   ergo fungar vice cotis, acutum
    reddere quae ferrum valet, exsors ipsa secandi;
    munus et officium, nil scribens ipse, docebo.
    (Horace, *Ars poetica* ll. 304–6, ed. and trans. H. Rushton Fairclough, Loeb Classical Library [Cambridge, Mass.: Harvard Univ. Press, 1955], pp. 474–77)

33 It is only a step away from these eroticized "instruments" of literary creation to the "sely instruments" of the Wife of Bath and her husbands.

34 Donaldson, "Chaucer's Three 'P's'," pp. 298–99.

35 See Donaldson, "The Ending of 'Troilus,'" p. 95; and Robert B. Burlin, *Chaucerian Fiction* (Princeton, N.J.: Princeton Univ. Press, 1977), pp. 131–33. Wetherbee acknowledges some anxiety and unresolved tension in the narrator's response to the tale in the ending, but suggests that most important is the narrator's discovery, through poetry, of transcendent spiritual experience (*Chaucer and the Poets*, pp. 20, 232).

36 Burlin quotes Erich Fromm, *Man for Himself* (New York: Rinehart, 1947), on the flight into "soothing and harmonious ideologies," in the chapter on *Troilus and Criseyde* in his *Chaucerian Fiction*, p. 133. I am indebted to Burlin's view of the end of the poem.

37 For varied discussions of precisely this point, see *Feminist Theory: A Critique of Ideology*, ed. Nannerl O. Keohane, Michelle Z. Rosaldo, and Barbara C. Gelpi (Chicago: Univ. of Chicago Press, 1982).

38 Waswo, "The Narrator of *Troilus and Criseyde*," p. 20.

39 Also noticing the *mise en abyme* of the text here, and analyzing the text's plurality, especially in reference to gesture, is John P. Hermann, "Gesture and Seduction in *Troilus and Criseyde*," *SAC* 7 (1985): 119. David Anderson traces the Theban subtext of the poem; see "Theban History in Chaucer's *Troilus*," *SAC* 4 (1982): 109–33.

40 Lee Patterson commented on the "central recursiveness" of Theban history in a lecture on *Anelida and Arcite* at the University of California at Berkeley in Spring 1985. See Patricia Parker, *Inescapable Romance: Studies in the Poetics of a Mode* (Princeton, N.J.: Princeton Univ. Press, 1979), on the "dilation" of romance.

41 Francis Grady develops this point in a reading of the first scene of book 2 in his provocative essay, "Thebes, Troy, and Prophecy in *Troilus and Criseyde*" (Department of English, University of California, Berkeley, 1985).

42 From this perspective, Calkas, the diviner, might be seen as feminized. Although his action is the paradigmatic patriarchal gesture in the poem—he keeps and moves Criseyde as his possession (she is a "moeble," just as is the rest of his furniture)—there are parallels between the father and the daughter. He is a traitor, of course, as will his daughter be; and, like Criseyde, he moves from the Trojan camp to the Greek camp (though by his own choice). Most interestingly, his reading of the stars—his "calkulynge"—is scorned in the poem, made fun of, dismissed—by Criseyde herself, in book 4.

43 I discuss hagiographic narrative form, based as it is on a principle of repetition, in detail in reference to the *Legend of Good Women*. Here, let it suffice to quote Gregory of Tours's oft-cited remark:

> Unde manifestum est, melius dici vitam patrum quam vitas, quia, cum sit diversitas meritorum virtutumque, una tamen omnes vita corporis alit in mundo.

> [It is better to talk about the life of the Fathers than the lives, because, though there may be some difference in their merits and virtues, yet the life of one body nourished them all in the world.]
> (*Gregorii episcopi Turonensis Liber vitae patrum*, ed. Bruno Krusch, in MGH, Scriptores rerum merovingicarum [Hannover: Hahn, 1885], 1:662–63; trans. Charles W. Jones, *Saints' Lives and Chronicles in Early England* (Ithaca, N.Y.: Cornell Univ. Press, 1947), p. 62)

44 For an excellent review of Criseyde's literary history, see Gretchen Mieszkowski, "The Reputation of Criseyde, 1155–1500," *Transactions of the Connecticut Academy of Arts and Sciences* 43 (1971): 71–153. She cites, for example, three works available to Chaucer, all of which represent Criseyde as an exemplum of fickleness: Benoît de Sainte-Maure, *Roman de Troie* (c. 1160), in which not only the narrator but Troilus excoriates Criseyde for her infidelity and predicts that she will take on even more lovers in the future (see *Le Roman de Troie par Benoît de Sainte-Maure*, vv. 13429–37, 20092–102, ed. Leopold Constans, SATF [Paris, 1904–12], 2:299–300, 3:282–83).; Guido delle Colonna, *Historia destruc-*

tionis Troiae (1287), in which the narrator blames Troilus' credulity (see *Guido de Columnis Historia destructionis Troiae*, ed. Nathaniel Edward Griffin [Medieval Academy of America, 1936], p. 164); and Boccaccio's *Il Filostrato*, whose narrator warns men in the end to be cautious in trusting women because of the example of Criseida (see *The Filostrato of Giovanni Boccaccio* 8.30 [ed. and trans. Nathaniel Edward Griffin and Arthur Beckwith Myrick (Philadelphia, 1929), pp. 496–97]). See, further, Mieszkowski's article, "R. K. Gordon and the *Troilus and Criseyde* Story" (*Chaucer Review* 15 [1980]:127–37), on the translations of Benoît and Boccaccio by Gordon in his anthology published in 1934, which continue to interpret Criseyde by excision and manipulation of texts.

45 Judith Fetterley, "Introduction: On the Politics of Literature," in her book *The Resisting Reader* (Bloomington: Indiana Univ. Press, 1978), pp. xi–xxvi.

46 Gayle Rubin, "The Traffic in Women: Notes on the 'Political Economy' of Sex," in *Toward an Anthropology of Women*, ed. R. R. Reiter (New York: Monthly Review Press, 1975), pp. 157–210; hereafter cited, by page number, in the text. Rubin in fact argues against such an imprecise use of the term "patriarchal": it doesn't, she claims, distinguish "between the human capacity and necessity to create a sexual world," on the one hand, and, on the other, "the empirically oppressive ways in which sexual worlds have been organized" (p. 168). But I follow Eve Kosofsky Sedgwick, in her *Between Men: English Literature and Male Homosocial Desire* (New York: Columbia Univ. Press, 1985), in finding the term generally useful. Sedgwick (p. 3) quotes Heidi Hartmann's definition of patriarchy as "relations between men, which have a material base, and which, though hierarchical, establish or create interdependence and solidarity among men that enable them to dominate women" (Heidi Hartmann, "The Unhappy Marriage of Marxism and Feminism: Towards a More Progressive Union," in *Women and Revolution*, ed. Lydia Sargent [Boston: South End Press, 1981], pp. 1–41; quotation is from p. 14).

47 Marcel Mauss, *Essai sur le don, forme archaïque de l'échange* (Paris, 1925); translated by Ian Cunnison, under the title *The Gift: Forms and Functions of Exchange in Archaic Societies* (New York: Norton, 1967).

48 Claude Lévi-Strauss, *Les Structures élémentaires de la parenté*, rev. ed. (Paris and The Hague: Mouton, 1967); translated by J. H. Bell, J. R. von Sturmer, and R. Needham, under the title *The Elementary Structures of Kinship* (Boston: Beacon Press, 1969), p. 65.

49 Judith Herman and Lisa Hirschman, "Father-Daughter Incest," *Signs* 2 (1977): 735–56.

50 See Maureen Fries, " 'Slydynge of Corage': Chaucer's Criseyde as

Feminist and Victim," in *The Authority of Experience: Essays in Feminist Criticism*, ed. Arlyn Diamond and Lee R. Edwards (Amherst: Univ. of Massachusetts Press, 1977), pp. 45–59, for an early feminist attempt to analyze Criseyde's position vis-à-vis the men around her in Troy. More recently, David Aers, in "Chaucer's Criseyde" (see n. 17 above), has provided a fuller articulation of Criseyde's position as woman in masculine society.

51 Charles Muscatine, *Chaucer and the French Tradition*, p. 164.

52 Donaldson, "The Masculine Narrator and Four Women of Style" (see n. 2 above), p. 57. Arlyn Diamond suggests that Criseyde's behavior is better seen as a series of adaptations to and negotiations with the structures of masculine control around her than as actions that proceed from a solid core of character (*"Troilus and Criseyde:* The Politics of Love," in *Chaucer in the Eighties*, ed. Julian N. Wasserman and Robert J. Blanch [Syracuse, N.Y.: Syracuse Univ. Press, 1986], pp. 93–103).

53 Shakespeare's *Troilus and Cressida* clearly and explicitly elaborates on the male bonding that is at the heart of patriarchal exchange of women. His representation includes the whole spectrum of homosocial-homoerotic relations (I use the terms as Eve Kosofsky Sedgwick has developed them, in *Between Men* [see note 46]), from Troilus and Pandarus (see 1.1.97; 1.2.231), to Hector and Ajax (4.5.135), to Achilles and Patroclus (3.3.222–235; 5.1.15).

54 For a discussion of the conventions and behaviors of "chivalry" as undertaken for masculine satisfactions only, see John F. Benton, "Clio and Venus: An Historical View of Medieval Love," in *The Meaning of Courtly Love*, ed. F. X. Newman (Albany: State Univ. of New York Press, 1968), pp. 34–35. See also E. Jane Burns, "The Man Behind the Lady in Troubadour Lyric," *Romance Notes* 25 (1985): 254–70.

55 Criseyde herself refers to the constitutive bonds between men in Troy, in arguing that Troilus must not leave Troy and his Trojan men for her, for a woman:

> But that ye speke, awey thus for to go
> And leten alle youre frendes, God forbede
> For any womman that ye sholden so,
> And namely syn Troie hath now swich nede
> Of help. . . .
>
> (4.1555–59)

56 As Patricia Klindienst Joplin suggests (using René Girard's theory of exchange of violence behind the exchange of women), Helen is just a pretext for maintaining violence between men—maintaining, that is, differentiated political groups: "In the ambiguities of his final plays,

Euripides comes as close as anyone to suggesting that Helen was always a pretext, and that the women who are violated (or, like Clytemnestra, who become violent) in exchanges between men are victims of the polis itself" ("The Voice of the Shuttle Is Ours," *Stanford Literature Review* 1 [1984]: 41).

57 For the suggestion that Pandarus has an autobiographical relevance to Chaucer, see Waswo ("The Narrator of *Troilus and Criseyde*"), who also comments that Chaucer, "constrained by necessity" as a bourgeois in an aristocratic court, had much in common with the aristocratic ladies as well (p. 14). For Criseyde as an autobiographical figure, see Mark Lambert, "*Troilus*, Books I–III: A Criseydan Reading," in *Essays on "Troilus and Criseyde,"* ed. Mary Salu, *Chaucer Studies* 3 (1979): 105–25.

58 As Gretchen Mieszkowski suggests in " 'Pandras' in Deschamps' Ballade for Chaucer" (*ChauR* 9 [1975]: 327–36), "pandras" is a probable reference to the character in Chaucer's *Troilus and Criseyde*. Eugen Lerch proposed this reading in "Zu einer Stelle bei Eustache Deschamps" (*Romanische Forschungen* 62 [1950]: 67–68), arguing against the prevailing reading established by Paget Toynbee in "The Ballade Addressed by Eustache Deschamps to Geoffrey Chaucer" (*Academy* 40 [1891]: 432), of "pandras" as Pandrasus, a character in Wace's *Brut*. Lerch's hypothesis went unnoticed until Mieszkowski resuscitated and argued for it.

CHAPTER TWO. *"The naked text in English to declare"*

1 As E. T. Donaldson comments on Criseyde's literary history, "From Benoît de Sainte Maure, who invented her, up to Dryden, who destroyed her by making her faithful, the Cressid figure had only a single raison d'être, her infidelity" ("Cressid False, Criseyde Untrue: An Ambiguity Revisited," in *Poetic Traditions of the English Renaissance*, ed. Maynard Mack and George deForest Lord [New Haven, Conn.: Yale Univ. Press, 1982], p. 68). See also Gretchen Mieszkowski, "The Reputation of Criseyde, 1155–1500," *Transactions of the Connecticut Academy of Arts and Sciences* 43 (1971): 71–153.

2 For a discussion of male authorial apologies to female readers that cites the *Legend* in making this point, see Susan Schibanoff, "Taking the Gold Out of Egypt: The Art of Reading as a Woman," in *Gender and Reading: Essays on Readers, Texts, and Contexts*, ed. Elizabeth A. Flynn and Patrocinio P. Schweickart (Baltimore: Johns Hopkins Univ. Press, 1986), pp. 83–106. Schibanoff analyzes the "immasculation" of woman's literary response, as I do here.

3 I wish to acknowledge a general indebtedness in my reading of the *Legend of Good Women* to Elaine Hansen, "Irony and the Antifeminist Narrator in Chaucer's *Legend of Good Women*," *JEGP* 82 (1983): 11–31, and John M. Fyler, "The *Legend of Good Women:* Palinode and Procrustean Bed," chapter 4 of his *Chaucer and Ovid* (New Haven, Conn.: Yale Univ. Press, 1979), pp. 96–123.

4 The F version (formerly called B) is found in Bodleian MS. Fairfax 16 and ten other manuscripts; the G version (formerly A) is extant in a single manuscript, Cambridge MS. Gg. 4.27. There has been considerable debate over the causes and chronology of the two versions, and the questions are still open; but critics generally agree these days that G is Chaucer's revision, made about eight years later, of the original F. If F dates from 1386–88, G dates subsequently from 1394–96—about the time, as Alfred David suggests, Chaucer must have been working on those other poems having to do with antifeminist thought, the Prologue to the *Wife of Bath's Tale* and the *Merchant's Tale; see The Strumpet Muse* (Bloomington: Indiana Univ. Press, 1976), p. 50.

5 See Eric Hicks, ed., *Le Débat sur "Le Roman de la rose"* (Paris: Champion, 1977) for the dossier of the *querelle.* John Fleming, "Hoccleve's 'Letter of Cupid' and the 'Quarrel' over the *Roman de la Rose*" (*Medium Aevum* 40 [1971]: 21–40), focuses on changing styles of reading the *Rose;* Christine de Pizan comes off rather badly in this analysis. It is interesting indeed to note Christine's totalizing, ideological techniques of reading as she argues against what she perceives as Jean de Meun's antifeminism: she alleges that Jean was simply untruthful in his excessive and impetuous defamation of women; even if some of these negative images were true, Christine goes on to say, they shouldn't be represented. The letter of the *Rose,* she argues, is not unambiguous, as it should be, and its female characters are not worthy of attention, let alone imitation. See Christine's letters to Jean de Montreuil (c. 1401) and Pierre Col (2 October 1402). In her revisionist feminist project, then, Christine would nevertheless keep the dangerous feminine in line. This accords with the admixture of revisionist and conservative social vision in Christine's work, especially *Le Livre de la cité des dames.* For a discussion of that admixture, see Sheila Delany, "Rewriting Woman Good: Gender and the Anxiety of Influence in Two Late-Medieval Texts," in *Chaucer in the Eighties,* ed. Julian N. Wasserman and Robert J. Blanch (Syracuse, N.Y.: Syracuse Univ. Press, 1986), pp. 75–92.

6 See Lee W. Patterson, "Ambiguity and Interpretation: A Fifteenth-Century Reading of *Troilus and Criseyde*" (*Speculum* 54 [1979]: 297–330), slightly revised as chapter 4 of *Negotiating the Past: The Histori-*

cal Understanding of Medieval Literature (Madison: Univ. of Wisconsin Press, 1987).

7 A passage in the early version of the Prologue to the *Legend* suggests that it was royally commissioned: Alceste instructs the narrator, "And whan this book ys maad, yive it the quene, / On my byhalf, at Eltham or at Sheene" (F: 496–97). The idea of a royal *command* seems to modern scholars to be a fiction, but it proved immediately useful and satisfying nonetheless: Lydgate mentions it in his notice of *Legend of Good Women* in the *Fall of Princes*: "This poete wrot, at request off the queen, / A legende off parfit hoolynesse, / Off Goode Women to fynde out nynteen / That dede excelle in bounte and fairnesse" (*Lydgate's Fall of Princes*, ed. Henry Bergen, EETS e.s. 121 [London: Oxford Univ. Press, 1924], 1.330–33). Discussions of the occasional nature of the poem dominated the scholarship in the late nineteenth century and early twentieth century; there seems to be a general sense these days that the poem did arise from some discussion at court. See Alfred David, "The Man of Law vs. Chaucer: A Case in Poetics" (*PMLA* 82 [1967]: 217–25), for the suggestion that the God of Love is "repeating objections to Chaucer's works made either seriously or in jest by members of his circle who thought that they knew best what he should write about" (p. 219). In the Prologue to the *Legend of Good Women*, according to David, "Chaucer is dramatizing the difficulties of a poet who writes for a small and opinionated audience" (p. 219). See also Robert B. Burlin, *Chaucerian Fiction* (Princeton, N.J.: Princeton Univ. Press, 1977), p. 34. As John M. Fyler comments in his *Chaucer and Ovid* (New Haven, Conn.: Yale Univ. Press, 1979), there is no way to know whether the *Legend of Good Women* resulted from adverse reaction to *Troilus and Criseyde;* he doesn't believe, however, that Chaucer's "penance" can be regarded as at all serious (p. 97).

8 For such an analysis of the *Book of the Duchess*, see D. W. Robertson, Jr., and B. F. Huppé, *Fruyt and Chaf* (Princeton, N.J.: Princeton Univ. Press, 1963), ch. 2.

9 H. Marshall Leicester, Jr., in "Dreaming and Writing: Temporality and Narrative in the Prologue to the *Legend of Good Women*," a talk presented at the 1984 Modern Language Association convention, analyzed the implications of this uncomfortable setting in a reading of the Prologue that stressed its dark, menacing aspects.

10 John M. Fyler, *Chaucer and Ovid*, p. 120.

11 Cupid's basic literary abilities are routinely assailed by critics. I take his objections to the narrator's works seriously and see that he is, in a sense, a paradigmatic reader: he is not incapable, or simpleminded, but is a particularly, defensively totalizing reader, a masculine reader.

For analyses of the God of Love that see him as simpleminded or frivolous, see David, "The Man of Law vs. Chaucer"; Lisa J. Kiser, *Telling Classical Tales* (Ithaca, N.Y.: Cornell Univ. Press, 1983), pp. 62–70; and Fyler, *Chaucer and Ovid*, pp. 96–123. It should be pointed out, however, that Cupid's taste for stories (his emphasis on plot, not style or treatment) does not alone brand him as a shallow or bad reader; it is shared by late-medieval writers in all genres, and his emphasis on the narrator's choice of material as the most important step in the process of writing reflects the traditional and rhetorical nature of medieval literary composition. See J. A. Burrow, *Ricardian Poetry: Chaucer, Gower, Langland, and the Gawain-Poet* (New Haven, Conn.: Yale Univ. Press, 1971), pp. 47–92; and Robert Worth Frank, *Chaucer and the "Legend of Good Women"* (Cambridge, Mass.: Harvard Univ. Press, 1972), pp. 30–36, 185–87. J. L. Lowes, in "Chaucer and the *Ovide moralisé*" (*PMLA* 33 [1918]: 318), suggests that Chaucer takes over from the *Ovide moralisé* "details which enhance the vividness and clarify the motivation of the narrative" (speaking in particular of the *Legend of Philomela*).

It's also important to note that Cupid's specific objection to the *Rose*—that in it,

> of myne olde servauntes thow mysseyest,
>
> . . . .
>
> And lettest folk to han devocyoun
> To serven me, and holdest it folye
> To truste on me
>
> (Prologue to the *Legend of Good Women*, G version, ll. 249–53)

—has been the thesis of a wide range of recent studies of the poem, from John V. Fleming's Robertsonian readings to Thomas D. Hill's discussion of the sterility of narcissistic courtly love. See, for example, Fleming's most recent book, *Reason and the Lover* (Princeton, N.J.: Princeton Univ. Press, 1984), as well as his earlier *Roman de la Rose: A Study in Allegory and Iconography* (Princeton, N.J.: Princeton Univ. Press, 1969); Hill, "Narcissus, Pygmalion, and the Castration of Saturn: Two Mythological Themes in the *Roman de la Rose*," *SP* 71 (1974): 404–26; Daniel Poirion, *Le Roman de la rose* (Paris: Hatier, 1973); Paul Zumthor, "Récit et anti-récit: *Le Roman de la rose*," in his *Langue, texte, énigme* (Paris: Seuil, 1975); and R. Howard Bloch, *Etymologies and Genealogies: A Literary Anthropology of the French Middle Ages* (Chicago: Univ. of Chicago Press, 1983), pp. 137–41.

12 For an analysis that suggests all of these positive values, see Kiser, *Telling Classical Tales*, the most recent of idealistic readings of Alceste. Burlin's *Chaucerian Fiction*, pp. 33–44, provides a complement. On

the other side, H. C. Goddard, "Chaucer's *Legend of Good Women*," (*JEGP* 7 [1908]: 87–129), reads Alceste as a comic figure, the butt of the poem's irony. Alfred David, in *The Strumpet Muse*, p. 46, recognizes both her ideal saintliness and her more aggressive actions but finds that the latter comfortingly humanizes the former. Delany ("Rewriting Woman Good," pp. 83–84) comments on Alceste as a "deeply ambiguous figure." A certain doubleness is suggested by Alceste's textual reputation itself: her powerful spiritual value in F is reduced considerably in G. See D. D. Griffith, "An Interpretation of Chaucer's *Legend of Good Women*," in *The Manly Anniversary Studies in Language and Literature* (Chicago: Univ. of Chicago Press, 1923).

13 As A. C. Spearing has pointed out in his *Medieval Dream-Poetry* (Cambridge: Cambridge Univ. Press, 1976), Alceste's "abrupt treatment" of the narrator here is similar to treatment of the narrator in Chaucer's earlier dream visions: he is "fiercely rebuked by the authoritative figure who confronts him" (p. 106).

14 Elaine Tuttle Hansen, in "Irony and the Antifeminist Narrator in Chaucer's *Legend of Good Women*" (*JEGP* 82 [1983]: 19), makes a related point in a different context, and quotes Eve Kosofsky Sedgwick on Dickens and Thackeray (from a paper read at the Mid-Atlantic Regional Meeting of the National Women's Studies Association, March 1980):

> "There is an unspoken rule of propaganda . . . that goes like this: whenever an ideological judgment against a woman is so crushingly cruel that even the institutions of the society cannot bring themselves to pronounce it—for instance, that a mother must give up her child, or that a wife must die to further her husband's moral growth—in those cases it is the woman herself who is forced to pronounce and justify the sentence."

15 Hippolyte Delehaye was the first to recognize and stress the conventionality of the form; see *Les Légendes hagiographiques*, 2d ed. (Brussels: Société des Bollandistes, 1906), and *Cinq leçons sur la méthode hagiographique* (Brussels: Société des Bollandistes, 1934). For an example of this conventionality, Charles W. Jones notes in his *Saints' Lives and Chronicles in Early England* (Ithaca, N.Y.: Cornell Univ. Press, 1947), p. 54, that Bede, in his *Life of Saint Cuthbert*, systematically eliminated all references to particular times, dates, and places. Donald Weinstein and Rudolph M. Bell, in *Saints and Society: The Two Worlds of Western Christendom, 1000–1700* (Chicago: Univ. of Chicago Press, 1982), provide a sociological analysis of this conventionality, well summarized in their quotation of the French sociologist Pierre Delooz:

> "The reputation of sanctity is the collective mental representation

of someone as a saint, whether based on a knowledge of facts that have *really* happened, or whether based on facts that have been at least in part *constructed* if not entirely imagined. But in truth, all saints, more or less, appear to be constructed in the sense that being necessarily saints in consequence of a reputation created by others and a role that others expect of them, they are remodelled to correspond to collective mental representations." (P. 9)

In regard to the conventionality of saints' lives, I have also benefitted from the studies by James W. Earl, "Typology and Iconographic Style in Early Medieval Hagiography," *Studies in the Literary Imagination*, 8 (1975): 15–46, and David L. Jeffrey, "English Saints' Plays," in *Medieval Drama*, ed. Neville Denny, Stratford-upon-Avon Studies 16 (London: Arnold Press, 1973), pp. 69–89.

16 Delehaye, *Les Légendes hagiographiques*, p. 115.

17 Weinstein and Bell, *Saints and Society*, p. 13.

18 Alexandra Hennessy Olsen, in "'De Historiis Sanctorum': A Generic Study of Hagiography" (*Genre* 13 [1980]: 407–29), defends the varieties within the genre against what she feels are reductionist readings of saints' lives. Her point is well taken, but there does exist a theory of imitation, abundantly enunciated in the documents, that is powerful in the Middle Ages. See Weinstein and Bell, *Saints and Society*, "Introduction: The Historian and the Hagiographer," for a discussion of the relation between two kinds of *vitae*, one which confines itself "to delineating the pattern of virtues" in order to demonstrate the saint's participation in the unified community of saints, and one which "departs from the routine pattern" and details the secular aspects of the saint's life (pp. 13–14). I am concerned with the first kind—what Weinstein and Bell call the "official" view—that clearly sets out a "routine pattern" or form, from which the second kind of *vita* is understood to deviate.

19   Et ubi inveni, quid illi certius fecerunt, vestris aspectibus allata sunt, et quod per seniores et longaevos audivi, vestris oculis non defraudavi; et ubi istoriam non inveni, aut qualiter eorum vita fuisset, nec per annosos et vetustos homines, neque per haedificationem, neque per quamlibet auctoritatem, ne intervallum sanctorum pontificum fieret, secundum ordinem, quomodo unus post alium hanc sedem optinuerunt, vestris orationibus me Deo adiuvante, illorum vitam composui, et credo non mentitum esse, quia et hortatores fuerunt castique et elemosinarii et Deo animas hominum adquisitores.

(Agnellus of Ravenna, *Agnelli Liber pontificalis ecclesiae Ravennatis*,

19.32, in MGH, Scriptores rerum langobardicarum et italicarum saec. VI–IX, p. 297; trans. Jones, *Saints' Lives and Chronicles*, p. 63)

"All things are common in the communion of saints," as Reginald of Canterbury, cited by Jones (p. 61), puts it. Reginald wrote a *Life of Saint Malchus*, in whose preface he states that since Malchus was just, holy, loved by God, and full of the spirit of all the just, Reginald did not deviate from the truth in ascribing *any* miracle to him. See Reginald of Canterbury, *The Vita Sancti Malchi of Reginald of Canterbury*, ed. Levi R. Lind (Urbana: Univ. of Illinois Press, 1942), pp. 40–41.

20   Unde manifestum est, melius dici vitam patrum quam vitas, quia, cum sit diversitas meritorum virtutumque, una tamen omnes vita corporis alit in mundo.

(Gregory of Tours, *Gregorii episcopi Turonensis Liber vitae patrum*, ed. Bruno Krusch, in MGH, Scriptores rerum merovingicarum, vol. 1, pp. 662–63; trans. Jones, *Saints' Lives and Chronicles*, p. 62)

21   The lion, agitated, ran,
                    Coming toward her, intending to adore,
                    Not to eat, the virgin.

Delehaye, *Les Légendes hagiographiques*, p. 90, recounts this transformation, though he seems to favor scribal error over deliberate interpretation as an explanation of it. For the dossier of the saint, see *Acta sanctorum*, January, 1: 568–69. There has been considerable disagreement about the date and location of her martyrdom and the authority of the documentation. There may, in fact, be two saints Marciana, one from Caesaria (whose feast is January 9) and one from Toledo (July 12): see *Bibliotheca hagiographica latina*, ed. Société des Bollandistes (Brussels: Société des Bollandistes, 1900–1901), pp. 780–81; and *Acta sanctorum*, July, 3: 233–34. See also *Analecta bollandiana* 24 (1905): 261–64; 58 (1940): 80–81; and 59 (1951): 305, for additional discussion of manuscript authority. (Hippolyte Delehaye, in his *Origines du culte des martyrs* [(Brussels: Société des Bollandistes, 1933), p. 391], suggests that the *Acta* of the saints of Mauritania should not be neglected, even though the manuscripts are not "des textes de premier choix.")

22 Athanasius, *The Life of Antony*, trans. Robert C. Gregg (New York: Paulist Press, 1980), p. 36.

23 Readers were encouraged to venerate the saints, to wonder at the miracles, to pray and ask for intercession, and to emulate the saints. This emulation was often the simple following of the moral example of the saint. See Earl, "Typology and Iconographic Style," p. 36. But in at least two cases it took the form of actual repetition of the actions

of the saint. In book 8 of the *Confessions,* Saint Augustine, moved by the story of the life of Saint Antony, who received a divine injunction from the Word of God, takes up his Bible and opens it to receive his own divine injunction. As John Freccero has noticed, Augustine then hands his Bible to Alypius, "thereby suggesting that his own text is to be applied metaleptically to the reader himself as part of the continual unfolding of God's Word in time" ("The Fig Tree and the Laurel: Petrarch's Poetics," *Diacritics* 5 [1975]: 37). And Petrarch, failed saint, exploited this pattern of reader's repetition by opening his volume of Augustine's *Confessions* atop Mount Ventoux. The reader's response to the saint's life—an *imitatio* of an *imitatio*—makes him a part of the great pattern of prefiguration and fulfillment that is scriptural history.

24 For Chaucer's use of his sources (which include Ovid, *Heroides, Metamorphoses, Fasti;* Boccaccio, *De claris mulieribus;* Virgil, *Aeneid;* Guido delle Colonne, *Historia destructionis Troiae),* see Fyler, *Chaucer and Ovid,* and Hansen, "Irony and the Antifeminist Narrator." Eleanor Winsor Leach, who earlier analyzed the *Legend* in "A Study in the Sources and Rhetoric of Chaucer's *Legend of Good Women* and Ovid's *Heroides* (Ph.D. diss., Yale University, 1963), writes in a more recent essay that the narrator does not merely "shape" the legends by applying principles of abbreviation and expansion (as she had argued earlier); he poetically "disfigure[s]" them. This shift in sensibility accompanies a shift in her sense that the poem is not only about rhetoric but about women. See Eleanor Winsor Leach, "Morwe of May: A Season of Feminine Ambiguity," in *Acts of Interpretation: The Text in Its Contexts, 700–1600,* ed. Mary J. Carruthers and Elizabeth D. Kirk (Norman, Okla.: Pilgrim Books, 1982), pp. 299–310.

25 In this way the narrator seems to be taking sides in the vexed question of Lucrece's culpability in the rape itself and in killing herself afterward. Unconscious, she couldn't possibly have consented to the rape, as she does in Livy—a fact which was to bother later redactors. See Ian Donaldson, *The Rapes of Lucretia: A Myth and Its Transformations* (Oxford: Clarendon, 1982), esp. 69–70.

26 See Augustine, *De civitate Dei,* 1. 19–22, CC 47 [Turnhout: Brepols, 1955], pp. 20–24). On female suicide as an act of signification, see Margaret Higonnet, "Speaking Silences: Women's Suicide," in *The Female Body in Western Culture: Contemporary Perspectives,* ed. Susan Rubin Suleiman (Cambridge, Mass.: Harvard Univ. Press, 1986), pp. 68–83.

27 Poe's *Philosophy of Composition* is quoted as an epigraph to Higonnet, "Speaking Silences," p. 68.

28 *Polychronicon Ranulphi Higden, Monachi Cestrensis, Together with the En-*

glish Translations of John Trevisa and of an Unknown Writer of the Fifteenth
Century 1.1.7, ed. Churchill Babington, Rolls Series (London: Long-
man, 1865), 1:9; C. Du Cange, Glossarium mediae et infimae latinitatis
(Paris: Firmin Didot, 1840–1860; rpt. Graz, 1954), s.v. "labyrinthus."

29 Donald R. Howard, in his Idea of the "Canterbury Tales" ([Berkeley and
Los Angeles: Univ. of California Press, 1976], pp. 326–32), analyzes
Chaucer's association of labyrinth with text. J. Hillis Miller, "Ariadne's
Thread: Repetition and the Narrative Line" (Critical Inquiry 3 [1976]:
57–77), analyzes the text (generic, timeless text; no claims of historical specificity are made) as labyrinth. For a provocative critique of
this text-as-labyrinth analysis that takes the gender of critic and text
into account and forces questions about masculine appropriation of
the feminine, see Nancy K. Miller, "Arachnologies: The Woman, The
Text, and the Critic," in The Poetics of Gender, ed. Nancy K. Miller (New
York: Columbia Univ. Press, 1986), pp. 270–95. Miller's reading of the
Ariadne legend as "a parable of women's writing" (p. 286) inspired
my analysis here.

30 Sheila Delany, "The Logic of Obscenity in Chaucer's Legend of Good
Women," Florilegium 7 (1985): 189–205.

31 Polychronicon Ranulphi Higden, 1.30; ed. Babington, 1:313.

32 Walter Map, De nugis curialium; Courtier's Trifles, ed. M. R. James, rev.
C. N. L. Brooke and R. A. B. Mynors (Oxford: Clarendon, 1983), pp.
288–311; quotation on p. 291.

33 Giovanni Boccaccio, Il Corbaccio, ed. Tauno Nurmela, Suomalaisen
Tiedakatemian Toimituksia, Annales Academiae Scientiarum Fennicae, ser. B, no. 146 (Helsinki: Academiae Scientiarium Fennicae 1968),
p. 52; an English translation, The Corbaccio, has been made by Anthony
K. Cassell (Urbana: Univ. of Illinois Press, 1975). Kiser cites Boccaccio's
text in her note on labyrinths (Telling Classical Tales, p. 117, n. 31).

34 See Sanford Brown Meech, "Chaucer and the Ovide moralisé: A Further
Study," PMLA 46 (1931): 182–204, esp. 187.

35 Le Jaloux, in the Roman de la rose (ed. Félix Lecoy, CFMA 95 [Paris:
Honoré Champion, 1970], vv. 9283–9330), yells to his profligate, un-
ruly wife that it's like mother, like daughter; to avoid women's handing
down the tricks of the trade of being uncontrollable wives, he implies,
men clearly ought to keep women apart.

36 Philomela has been taken as an emblem of the female writer by recent feminist critics: see, for example, Cheryl Walker, The Nightingale's
Burden: Women Poets and American Culture before 1900 (Bloomington:
Indiana Univ. Press, 1982); and Jane Marcus, "Liberty, Sorority, Misogyny," in The Representation of Women in Fiction, ed. Carolyn G. Heilbrun and Margaret R. Higonnet, Selected Papers of the English In-

stitute, 1981, n.s. 7 (Baltimore: Johns Hopkins Univ. Press, 1983), pp. 60–97. Walker (pp. 21–22) argues against Geoffrey Hartman's use of the legend to describe a genderless voice; see his essay, "The Voice of the Shuttle," in *Beyond Formalism* (New Haven, Conn.: Yale Univ. Press, 1970), pp. 337–55. Walker contends that the legend has a particular, gendered value: the figure of the poet, after all, is a raped woman whose tongue has been cut out. For another comment on Hartman's essay and a strong analysis of the Philomela legend, see Patricia Klindienst Joplin, "The Voice of the Shuttle Is Ours," *Stanford Literature Review* 1 (1984): 25–53.

37 See my discussion of Pandarus as "courtly lover" in the previous chapter. I contend that his obscure, unrequited love is but a fiction, an obfuscation of his fundamental engagement in the exchange of women (which structure precludes any sense of a woman as uniquely desirable).

38 As Gayle Rubin notes in "The Traffic in Women: Notes on the 'Political Economy' of Sex" (in *Toward an Anthropology of Women*, ed. R. R. Reiter [New York: Monthly Review Press, 1975], p. 182), the woman traded had best conform her desire to the man in possession of her in the patriarchal social structure which regards women as objects to be traded. The resistant raped woman is one who presumably does not consider herself the possession of the man attempting to take her, and consequently does not docilely conform her desire.

39 It is no surprise, then (although Frank, p. 139, alludes to a possible "mystery" here), that the Philomela legend should be both treated in the palinode for *Troilus and Criseyde* and elided in lists of the legends: in the Man of Law's Introduction, in the "Cronycle made by Chaucier," and in the Prologue's Balade, no mention of Philomela is made. (The Man of Law also omits Cleopatra, and the Balade omits Medea.) For the "Cronycle," a nine-stanza summary of the *Legend of Good Women* in MS. Ashmole 59, fol. 38v. (copied between 1447 and 1456), see *Odd Texts of Chaucer's Minor Poems*, ed. F. J. Furnivall, Chaucer Society, 1st ser., nos. 23, 60 (London: Trübner, 1868–80).

40 Anne Middleton, "The *Physician's Tale* and Love's Martyrs: 'Ensamples mo than ten' as a Method in the *Canterbury Tales*," *ChauR* 8 (1973): 29. As far as I know, Middleton is the only critic who has noted this in the *Legend of Hypermnestra*. Pat Trefzger Overbeck, in "Chaucer's Good Woman" (*ChauR* 2 [1967]: 78), comments on the familial situations of the heroines but links these to the women's rejection of authority.

41 There is, as Robert Worth Frank argues in *Chaucer and the "Legend of Good Women,"* plenty of *occupatio* and *abbreviatio* in the *Legend*. Phrases

such as "And shortly, lest this tale be to long" (2675), "But shortly
to the ende I telle shal" (2221), "But now to purpos; in the story I
rede" (1825), "Now to th'effect, now to the fruyt of al" (1160), "Who
coude wryte which a dedly cheere / Hath Thisbe now" (869–70), do
not, *in themselves*, indicate boredom or weariness; Frank contends that
they are necessary devices for responsibly pruning sources to form
compressed and specific narratives. But there is another agenda motivating the narrator's constantly visible shaping hand. Combined with
the protestations of weariness, these rhetorical interjections, I argue,
serve to characterize a narrator who simply refuses to go into the
more complicated—the difficult, the hard to interpret—aspects of his
stories of "good women." He turns away, that is, from the feminine
as it threatens to disrupt the patriarchal project that would constrain
it. Countering the legend of Chaucer's boredom, Frank argues firmly
that Chaucer was far from bored when writing the *Legend of Good
Women*. And I agree: Chaucer was busy depicting sheer boredom,
utter weariness in his narrator, and revealing it as a specifically masculine defense against the feminine. Elaine Tuttle Hansen, in "Irony
and the Antifeminist Narrator," makes a similar claim about the narrator's boredom: it is, she writes, "undisguised" (p. 29), and it must
be distinguished from Chaucer's motives.

42 Peter L. Allen discussed such implications of this line in " 'And trusteth, as in love, no man but me': Irony and the Narrator in *The Legend
of Good Women*," a talk presented at the Nineteenth International Congress on Medieval Studies, The Medieval Institute, Western Michigan
University, Kalamazoo, in May 1984, later expanded into "Reading
Chaucer's Good Women," *ChauR* 21 (1987): 419–34.

43 Boredom—the flip side of aggression, as modern psychologists suggest—is an affect in itself. For a thorough discussion and extensive
bibliography on boredom, see Franz R. Goetzl, "Root of Discontent
and Aggression," in *Boredom: Root of Discontent and Aggression*, ed.
Franz R. Goetzl (Berkeley, Calif.: Grizzly Peak Press, 1975), pp. 55–
109. For a brilliant analysis of the boring in Trollope that has influenced
my discussion here of *Legend of Good Women*, see D. A. Miller, "The
Novel as Usual: Trollope's *Barchester Towers*," in *Sex, Politics, and Science in the Nineteenth-Century Novel*, ed. Ruth Bernard Yeazell, Selected
Papers from the English Institute, 1983–84, n.s., no. 10 (Baltimore:
Johns Hopkins Univ. Press, 1986), pp. 1–38.

44 Allen, "Reading Chaucer's Good Women," p. 429.

45 Ibid.

CHAPTER THREE. *The Law of Man and Its "Abhomynacions"*

1 Martin Stevens, "The Royal Stanza in Early English Literature" (*PMLA* 94 [1979]: 62–76), suggests that "prose" here in fact refers to the rime royal stanza, and develops his argument with a discussion of Chaucer's artistic use of rime royal in the *Canterbury Tales*. But, as Stevens also acknowledges, Chaucer uses "prose" three other times in the *Tales;* the word is used twice to denote works written in what we know now as prose (the *Melibee* and the *Parson's Tale*) and once in a context that appears to contrast prose to poetry (in the headlink to the *Monk's Tale*). Patricia J. Eberle, in her Explanatory Notes in the *Riverside Chaucer*, comments that "most critics have inclined to the view that the reference to *prose* indicates a prose tale was to follow" (p. 854).

2 See the Explanatory Notes in *The Works of Geoffrey Chaucer* (ed. F. N. Robinson, 2d ed. [Boston: Houghton Mifflin, 1957], p. 690), for additional "puzzling problems," and Eberle's updated account of these problems in the *Riverside Chaucer* (pp. 854–63).

3 Margaret Schlauch, *Chaucer's Constance and Accused Queens* (1927; rpt. New York: Gordian Press, 1969), thoroughly demonstrates that incest is the narrative motive of a large number of folktale sources and analogues of the *Man of Law's Tale*. See also Elizabeth Archibald, "The Flight from Incest: Two Late Classical Precursors of the Constance Theme," *ChauR* 20 (1986): 259–72; she argues that the flight from incest has an ancient and lasting connection with the Accused Queen theme. Here I would like to acknowledge my indebtedness to Lawrence Howe's excellent unpublished paper, "The Man of Law's Obsession" (Department of English, University of California, Berkeley), which first convinced me of the pervasiveness of incest in the thematics and language of the *Tale*. See also Peter Goodall's brief article, " 'Unkynde abhomynaciouns' [*sic*] in Chaucer and Gower" (*Parergon* 5 [1987]: 94–102), arguing for the Man of Law's suppression of incest, which I read after I finished this chapter.

4 For an analysis in gender terms of such active not-reading, see Susan Schibanoff, "Taking Jane's Cue: *Phyllyp Sparowe* as a Primer for Women Readers," *PMLA* 101 (1986): 832–47.

5 The Man of Law's comments about the tales of Canacee and Apollonius of Tyre were taken as evidence of a quarrel between Chaucer and Gower, hypothesized first by Tyrwhitt in his edition of Chaucer (1775–78); the idea had a continuous following through the nineteenth century and into the twentieth (Skeat and Tatlock, e.g., were believ-

ers). Robinson comments that "Chaucer very probably intended the passage as a fling at Gower," but goes on to note that "there is no positive evidence" of an estrangement between the two poets (*Works of Geoffrey Chaucer*, p. 690); and Eberle (*Riverside Chaucer*, p. 854) reports the hypothesis but reiterates the fact that no other evidence is extant. John H. Fisher, in *John Gower: Moral Philosopher and Friend of Chaucer* (New York: New York Univ. Press, 1964), summarizes the critical tradition of the quarrel hypothesis (pp. 26–36) and, further on (pp. 286–92), interprets the Man of Law's headlink in context of the relationship between the two poets.

The unfinished nature of the *Canterbury Tales* has been advanced to explain both the Man of Law's declaration that he will "speke in prose" and his delivery of a poem in rime royal: the suggestion is that either the *Melibee* or Innocent III's *De contemptu mundi* ("the Wreched Engendrynge of Mankynde" [*Legend of Good Women*, G: 414]) was originally intended for the Man of Law. The latter suggestion would also explain the "far-fetched" (Robinson, *Works of Geoffrey Chaucer*, p. 691) connection between the Prologue and the *Tale*, which Eberle's notes continue to see as problematic (*Riverside Chaucer*, p. 856): see J. L. Lowes, "The Prologue to the *Legend of Good Women* Considered in Its Chronological Relations," *PMLA* 20 (1905): 793–96. Recently, Charles A. Owen, Jr., has emphasized the unfinishedness of the *Canterbury Tales*, stressing its nature as a work in progress, in "The Alternative Reading of *The Canterbury Tales*: Chaucer's Text and the Early Manuscripts," *PMLA* 97 (1982): 237–50.

Among the many implicit and explicit condemnations of the *Man of Law's Tale* as one of Chaucer's more unfortunate productions, Robert B. Burlin's brusque treatment dismisses it as an aesthetic failure on Chaucer's part (*Chaucerian Fiction* [Princeton, N.J.: Princeton Univ. Press, 1977], pp. 138–40). Alfred David, in "The Man of Law vs. Chaucer: A Case in Poetics" (*PMLA* 82 [1967]: 217–25), rehabilitates the *Man of Law's Tale* (and addresses the problem of the Man of Law's tone) by suggesting that it is Chaucer's deft indictment of the Man of Law's literary taste—the taste of the humorless moralists around Chaucer in court. Hope Weissman, in her excellent article, "Late Gothic Pathos in *The Man of Law's Tale*" (*JMRS* 9 [1979]: 133–53), addresses the problem of Constance's contradictory roles by suggesting that Chaucer was exposing the vapidity not only of literary taste but of an entire devotional style.

6 John Matthews Manly, *Some New Light on Chaucer* (1926; rpt. Gloucester, Mass.: Peter Smith, 1959), pp. 131–32. (But see Eberle [*Riverside*

Chaucer, p. 855], who suggests that "the terms *sergeant* and *man* of law seem to have been interchangeable," citing evidence from Gower's *Mirour de l'omme*.)

7 For a recent, methodologically similar analysis of a Chaucer work, an analysis focusing on ideological dissonances within the text, see Britton J. Harwood, "Chaucer and the Silence of History: Situating the *Canon's Yeoman's Tale*," *PMLA* 102 (1987): 338–50.

8 Louis Althusser's "Ideology and Ideological State Apparatuses (Notes towards an Investigation)" has informed my understanding and use of the term "ideology" here. See his *"Lenin and Philosophy" and Other Essays*, trans. Ben Brewster (New York: Monthly Review Press, 1971), pp. 127–86. See also Terry Eagleton's brief discussion, *Marxism and Literary Criticism* (Berkeley and Los Angeles: Univ. of California Press, 1976). I have also found Susan Griffin's "The Way of All Ideology" (in *Feminist Theory: A Critique of Ideology*, ed. Nannerl O. Keohane, Michelle Z. Rosaldo, and Barbara C. Gelpi [Chicago: Univ. of Chicago Press, 1982], pp. 273–92), invigorating and useful. For the idea of a text as ruptured, revealing the limits of its own ideology, see Pierre Macherey, *A Theory of Literary Production*, trans. Geoffrey Wall (London: Routledge and Kegan Paul, 1978). And for an extension of Macherey's theory into feminist literary criticism, see Toril Moi, *Sexual/Textual Politics: Feminist Literary Theory*, New Accents Series (London: Methuen, 1985), esp. pp. 26, 91–95.

9 For the Man of Law's culpability, compare Muriel Bowden, *A Commentary on the General Prologue to the "Canterbury Tales"* (2d ed. [London: Macmillan, 1967], pp. 170–71), and Jill Mann, *Chaucer and Medieval Estates Satire* ([Cambridge: Cambridge Univ. Press, 1973], pp. 86–91).

10 Theodore F. T. Plucknett, *A Concise History of the Common Law*, 5th ed. (Boston: Little, Brown, 1956), p. 711.

11 Jack Goody, Introduction to *Family and Inheritance: Rural Society in Western Europe, 1200–1800*, ed. J. Goody, J. Thirsk, and E. P. Thompson, Past and Present Publications (Cambridge: Cambridge Univ. Press, 1976), pp. 1–9.

12 After the Fourth Lateran Council in 1215, the Church reduced its prohibition of marriage from the seventh degree of consanguinity to the fourth; it also restricted marriage between affines and spiritual kin. In regard to monogamy, the Church condemned adultery and advised against remarriage. For discussion of the ecclesiastical model of marriage and its conflict with the lay model, see Georges Duby, *Medieval Marriage: Two Models from Twelfth-Century France*, trans. Elborg Forster (Baltimore: Johns Hopkins Univ. Press, 1978). For the influence of canon law on the common law of marriage, and the interaction be-

tween the two laws, see Frederick Pollock and Frederic Maitland, *The History of English Law before the Time of Edward I* (Cambridge: Cambridge Univ. Press, 1895), 2: 364–70. For general discussion of marriage, see David Herlihy, *Medieval Households* (Cambridge, Mass: Harvard Univ. Press, 1985).

13 Pope Alexander III's innovations in the canon law of marriage were thoroughgoing and influential in later legal development. His decretal *Veniens ad nos* (c. 1176–80) ruled, as James A. Brundage puts it,

> that a valid marriage might be contracted either by the free and voluntary exchange of present consent between persons of legal age who were free to marry each other, or by the free and voluntary exchange of future consent between two parties legally able to marry one another, if that consent was ratified by subsequent sexual intercourse.
>
> (*Law, Sex, and Christian Society in Medieval Europe* [Chicago: Univ. of Chicago Press, 1987], p. 334)

For later canonists on consent in marriage, see Brundage, *Law, Sex, and Christian Society*, pp. 351–55. For qualifications of paternal authority in the common law of marriage, see David Herlihy, *Medieval Households*, pp. 80–82, and Pollock and Maitland, *History of English Law* 2:369–70. But David Herlihy suggests in fact that "it is possible that the Church's denial of a parental (meaning paternal) veto over marriages of the children was meant to counteract a contemporary resurgence of the father's authority within the medieval kindred" (*Medieval Households*, p. 82). Herlihy goes on to note the rise of patrilineage in elite western European circles in the eleventh and twelfth centuries. And "despite the insistence of lawmakers and jurists that the essence of marriage lay in free consent to wed a partner freely chosen," writes Brundage of the late fourteenth and fifteenth centuries, "people often married in ways that emphasized *traditio* and the transfer of property between families" (*Law, Sex, and Christian Society*, pp. 547–48). Thus legal qualifications of paternal power may have reflected a rise in paternal authority and often may not after all have affected behavior.

14 Pollock and Maitland, *History of English Law* 2: 420.

15 Plucknett, *A Concise History of the Common Law*, p. 715.

16 Contract law was late in developing in English common law, but there were adumbrations of contractual agreements in the commercial usages of the late Middle Ages; see ibid., pp. 628–70.

17 R. Howard Bloch, *Etymologies and Genealogies: A Literary Anthropology of the French Middle Ages* (Chicago: Univ. of Chicago Press, 1983).

18 Jack Goody, *The Development of the Family and Marriage in Europe* (Cam-

bridge: Cambridge Univ. Press, 1983), pp. 103–56, 215. (For a brief critique, see Brundage, *Law, Sex, and Christian Society,* "Appendix 2: Marriage Law and the Economic Interests of the Medieval Church," pp. 606–7.)

19 Jacques Le Goff, "Merchant's Time and Church's Time in the Middle Ages," in *Time, Work, and Culture in the Middle Ages,* trans. Arthur Goldhammer (Chicago: Univ. of Chicago Press, 1980), esp. pp. 34–35, 50–51. For a general overview of the establishment of commerce in the Middle Ages, see Robert S. Lopez, *The Commercial Revolution of the Middle Ages, 950–1350* (Cambridge: Cambridge Univ. Press, 1976).

20 See Le Goff, p. 35, and David S. Landes, *Revolution in Time: Clocks and the Making of the Modern World* (Cambridge, Mass.: Harvard Univ. Press, 1983), esp. pt. 1, "Finding Time."

21 Domenico Calva, *Disciplina degli Spirituali,* ed. G. Bottari (1838), chs. 19–20; cited by Le Goff, *Time, Work, and Culture in the Middle Ages,* pp. 50–51.

22 In her provocative recent book, *Literary Fat Ladies: Rhetoric, Gender, Property* (London and New York: Methuen, 1987), Patricia Parker discusses the wide, broad, expansive female figure as an image, pervasive in Western literature, of disruption or transgression of narrative and social control.

23 Virginity's superior value to gold is the stuff of commonplace: Saint Jerome makes the comparison, claiming, for example, that no gold or silver vessel is so dear to God as the virgin's body. See letter 22 (to Eustochium), par. 23, in *Epistulae,* ed. Isidorus Hilberg, CSEL 54 (Vienna: F. Tempsky, 1912), pt. 1, pp. 175–76.

24 Medieval discussions of virginity stress purity, integrity, spotlessness. For a sampling, see Saint Cyprian, *De habitu virginum;* Saint Methodius, *Symposium;* Tertullian, *De virginibus velandis* and *De exhortatione castitatis;* Saint Jerome, *Adversus Jovinianum;* and *Hali Meidenhad.* The usual iconography emphasizes closure: the closed chamber, door, garden (Methodius' image of the sealed timbers on a boat prefigures Constance in her boat). Methodius stresses the fullness of the virgin (in whom there is "nothing of emptiness"). Chaucer's *Man of Law's Tale* focuses on the virgin—and more generally, on woman—as blank, and thereby, I argue, indicts the Man of Law as patriarchal ideologue, creating woman as Other, as lack, as nothing. For the interesting argument that virginity as a religious ideal used women's sexuality as a commodity to be traded, see Elizabeth Castelli, "Virginity and Its Meaning for Women's Sexuality in Early Christianity," *Journal of Feminist Studies in Religion* 2 (1986): 61–86.

25 Hugh of Saint Victor, in his *Didascalicon*, demonstrates an understanding of trade or commerce as a kind of discourse:

> Commerce contains every sort of dealing in the purchase, sale, and exchange of domestic or foreign goods. This art is beyond all doubt a peculiar sort of rhetoric—strictly of its own kind—for eloquence is in the highest degree necessary to it. Thus the man who excels others in fluency of speech is called a *Mercurius*, or Mercury, as being a *mercatorum kirrius* (=*kyrios*)—a very lord among merchants.
>
> (Trans. Jerome Taylor [New York: Columbia Univ. Press, 1961], bk. 2, ch. 23)

Cited in Eugene Vance, "Chrétien's *Yvain* and the Ideologies of Change and Exchange," in *Mervelous Signals: Poetics and Sign Theory in the Middle Ages* (Lincoln and London: Univ. of Nebraska Press, 1986), p. 118.

26 John Gower, *Confessio amantis* 5.6114 (in *English Works of John Gower*, ed. G. C. Macaulay, EETS, e.s. 82 [1900; rpt. Oxford: Oxford Univ. Press, 1957], 2:113); *Piers Plowman* B. 15.105; *Hali Meidenhad*, MS. Bodley 34 and Cotton MS. Titus D. 18. (ed. F. J. Furnivall [1922; rpt. New York: Greenwood, 1969], pp. 12–13, 36–37).

27 Claude Lévi-Strauss, *The Elementary Structures of Kinship*, trans. James Harle Bell, John Richard von Sturmer, and Rodney Needham, rev. ed. (Boston: Beacon Press, 1969); hereafter cited, as *ES*, in the text. *Les Structures élémentaires de la parenté*, first published in France in 1949, appeared in a revised edition in France in 1967.

28 See Marcel Mauss, *Essai sur le don, forme archaïque de l'échange* (1925); translated by Ian Cunnison, under the title *The Gift: Forms and Functions of Exchange in Archaic Societies* (New York: Norton, 1967); and Gayle Rubin, "The Traffic in Women: Notes on the 'Political Economy' of Sex," in *Toward an Anthropology of Women*, ed. R. R. Reiter (New York: Monthly Review Press, 1975), pp. 157–210.

29 Georges Duby notes that "marriage is at the core of all social institutions," and marriage is a "treaty . . . concluded between two houses": "Under such a pact, one of the houses would give up, the other receive or acquire, a woman. The exchange, then, involved a woman" (*Medieval Marriage*, p. 4). David Herlihy suggests a Lévi-Straussian analysis of constitutive social exchange (of signs, money, and women) when he links women and money: analyzing high- and late-medieval rules of inheritance, he notes that in the common medieval view such rules were tied to exogamy. Referring to the eleventh-century Peter Damian, Herlihy comments: "The woman must marry out, and she inevitably

takes some property with her. The circulation of women thus also produced a circulation of capital" (*Medieval Households*, p. 136).

30 Claude Lévi-Strauss, "The Family," in *Man, Culture, and Society*, ed. H. Shapiro (London: Oxford Univ. Press, 1971), p. 278.

31 Herlihy, *Medieval Households*, p. 61.

32 Rubin, "The Traffic in Women," p. 174.

33 In "The Family," Lévi-Strauss—again at the end of the work—acknowledges this uneasiness and tries to provide reassurance:

> The female reader, who may be shocked to see womankind treated as a commodity submitted to transactions between male operators, can easily find comfort in the assurance that the rules of the game would remain unchanged should it be decided to consider the men as being exchanged by women's groups. As a matter of fact, some *very few* societies, of a highly developed matrilineal type, have *to a limited extent attempted* to express things that way.
>
> (P. 284; my emphasis)

The heavy qualification here works, in my view as female reader, against such "assurance."

34 Robert F. Murphy, from the *Saturday Review*, is the reviewer quoted on the back cover whom I cite here. Gayle Rubin writes of these last paragraphs of Lévi-Strauss, as well as of similar paradoxical passages in Freud:

> It is precisely at such points that the implications of the theory are ignored, and are replaced with formulations whose purpose is to keep those implications firmly lodged in the theoretical unconscious. It is at these points that all sorts of mysterious chemical substances, joys in pain, and biological aims are substituted for a critical assessment of the costs of femininity.
>
> ("The Traffic in Women," pp. 202–3)

35 See Judith Herman and Lisa Hirschman, "Father-Daughter Incest," *Signs* 2 (1977): 735–56, for an analysis of "the asymmetrical nature of the incest taboo under patriarchy": "Because the taboo is created and enforced by men, we argue that it may also be more easily and frequently violated by men." But "a patriarchal society . . . most abhors the idea of incest between mother and son, because this is an affront to the father's prerogatives" (pp. 740–41). Herman and Hirschman present a clinical report of fifteen victims of father-daughter incest.

36 Schlauch, *Chaucer's Constance and Accused Queens*, pp. 132–33.

37 Macherey, *A Theory of Literary Production*, p. 194.

38 Schlauch notes that father-daughter incest in the folktales may be the vestige of an earlier matrilineal social organization in Western Europe: the king wants to marry the daughter, after the mother's decease, in order to retain his regal status. The daughter's refusal of her father's advances would, then, suggest a new kind of social organization—patrilineage—and the tale would itself document a transition from female determination of social organization to male determination (*Chaucer's Constance and Accused Queens*, pp. 43–45).

39 Christianity—an ideology that subsumes patriarchy—maintains its sovereignty by denying heathens identity with the rest of humankind, converting them, or killing them. Patriarchy employs parallel methods of suppression, marginalization, appropriation, obliteration. Indeed, in the *Man of Law's Tale* both "lawes"—"mannes governance" and the "newe lawe" of Christianity—create an Other, on whom each is said to impose "thraldom and penance" (286, 338).

40 Note that this scene does not occur in Gower; and, although the word "pavement" seems to have been derived from the Latin version, Antiochus there does not throw his daughter to the ground (see *Historia Apollonii regis Tyri*, ed. A. Riese, 2d ed. [Leipzig: Teubner, 1893], pp. 2–3). See the note on line 81 in Robinson, *The Works of Geoffrey Chaucer*, 2d ed., p. 691. This gesture, with its symmetry to Constance's later gestures, seems to be Chaucer's innovation.

41 A vow made at Easingwold in 1484, typical of late-medieval marriage vows, recorded in *Acts of the Chapter of the Collegiate Church of Saints Peter and Wilfred, Ripon, 1452–1506* (Durham: Surtees Society, 1875), 64:162; my emphasis.

42 Rubin makes this point well:

> If a girl is promised in infancy, her refusal as an adult would disrupt the flow of debts and promises. It would be in the interests of the smooth and continuous operation of such a system if the woman in question did not have too many ideas of her own about whom she might want to sleep with. From the standpoint of the system, the preferred female sexuality would be one which responded to the desire of others, rather than one which actively desired and sought a response.
>
> ("The Traffic in Women," p. 182)

See also Margaret Gist:

> It is a commonplace that throughout the Middle Ages marriage was an arrangement of convenience, an enforced legal contract. . . . With such ends in view, it was inevitable that the desire of the woman should be the least significant element in the bargain.

(*Love and War in the Middle English Romances* [Philadelphia: Univ. of Pennsylvania Press, 1947], p. 17)

43 Schlauch, *Chaucer's Constance and Accused Queens,* esp. 33–34.

44 Nicholas Trivet, *Les Chroniques écrites pour Marie d'Angleterre, fille d'Edward I,* in *Sources and Analogues of Chaucer's "Canterbury Tales,"* ed. W. F. Bryan and G. Dempster (New York: Humanities Press, 1958), p. 167; John Gower, *Confessio amantis* 2.648–49 (in *English Works of John Gower,* 1:148). On Chaucer's use of these two sources in this scene, see Schlauch, p. 134.

45 Trivet, *Les Chroniques écrites pour Marie d'Angleterre,* p. 172.

46 "Verum enimvero hac in parte verum habetur cuiusdam saecularis prudentia dictum quod omnes socrus oderunt nurus" (*La Vie ancienne de sainte Godelive de Ghistelles par Drogon de Bergues, Analecta bollandiana* 44 [1926]: 128); Schlauch, *Chaucer's Constance and Accused Queens,* p. 34. Drogon honors Godelive for her patience in the teeth of marital abuse (she was tormented by both husband and mother-in-law). Herlihy, *Medieval Households,* p. 114, mentions this saint's life; we remember another Godelive who forms a neat contrast: Harry Bailly's brawny, aggressive wife Goodelief, who, reversing the power relations between husband and wife, strikes fear into her husband (ruefully reported by the Host in the headlink to the *Monk's Tale,* after *Melibee*). Harry remarks that she acts nothing like Melibee's Prudence—and we might suspect that she has never read the *vita* of her namesake, either.

47 My analysis in this section is indebted to Sheila Delany's chapter, "Womanliness in *The Man of Law's Tale,*" in her *Writing Woman: Women Writers and Women in Literature, Medieval to Modern* (New York: Schocken, 1983), pp. 36–46. Delany problematizes the Man of Law's breaks in style and tone, identifies a reductive conception of femininity, and observes the lack of femaleness of Constance's mothers-in-law.

48 Rodney Delasanta, "And of Great Reverence: Chaucer's Man of Law," *ChauR* 5 (1971): 288–310.

49 Infidels were not necessarily viewed in the Middle Ages as entirely outside the realm of humankind: as Stephen G. Nichols, Jr., pointed out to me, John Scottus Eriugena, e.g., thought them to represent that half of humanity which rejected God and became the race of Cain. See bk. 5, sec. 38 of his *Periphyseon* or *De divisione naturae* (*PL* 122: 1011).

50 Note that the Sowdanesse herself instigates a trade, thus usurping the masculine role of exchanger: she vows to "quite" the Sultan in his change of religion (354).

51 "Embodiments of men's projected needs" is a phrase from Catherine

A. MacKinnon's pithy article, "Feminism, Marxism, Method, and the State," in *Feminist Theory: A Critique of Ideology* (see n. 8 above), p. 20.

52 For a discussion of the architectural iconography of the Virgin as closed chamber, see Gail McMurray Gibson, "'Porta haec clausa erit': Comedy, Conception, and Ezekiel's Closed Door in the *Ludus Coventriae* Play of 'Joseph's Return,'" *JMRS* 8 (1978): 137–56.

53 Simone de Beauvoir, *The Second Sex*, trans. H. M. Parshley (New York: Knopf, 1957), p. 160. Marina Warner cites this phrase from *The Second Sex* in her lively and useful discussion of the Virgin's motherhood in *Alone of All Her Sex: The Myth and the Cult of the Virgin Mary* (New York: Random House, 1976), p. 183.

54 Cf. Luce Irigaray's comments on the traffic in women: the exchange of women establishes the operations of patriarchal society, and thus presupposes, among other conditions, "the equality of women among themselves, but in terms of laws of equivalence that remain external to them" ("Women on the Market," in *This Sex Which Is Not One*, trans. Catherine Porter [Ithaca, N.Y.: Cornell Univ. Press, 1985], pp. 184–85).

55 See Lee Patterson's comments on the *Man of Law's Tale* in his article, "'For the Wyves love of Bathe': Feminine Rhetoric and Poetic Resolution in the *Roman de la Rose* and the *Canterbury Tales*" (*Speculum* 58 [1983]): Constance's "redemptive mission is an effect of her father's tyranny" (p. 692).

56 Sandra M. Gilbert and Susan Gubar, *The Madwoman in the Attic: The Woman Writer and the Nineteenth-Century Literary Imagination* (New Haven, Conn.: Yale Univ. Press, 1979), p. 25.

57 I would maintain, in an argument that is beyond the scope of the present chapter, that those very romance hagiographies forming the horizon of expectation for Constance's self-presentation here (and for the Man of Law's performance in general) have the same effect as the one I have analyzed for the *Man of Law's Tale:* they uncritically generate, reconfirm, and perpetuate patriarchal ideology. For an example picked more or less at random from an enormous body of literature, consider the popular legend of Saint Mary Magdalene (fourteenth-century text found in the *South English Legendary*, ed. Charlotte d'Evelyn and Anna J. Mill, EETS 235 [London: Oxford Univ. Press, 1956], 1:302–15; fifteenth-century representation in the Digby play of *Mary Magdalene*, in *Medieval Drama*, ed. David Bevington [Boston: Houghton Mifflin, 1975], pp. 687–753), with its emphasis on conversion, proper lineage, and typological reenactment of Christ's life—properly patriarchal preoccupations, as I have suggested.

CHAPTER FOUR. *"Glose/bele chose"*

1 The ascription of speaker to these lines is uncertain. The entire Epilogue to the *Man of Law's Tale* presents textual difficulties: it does not appear in twenty-two of the fifty-seven manuscripts of the *Canterbury Tales*, including Ellesmere, a condition that suggests to Robinson that Chaucer abandoned it in his developing plan for the *Tales.* But, as Robinson goes on to state, there is no question of its genuineness as Chaucerian. *Who* interrupts the Host at line 1178 is uncertain from the textual evidence: manuscripts ascribe the speech to the Shipman, the Squire, or the Summoner (see Robinson's summary account, in *The Works of Geoffrey Chaucer,* ed. F. N. Robinson, 2d ed. [Boston: Houghton Mifflin, 1957], pp. 696–97). I follow Robert Pratt's argument in his classic article, "The Development of the Wife of Bath" (in *Studies in Medieval Literature in Honor of Professor Albert Croll Baugh,* ed. MacEdward Leach [Philadelphia: Univ. of Pennsylvania Press, 1961], pp. 45–79), that the lines were originally written for the Wife of Bath in order to link the *Man of Law's Tale* to her tale (which was later reassigned to the Shipman after Chaucer wrote a new prologue and tale for her). Pratt, of course, follows the Bradshaw shift in putting the *Shipman's Tale* after this endlink (Fragment B²), but his argument about the lines' speaker doesn't necessitate this move. (For a defense of the Ellesmere order, see E. T. Donaldson, "The Ordering of the *Canterbury Tales,"* in *Medieval Literature and Folklore Studies: Essays in Honor of Francis Lee Utley,* ed. Jerome Mandel and Bruce A. Rosenberg [New Brunswick, N.J.: Rutgers Univ. Press, 1970], pp. 193–204.) The verbal echoes of the Man of Law's Epilogue in the *Shipman's Tale*—and in the later Wife of Bath's Prologue and *Tale*—are unmistakable: "joly body," for example, occurs at line 423 of the *Shipman's Tale.* Although the second and third editions of Robinson print "Seyde the Shipman" at line 1179, both Fisher and Donaldson, in their editions, emend the text to make the Wife of Bath the speaker of these lines.

Lee Patterson, " 'For the Wyves love of Bathe': Feminine Rhetoric and Poetic Resolution in the *Roman de la Rose* and the *Canterbury Tales,"* *Speculum* 58 (1983): 656–95, has explicated the significance of the Wife of Bath's "joly body" in terms that prefigure my own, and makes many related points. As he puts it, "The Wife's text . . . solicits both body and mind, and it requires for its explication both an erotics and a hermeneutic" (p. 658). In observing that "the language of poetry, as enacted by the poet and received by the reader, is habitually conceived in the Middle Ages in sexual, and specifically in feminine terms" (p. 659), he suggests a structure of sexualized poetics consonant with the one I describe here, and he undertakes, as I do, to determine what the creation of the Wife means to Chaucer's masculine poetic self-definition. The Wife proposes, in Patterson's terms, a "reading at once both literal and moral" (p. 694); but while I stress the patriarchal gratifications of such a hermeneutic, Patterson proposes a more fully subversive cultural value for it.

2 The Wife's clothing seems to have been an essential part of her character from her very beginnings as teller of the *Shipman's Tale*, as several critics, including Pratt, have observed (see n. 1 above, on the Wife of Bath as original teller of that tale). The narrator's voice, as the *Shipman's Tale* opens, insists that husbands must clothe their wives properly, "in which array we daunce jolily" (7:14). The wife in the tale needs money to pay for new clothes, so she borrows from the lascivious monk John (and pays for these "frankes" with her "flankes" [201–2]). But clothes are absorbed into the larger economic nexus of the *Shipman's Tale*: see Gerhard Joseph, "Chaucer's Coinage: Foreign Exchange and the Puns of the *Shipman's Tale*," *ChauR* 17 (1983): 341–57; and Thomas Hahn, "Money, Sexuality, Wordplay, and Context in the *Shipman's Tale*," in *Chaucer in the Eighties*, ed. Julian N. Wasserman and Robert J. Blanch (Syracuse, N.Y.: Syracuse Univ. Press, 1986), pp. 235–49. As Patterson, in "For the Wyves love of Bathe," has also suggested, although an association of the literary and the sexual is suggested in the triple pun on "taillying" at the end of the tale, it remains for the Wife of Bath, in her present Prologue and *Tale*, to develop the full hermeneutic value of her "joly body" in her fine and showy dress.

3 It is along this continuum defined by the Hieronymian paradigm—compliant, passive, silent brides on the one end, vocal Others on the other end—that almost all the female characters of the *Canterbury Tales* can in fact be read: Alisoun of the *Miller's Tale*, May of the *Merchant's Tale*, the Prioress (a bride of Christ), and Pertelote, to name a few.

4 For an argument supporting the claim that Chaucer intends to show respect for literal reading in his creation of the Wife as literal exegete, see Lawrence Besserman, " 'Glosynge Is a Glorious Thyng': Chaucer's Biblical Exegesis," in *Chaucer and Scriptural Tradition*, ed. David Lyle Jeffrey (Ottawa: Univ. of Ottawa Press, 1984), pp. 65–73. Besserman suggests that Chaucer's increasing respect for the letter might have derived from the contemporary, antifraternal movement as well as from late fourteenth-century English biblical translators. (On the issue of the literal, see also Douglas Wurtele, "Chaucer's *Canterbury Tales* and Nicholas of Lyre's *Postillae litteralis et moralis super totam Bibliam*," in *Chaucer and Scriptural Tradition*, pp. 89–107.) I shall discuss Chaucer's possible response to these late fourteenth-century movements in my

treatment of the *Pardoner's Tale,* in Chapter 6, agreeing with Besserman's idea but also suggesting that a good deal of anxiety about the integrity of the letter motivates that growing "respect." The argument about Chaucer's respect for literal exegesis goes counter to D. W. Robertson's famous pronouncements about the Wife in *A Preface to Chaucer* (Princeton, N.J.: Princeton Univ. Press, 1962), pp. 317–31. For more recent articulations of a basically Robertsonian position, see Graham D. Caie, "The Significance of the Early Chaucer Manuscript Glosses (with Special Reference to the *Wife of Bath's Prologue*)," *ChauR* 10 (1976): 350–60; and Sarah Disbrow, "The Wife of Bath's Old Wives' Tale," *SAC* 8 (1986): 59–71.

5 The exact source of the *Wife of Bath's Tale* is unknown, but of the known analogues (including *The Marriage of Sir Gawain, The Wedding of Sir Gawen and Dame Ragnell,* and the *Tale of Florent* in Gower's *Confessio amantis*), none includes a rape. For a summary of possible narrative sources of the rape, see the *Riverside Chaucer,* 872–73; and see, for contrast to my discussion, Bernard F. Huppé's "Rape and Woman's Sovereignty in the *Wife of Bath's Tale*" (*Modern Language Notes* 63 [1948]: 378–81), for an analysis of the rape as an "indication of the structural perfection" (p. 378) of the tale.

6 Luce Irigaray, *This Sex Which Is Not One,* trans. Catherine Porter (Ithaca, N.Y.: Cornell Univ. Press, 1985), p. 76. For an expression of the view that the Wife of Bath is "confined within the prison house of masculine language," see Patterson, p. 682; see also Hope Phyllis Weissman, "Antifeminism and Chaucer's Characterization of Women," in *Geoffrey Chaucer,* ed. George D. Economou (New York: McGraw-Hill, 1975), esp. pp. 104–10; and Susan Crane, "Alison's Incapacity and Poetic Instability in the *Wife of Bath's Tale,*" *PMLA* 102 (1987): 20–28.

7 Pratt, "The Development of the Wife of Bath," p. 45.

8 Robert B. Burlin, in his *Chaucerian Fiction* ([Princeton, N.J.: Princeton Univ. Press, 1977], pp. 217–27), provides an optimistic analysis of the Wife's ability to "transcen[d] the limits of [her] own fictive universe": "When the Wife of Bath attacks Jankyn's book, which is both her enemy and the source of her being, it is as if she were usurping the role of creator, destroying the 'original' so that she might recast herself in her own image" (pp. 225, 227). But that "as if" is crucial: Chaucer is, of course, still and ever her creator, and we must ask what purpose it serves him to create a woman who *seems* to usurp the role of creator.

9 Sheila Delany uses this term in her chapter, "Sexual Economics, Chaucer's Wife of Bath, and *The Book of Margery Kempe,*" in her *Writing*

Woman: Women Writers and Women in Literature, Medieval to Modern (New York: Schocken, 1983), pp. 76–92. She defines it as "the psychological effects of economic necessity, specifically upon sexual mores" (p. 77) and analyzes the Wife's successful exploitation of her own commodification in terms of the profit motive and the law of supply and demand.

10 Claude Lévi-Strauss, *The Elementary Structures of Kinship*, trans. James Harle Bell, John Richard von Sturmer, and Rodney Needham, rev. ed. (Boston: Beacon, 1969), pp. 36–38; Irigaray, "Women on the Market," in *This Sex Which Is Not One*, pp. 170–71.

11 Patterson, " 'For the Wyves love of Bathe,' " provides full documentation of various antifeminist texts and Chaucer's possible use of them in creating the Wife. See, further, R. Howard Bloch's "Medieval Misogyny" (*Representations* 20 [Fall 1987]: 1–24), for a discussion of the repetitiveness and monotony of antifeminist writers, and of the ways in which antifeminist writers are themselves inescapably feminized in their ceaselessly talking against women who ceaselessly talk.

12 Saint Jerome, *Adversus Jovinianum*, trans. W. H. Fremantle, in *A Select Library of Nicene and Post-Nicene Fathers of the Christian Church* (Grand Rapids, Mich.: Eerdmans, n.d.), 6:383.

> Deinde per noctes totas garrulae conquestiones: Illa ornatior procedit in publicum: haec honoratur ab omnibus, ego in conventu feminarum misella despicior. Cur aspiciebas vicinam? quid cum ancillula loquebaris?
> (Saint Jerome, *Adversus Jovinianum* 1. 47, in *PL* 23:276)

13 Guillaume de Lorris and Jean de Meun, *Le Roman de la rose*, trans. Charles Dahlberg, under the title *The Romance of the Rose* (Princeton, N.J.: Princeton Univ. Press, 1971), p. 227.

> . . . jurt que, s'il eüst volu
> soffrir que par autre fust prise
> sa rose, qui bien est requise,
> d'or fust chargiez et de joiaus;
> mes tant est ses fins queur loiaus
> que ja nus la main n'i tendra
> fors cil seus qui lors la tendra.
> (*Le Roman de la rose*, vv. 13082–88 [ed. Félix Lecoy, CFMA 98 (Paris: Honoré Champion, 1970)])

14 Irigaray, "This Sex Which Is Not One," p. 76.

15 In the following general comments about glossing, I have drawn on:

the summary article by Francis E. Gigot in *The Catholic Encyclopedia* (New York: Appleton, 1909), 6: 586–88; Beryl Smalley, *The Study of the Bible in the Middle Ages,* 3d ed. (Oxford: Basil Blackwell, 1983); Henri de Lubac, *Exégèse médiévale,* 4 vols. (Paris: Aubier, 1959); C. Spicq, *Esquisse d'une histoire de l'exégèse latine au moyen âge,* Bibliothèque thomiste 26 (Paris: J. Vrin, 1944), esp. pp. 62–108, 202–88; *Cambridge History of the Bible,* ed. P. R. Ackroyd, C. F. Evans, G. W. H. Lampe, S. L. Greenslade, 3 vols. (Cambridge: Cambridge Univ. Press, 1963–70); and Hennig Brinkmann, *Mittelalterliche Hermeneutik* (Tübingen: Max Niemeyer, 1980), esp. pp. 154–163.

16 See the *Prefatio* to his *Sententie,* in *Oeuvres de Robert de Melun,* ed. Raymond M. Martin, O.P., Spicilegium Sacrum Lovaniense (Louvain, 1947), 3:12, and Smalley's discussion of it (*The Study of the Bible,* pp. 215–30). Robert attacked not only the practice of glossing, with its removal of passages from contexts and alterations of syntax and diction (he speaks of the violence [*violentia*] done to the text [p. 17]), but also the very idea of glossing: if the gloss only repeats what the text says, it is worthless; if it changes what the text says, it is worse than worthless (pp. 13–14). As Smalley points out, Robert's critique of the authority of glosses is founded on a reverence for the inviolate word of Scripture itself. This is an impractical position for the teaching of scriptural interpretation, as Smalley says; nonetheless, it demonstrates an anxiety about the deformation and appropriation of the text by glossing (see *The Study of the Bible,* pp. 229–30).

17 Caie, "The Significance of the Early Chaucer Manuscript Glosses," p. 350.

18 Robert of Melun, *Prefatio,* p. 18, describes the masters as ready to fight for their glosses ("*usque ad sanguinem* pro eis, si opus esset, decertare parati" [emphasis in original]), and speaks of the violence to the literal text on p. 17; Christine de Pizan, letter 14, in *La Querelle de la Rose: Letters and Documents,* ed. and trans. Joseph L. Baird and John R. Kane (Chapel Hill: Univ. of North Carolina Dept. of Romance Languages, 1978), p. 140. "Voire, come dist le proverbe commun des gloses d'Orliens, qui destruisent le texte" (Christine de Pizan, "A Maistre Pierre Col, Secretaire du Roy Nostre Sire," in *Le Débat sur "Le roman de la rose,"* ed. Eric Hicks [Paris: Honoré Champion, 1977], p. 144).

19 See n. 4 above for critical discussions of the Wife's literality as an exegete.

20 For criticism that focuses on the Wife of Bath, glossing, and glossators, see Daniel S. Silvia, Jr., "Glosses to the *Canterbury Tales* from St. Jerome's *Epistola Adversus Jovinianum,*" *SP* 62 (1965): 28–39; and

Graham D. Caie, "The Significance of the Early Chaucer Manuscript Glosses." Anne Kernan, in "The Archwife and the Eunuch" (*ELH* 41 [1974]: 1–25), observes in detail the Wife's relationship to exegetical commentary (which I am including under the general rubric "glossing"). The *locus classicus* for the Wife's relation to exegetes is Robertson, *Preface to Chaucer*, pp. 317–31.

21 For comments on Jerome's pseudologicality and rhetorical excesses in *Adversus Jovinianum,* see E. Talbot Donaldson, "Designing a Camel; or, Generalizing the Middle Ages," *Tennessee Studies in Literature* 22 (1977): 1–16; Kernan, "The Archwife and the Eunuch," pp. 16–19; and Mary Carruthers, "The Wife of Bath and the Painting of Lions," *PMLA* 94 (1979): 211. Pammachius, whose initiative inspired Jerome to refute Jovinian in the first place, saw Jerome's polemic as excessive and suppressed as many copies of the treatise as he could—and this action was taken with Jerome's own approval. Douglas Wurtele, however, in "The Predicament of Chaucer's Wife of Bath: St. Jerome on Virginity" (*Florilegium* 5 [1983]: 208–36), performing a point-by-point summary and analysis of Jerome and the Wife's Prologue, finds Jerome's argument effective and the hapless Wife unable to refute it.

22 De Lubac speaks of one of the common faults of late fourteenth-century exegesis as "la pulverization du texte" (see *Exégèse médiévale,* vol. 2, pt. 2, ch. 9, "L'Age scolastique," esp. pp. 350–53, and ch. 10, "Humanistes et spirituels," pp. 369–513).

23 See Donald R. Howard, *The Idea of the Canterbury Tales* (Berkeley and Los Angeles: Univ. of California Press, 1976), pp. 247–55; see also H. Marshall Leicester, Jr., "Of a Fire in the Dark: Public and Private Feminism in the *Wife of Bath's Tale,*" *Women's Studies* 11 (1984): 157–78.

24 For a sophisticated analysis of the use of the romance in the Wife's performance, see Louise O. Fradenburg, "The Wife of Bath's Passing Fancy," *SAC* 8 (1986): 31–58. Fradenburg argues that the romance, in the late fourteenth century, became the genre in which the problematics of the categories of the past and of woman intersected.

25 Patterson's " 'The Wyves love of Bathe' " analyses the whole phenomenon of the Wife's rhetorical strategy as one of dilation, delay; his comments on her Midas digression appear on pp. 656–58.

26 For a less sympathetic reading of the Wife's deafness, see Melvin Storm, "Alisoun's Ear," *MLQ* 42 (1981): 219–26. Storm supports the reading of Robertson: her deafness is an iconographic representation of her unregenerate Pauline oldness.

27 Christine de Pizan, letter 14, in *La Querelle de la Rose,* trans. Baird and Kane, p. 136.

Je oÿ dire, n'a pas moult, a ·i· de ces compaingnons de l'office
dont tu es et que tu bien congnois, et homme d'auctorité, que il
congnoit ung home marié, lequel ajouste foy au *Ronmant de la Rose*
comme a l'Euvangile; celluy est souverainnement jaloux, et quant
sa passion le tient plus aigrement il va querre son livre et list devant sa fame, et puis fiert et frappe sus et dist: "Orde, telle come
quelle il dist, voir que tu me fais tel tour. Ce bon sage homme
maistre Jehan de Meung savoit bien que femmes savoient fere!"
Et a chascun mot qu'il treuve a son propos il fiert ung coup ou
deux du pié ou de la paume; si m'est advis que quiconques s'en
loe, telle povre famme le compere chier.

(Christine de Pizan to Pierre Col, *Le débat sur "Le Roman de la rose,"*
pp. 139–40)

CHAPTER FIVE. *Griselda Translated*

1 For a full account and texts of the sources of Chaucer's redaction,
see the classic study by J. Burke Severs, *The Literary Relationships of
Chaucer's "Clerkes Tale"* (New Haven, Conn.: Yale Univ. Press, 1942).
For an interesting and persuasive discussion of Chaucer's use of multiple sources in his translations, see Tim William Machan, *Techniques
of Translation: Chaucer's "Boece"* (Norman, Okla.: Pilgrim Books, 1985),
ch. 6.

2 Anne Middleton, in "The Clerk and His Tale: Some Literary Contexts,"
SAC 2 (1980): 121–50, analyzes the Clerk's performance as "a guided
tour of several specifically secular literary canons and ideals current
at the end of the fourteenth century" (p. 150), particularly those of
exemplary literature, Humanistic affect, and story collections.

3 For another example of fourteenth-century outrage at Walter, see *Le
Ménagier de Paris*, ed. J. Pichon (Paris: Société des Bibliophiles Français,
1846).

4 Paul G. Ruggiers, *The Art of the Canterbury Tales* (Madison: Univ. of
Wisconsin Press, 1965), p. 221.

5 The test of the strength of the wife can be seen to be at the same
time the test of the power of the text, and both pass magnificently:
Griselda's unflinching conformity to masculine desire never fails, and
Petrarch's translation provokes strong reactions in its readers (the
Paduan bursts into tears and cannot even finish it, while the Vero-
nese rigidly suppresses his emotions, admitting that "the style is well
adapted to call forth tears" but not yielding because he knows the
tale is not true). See *Seniles* 17.4 in *Originals and Analogues of Some
of Chaucer's Canterbury Tales*, Part 2, gen. ed. F. J. Furnivall, Chaucer

Society, 2d ser., no. 10 (London: Trübner, 1875), pp. 170–72; an English translation is printed in James Harvey Robinson and Henry Winchester Rolfe, *Petrarch: The First Modern Scholar and Man of Letters,* 2d ed. (New York: Putnam's Sons, 1914), pp. 191–96. See also *Seniles* 17.3 in Severs, *Literary Relationships of Chaucer's "Clerkes Tale,"* and my fuller discussion of the patriarchal implications of Petrarch's translation at the end of this chapter.

6 In " 'Whan she translated was': A Chaucerian Critique of the Petrarchan Academy," a paper presented at the 1986 New Chaucer Society meeting in Philadelphia, David Wallace analyzed the "translation" of the female body and discussed Walter and Petrarch as elitist and masculinist "translators." In his witty and provocative paper, which I read in manuscript after finishing the major outlines of my argument, Wallace suggests that Chaucer provides in the *Clerk's Tale* a critique of this "translation"; Wallace, further, situates Chaucer's critique within the sociopolitical climate of late fourteenth-century Italy.

7 Severs has shown that for details of Griselda's robing and disrobing Chaucer turned to his French source to fill out the Petrarch text (*Literary Relationships of Chaucer's "Clerkes Tale,"* pp. 245–46). And, as I shall note below, Chaucer adds particular emphasis at other sartorial moments in the narrative.

8 Hastings Rashdall, in *The Universities of Europe in the Middle Ages,* ed. F. M. Powicke and A. B. Emden, new ed., 3 vols. (London: Oxford Univ. Press, 1936), 3: 5–7, reports this myth of *translatio studii.* John Rous (or Rosse), chantry-priest of Warwick, in his *Historia regum Angliae* mentions the Mempric legend for what appears to be the first time. Ralph Higden (d. 1364), in his *Polychronicon* 6.1, Rolls Series (ed. J. R. Lumby [London: Longman and Co., 1876], 6: 352–54), mentions an Alfredian connection with Oxford University, and he is apparently the first to do so. But Rashdall dismisses "the whole story, with the vast cycle of legend of which it is the nucleus" as material for students of "the pathology of the human mind" (pp. 5–6).

9 See Judith Ferster, *Chaucer on Interpretation* (Cambridge: Cambridge Univ. Press, 1985), pp. 101–2. Ferster's discussion of Griselda's paradoxical self-assertiveness (and her observation of the Clerk's literary assertiveness) is the fullest and most sensitive I have seen.

10 In the context of the Clerk's aggressive stance toward Petrarch and Griselda's similar posture toward Walter, the famous tag from the General Prologue, happily quoted by generations of professors, must be reread: the Clerk "gladly" teaches; and he describes Griselda's actions several times with the same word. In turn, she says she'll "gladly" yield her place to Walter's new bride—but in a speech that includes

an unmistakable assertion of self ("*my* place" is what she'll yield) and a warning to Walter. Actions performed "gladly" may not, in fact, be done with unalloyed selflessness but may be mixed with a good deal of defensive self-assertion.

11 Stephen G. Nichols, Jr., in *Romanesque Signs: Early Medieval Narrative and Iconography* (New Haven, Conn.: Yale Univ. Press, 1983), suggests this appropriative function of *translatio* in the historical narratives of the early Middle Ages: "*Translatio* was a metaphoric process whereby one construct assumed the symbolic signification of another considered greater than itself" (p. 20). See also Ernst Robert Curtius, *European Literature and the Latin Middle Ages*, trans. Willard R. Trask (Princeton, N.J.: Princeton Univ. Press, 1953), pp. 28–30.

12 See Jacques Lacan's extension of Freudian transference into the very mechanism of the functioning of authority, in his *Four Fundamental Concepts of Psycho-Analysis*, ed. J.-A. Miller, trans. Alan Sheridan (New York: Norton, 1981), esp. pp. 230–36, 253–55. I have found Shoshana Felman's article, "Psychoanalysis and Education: Teaching Terminable and Interminable" (*YFS* 63 [1982]: 21–44), very valuable in its discussion of Lacan on transference. For Freud's use of the term "translation" (*Übersetzung*), see Patrick Mahony's comments in *The Ear of the Other: Otobiography, Transference, Translation; Texts and Discussions with Jacques Derrida* (ed. Christie V. McDonald [New York: Schocken Books, 1985]):

> While he considers repression to be a rift or fault in the translation, on several occasions in his writings he implicitly conceives all of the following to be translations: hysterical, phobic, and obsessional symptoms, dreams, recollections, parapraxes, the choice of the means of suicide, the choice of fetish, the analyst's interpretations, and the transpositions of unconscious material to consciousness.
>
> (Pp. 96–97)

13 Valery Larbaud, *An Homage to Jerome: Patron Saint of Translators*, trans. Jean-Paul de Chezet (Marlboro, Vt.: Marlboro Press, 1984). For Jerome's career as translator, see J. N. D. Kelly, *Jerome: His Life, Writings, and Controversies* (London: Duckworth, 1975), and Jean Steinmann, *Saint Jerome and His Times*, trans. Ronald Matthews (Notre Dame, Ind.: Fides Publishers, 1959).

14 Saint Jerome, Preface to his *Interpretatio Chronicae Eusebii Pamphili*, in *PL* 27: 36; trans. W. H. Fremantle, in *The Principal Works of St. Jerome*, Select Library of Nicene and Post-Nicene Fathers of the Christian Church (Grand Rapids, Mich.: Eerdmans, n.d.), 6:483.

15 Jerome, *Epistulae,* letter 57 (to Pammachius), ed. Isidorus Hilberg, CSEL 54 (Vienna: F. Tempsky, 1912), pt. 1, p. 512; trans. Fremantle, in *Principal Works of St. Jerome,* p. 115.

16 That translation (transfer, substitution) is the mechanism of rhetorical trope in general is apparent in Quintilian, *Institutio oratoria* 9.1.4–7 (ed. and trans. H. E. Butler, Loeb Classical Library [Cambridge: Harvard Univ. Press, 1959]), quoted above, in n. 21 to Chapter 1. See also Donatus, *Ars grammatica* 3.6, and Geoffrey of Vinsauf, *Poetria nova* ll.765–67a, both cited in n. 21 to Chapter 1.

The interpretive function of translation is suggested by Roman Jakobson's categorization (in "On Linguistic Aspects of Translations" in *On Translation,* ed. Reuben A. Brower [Cambridge, Mass.: Harvard University Press, 1959]) of the translation of verbal signs into three classes: *rewording* (or intralingual translation, "an interpretation of verbal signs by means of other signs of the same language"); *translation proper* (or interlingual translation, "an interpretation of verbal signs by means of some other language"); and *transmutation* (or intersemiotic translation, "an interpretation of verbal signs by means of nonverbal sign systems" [p. 233]). Rewording and translation proper are obviously interrelated, insofar as both produce verbal interpretations of the original message; and the categorization of transmutation as translation makes the interpretive function of translation explicit. For useful bibliography of literature on translations, see George Steiner, *After Babel: Aspects of Language and Translation* (London: Oxford Univ. Press, 1975). See also Susan Bassnett-McGuire, *Translation Studies,* New Accents Series (New York: Methuen, 1980).

17 On the currency of both *interpretatio* and *translatio* and the emerging prominence of the latter, Eugene Vance, in his *Mervelous Signals: Poetics and Sign Theory in the Middle Ages* (Lincoln: Univ. of Nebraska Press, 1986), pp. 318–19, cites Gianfranco Folena, "'Volgarizzare' e 'tradurre,'" in *La traduzione: Saggi e studi,* ed. Centro per lo studio dell'insegnamento all'estero dell'italiano, Universita degli studi de Trieste (Trieste: Lint, 1973), pp. 59–120. See Vance's discussion of translation in Chaucer and Spenser (*Mervelous Signals,* pp. 311–51). Rita Copeland's excellent essay, "Rhetoric and Vernacular Translation in the Middle Ages" (*SAC* 9 [1987]: 41–75), discusses the hermeneutic value of classical and medieval translation.

18 Saint Jerome, Preface to his translation of Eusebius' *Onomastikon,* in *Eusebius Werke,* ed. Erich Klostermann, Griechischen christlichen Schriftsteller, no. 11 (Leipzig: Hinrichs'sche, 1904), p. 3. Cited in Steinmann, *Saint Jerome,* p. 195.

19 Saint Jerome, *Epistulae*, letter 57 (to Pammachius), pt. 1, p. 512; trans. Fremantle, in *Principal Works of St. Jerome*, p. 115. Jerome articulates the problematics of translation early on, in his Preface to Eusebius' *Chronicle* (the earliest of his translations made in Constantinople [A.D. 381–82]): "Si ad verbum interpretor, absurde resonat; si ob necessitatem aliquid in ordine, vel in sermone mutavero, ab interpretis videbor officio recessisse" ("A literal translation sounds absurd; if, on the other hand, I am obliged to change either the order or the words themselves, I shall appear to have forsaken the duty of a translator" [*PL* 27:35; trans. Fremantle, *Principal Works of St. Jerome*, 6:483]). In this preface he goes on to suggest his solution, later explicitly formulated in letter 57, of translating the *sense:* he suggests here that under the ugly garb of words can be found the fair body of meaning. The sense must be maintained as unaltered as possible, even if he strives to preserve the grace of Latin style; see letters 57, sec. 5; 106, sec. 3; 26; 29; 54; and Preface to Job (*PL* 28: 1081) and Preface to Judith (*PL* 29: 39).

20 See Jerome's Preface to Samuel and Kings, the so-called *Prologus galeatus* (*PL* 28:5476–58), for his assertive protest of fidelity to the original Hebrew; see his Preface to Isaiah for a strong statement of his worthiness as a translator in comparison to his post-Septuagint Greek predecessors (Aquila, Symmachus, Theodotion); and see the beginning of *Hebraicae quaestiones* for the explicit statement of the necessity of the return to Hebrew to recover the original authority of the sacred Word. R. Howard Bloch, in *Etymologies and Genealogies: A Literary Anthropology of the French Middle Ages* ([Chicago: Univ. of Chicago Press, 1983], pp. 59–60), discusses Jerome's use of etymology—returning to the Hebrew—as a principle of exegesis. Also, for analysis of medieval translation in terms of a general ethics of speech, see Vance, *Mervelous Signals*, pp. 311–19.

21 For a discussion of medieval linguistic nostalgia, see Bloch, *Etymologies and Genealogies*, esp. pp. 30–63. See also Walter Benjamin's 1923 essay, "The Task of the Translator: An Introduction to the Translation of Baudelaire's *Tableaux parisiens*" (in *Illuminations*, ed. Hannah Arendt, trans. Harry Zohn [New York: Schocken Books, 1969]), on the goal of translation as a rediscovery of the original oneness of language.

22 Augustine, *De doctrina christiana* 2.6.8 (ed. J. Martin, CC 32 [Turnhout: Brepols, 1962]), referring to the pleasant and stimulating labor of interpretation; Geoffrey of Vinsauf, *Poetria nova* ll.767–69.

23 See Margaret F. Nims, IBVM, "*Translatio:* 'Difficult Statement' in Medieval Poetic Theory," *University of Toronto Quarterly* 43 (1974): 215–30. See also Lisa J. Kiser's discussion of figurative language in *Telling Classical Tales: Chaucer and the "Legend of Good Women"* (Ithaca, N.Y.: Cornell

Univ. Press, 1983), pp. 50–70. For the Chartrians, see Brian Stock, *Myth and Science in the Twelfth Century: A Study of Bernard Sylvester* (Princeton, N.J.: Princeton Univ. Press, 1972), pp. 227–83, cited by Vance, *Mervelous Signals*, p. 312. Stock notes (p. 275) that Bernard's *Cosmographia*, in numerous late-medieval codices, is bound with treatises on composition (such as that of Geoffrey of Vinsauf) or twelfth-century poetry (such as that of Alain de Lille).

24 Nims, "*Translatio*," pp. 221, 223.

25 Ibid., pp. 217–18.

26 Ibid., p. 220.

27 On the Creation as the utterance of the Word, see Augustine, for example. Wary, as usual, of human language's ability to express the divine, he nevertheless describes with wonder the power of the original translation:

> Postremo cetera dici possunt utcumque: ille solus est ineffabilis, qui dixit, et facta sunt omnia. Dixit, et facti sumus: sed nos eum dicere non possumus. Verbum eius quo dicti sumus, Filius eius est.

> [Lastly, all other things can be spoken in some way; He alone, Who spoke, and all things were made, is ineffable. He spake, and we were made: but we cannot speak of Him. His Word, by Whom we were uttered, is His Son.]

> (*Enaratio in Psalmum* 99, sec. 6 [in *Enarationes in Psalmos*, ed. D. Eligius Dekkers and Iohannes Fraipont, CC 39 (Turnhout: Brepols, 1956)]; the English translation is in Marcia Colish, *The Mirror of Language*, 2d ed. [Lincoln: Univ. of Nebraska Press, 1983], p. 26)

Nims cites both Hugh of Saint Victor and Vincent of Beauvais on the unity or mimetic relationship of God's Word and humankind's language. According to Nims, "*Translatio*," p. 229 n. 17, Hugh describes the unity of "the word of man, the word of God spoken in creation, and the uncreated Word of God" in his *De arca Noe morali* 2.13, "De tribus verbis." And Vincent of Beauvais, in his *Speculum naturale*, writes:

> Ita enim verbum nostrum vox quoddamodo corporis fit, assumendo eam in qua manifestetur sensibus hominum; sicut Verbum Dei caro factum est, assumendo eam in qua et ipsum manifestetur sensibus hominum.

> [Man, in uttering a word, is incarnating the word of his mind in order that it may be made manifest to human senses, just as the

Word of God was made flesh in order that He might be made
manifest to human senses.]
   (27.6.1921b [trans. Nims, "*Translatio*," p. 221])

28   The positing of a name departs from its normal process when the
condition of being man passes over to the realms of godhead.
Speaking in figure, a new trope (a new turning) is created, a new
verbal construction formed; there is a new stylistic beauty in this
joining, a new *translatio* has entered the world. In this uniting of
the Word with flesh, every rule stands stupefied.
   (Alain de Lille, *Rithmus de incarnatione Domini* [in "Alain de Lille
   et la *Theologia*," by M.-T. d'Alverny, in *L'Homme devant Dieu: Mélanges offerts au Père Henri de Lubac* (Paris, 1964), 2:126–28; quoted
   and trans. Nims, "*Translatio*," pp. 220, 229])

29   See Jerome's Preface to his *Interpretatio libri Didymi de Spiritu sancto*
(*PL* 23:105); and Preface to his translation of Origen, in *Die Homilien
zu Lukas*, in *Origenes Werke*, ed. Max Rauer, Griechischen christlichen
Schriftsteller, no. 49 (Berlin: Akademie Verlag, 1959), p. 1. On the con-
troversy between Jerome and Ambrose of Milan, see J. N. D. Kelly,
Jerome, pp. 143–44.

30   Kelly, *Jerome*, p. 266.

31   Donatus, *Ars grammatica* 3.6 (see n. 16 above).

32   George Puttenham writes of the "courtly figure *Allegoria*":

   Of this figure therefore which for his duplicitie we call the figure of
   [false semblant or dissimulation] we will speake first as of the chief
   ringleader and captaine of all other figures. . . . To be short every
   speach wrested from his owne naturall signification to another
   not altogether so naturall is a kind of dissimulation, because the
   words beare contrary countenaunce to th'intent.
   (*The Arte of English Poesie* [1589; rpt. Menston, England: Scolar
   Press, 1968], bk. 3 "Of Ornament," ch. 18, p. 155)

33   On figurative language as exile, see Margaret W. Ferguson, "Saint
Augustine's Region of Unlikeness: The Crossing of Exile and Language," *Georgia Review* 29 (1975): 842–64.

34   If the metaphor performs an inappropriate substitution, there is disruption of surface coherence and a discord between word and meaning below the surface as well. As Bloch notes (*Etymologies and Genealogies*, p. 118), Peter Helias distinguishes between appropriate and
inappropriate, proper and improper figures; when the transfer of a
word does not retain "the similitude of the elements conjoined," it is
improper ("Vitiosa est locutio ubi est translatio inconveniens"). See

Charles Thurot, *Notices et extraits de divers manuscrits latins* (1869; rpt. Frankfurt: Minerva, 1964), p. 234.

35 See Severs, *Literary Relationships of Chaucer's "Clerkes Tale,"* p. 274.

36 Alfred David, in *The Strumpet Muse: Art and Morals in Chaucer's Poetry* (Bloomington: Indiana Univ. Press, 1976), pp. 159–69, finds that melodrama in fact renders the last parts of the tale difficult to take seriously (but there is, he argues, too little of this oversentimentality to force us into an ironic reading; it simply makes us uneasy).

37 Quintilian, *Institutio oratoria* 9.1.4: a trope is "dictio ab eo loco, in quo propria est, translata in eum, in quo propria non est" ("the transference of words and phrases from the place which is strictly theirs to another to which they do not properly belong" [ed. and trans. Butler, pp. 350–51]). See n. 16 above.

38 The prominence of clothing imagery in the *Tale* has been remarked often, and its source and significance have been the subjects of considerable speculation. See Kristine Gilmartin Wallace's excellent article, which includes discussion of Chaucer's alterations of his sources, and her inclusive notes: "Array as Motif in the *Clerk's Tale,*" *Rice University Studies* 62 (1976): 99–110. The major critical explanation was advanced by D. D. Griffith, who argues for a folklore origin for this imagery, making the clothing demarcate the border between the world of mortals and the supernatural world; see his *Origin of the Griselda Story*, Univ. of Washington Publications in Language and Literature, no. 8 (Seattle: Univ. of Washington Press, 1931), pp. 92–93. Severs agrees that the clothes are folklore relics, but finds them "impertinent" to literary versions (*Literary Relationships of Chaucer's "Clerkes Tale,"* pp. 5–6). Other critical analyses advance various religious significances: Griselda's humiliating stripping recalls Christ's Passion (Elizabeth Salter, *Chaucer: The "Knight's Tale" and the "Clerk's Tale"* [London: Edward Arnold, 1962]), pp. 47–48); her clothing is an index of her proper Christian submission (John P. McCall, "The *Clerk's Tale* and the Theme of Obedience," *MLQ* 27 [1966]: 260–69); her "despoiling" and "translation" suggest conversion and transfiguration (Bertrand H. Bronson, *In Search of Chaucer* [Toronto: Univ. of Toronto Press, 1960], p. 108).

39 See Kristine Gilmartin Wallace, "Array as Motif," p. 101.

40 For a different, less generous reading of Griselda's words here, see Donald H. Reiman, who claims in "The Real *Clerk's Tale*; or, Patient Griselda Exposed" (*Texas Studies in Literature and Language* 5 [1963]: 356–73), that Griselda simply—and sinfully—cannot tell the difference between literal and figurative: "Griselda did not sell her conscience for the fine clothes and jewels of a marquesa, but simply lacked the

understanding to distinguish between her old clothes and her 'liberty and will,' or between her husband and her God" (p. 366).

41 Major studies arguing a largely symbolic value for Griselda and her experience (Abraham, Job, Virgin Mary, Rebecca, Rachel) include Charles Muscatine, *Chaucer and the French Tradition* (Berkeley and Los Angeles: Univ. of California Press, 1957), pp. 195–97; Salter, *Chaucer,* pp. 45–46); D. W. Robertson, *A Preface to Chaucer* (Princeton, N.J.: Princeton Univ. Press, 1962), pp. 82–83; Bernard F. Huppé, *A Reading of the "Canterbury Tales"* (Albany: State Univ. of New York, 1964), pp. 143–46, 260–69; and Francis Lee Utley, "Five Genres in the *Clerk's Tale,*" *ChauR* 6 (1972): 217–26.

42 Critics have noted such doubleness on the general narrative level: see, for example, Salter, who speaks of "the double preoccupation of poet or clerkly narrator in this *Tale*—the desire to interpret the story as a human document at the same time as establishing its meaning on a higher spiritual plane" ("The Clerk's Tale," in *Chaucer,* p. 51).

43 J. Mitchell Morse, in "The Philosophy of the Clerk of Oxenford" (*MLQ* 19 [1958]: 3–20), suggests that Walter's "realism" prevents him from treating Griselda as an individual; he is interested in her "wommanheede," not the individual woman. Morse contends that the Clerk, on the other hand, is "nominalist" (he is from Oxford) in his democratic regard for Griselda's individuality and experience. Morse's analysis, in the terms of fourteenth-century philosophical currents, of Walter's and the Clerk's treatments of Griselda complements my own analysis of translation as a literary gesture with social consequences—the elimination of Griselda's particular experience.

44 Ruggiers, *The Art of the Canterbury Tales,* p. 221. Judith Ferster, in *Chaucer on Interpretation* (Cambridge: Cambridge Univ. Press, 1985), makes an observation that is relevant here. While I argue that Griselda consciously articulates the consequences of figuration, Ferster reads Griselda's swoon just after her description of Walter as "benyngne fader" (1097) as a bodily index of her deep resistance to her own euphemistic treatment of Walter (p. 107).

45 For an allegorical reading here of Griselda's old clothes as her "wyl and al my libertee," her old self which is now hard to find, see Wallace, "Array as Motif in the *Clerk's Tale,*" p. 103.

46 Hans Baron's *The Crisis of the Early Italian Renaissance* (rev. ed. [Princeton, N.J.: Princeton Univ. Press, 1966]) traces the appraisal of Petrarch by humanists, early and late; Petrarch's discovery of Christian wisdom in the act of translation of texts into Latin was lauded by Salutati (as late as 1405) as the pinnacle of humanistic achievement (pp. 257–58).

47 Petrarch, *Seniles* 17.3, in Severs, *Literary Relationships of Chaucer's*

"Clerkes Tale," p. 288; trans. James Harvey Robinson and Henry Winchester Rolfe, in *Petrarch: The First Modern Scholar and Man of Letters,* 2d ed. (New York: Putnam's Sons, 1914), p. 194.

48 Dante Alighieri, *De vulgari eloquentia,* ed. Aristide Marigo, 3d ed. (Florence: Felice le Mounier, 1957), esp. chs. 1 and 6. See Robert Hollander, "Babytalk in Dante's *Commedia"* (*Mosaic* 8 [1975]: 73–84): Dante accords the highest linguistic and theological value to this "babytalk," whereas Petrarch (*Seniles* 5.2) and Boccaccio (*Vita di Dante*) see its use as the sign of an immature work.

49 Anne Middleton, "The Clerk and His Tale: Some Literary Contexts," *SAC* 2 (1980): 129.

50 See, e.g., Helen Cooper, in *The Structure of the Canterbury Tales* (Athens: Univ. of Georgia Press, 1984), p. 138.

51 Petrarch, in Severs, *Literary Relationships of Chaucer's "Clerkes Tale,"* p. 288; trans. Robinson, in *Petrarch,* p. 194.

52 Salter, "The Clerk's Tale," in *Chaucer,* p. 63.

53 The juxtaposition of alloyed coins here with modern wives associates women with the rupture and discontinuity of the still-emergent money economy. See Bloch, *Etymologies and Genealogies;* and Vance, *Mervelous Signals,* ch. 5, "Chretien's 'Yvain' and the Ideologies of Change and Exchange." Griselda herself in this context becomes a nostalgic figure, a lost unity and plenitude; writes Muscatine, for example: "In all, the tale of Griselda is a latter-day parable. . . . It yearns for the naked, simple, uncompromising virtue of original Christianity" (*Chaucer and the French Tradition,* p. 197).

54 Helen Cooper takes this song as a summation of the Clerk's attitude throughout his tale: "In spite of Alisoun and Griselda being diametrically opposite types of wifehood, the outlook finally presented by the Wife's and the Clerk's tales is astonishingly close" (*The Structure of the Canterbury Tales,* p. 139). Other critics who take the Envoy straight, as hyperbolic but not sarcastic, are D. H. Reiman and J. M. Morse.

55 The memorable phrase "relentless submissiveness," which Ferster also picks up (*Chaucer on Interpretation,* p. 101), is from Robert Longsworth, "Chaucer's Clerk as Teacher," in *The Learned and the Lewed,* ed. Larry D. Benson (Cambridge, Mass.: Harvard Univ. Press, 1974), p. 63. Salter sums up this view: in contrast to the Wife, she writes, Griselda is made a "more acceptable, less preposterous creation than the Wife of Bath and 'archewyves' of her kind" ("The Clerk's Tale" in *Chaucer,* p. 65).

56 Robert B. Burlin, in his *Chaucerian Fiction* (Princeton, N.J.: Princeton Univ. Press, 1977), p. 144, picks up Muscatine's interpretive suggestion and felicitous phrase, "concessive comedy," and argues that the success of the *Clerk's Tale* depends on this inclusive view. I owe much

to Burlin's problematization of the end of the poem, although my solution finally diverges from his.

57 See n. 10 above.

58 See, for example, Charlotte C. Morse, "The Exemplary Griselda," *SAC* 7 (1985): 83.

59 Cf. Salter's claim that it is a " 'human view' which is irresistible to Chaucer, and which urges him to dramatise and *then* criticise what he has created" ("The Clerk's Tale" in *Chaucer*, p. 62). It seems to me that Salter and others who point in various ways to conflicting points of view or mores in the Clerk's performance (e.g., Bronson, Cooper, Warren Ginsberg [*The Cast of Character* (Toronto: Univ. of Toronto Press, 1983), pp. 151–65]) use "human" here to denote all that is erased or marginalized by the rigorously Christian meaning or interpretation imposed at the end. I agree with the structure of such an analysis but argue that "human" must itself be analyzed in terms of gender. The issue in this narrative is the treatment of a woman. Chaucer's engagement with the marginal is with the female here; *translatio*, in particular, is represented as enacted on the body of a woman in this tale. More generally, I would argue that issues of exclusion in Chaucer are raised in reference to, or are based on, the gendered body; they are posed as or become gender issues.

60 Cf. H. Marshall Leicester, Jr.'s comments on the *Tales* in "The Art of Impersonation: A General Prologue to the *Canterbury Tales*," *PMLA* 95 (1980): 213–24: "The enterprise of the poem involves the continual attempt, continually repeated, to see from another's point of view, to stretch and extend the self by learning to speak in the voices of others" (p. 221).

CHAPTER SIX. *Eunuch Hermeneutics*

1 I take "trowe" here in its most common Middle English usage as denoting a speculation, a guess. See the *Oxford English Dictionary*, s.v. "trow" 3.b: "To believe or suppose (a thing or person) to be (so and so)"; and *A Chaucer Glossary*, ed. Norman Davis et al. (Oxford: Clarendon Press, 1979), s.v. "trowe(n)" 1: "Believe; think, judge." C. David Benson comments:

> This word most commonly indicates speculation, but even if we take it in its less usual meaning of certainty, is this the assertion of the same narrator who agrees with the Monk's idea of cloistered duty and find the murderous Shipman a good fellow? Certainly the phrase "I trowe" qualifies what is to follow to some degree.
>
> ("Chaucer's Pardoner: His Sexuality and Modern Critics," *Mediaevalia* 8 [1985 for 1982]: 339)

We can't read "trowe" here too easily and ironically; Benson stresses the uncertainty of any knowledge of the Pardoner's sexual makeup. Moreover, he suggests that recent critical emphasis on the Pardoner's sexuality is a modern distortion: "The real perversion of this pilgrim is not sexual but moral" (p. 346). While I agree with Benson that the Pardoner's portrait confounds any sure knowledge of his sexuality, I would argue that the issue of sexuality was in fact central to medieval audiences of this text: as James A. Brundage has recently stated, sexual practices, from the late twelfth century on, were "taken as indicators of doctrinal orthodoxy," so that sexual deviance implied spiritual deviance (*Law, Sex, and Christian Society in Medieval Europe* [Chicago: Univ. of Chicago Press, 1987], pp. 256–324, esp. 313–14]). Indeed, the moral cannot be opposed to the sexual, but is deeply implicated in it.

2 For a discussion of the "obligatory heterosexuality" in the exchange model of society (and the implied ban on homosexual relations, even though the society is "homosocial"—i.e., constituted by bonds between men), see Gayle Rubin, "The Traffic in Women: Notes on the 'Political Economy' of Sex," in *Toward an Anthropology of Women*, ed. R. R. Reiter (New York: Monthly Review Press, 1975), pp. 179–80; Eve Kosofsky Sedgwick, *Between Men: English Literature and Male Homosocial Desire* (New York: Columbia Univ. Press, 1985); and Craig Owens, "Outlaws: Gay Men in Feminism," in *Men in Feminism*, ed. Alice Jardine and Paul Smith (New York: Methuen, 1987), pp. 219–32.

3 Robert B. Burlin, *Chaucerian Fiction* (Princeton, N.J.: Princeton Univ. Press, 1977), p. 170; Lee W. Patterson, "Chaucerian Confession: Penitential Literature and the Pardoner," *Medievalia et Humanistica*, n.s. 7 (1976): 153–73, esp. p. 163. H. Marshall Leicester, Jr., in *The Disenchanted Self: Representing the Subject in the "Canterbury Tales"* (forthcoming, Univ. of California Press), also stresses the Pardoner's hiding his intentions from others. Leicester's reading of the Pardoner as an embodiment of lack has much in common with mine; and his contrast of "the feminine" in the Wife of Bath and in the Pardoner runs parallel to my contrast, below, of the Clerk (and Chaucer) and the Pardoner as they occupy the "feminine" position.

4 For a discussion of the hermeneutic provocations of retaining such a veil, see D. A. Miller, "The Administrator's Black Veil: A Response to J. Hillis Miller," *ADE Bulletin* 88 (1987): 49–53.

5 For an account of the Pardoner's literary reception from medieval to modern times, see Betsy Bowden, *Chaucer Aloud: The Varieties of Textual Interpretation* (Philadelphia: Univ. of Pennsylvania Press, 1987), pp. 77–173. "About the Pardoner," she writes, "critics have almost always agreed to disagree" (p. 79).

6 R. Howard Bloch, in "Silence and Holes: The *Roman de Silence* and the

Art of the Trouvère" (in *Images of Power: Medieval History/Discourse/ Literature*, ed. Stephen G. Nichols and Kevin Brownlee, *YFS* 70 [1986]: 81–99), reads Macrobius in precisely this way. Looking at Macrobius' commentary on the *Somnium Scipionis*, Bloch sees that Macrobius discusses the wont of Nature to wrap her truths in allegorical texts:

> sicut vulgaribus hominum sensibus intellectum sui vario rerum tegmine operimentoque subtraxit, ita a prudentibus arcana sua voluit per fabulosa tractari.

> [Just as she has withheld an understanding of herself from the uncouth senses of men by enveloping herself in variegated garments, [she] has also desired to have her secrets handled by more prudent individuals through fabulous narratives.]

Further on in this prefatory section, Macrobius describes the tradition of representing divinities, such as Nature or the Eleusinian goddesses:

> adeo semper ita se et sciri et coli numina maluerunt qualiter in vulgus antiquitas fabulata est, quae et imagines et simulacra formarum talium prorsus alienis, et aetates tam incrementi quam diminutionis ignaris, et amictus ornatusque varios corpus non habentibus adsignavit.

> [In truth, divinities have always preferred to be known and worshiped in the fashion assigned to them by ancient popular tradition, which made images of beings that had no physical form, represented them as of different ages, though they were subject neither to growth nor decay, and gave them clothes and ornaments, though they had no bodies.]

> (Macrobius, *Commentarii in Somnium Scipionis*, ed. J. Willis [Leipzig: Teubner, 1963], pp. 7–8; trans. William Harris Stahl [New York: Columbia Univ. Press, 1952], pp. 86–87)

Macrobius' comment here may be taken to refer to the idea that the gods are transcendent entities—that deities have no real bodies and thus are transcendent signifieds. But Bloch uses the context of the preface to suggest that the nature of all representation is implicated:

> The relation of truth, Nature, to its representation or image is thus that of the body to the clothes which are a potent paradigm of representation in Macrobius's terms—bodiless, empty, less capable of expressing a reality exterior to it than of covering up an absence that is also, finally, scandalous.

> ("Silence and Holes," p. 95)

There are varieties of response to such an idea about representation: if, say, Ovid can gaily face such a possibility—in the *Remedia* he blithely remarks, "Auferimur cultu; gemmis auroque teguntur / Omnia; pars minima est ipsa puella sui" ("We're dazzled by feminine adornment, by the surface; all is concealed by gold and jewels; a woman is the least part of herself")—others might find it terrifying, the possibility of a radical absence unbearable. I shall suggest that the Pardoner poignantly demonstrates the latter response. (For the Ovid, see the *Remedia amoris* 343–44, in *"The Art of Love" and Other Poems*, ed. and trans. J. H. Mozley, Loeb Classical Library [London: William Heinemann, 1929], p. 200; I combine Mozley's English translation with Peter Green's in *Ovid: The Erotic Poems* [Harmondsworth: Penguin, 1982], p. 249.)

7 The narrator's perception of lack is what Donald R. Howard stresses in his reading of the line, "I trowe he were a geldyng or a mare"; see his *The Idea of the "Canterbury Tales"* (Berkeley and Los Angeles: Univ. of California Press, 1976), p. 343. Howard seeks to restore the sense of the Pardoner's inexplicably strange presence among the pilgrims but accepts, nonetheless, Curry's determination that the Pardoner is a eunuch (see n. 8 below and the excellent critical analysis of critical analyses of the Pardoner in Monica McAlpine's "The Pardoner's Homosexuality and How It Matters," *PMLA* 95 [1980]: 8–22).

8 The gloss of "geldyng" as "eunuch" is attested by both the *Middle English Dictionary* and the *Oxford English Dictionary*. The wide acceptance of eunuchry as the description of the Pardoner's condition derives ultimately from "The Secret of Chaucer's Pardoner," W. C. Curry's ground-breaking article (*JEGP* 18 [1919]: 593–606; later appearing in his *Chaucer and the Mediaeval Sciences*, rev. ed. [New York: Barnes and Noble, 1960], pp. 54–90). Curry was the first to bring the inference of eunuchry under critical scrutiny, attempting to provide evidence from classical and medieval scientific discourse. Curry's particular interpretation of this evidence—his conclusion that the Pardoner is a congenital eunuch, a *eunuchus ex nativitate*, rather than a castrated one—has come under attack: see Muriel Bowden, *A Commentary on the General Prologue to the "Canterbury Tales"* (New York: Macmillan, 1957), pp. 274–76; Beryl Rowland, "Chaucer's Idea of the Pardoner," *ChauR* 14 (1979): 140–54; McAlpine, "The Pardoner's Homosexuality and How It Matters"; and Benson, "Chaucer's Pardoner: His Sexuality and Modern Critics." Curry bases his diagnosis on his own interpretation of the Pardoner's character and not on the medieval physiognomists (according to whom all eunuchs look alike). And his medieval evidence is not, as Benson points out, as compelling or conclusive as is often assumed by modern critics. Still, the reading of the equine figure "geldyng" as "eunuch," either congenital or castrated, is supported by physical details in the General Prologue; as McAlpine concedes, Chaucer does evoke the medieval stereotype of the eunuch in details

of the Pardoner's portrait. Robert P. Miller has provided the scriptural background that supports the diagnosis *eunuchus* (see his classic article, "Chaucer's Pardoner, the Scriptural Eunuch, and the Pardoner's Tale," *Speculum* 30 [1955]: 180–99); Chaucer's detailing of the Pardoner's physical condition, Lee Patterson argues, renders it meaningful both in the realm of science and of religious symbol ("Chaucerian Confession: Penitential Literature and the Pardoner"). As I hope to demonstrate, eunuchry as a figure has a powerful psychological value in the Prologue and *Tale*.

"Mare" is defined in the *MED* (s.v. "mere," n.(1) 2.e) as figuratively denoting "a bad woman, a slut"; attestations include *Handlyng Synne* and the *Castle of Perseverance*. Sexually wayward femininity can thus be evoked by this term. The gloss of "mare" as "effeminate male" is not attested by the *MED* or *OED* but is a likely reading of this equine figure in context of a description of a male; such a gloss was suggested by Curry ("The Secret of Chaucer's Pardoner," p. 58) and has been reiterated by McAlpine:

> "Mare" must be a term commonly used in Chaucer's day to designate a male person who, though not necessarily sterile or impotent, exhibits physical traits suggestive of femaleness, visible characteristics . . . that were thought to have broad effects on the psyche and on character.
>
> ("The Pardoner's Homosexuality," p. 11)

See also Benson, who seems to accept the reading of "mare" as "effeminate in some way" ("Chaucer's Pardoner," p. 339).

Other analyses of the Pardoner's sexuality—that he is a "testicular pseudo-hermaphrodite of the feminine type" (Beryl Rowland, "Animal Imagery and the Pardoner's Abnormality," *Neophilologus* 48 [1964]: 56–60), or a combination pervert, e.g., "a manic depressive with traces of anal eroticism, and a pervert with a tendency toward alcoholism" (Eric W. Stockton, "The Deadliest Sin in the *Pardoner's Tale*," *Tennessee Studies in Literature* 6 [1961]: 47)—seem far more specific and certain than is warranted by the portrait and performance of the character.

9 McAlpine argues at length for the possibility of reading "mare" as "a possibly homosexual male," suggesting that "certain types of feminized behavior and appearance in males were sometimes interpreted as evidence of homosexuality" ("The Pardoner's Sexuality," p. 12). Citing a variety of medieval examples, she bases her discussion on the apparent conflation of sexual categories—effeminacy, homosexuality, eunuchry, hermaphroditism, impotence—in common medieval understanding. I shall treat this apparent conflation in more detail in n. 16 below. McAlpine mentions the anachronism of the term "homo-

sexual" in this context (p. 11), but she retains it nonetheless to refer not just to sexual acts but to sexual and moral identity. For a thorough and clear discussion of appropriate terminology for older literatures, see John Boswell, *Christianity, Social Tolerance, and Homosexuality: Gay People in Western Europe from the Beginning of the Christian Era to the Fourteenth Century* (Chicago: Univ. of Chicago Press, 1980), pp. 43–46: Boswell distinguishes between "homosexuality" (referring to the "general phenomenon of same-sex eroticism") and "gay" (referring to "persons who are conscious of erotic inclination toward their own gender as a distinguishing characteristic"). I shall use the more general term; my point about the Pardoner's character is not as specific as that he is "gay."

10 I wish to acknowledge a general indebtedness in the development of my idea of eunuch hermeneutics to R. Howard Bloch, *The Scandal of the Fabliaux* (Chicago: Univ. of Chicago Press, 1986).

11 See Robert P. Miller, "Chaucer's Pardoner, the Scriptural Eunuch, and the Pardoner's Tale." Augustine's analyses of spiritual conditions are powerful psychological analyses as well, as Donald R. Howard comments in his discussion of the Pardoner in his *Idea of the "Canterbury Tales,"* pp. 355–56. Janet Adelman, in " 'That We May Leere Som Wit' " (in *Twentieth-Century Interpretations of the Pardoner*, ed. Dewey R. Faulkner [Englewood Cliffs, N.J.: Prentice-Hall, 1973], pp. 96–106), discusses *aesthetic* implications of *cupiditas*, seeing in the *Tale*'s use of parody and analogy a pattern of false substitution.

12 About the eunuch in the Acts, Richard remarks:

> Solus amor libri totum sibi vindicaverat domicilium castitatis, quo disponente mox fidei ianuam meruit introire.

> [Love of his book alone had wholly engrossed this domicile of chastity, under whose guidance he soon deserved to enter the gate of faith.]

> (*The Philobiblon of Richard Bury*, ed. and trans. Ernest C. Thomas [London: Kegan, Paul, Trench and Co., 1888], ch. 15, sec. 203 [pp. 121, 231])

See also *Philobiblon*, ch. 15, sec. 193 (pp. 115, 227) for citation of Origen.

13 J. T. Muckle, ed., "Abelard's Letter of Consolation to a Friend," *Mediaeval Studies* 12 (1950): esp. 182. See letter 4, from Abelard to Heloise, for remarks regarding Origen (Muckle, ed., *Mediaeval Studies* 15 [1953]: 89–90). R. Howard Bloch's discussion in *Etymologies and Genealogies: A Literary Anthropology of the French Middle Ages* ([Chicago: Univ. of Chicago Press, 1983], "Philosophy and the Family: Abelard," pp. 141–49) suggests ways in which castration informs Abelard's theological formulations and his radical break from philosophical tradition.

14 Abelard's castration was not voluntary, of course, however salutary
   he later found it. He notes that Origen acted impetuously and was
   worthy of blame:

   > Culpam tamen non modicam Origines [*sic*] incurrit dum per poe-
   > nam corporis remedium culpae quaerit, zelum quippe dei habens,
   > sed non secundam scientiam, homicidii incurrit reatum, inferendo
   > sibi manum.

   > [Yet Origen is seriously to be blamed because he sought a remedy
   > for blame in punishment of his body. True, he has zeal for God,
   > but an ill-informed zeal, and the charge of homicide can be proved
   > against him for his self-mutilation.]

   >   (Letter 4 [*Mediaeval Studies*, p. 90; trans. Betty Radice, *The Letters
   >   of Abelard and Heloise* (New York: Penguin, 1974), p. 149])

   Similarly, John of Salisbury, one of Abelard's students in Paris, commends Origen for his zeal but remarks on his lack of good sense
   (*Polycraticus* 8.6 [in *PL* 199: 724D–25D]). For summary discussion of
   medieval attitudes toward castration, see John T. Noonan, Jr., *Contraception: A History of Its Treatment by the Catholic Theologians and Canonists*
   (Cambridge, Mass.: Harvard Univ. Press, 1966), pp. 95, 247. The idea
   that self-castration was blameworthy was current throughout the Middle Ages; voluntary self-castration was not approved of even by the
   early Church: opposing Gnostic opinion regarding self-castration, the
   Council of Nicea (A.D. 325) enunciated the belief that nature should not
   be mutilated. Aquinas summed up medieval opinion when he stressed
   that God intended, through nature, that the human body be integral
   in all its members (*Summa theologica* 2a.2ae.65 ["De mutilatione membrorum"] [*Opera omnia* (Parma, 1852–73; rpt. New York: Musurgia,
   1948), 3:244–45]). Nature (vv. 17022–29) and Genius (vv. 20007–52) in
   the *Roman de la rose* (ed. Félix Lecoy, CFMA 98 [Paris: Honoré Champion, 1970]) similarly stress the natural integrity of the body. Richard
   of Bury does, it is true, acknowledge that Origen's self-castration was
   a "hasty remedy," "nec naturae tamen consentaneum nec virtuti" ("repugnant alike to nature and to virtue," in Thomas' emphatic translation) but ends the chapter with his vigorous commendation of the
   New Testament castrato; the metaphoric charge of Richard's discourse
   is most important here (*Philobiblon*, ch. 15, sec. 203).
15 See Raison, in *Le Roman de la rose*, vv. 5505–628; Genius also explicitly
   connects castration to the loss of the Golden Age (vv. 20007–52). For
   a detailed analysis of the Golden Age in reference to these passages
   in the *Roman de la Rose*—divergent from the one I shall propose here
   —see John V. Fleming, *Reason and the Lover* (Princeton, N.J.: Princeton
   Univ. Press, 1984), pp. 97–135.

16 McAlpine briefly documents the conflation of sexual categories in the Middle Ages, citing among other writings a thirteenth-century fabliau by Gautier le Leu, "La Veuve," in which impotence, eunuchry, homosexuality, and heresy are equated ("The Pardoner's Homosexuality," p. 12). "La Veuve," Charles Muscatine has argued, may have influenced Chaucer's characterization of the Wife of Bath; see "The Wife of Bath and Gautier's 'La Veuve,'" in *Romance Studies in Memory of Edward Billings Ham*, ed. U. T. Holmes, California State College Publications 2 (Hayward, Calif., 1967), pp. 109–14.

17 Boswell, *Christianity, Social Tolerance, and Homosexuality*, p. 53. See [Aristotle], *Problems* 4.24–26 (trans. E. S. Forster, in *The Complete Works of Aristotle*, ed. Jonathan Barnes [Princeton, N.J.: Princeton Univ. Press, 1984], pp. 1356–57). Boswell goes on to mention Caelius Aurelianus (fifth-century translator of Soranus), who himself cites Parmenides' *On Nature*, in considering homosexuality to be the result of a birth defect. Caelius Aurelianus mentions others (*multi sectarum principes*) as well who considered homosexuality an inherited disease; see *On Chronic Diseases*, ed. and trans. I. E. Drabkin (Chicago: Univ. of Chicago Press, 1950), pp. 900–905. Aurelianus' works were apparently not important in the development of medieval medical thought, but Aquinas' certainly were. I have already discussed Aquinas on the conception of females in my Introduction (see p. 19 and n. 47); Aquinas' position on homosexuality in the *Summa theologica*, the repository of orthodox Christian sentiment for centuries to come, is acutely analyzed by Boswell, in *Christianity, Social Tolerance, and Homosexuality*, pp. 318–30. Aquinas' discussion is of particular interest here: homosexuality might be quite "natural" to a given individual because of a "defect of nature in him":

> Ita igitur contingit quod id quod est contra naturam hominis vel quantum ad rationem, vel quantum ad corporis conservationem, fiat huic homini connaturale propter aliquam corruptionem naturae in eo existentem.

> [Thus it may happen that something which is against human nature, in regard either to reason or to the preservation of the body, may become natural to a particular man, owing to some defect of nature in him.]
>
> (*Summa theologica* 2a.31.7; trans. Boswell, in *Christianity, Social Tolerance, and Homosexuality*, p. 326)

Females, too, are produced by "defective" circumstances—Aquinas follows Aristotle here—and, as I noted in the Introduction, this leads the scholastic philosopher into a difficulty regarding the morality and

goodness of the condition of femaleness ("Utrum mulier debuerit produci in prima rerum productione" [*Summa theologica* 1a.92.1]). Boswell
argues that, in Aquinas, "neither homosexuality nor femaleness can
be shown to be 'immoral' simply because it does not represent the
primary intent of 'nature,' and both are in fact 'natural' to the indi-
viduals in question" (p. 327). Aquinas condemns homosexuality as
"unnatural," Boswell contends, in "a concession to popular sentiment
and parlance" rather than in a theological proof (p. 328). For more on
the "unnatural" in medieval discussions of homosexuality, see Vern L.
Bullough, "The Sin against Nature and Homosexuality," in *Sexual Practices and the Medieval Church,* ed. Vern L. Bullough and James Brundage (Buffalo, N.Y.: Prometheus Books, 1982), pp. 55–71; and James A.
Brundage, *Law, Sex, and Christian Society in Medieval Europe* (see n. 1
above).

18 For a discussion and translation of Rhazes' treatise, see Franz Rosenthal, "Ar-Rāzī on the Hidden Illness," *Bulletin of the History of Medicine*
52 (1978): 45–60. For a general treatment of Rhazes in the context of
Islamic medicine, see Manfred Ullmann, *Islamic Medicine* (Edinburgh:
Edinburgh Univ. Press, 1978). Helen Rodnite Lemay mentions Rhazes
in her general discussions of human sexuality in the medical writings
of the medieval West; see "William of Saliceto on Human Sexuality,"
Viator 12 (1981): 165–81; and "Human Sexuality in Twelfth- through
Fifteenth- Century Scientific Writings," in *Sexual Practices and the Medieval Church,* pp. 187–205.

19 Jacques Lacan, "The mirror stage as formative of the function of the
I as revealed in psychoanalytic experience," in his *Ecrits: A Selection,*
trans. Alan Sheridan (New York: Norton, 1977), p. 4.

20 Alfred L. Kellogg, "Chaucer's Satire of the Pardoner," in his *Chaucer,
Langland, Arthur: Essays in Middle English Literature* (New Brunswick,
N.J.: Rutgers Univ. Press, 1972), pp. 212–44.

21 I have found Jonathan Sumption, *Pilgrimage: An Image of Mediaeval Religion* (London: Faber, 1975), especially useful—well documented and
lively—on the subject of relics. Other interesting, general treatments I
have used include Hippolyte Delehaye, *Les Origines du culte des martyrs,*
2d ed., rev. (Brussels: Société des Bollandistes, 1933); P. Sejourné, "Reliques," in *Dictionnaire de théologie catholique* (Paris: Librairie Letouzey
et Ané, 1937), 13:2311–75; and Peter Brown, *The Cult of the Saints: Its
Rise and Function in Latin Christianity* (Chicago: Univ. of Chicago Press,
1981). In the brief discussion that follows, I have cited sources from the
early through the late Middle Ages; veneration of relics varied through
the age, but the essential theological idea of relics remained fairly con-

stant. Sumption suggests that the early Church's defenses of relics are echoed "in every major apologist of the Middle Ages" (*Pilgrimage*, p. 23).

22 See A. Frowlow, *La Relique de la vrai croix: Recherches sur le développement d'un culte*, Archives de l'orient chrétien, no. 7 (Paris: Institut français d'études byzantines, 1961), pp. 60–61, 161–65.

23 Theodoret of Cyrus, *Graecarum affectionum curatio* 8; quoted in Sumption, *Pilgrimage*, p. 28. See also Victricius of Rouen (*De laude sanctorum* 10–11 [*PL* 20:454B]), who speaks of saints' bodies, wherein all fragments are "totius vinculo aeternitatis astricti"—"linked by a bond to the whole stretch of eternity" in Brown's elegant translation; see Brown's discussion of Victricius, in *The Cult of the Saints*, pp. 78–79.

24 Sumption, *Pilgrimage*, p. 28.

25 Guibert of Nogent traces corruption and fraudulent claims to the practice of dismemberment and translation:

> Quod totum contentionis malum inde sumit originem quod sancti non permittuntur habere debitae et immutabilis sepulturae quietem.
>
> [All the evil of contention [over relics] originates in the fact that the saints are not permitted the repose of a proper and immutable burial place.]
>
> (*Gesta Dei per Francos* 1.5 [*PL*, 156:695A])

See Sumption's discussion of Guibert in *Pilgrimage*, pp. 27, 42–44.

26 Guibert of Nogent, in *De pignoribus sanctorum* 1.3.2 (*PL* 156:624D), points to the competing claims of Constantinople and Angeli to the head of the Baptist, and remarks: "Quid ergo magis ridiculum super tanto homine praedicetur, quam si biceps esse ab utrisque dicatur?" ("What, therefore, is more ridiculous than to suppose that this great man had two heads?"). See Delehaye for a specific history of the head (*Les origines du culte des martyrs*, pp. 82–83); Sumption summarizes the history of Christ's foreskin (*Pilgrimage*, p. 46).

27 *Mandeville's Travels*, ed. P. Hamelius, from BM Ms. Cotton Titus C. XVI, EETS o.s 153 (London: Kegan Paul, 1919 for 1916), p. 71.

28 Sumption, *Pilgrimage*, pp. 50–51.

29 Leo Steinberg, *The Sexuality of Christ in Renaissance Art and in Modern Oblivion* (New York: Pantheon, 1983). For a recent study of Chaucerian comedy that uses Steinberg's analysis of Christ's private parts ("Goddes pryvetee"), see Laura Kendrick, *Chaucerian Play: Comedy and Control in the "Canterbury Tales"* (Berkeley and Los Angeles: Univ. of California Press, 1988), pp. 5–19.

30 M. T. Clanchy, *From Memory to Written Record: England, 1066–1307* (Cambridge, Mass.: Harvard Univ. Press, 1979), p. 126. See also Delehaye, *Les Origines du culte des martyrs.*

31 My idea of a "partial object" here is different from Melanie Klein's "part-object." Klein establishes that in early infancy "all the baby knows or experiences is a breast (a 'part-object') and that it takes time and development for the baby to become aware of the mother in her completeness ('whole-object')" (Harry Guntrip, *Personality Structure and Human Interaction* [New York: International Universities Press, 1961], p. 226). The "part-object," to the infant, is not partial; it is a whole-object to the baby and is partial only in the adult's eyes. In my adaptation of the term, the partialness of the object, from the subject's point of view, is important: the object is a substitute for a formerly known whole and is recognized to be defective in relation to that lost whole. Klein stresses that part-objects remain active as representations of the mother even after the infant has perceived her as a whole, and analysts following Klein have pointed to situations in which older children treat people as part-objects. See, for example, Emilio Rodrigué, "An Analysis of a Three-Year-Old Mute Schizophrenic," in *New Directions in Psycho-Analysis,* ed. Melanie Klein, Paula Heimann, and R. E. Money-Kyrle (New York: Basic Books, 1955), pp. 140–79. It's this afterlife of the Kleinian part-object that led me to the idea that the part has an important function *after* perception of and loss of the whole—that it is, in fact, fetishized. But more on fetishes later.

32 Sigmund Freud, "Fetishism," in *The Standard Edition of the Complete Psychological Works,* ed. and trans. James Strachey (London: Hogarth Press, 1953–56), 21:153. See also Freud, "The Dissolution of the Oedipus Complex," in *Standard Edition,* 19:173–79.

33   C'est donc plutôt l'assomption de la castration qui crée le manque dont s'institue le désir. Le désir est désir de désir, désir de l'Autre, avons-nous dit, soit soumis à la Loi.

[It is, therefore, the assumption of castration which creates the lack through which desire is instituted. Desire is the desire for desire, the desire of the Other and it is subject to the Law.]
(Lacan, "Du *Trieb* de Freud et du désir du psychanalyste," in *Ecrits* [Paris: Seuil, 1966], p. 852; trans. David Macey, in *Jacques Lacan,* by Anika Lemaire [London: Routledge and Kegan Paul, 1977])

I was pointed to this passage by Margaret Homans, *Bearing the Word: Language and Female Experience in Nineteenth-Century Women's Writing* (Chicago: Univ. of Chicago Press, 1986), p. 8. See also David Carroll, *The Subject in Question: The Languages of Theory and the Strategies of Fic-*

tion (Chicago: Univ. of Chicago Press, 1982), for fine discussion of the implications of castration in literary texts.

34 Anthony Wilden, "Lacan and the Discourse of the Other," in *Speech and Language in Psychoanalysis*, by Jacques Lacan, trans. with notes and commentary by Anthony Wilden (Baltimore: Johns Hopkins Univ. Press, 1968), p. 163. Lacan, in "The Function and Field of Speech and Language in Psychoanalysis" (in *Ecrits: A Selection*, pp. 102–4), reinterprets Freud's analysis of his grandson's game of *Fort!/Da!*, analyzing the partial object as itself conveying absence. The partial object attempts to fill a lack created by a loss of ideal plenitude; Lacan analyzes the restless movement of desire opened up by the loss of the *objet a*, the loss of the relation to an other who is not conceived of as an object. The substitutes will always be partial. This lost "object a" is in particular the mother's body; in Lacan's interpretation of the Oedipal situation, the father interrupts the symbiotic relationship of mother and child; the phallus represents sexual difference and thus is a sign of castration. See "Of the Gaze as *Objet Petit a*," in *Four Fundamental Concepts of Psychoanalysis*, ed. J.-A. Miller, trans. Alan Sheridan (New York: Norton, 1981), pp. 67–119, esp. 67–77.

35 I am indebted to Margaret Homans' discussion of Lacan's androcentrism in her *Bearing the Word*, pp. 1–39. I've also found useful Jacqueline Rose's remarks in *Feminine Sexuality: Jacques Lacan and the école freudienne*, ed. Juliet Mitchell and Jacqueline Rose, trans. Jacqueline Rose (New York: Norton, 1982), pp. 27–57. Two works have proved most helpful on Freud's androcentrism: Sarah Kofman, *The Enigma of Woman: Woman in Freud's Writings*, trans. Catherine Porter (Ithaca, N.Y.: Cornell Univ. Press, 1985); and Luce Irigaray, *Speculum of the Other Woman*, trans. Gillian C. Gill (Ithaca, N.Y.: Cornell Univ. Press, 1985).

36 Sarah Kofman, *The Enigma of Woman*, p. 82.

37 Anthony Wilden quotes Lacan from the seminar of April–June 1958, "Les formations de l'inconscient," in his commentary in *Speech and Language in Psychoanalysis*, pp. 187–88.

38 Homans, *Bearing the Word*, pp. 8–9. Homans extends the implications of Nancy Chodorow's feminist revision of Freud to Lacanian theory (see Chodorow, *The Reproduction of Mothering: Psychoanalysis and the Sociology of Gender* [Berkeley and Los Angeles: Univ. of California Press, 1978]).

39 "Necessary symbolisation and the privileged status of the phallus appear as interdependent in the structuring and securing (never secure) of human subjectivity" (Rose, *Feminine Sexuality*, p. 56).

40 Julia Kristeva's remarks are from her *In the Beginning Was Love: Psycho-*

analysis and Faith, trans. Arthur Goldhammer (New York: Columbia
Univ. Press, 1987), p. 41. See also Jacqueline Rose's comments on the
difficulty of subjectivity, *Feminine Sexuality*, esp. pp. 40–41.

41 Terry Eagleton, *Literary Theory: An Introduction* (Minneapolis: Univ. of
Minnesota Press, 1983), p. 168.

42 *The Gouernaunce of Prynces*, trans. James Yonge, in *Three Prose Versions
of the "Secreta Secretorum,"* ed. Robert Steele, EETS e.s. 74 (London:
Kegan Paul, Trench, and Trübner, 1898), p. 231; cited by Curry, "The
Secret of Chaucer's Pardoner," pp. 57–58.

43 This Freudian reading may seem less fanciful when we recall the
Host's rueful remarks (following the *Melibee*) about his own fearsome,
threatening wife, Goodelief:

> Whan she comth hoom she rampeth in my face,
> And crieth, "False coward, wrek thy wyf!
> *By corpus bones, I wol have thy knyf,*
> *And thou shalt have my distaf and go spynne!"*
> Fro day to nyght right thus she wol bigynne.
> "Allas," she seith, "that evere I was shape
> To wedden a milksop, or a coward ape,
> That wol been overlad with every wight!"
>
> . . . .
>
> I woot wel she wol do me slee som day
> Som neighebor, and thanne go my way;
> *For I am perilous with knyf in honde,*
> *Al be it that I dar nat hire withstonde,*
> *For she is byg in armes, by my feith.*
> (7:1904–21, emphasis mine)

We recall the epithets for male members in the *Legend of Good Women*;
if Goodelief has wished that she had the Host's "knyf," the Host
ferociously strikes out at the lacking Pardoner, desiring to reassert,
reinscribe the latter's utter difference from him.

44 See *Le Roman de la rose*, vv. 6898–7200.

45   Si ne vos tiegn pas a cortaise
                          quant ci m'avez coilles nomees,
                          qui ne sunt pas bien renomees
                          en bouche a cortaise pucele.
                          (Ibid., vv. 6898–6901)

Bloch, *Etymologies and Genealogies*, p. 138, also makes this point. *Le
Roman de la rose* will hereafter be cited, as *Rose*, in the text.

46 Fleming, *Reason and the Lover*, p. 101. Fleming has written the most
recent analysis of this scene in his chapter 3, "Words and Things." He
identifies Augustine as the most important influence here (the "super-

text," to use his term), as I also do; but our conclusions are somewhat different. My discussion coincides more closely with that of R. Howard Bloch, in *Etymologies and Genealogies*, pp. 137–41.

47 Bloch, *Etymologies and Genealogies*, pp. 44–53.

48 My analysis of Augustine is indebted to Marcia Colish's discussion of Augustine's lifelong engagement with the problematic of language and of his development of a "redeemed rhetoric." See *The Mirror of Language: A Study in the Medieval Theory of Knowledge*, 2d ed. (Lincoln: Univ. of Nebraska Press, 1983), pp. 7–54. Colish posits that an understanding of the Incarnation was critical in Augustine's intellectual movement toward Christianity. See also Bloch, *Etymologies and Genealogies*, pp. 47–48, and Vance, *Mervelous Signals*, pp. 256–64.

49 See, for example, R. A. Markus, "St. Augustine on Signs," in *Augustine: A Collection of Critical Essays*, ed. R. A. Markus (New York: Doubleday Anchor, 1972), p. 78.

50 Augustine, *De doctrina christiana* 2.24; trans. D. W. Robertson, Jr., under the title *On Christian Doctrine* (Indianapolis: Bobbs-Merrill, 1958), pp. 60–61.

> et beta uno eodemque sono apud Graecos litterae, apud Latinos holeris nomen est; et cum dico "lege," in his duabus syllabis aliud Graecus, aliud Latinus intellegit—sicut ergo hae omnes significationes pro suae cuiusque societatis consensione animos mouent et, quia diuersa consensio est, diuerse mouent, nec ideo consenserunt in eas homines, quia iam ualebant ad significationem, sed ideo ualent, quia consenserunt in eas . . .
> (Augustine, *De doctrina christiana* 2.24, ed. J. Martin, CC 32 [Turnhout: Brepols, 1962], pp. 59–60)

51 Augustine, *De magistro* 11.36, ed. K.-D. Daur, CC 29 (Turnhout: Brepols, 1970), p. 194.

52 *De dialectica* is a work whose authorship has been disputed but one which has been taken by its most recent translator and by Fleming as genuinely Augustinian; see the Introduction to *De dialectica*, ed. Jan Pinborg, trans. (with introduction and notes) B. Darrell Jackson (Boston: D. Reidel, 1975). Augustine begins chapter 6 by suggesting that a word's origin may indeed be a matter of indifference, as long as its meaning is understood; he suggests that the pursuit of the origin of words is a potentially endless task, dependent on the researcher's own ingenuity; and some words' origins can't ever be accounted for. But he asserts, in the same chapter, that there are many cases of natural resemblance between word and referent: the impressions made on the senses by the sounds of such words as *lene* and *asperitas* are in harmony (*concordarent*) with the impressions made by the referents them-

selves. Further on, Augustine specifically discusses the *vis* of words
—the affective power of words—suggesting that the sensible qualities
of words convey a meaning that is in accord with the referent itself.
Sound and referent—physical property of word and physical property of thing—are linked: the word shares the natural property of the
thing.

53 Bloch makes this observation (*Etymologies and Genealogies*, p. 36) and
cites Augustine:

> Sicut autem Cain, quod interpretatur possessio, terrenae condi-
> tor ciuitatis, et filius eius, in cuius nomine condita est, Enoch,
> quod interpretatur dedicatio, indicat istam ciuitatem et initium et
> finem habere terrenum, ubi nihil speratur amplius, quam in hoc
> saeculo cerni potest: ita Seth quod interpretatur resurrectio, cum
> sit generationum seorsus commemoratarum pater, quid de filio
> eius sacra haec historia dicat, intuendum est.

> [Now as Cain, signifying possession, the founder of the earthly
> city, and his son Enoch, meaning dedication, in whose name it
> was founded, indicate that this city is earthly both in its beginning
> and in its end—a city in which nothing more is hoped for than
> can be seen in this world—so Seth, meaning resurrection, and
> being the father of generations registered apart from the others,
> we must consider what this sacred history says of his son.]
>   (*De civitate Dei* 15.17, CC 47 [Turnhout: Brepols, 1955], p. 480;
>   trans. M. Dods, in *Basic Writings of Saint Augustine*, ed. Whitney J.
>   Oates [New York: Random House, 1948], 2:300)

54 Augustine, *De magistro* 13.43.
55 Colish, *The Mirror of Language*, pp. 7–54.
56 See Augustine, *Confessiones* 1.4, and *De trinitate* 11, 15, ed. W. J. Mountain, CC 50 (Turnhout: Brepols, 1968), for the explication of the relationship between word and Word. And note his final protestation of
the ineffability of God and the shortcomings of language:

> Sapiens quidam cum de te loqueretur in libro suo qui ecclesias-
> ticus proprio nomine iam uocatur: *Multa,* inquit, *dicimus et non*
> *peruenimus, et consummatio sermonum uniuersa est ipse.* Cum ergo
> peruenerimus ad te, cessabunt *multa* ista quae *dicimus et non perue-*
> *nimus,* et manebis unus *omnia in omnibus.* . . .

> [When the wise man spake of Thee in his book, which is now
> called by the special name of *Ecclesiasticus,* "We speak," he said,
> "much, and yet come short; and in sum of words, He is all."
> When, therefore, we shall have come to Thee, these very many

things that we speak, and yet come short, will cease; and Thou, as One, wilt remain "all in all."]

(*De trinitate* 15.28, pp. 533–35; trans. A. W. Hadden, rev. W. G. T. Shedd, in *Basic Writings of Saint Augustine*, 2:878)

57 Augustine, *De catechizandis rudibus*, ed. I. B. Bauer, CC 46 (Turnhout: Brepols, 1969), pp. 122–23.

58 Bloch, *Etymologies and Genealogies*, p. 44.

59 Deus enim, post hominem institutum praedicavit, nomen praedicationis extendendo, dicens Adae, Gen. 2: *In quocumque die comederis ex eo, morte morieris.* Haec enim fuit prima persuasio de qua in Scriptura legimus. . . . Et tandem Ipse, corpus humanum et animam in unitate suppositi assumens, veniens praedicavit etiam idem thema quod praeco suus prius praedicaverat, ut habetur Matth. 4.

[After creating man, God preached (if we extend the word 'preaching'), saying to Adam (Gen. 2:17): *For in what day soever thou shalt eat of it, thou shalt die the death.* This was the first persuasion of which we read in Scripture. . . . And at last He Himself, taking on a human soul and body in the unity of substance, came preaching the same theme which his precursor had preached before, as is seen in Matt. 4:17.]

(Robert of Basevorn, *Forma praedicandi* 6 [in *Artes praedicandi*, ed. Th.-M. Charland, O. P., Publications de l'Institut d'Etudes Médiévales d'Ottawa (Ottawa, 1936), pp. 243–44]; trans. Leopold Krul, O.S.B., in *Three Medieval Rhetorical Arts*, ed. James J. Murphy [Berkeley and Los Angeles: Univ. of California Press, 1971], pp. 126–27)

See also Thomas Waleys, *De modo componendi sermones cum documentis* 1, in *Artes praedicandi*, pp. 329–41. I have benefitted from the surveys of sermon rhetoric in James J. Murphy, *Rhetoric in the Middle Ages: A History of Rhetorical Theory from St. Augustine to the Renaissance* (Berkeley and Los Angeles: Univ. of California Press, 1974), pp. 269–355; Etienne Gilson, "Michel Menot et la technique du sermon médiéval," in his *Les Idées et les lettres*, 2d ed. (Paris: J. Vrin, 1955), pp. 93–154; and Margaret Jennings, C.S.J., "The *Ars componendi sermones* of Ranulph Higden," in *Medieval Eloquence: Studies in the Theory and Practice of Medieval Rhetoric*, ed. J. J. Murphy (Berkeley and Los Angeles: Univ. of California Press, 1978), pp. 112–26.

60 . . . si non esset praedicatio, per quam verbum Dei seminatur, totus mundus esset sterilis, et sine fructu.

[Without preaching, which scatters the word of God like seed, the world would be sterile and produce no fruit.]

(Humbert of Romans, *De eruditione praedicatorum* 1.3 [ed. J. J. Berthier (Rome: A. Befani, 1889), p. 377]; translation under the title *Treatise on Preaching* by the Dominican Students, Province of Saint Joseph, ed. Walter M. Conlon [Westminster, Md.: Newman Press, 1951], p. 5)

61 For the major attack on the friars in the mid-thirteenth century, see William of Saint-Amour ("mestre Guillaume de Saint Amour," whom Faus Semblant discusses as antagonist in *Le Roman de la rose*, vv. 11453–94), *De periculis novissimorum temporum* (1255). William, a secular master embroiled in the controversy at the University of Paris with the friars, represented the friars as (among other things) false prophets, *pseudo-apostoli,* and *pseudo-praedicatores;* see *De periculis,* esp. chs. 2 and 3 (ed. Max Bierbaum, *Bettelorden und Weltgeistlichkeit an der Universität Paris, Franziskanische Studien* 2 [1920]: 1–36). Bierbaum prints selections (the Prologue and chs. 1–3, 5, 8, 11–12); the whole is printed in *Opera omnia* (Constance [actually Paris]: Alitophilos, 1632). See notes in Lecoy, *Rose* 2:281–90, and Dahlberg, *The Romance of the Rose,* pp. 395–98. A schematic chronology of events surrounding William is provided by P. Glorieux, "Le conflit de 1252–1257 à la lumière du Mémoire de Guillaume de Saint-Amour," *Recherches de théologie ancienne et médiévale* 24 (1957): 364–72. For Rutebeuf's mid-century antimendicant poems, in particular, the "Complainte de Guillaume," in which the personified Faus Semblant appears, see *Œuvres complètes,* ed. Edmond Faral and Julia Bastin (Paris: Picard, 1959), 1:238–335, esp. 256–66.

62 This accusation is a fundamental one in Wycliffe's continual antifraternal polemic. For examples in English, see his vernacular version of his Latin *De officio pastorali* (c. 1377):

> . . . thus ther ben many causis that letten goddis word to renne. . . . The fourthe cause is bringing in of false freris bi many cuntreys; for, as it is seid bifore, thei letten trewe preching to renne and maken curatis bi many weyes to leeue this moost worthy offiss. First they robben hem many weyes and maken hem bisy for to lyue, for they deprauen hem to ther parischens bi floriyshid wordis that they bringen yn; and no drede they shapen ther sermouns by dyuysiouns and othere iapis that they maken moost plese the puple. And thus they erren in bileue and maken the puple to trowe to hem that sermouns ben nought but in ther foorme.

(Ch. 26, in *The English Works of Wyclif, Hitherto Unprinted*, ed. F. D. Matthew, EETS, n.v. [London, Trübner, 1880], pp. 445–46)

Another example is sermon 111, on the Feast of the Seven Brethren:

> Thes wordis of Crist ben scorned of gramariens and devynes. Gramariens and filosophris seien, that Crist knewe not his gendris; and bastard dyvynes seien algatis that thes wordis of Crist ben false, and so no wordis of Crist bynden, but to the witt that gloseris tellen. But here we seien to thes trowauntis that thei blaiberen thus for defaute of witt. Leeve we thes heretikes as foolis, and seie we sum witt that God hath yovon us.
>
> (*Select English Works of John Wyclif*, ed. Thomas Arnold [Oxford: Clarendon Press, 1869], 1:375–76)

See G. R. Owst, *Preaching in Medieval England: An Introduction to Sermon Manuscripts of the Period, c. 1350–1450* (New York: Russell and Russell, 1965), for a discussion of fraternal preaching; and *Literature and Pulpit in Medieval England* (Oxford: Basil Blackwell, 1961], pp. 56–109, for literal and allegorical uses of Scripture in sermons. Dom David Knowles, in *The Religious Orders in England* (Cambridge: Cambridge Univ. Press, 1957), 2:61–73, 90–115, provides a good discussion of mendicant orders and their critics.

63 Arnold Williams cites a sermon by FitzRalph (B.M. MS. Lansdowne 393, fol. 108r) in which FitzRalph remarks that "when he challenged the friars to produce one scriptural text commanding poverty or proving that Christ ever begged voluntarily or spontaneously, they complained that he respected only the text of Scripture, not the gloss"; see Williams, "Chaucer and the Friars," *Speculum* 28 (1953): 511.

64 Even some friars themselves admitted that they preached sometimes "with hatred in their hearts," not with the *caritas* that is the proper significator of all language: see Owst, *Preaching in Medieval England*, p. 77.

65 See Germaine Dempster, "The Pardoner's Prologue," in *Sources and Analogues of Chaucer's "Canterbury Tales,"* ed. W. F. Bryan and Germaine Dempster (New York: Humanities Press, 1958), p. 409; Dean S. Fansler, *Chaucer and the "Roman de la Rose"* (New York: Columbia Univ. Press, 1914), pp. 162–66 (discussing Chaucer's use of Faus Semblant in the creation of both the Friar and the Pardoner); and P. M. Kean, *Chaucer and the Making of English Poetry* (London: Routledge and Kegan Paul, 1972), 2:96–109. See also Patterson, "Chaucerian Confession," for the problematics of literary confession in both Faus Semblant and Pardoner.

66 O. Mannoni, *Clefs pour l'imaginaire* (Paris: Seuil, 1969), pp. 9–33.

67 Freud, "Fetishism," pp. 152–53.

68 Ibid., p. 157. My emphasis is on the fetish's role in allowing a belief in nondifferentiation and plenitude here. Although I shall not directly deal with other emphases, it is clear that the fetish protects the child from the terror of the female genitals, too. If the mother is castrated, she threatens the child with castration thereby, as Freud has said: "If a woman ha[s] been castrated, then his own possession of a penis [is] in danger" (p. 152). Freud's short note on "Medusa's Head" is relevant to this view:

> To decapitate = to castrate. The terror of Medusa is thus a terror of castration that is linked to the sight of something. Numerous analyses have made us familiar with the occasion for this: it occurs when a boy, who has hitherto been unwilling to believe the threat of castration, catches the sight of the female genitals, probably those of an adult, surrounded by hair, and essentially those of his mother.
>
> (*Standard Edition* 18:273)

69 Sarah Kofman, in *The Enigma of Woman* (pp. 86–87), quotes Derrida's *Glas* on the undecidable nature of the fetish: it may be possible, writes Derrida, "to reconstruct from Freud's generalization a 'concept' of fetish that can no longer be contained within the traditional opposition *Ersatz/non Ersatz* or even within opposition at all." See Jacques Derrida, *Glas*, trans. John P. Leavey, Jr., and Richard Rand (Lincoln: Univ. of Nebraska Press, 1986).

70 Bloch, *Scandal*, p. 119. D. W. Winnicott, in "Transitional Objects and Transitional Phenomena: A Study of the First Not-Me Possession" (*International Journal of Psycho-Analysis* 34 [1953]: 95–96), contrasts the fetish with the transitional object in order to emphasize the abnormality of the fetishist. The fetish, based as it is on a "delusion of a maternal phallus," is not a normal phenomenon, whereas the transitional object, based on illusion (an area "between primary creativity and objective reality based on reality testing"), is healthy and universal. Phyllis Greenacre, in "The Fetish and the Transitional Object" (*Psychoanalytic Study of the Child* 24 [1969]: 144–65), also stresses the fetishist's arrested development.

71 Mannoni, *Clefs pour l'imaginaire*, p. 12.

72 Among the many recent critics who have discussed narrative elements of the *Tale* as representations or projections of the Pardoner himself, see H. Marshall Leicester, Jr., "'Synne Horrible': The Pardoner's Exegesis of His Tale, and Chaucer's," in *Acts of Interpretation: The Text in*

Its Contexts, 700–1600, ed. Mary J. Carruthers and Elizabeth D. Kirk (Norman, Okla.: Pilgrim Books, 1982), pp. 25–50; Alfred David, *The Strumpet Muse* (Bloomington: Indiana Univ. Press, 1976), pp. 193–204; Patterson, "Chaucerian Confession" (see n. 3 above), pp. 166–67; and Howard, *The Idea of the "Canterbury Tales"* (see n. 7 above), pp. 357–63.

My sense of the patriarchal atmosphere of the *Tale* is empirically confirmed by Betsy Bowden in *Chaucer Aloud* (see n. 5 above), who notes that among her group of male and female performers (oral interpreters) of the Pardoner's Prologue and *Tale*, women consistently avoided the Old Man scene and "produced decidedly less distinctive performances," several even skipping over the whole *Tale* (p. 151).

73 Lee Patterson, in "Childishness and Authorship in the *Canterbury Tales*," a paper presented at the Twentieth International Congress on Medieval Studies, Western Michigan University, Kalamazoo, Michigan, May 1985, discussed the Old Man in these terms; earlier, in "Chaucerian Confession," p. 166, he analyzed the Old Man as "a figure who accurately reflects [the Pardoner's] own irreducible contradictions."

74 Bloch analyzes the psychologically and socially conservative functions of the *fabliaux* in similar terms in his *Scandal of the Fabliaux*, speaking, for example, of "their apparent gratuity and their essentially resolved form" (p. 126).

75 Leigh Hunt's 1846 plot summary emphasizes this static quality of the exemplum:

> Three drunken ruffians, madly believing Death to be an embodied person, go out to kill him. They meet him in the shape of an old man, who tells them where Death is to be found; and they find him accordingly.
> (*Stories in Verse* [London: George Routledge, 1855], p. 264; cited in Bowden, *Chaucer Aloud*, p. 133)

76 "Nous voyons déjà qu'il y a plusieurs manières de croire et de ne pas croire" ("We have already seen that there are several ways to believe and not to believe") (Mannoni, *Clefs pour l'imaginaire*, p. 24). The swindler believes, in a certain fashion, in his admittedly false inventions, using the fetishist's belief "even so." Belief is the key to the creation of illusion or of the successful swindle—and as Mannoni suggests, it is the swindler's own belief that makes the job work. "Il n'y a pas de doute, on le voit, que la Verleugnung suffit pour créer le magique" ("Clearly, there is no doubt that disavowal is enough to create magic") (p. 29).

77 See Augustine, *Contra Julianum Pelagianum* (PL 44:787): "Ita concupis-

centia carnis . . . et peccatum est . . . et poena peccati . . . et causa peccati" ("Thus concupiscence of the flesh . . . is at once sin . . . and punishment of sin . . . and cause of sin") (Latin quoted in Alfred L. Kellogg, "An Augustinian Interpretation of Chaucer's Pardoner," in his *Chaucer, Langland, Arthur,* pp. 245–68). See also Howard, *The Idea of the "Canterbury Tales,"* pp. 355–57.

78 Nicolas James Perella, in *The Kiss Sacred and Profane: An Interpretive History of Kiss Symbolism and Related Religio-Erotic Themes* (Berkeley and Los Angeles: Univ. of California Press, 1969), pp. 124–57, esp. 130–31, describes the late-medieval romance motif of kiss of peace on the mouth that is an "establishment of something approaching brotherhood or, at the very least, membership in the group or clan" (p. 130). Chaucer critics disagree widely as to the "reconciliation" effected; Burlin doubts that one has indeed occurred (*Chaucerian Fiction,* p. 175).

79 A language of presence, a language of the female body, has been theorized by various feminist theorists seeking to find alternatives to the dominant figurative, symbolic, masculine language based on absence. Lacan, as I've discussed above, derives the origin of symbolization from lack, the lack of the mother's body; thus language presupposes and proceeds from the absence of the object. But if absence and separation—from the mother's body, in the first place—are not so complete as Lacanian theory purports, language might be informed by presence, not absence, might somehow partake of the things signified; representation might not necessarily mean absence, as Homans suggests, following and extending Nancy Chodorow's revision of Freud into a "revisionary myth of women and language" (*Bearing the Word,* pp. 1–39). Julia Kristeva has suggested a poetic language which she calls the "semiotic," closely linked to the mother's body and consisting of gesture, body language, and prerepresentational sounds (see, e.g., "From One Identity to an Other," in her *Desire in Language: A Semiotic Approach to Literature and Art,* ed. Leon S. Roudiez, trans. Thomas Gora, Alice Jardine, and Leon S. Roudiez [New York: Columbia Univ. Press, 1980], pp. 124–47). Luce Irigaray, in "When Our Lips Speak Together" (in *This Sex Which Is Not One,* trans. Catherine Porter [Ithaca, N.Y.: Cornell Univ. Press, 1985], pp. 205–18) and Hélène Cixous, in "The Laugh of the Medusa" (in *New French Feminisms,* ed. Elaine Marks and Isabelle de Courtivron [New York: Schocken, 1981], pp. 245–64), both oppose women's literal, bodily experience to the figurative discourse of Western patriarchy.

There are compelling arguments to be made against such a language of the body, or the semiotic, or *l'écriture féminine,* which Ann Rosalind Jones summarizes well: the theories have been criticized as idealist and essentialist, bound up in the very system they claim to undermine; they have been attacked as theoretically fuzzy and as fatal to constructive political action.

> ("Writing the Body: Toward an Understanding of *l'Écriture féminine*," in *The New Feminist Criticism*, ed. Elaine Showalter [New York: Pantheon, 1985], p. 367)

But Jones acknowledges, too, that the power of such theories lies in their radical critique of phallocentrism in all its forms and in their capacity to open up new ways of thinking after "phallocentric delusion" has been discovered (pp. 366, 374–75).

It may seem contradictory that the language associated with the mother's body in psychoanalysis is finally linked in my argument to the language of the Christian Father and Son. Judson Boyce Allen has suggested, indeed, a revision of Lacanian theory in regard to another eunuch, Abelard, so that the fullness of the Imaginary is located in the Father; see Allen, "Exemplum as Autobiography: Abelard's Complaints and Lacan" (paper delivered at the International Congress on Medieval Studies, Western Michigan University, Kalamazoo, Michigan, May 1985). The Christian trinitarian schema is, of course, characterized in patriarchal terms, and the redemptive scheme of history may be seen to be based, as Kristeva suggests, on masculine Oedipal desires; see her *In the Beginning Was Love: Psychoanalysis and Faith*, trans. Arthur Goldhammer (New York: Columbia Univ. Press, 1987). Surely these patriarchal terms of the Christian scheme were deeply meaningful in the personal devotion and powerful in the sociopolitical organization of the later Middle Ages. But they were also open to revision: "the use of explicit and elaborate maternal imagery to describe God and Christ" flowered in the later Middle Ages, as Caroline Walker Bynum has found, and gender associations could indeed shift; see her *Jesus as Mother: Studies in the Spirituality of the High Middle Ages* (Berkeley and Los Angeles: Univ. of California Press, 1982), pp. 110–69, esp. p. 112. I suggest here that the concept of God as absolute presence finally *obviates* division and distinctions, by which gender and the hermeneutic processes that are based on those power-asymmetrical categories are constituted.

80 On the deathbed scenario Thomas Gasgoigne reports and its relation to the *Retractions*, see Douglas Wurtele, "The Penitence of Geoffrey Chaucer," *Viator* 11 (1980): 335–59. Wurtele argues that lines 1081–84 and 1090(b)–92 were originally meant for the Parson's concluding address; lines 1085–90(a), the retractions proper, should be read separately "as a later interpolation by, or at the behest of, Chaucer himself" (p. 342). This multiplication of voices seems unnecessary to me,

despite Wurtele's careful argumentation; I read the voice of the *Retractions* as many critics—Donald Howard, for example, in his *Idea of the Canterbury Tales* (p. 387)—do: Chaucer the unimpersonated poet breaks the fictional frame of the *Tales* and reflects on the *Parson's Tale* (the "litel tretys" that has just concluded) and on all of his works.

Bibliography

Primary Sources

Acts of Chapter of the Collegiate Church of Saints Peter and Wilfred, Ripon, 1452–1506. Publications of the Surtees Society, 64. Durham: Surtees Society, 1875 for 1874.

Abelard, Peter. "Abelard's Letter of Consolation to a Friend." Ed. J. T. Muckle. *Mediaeval Studies* 12 (1950): 163–213. ["*Historia calamitatum*"]

Abelard, Peter. "Abelard's Rule for Religious Women." Ed. T. P. McLaughlin, C.S.B. *Mediaeval Studies* 18 (1956): 241–92. [Letter 7]

Abelard, Peter. "The Letter of Heloise on Religious Life and Abelard's First Reply." Ed. J. T. Muckle. *Mediaeval Studies* 17 (1955): 240–81. [Letters 5-6]

Abelard, Peter. *The Letters of Abelard and Heloise.* Trans. Betty Radice. New York: Penguin, 1974.

Abelard, Peter. "The Personal Letters between Abelard and Heloise." Ed. J. T. Muckle. *Mediaeval Studies* 15 (1953): 47–94. [Letters 1-4]

Agnellus of Ravenna. *Agnelli Liber pontificalis ecclesiae Ravennatis.* Ed. O. Holder-Egger. Pp. 265–391. MGH. Scriptores rerum langobardicarum et italicarum saec. VI–IX. Hannover, 1878.

Alanus de Insulis (Alain de Lille). *De planctu naturae.* Ed. Nikolaus Häring. *Studi medievali.* 3d ser., no. 19 (1978), pp. 797–879.

Alanus de Insulis. *The Plaint of Nature.* Trans. James J. Sheridan. Toronto: Pontifical Institute of Mediaeval Studies, 1980.

Alanus de Insulis. "Rithmus de incarnatione Domine." In "Alain de Lille et la *Theologia*," by M.-T. d'Alverny. In *L'Homme devant Dieu: Mélanges offerts au Père Henri de Lubac,* vol. 2, pp. 111–28. Paris: Aubier, 1964.

Albertus Magnus. *Quaestiones super De animalibus.* Ed. Ephrem Filthaut. In *Opera omnia,* vol. 12. Monasterii Westfalorum in Aedibus Aschendorff, 1955.

Ambrose, Saint. *Expositio evangeliis secundum Lucam. PL* 15:1525–1850.

Ancrene Riwle. See *The English Text of the Ancrene Riwle.*

Aristotle. *Generation of Animals.* Ed. and trans. A. L. Peck. Loeb Classical Library. Cambridge, Mass.: Harvard Univ. Press, 1953.

Aristotle. *Parts of Animals.* Ed. and trans. A. L. Peck. Loeb Classical Library. Cambridge, Mass.: Harvard Univ. Press, 1937.

Aristotle. *Politics*. Trans. Benjamin Jowett. In vol. 2 of *The Complete Works of Aristotle*, ed. Jonathan Barnes, pp. 1986–2129. Princeton, N.J.: Princeton Univ. Press, 1984.

Aristotle. *Problems*. Trans. E. S. Forster. In vol. 2 of *The Complete Works of Aristotle*, ed. Jonathan Barnes, pp. 1319–1527. Princeton, N.J.: Princeton Univ. Press, 1984.

Athanasius. *Life of Antony*. Trans. Robert C. Gregg. New York: Paulist Press, 1980.

Augustine, Saint. *Basic Writings of Saint Augustine.* Ed. Whitney J. Oates. 2 vols. New York: Random House, 1948.

Augustine, Saint. *Confessionum*. Ed. Lucas Verheijen. CC 27. Turnhout: Brepols, 1981.

Augustine, Saint. *Contra Julianum Pelagianum*. PL 44:637–874.

Augustine, Saint. *De catechizandis rudibus*. Ed. I. B. Bauer. CC 46. Turnhout: Brepols, 1969.

Augustine, Saint. *De civitate Dei*. Ed. Bernardus Dombart and Alphonsus Kalb. CC 47–48. Turnhout: Brepols, 1955.

Augustine, Saint. *De dialectica*. Ed. Jan Pinborg. Trans. (with introduction and notes) B. Darrell Jackson. Boston: D. Reidel, 1975.

Augustine, Saint. *De doctrina christiana*. Ed. J. Martin. CC 32. Turnhout: Brepols, 1962.

Augustine, Saint. *On Christian Doctrine*. Trans. D. W. Robertson, Jr. Indianapolis: Bobbs-Merrill, 1958.

Augustine, Saint. *De magistro*. Ed. K.-D. Daur. CC 29. Turnhout: Brepols, 1970.

Augustine, Saint. *De sermone Domini in monte*. Ed. A. Mutzenbecher. CC 35. Turnhout: Brepols, 1967.

Augustine, Saint. *De trinitate*. Ed. W. J. Mountain and Fr. Glorie. CC 50–50A. Turnhout: Brepols, 1968.

Augustine, Saint. *Enarationes in Psalmos*. Ed. D. Eligius Dekkers and Iohannes Fraipont. CC 38–40. Turnhout: Brepols, 1956.

Averroës. *Aristotelis opera cum Averrois commentariis*. Frankfurt am Main: Minerva Verlag, 1962.

Benoît de Sainte-Maure. *Le Roman de Troie par Benoît de Sainte-Maure*. Ed. Leopold Constans. 6 vols. SATF. Paris, 1904–12.

Bevington, David, ed. *Medieval Drama*. Boston: Houghton Mifflin, 1975.

Boccaccio, Giovanni. *Boccaccio on Poetry*. Trans. Charles G. Osgood. Library of Liberal Arts. Indianapolis: Bobbs-Merrill, 1956.

Boccaccio, Giovanni. *Il Corbaccio*. Ed. Tauno Nurmela. Suomalaisen Tiedakatemian Toimituksia. Annales Academiae Scientiarum Fennicae, ser. B, no. 146. Helsinki, 1968.

Boccaccio, Giovanni. *The Corbaccio*. Trans. Anthony K. Cassell. Urbana: Univ. of Illinois Press, 1975.

Boccaccio, Giovanni. *The Filostrato of Giovanni Boccaccio.* Ed. and trans. Nathaniel Edward Griffin and Arthur Beckwith Myrick. 1929. Rpt. New York: Octagon Books, 1978.

Boccaccio, Giovanni. *Genealogia deorum gentilium.* Ed. Vincenzo Romano. Bari: Laterza, 1951.

Bryan, W. F., and Germaine Dempster, eds. *Sources and Analogues of Chaucer's "Canterbury Tales."* New York: Humanities Press, 1958.

Caelius Aurelianus. *On Acute Diseases and On Chronic Diseases.* Ed. and trans. I. E. Drabkin. Chicago: Univ. of Chicago Press, 1950.

Chaucer, Geoffrey. *Odd Texts of Chaucer's Minor Poems.* Ed. F. J. Furnivall. Chaucer Society, 1st ser., nos. 23, 60. London: Trübner, 1868–80.

Chaucer, Geoffrey. *Originals and Analogues of Some of Chaucer's Canterbury Tales.* Part 2. Ed. F. J. Furnivall. Chaucer Society, 2d ser., no. 10. London: Trübner, 1875.

Chaucer, Geoffrey. *The Riverside Chaucer.* Gen. ed. Larry D. Benson. 3d ed. Boston: Houghton Mifflin, 1987.

Chaucer, Geoffrey. *Troilus and Criseyde.* Ed. B. A. Windeatt. London: Longman, 1984.

Chaucer, Geoffrey. *The Works of Geoffrey Chaucer.* Ed. F. N. Robinson. 2d ed. Boston: Houghton Mifflin, 1957.

Chaucer Life-Records. Ed. Martin M. Crow and Clair C. Olson. Oxford: Clarendon Press, 1966.

Dante Alighieri. *The Divine Comedy.* Ed. and trans. Charles S. Singleton. 6 vols. Bollingen Series, no. 80. Princeton, N.J.: Princeton Univ. Press, 1970.

Dante Alighieri. *Literary Criticism of Dante Alighieri.* Ed. and trans. Robert S. Haller. Lincoln: Univ. of Nebraska Press, 1973.

Dante Alighieri. *De vulgari eloquentia.* Ed. Aristide Marigo. 3d ed. Florence: Felice le Mounier, 1957.

Delisle, Leopold. "Notice sur la *Rhétorique de Cicéron,* traduite par Maître Jean D'Antioche, ms. 590 de Musée Conde." *Notices et extraits* 36 (1899): 207–65.

"De S. Marciana, Virgine Martyre." *Acta sanctorum.* January. Ed. Joannes Bollandus et al. Brussels: Alphonsum Greuse, 1853. 1:568–70.

Donatus. *Ars grammatica.* Vol. 4 of *Grammatici Latini,* ed. Henricus Keil, pp. 353–402. Hildesheim: Georg Olms, 1961.

Drogon of Bergues. *La Vie ancienne de sainte Godelive de Ghistelles par Drogon de Bergues. Analecta bollandiana* 44 (1926): 102–37.

Eike von Repgow. *Sächsische Weltchronik.* Ed. Gesellschaft für ältere deutsche Geschichtskunde. *Deutsche Chroniken und andere Geschichtsbücher des Mittelalters.* MGH. Scriptores qui vernacula lingua usi sunt, no. 2. Hannover: Hahn, 1877.

Eike von Repgow. *Das Zeitbuch des Eike von Repgow in ursprünglich nieder-*

deutscher Sprache und in früher lateinischer Übersetzung. Ed. H. F. Massmann. Bibliothek des Litterarischen Vereins in Stuttgart. Stuttgart: Litterarische Verein, 1887.

The English Text of the Ancrene Riwle. Magdalene College, Cambridge MS. Pepys 2498. Ed. A. Zettersten. EETS o.s. 274. London: Oxford Univ. Press, 1976.

Eriugena, John Scottus. *Periphyseon; or, De divisione naturae.* PL 122:439–1022.

Fifty Earliest English Wills in the Court of Probate, London, A.D. 1387–1439. Ed. Frederick J. Furnivall. EETS o.s. 78. London: Trübner, 1882.

Galen. *On the Usefulness of the Parts of the Body.* Trans. Margaret Tallmadge May. Ithaca, N.Y.: Cornell Univ. Press, 1968.

Geoffrey of Vinsauf. *Poetria nova.* In *Les Arts poétiques du XIIe et du XIIIe siècles,* ed. E. Faral. Paris: Honoré Champion, 1958.

Gerson, Jean. *De probatione spirituum.* In vol. 9 of *Oeuvres complètes,* ed. P. Glorieux, pp. 177–85. Paris: Desclée, 1960–73.

The Gouernaunce of Prynces. Trans. James Yonge. In *Three Prose Versions of the "Secreta Secretorum,"* ed. Robert Steele, pp. 121–248. EETS e.s. 74. London, 1898.

Gower, John. *Confessio amantis.* In *The English Works of John Gower,* ed. G. C. Macaulay. EETS e.s. 81 and 82. Oxford: Clarendon, 1899–1902.

Gregory of Tours. *Gregorii episcopi Turonensis Liber vitae patrum.* Ed. Bruno Krusch. MGH. Scriptores rerum merovingicarum, vol. 1, pp. 661–744. Hannover: Hahn, 1885.

Guibert of Nogent. *De pignoribus sanctorum.* PL 156:607–80.

Guibert of Nogent. *Gesta Dei per Francos.* PL 156:679–838.

Guido delle Colonna. *Guido de Columnis Historia destructionis Troiae.* Ed. Nathaniel Edward Griffin. Cambridge, Mass.: Medieval Academy of America, 1936.

Guillaume de Lorris and Jean de Meun. *Le Roman de la rose.* Ed. Félix Lecoy. CFMA 92, 95, 98. Paris: Honoré Champion, 1965–1970.

Guillaume de Lorris and Jean de Meun. *The Romance of the Rose.* Trans. Charles Dahlberg. Princeton, N.J.: Princeton Univ. Press, 1971.

Guillaume de Saint-Amour. *De periculis novissimorum temporum.* Ed. Max Bierbaum. *Bettelorden und Weltgeistlichkeit an der Universität Paris. Franziskanische Studien* 2 (1920): 1–36. [Selections: prologue, chapters 1–3, 5, 8, 11–12]

Guillaume de Saint-Thierry. *Expositio super Cantica canticorum.* PL 180:473–546.

Hali Meidenhad. MS. Bodley 34 and Cotton MS. Titus D. 18. Ed. F. J. Furnivall. EETS o.s. 18. Rev. ed., 1922. Rpt. New York: Greenwood, 1969.

Hicks, Eric, ed. *Le Débat sur "Le Roman de la rose."* Paris: Honoré Champion, 1977.

Higden, Ranulph. *Polychronicon, Together with the English Translations of John Trevisa and an Unknown Writer of the Fifteenth Century.* Ed. Churchill Babington and Joseph R. Lumby. Rolls Series. 9 vols. London: Longman, 1865–86.

Historia Apollonii regis Tyrii. Ed. A. Riese. 2d ed. Leipzig: Teubner, 1893.

Horace. *Ars poetica.* Ed. and trans. H. Rushton Fairclough. Loeb Classical Library. Cambridge, Mass.: Harvard Univ. Press, 1955.

Hugh of St. Victor. *Didascalicon.* Trans. Jerome Taylor. New York: Columbia Univ. Press, 1961.

Humbert of Romans. *De eruditione praedicatorum.* Ed. J. J. Berthier. Rome: A. Befani, 1889.

Humbert of Romans. *Treatise on Preaching.* Trans. the Dominican Students, Province of Saint Joseph. Ed. Walter M. Conlon, O.P. Westminster, Md.: Newman Press, 1951.

Jean de Hareng (Jean d'Antioche), trans. See Leopold Delisle.

Jean de Meun, trans. "Boethius' *De consolatione* by Jean de Meun." Ed. V. L. Dedeck-Héry. *Mediaeval Studies* 14 (1952): 165–275. [Jean de Meun's trans. of the *De consolatione philosophiae*]

Jerome, Saint. *Adversus Jovinianum.* PL 23:205–338.

Jerome, Saint. *Commentariorum in Epistolam ad Ephesios.* PL 26:439–554.

Jerome, Saint. *Epistulae.* Ed. Isidorus Hilberg. CSEL 54–56. 3 vols. Vienna: F. Tempsky, 1912.

Jerome, Saint. *Hebraicae quaestiones in libro Geneseos.* CC 72. Turnhout: Brepols, 1959.

Jerome, Saint. *The Principal Works of Saint Jerome.* Trans. W. H. Fremantle. Vol. 6 of *A Select Library of Nicene and Post-Nicene Fathers of the Christian Church.* 1892. Rpt. Grand Rapids, Mich.: Eerdmans, n.d.

Jerome, Saint, trans. *Die Homilien zu Lukas,* by Origen. In *Origenes Werke,* ed. Max Rauer. Griechischen christlichen Schriftsteller, no. 49. Berlin: Akademie Verlag, 1959.

Jerome, Saint, trans. *Interpretatio Chronicae Eusebii Pamphili.* PL 27:33–676.

Jerome, Saint, trans. *Interpretatio libri Didymi de Spiritu sancto.* PL 23:101–54.

Jerome, Saint, trans. *Onomasticon,* by Eusebius. In *Eusebius Werke,* ed. Erich Klostermann. Griechischen christlichen Schriftsteller, no. 11. Leipzig: Hinrichs'sche, 1904.

Jerome, Saint, trans. *Divinae bibliothecae pars prima.* PL 28 [The Vulgate, Genesis through Esther]

Jerome, Saint, trans. *Divinae bibliotheca pars secunda.* PL 29. [The Vulgate, Tobias through Revelation]

John of Garland. *Parisiana poetria*. Ed. and trans. Traugott Lawler. New Haven, Conn.: Yale Univ. Press, 1974.

John of Salisbury. *Polycraticus*. PL 199:379–822.

John the Scot. See Eriugena, John Scottus.

Juvenal. *Satires*. Ed. and trans. G. G. Ramsay. Loeb Classical Library. Cambridge, Mass.: Harvard Univ. Press, 1940.

Lydgate, John. *Lydgate's Fall of Princes*. Ed. Henry Bergen. EETS e.s. 121. London: Oxford Univ. Press, 1924.

Macrobius, Ambrosius Theodosius. *Commentarii in Somnium Scipionis*. Ed. J. Willis. Leipzig: Teubner, 1963.

Macrobius, Ambrosius Theodosius. *Commentary on the Dream of Scipio*. Trans. William Harris Stahl. New York: Columbia Univ. Press, 1952.

Mandeville, Sir John. *Mandeville's Travels*. Ed. P. Hamelius. EETS o.s. 153. London: Kegan Paul, 1919 (for 1916).

Map, Walter. *De nugis curialium; Courtiers' Trifles*. Ed. and trans. M. R. James, rev. C. N. L. Brooke and R. A. B. Mynors. Oxford: Clarendon, 1983.

Le Ménagier de Paris. Ed. J. Pichon. 2 vols. Paris: Société des Bibliophiles Français, 1846.

Origen. *The Song of Songs: Commentary and Homilies*. Trans. (and notes) R. P. Lawson. Westminster, Md.: Newman Press, 1957.

Ovid. *"The Art of Love" and Other Poems*. Ed. and trans. J. H. Mozley. Loeb Classical Library. London: William Heinemann, 1929.

Owen, S. G. "A Medieval Latin Poem." *English Historical Review* 2 (1887): 525–26. ["Clericus Adam"]

Pascal, Carlo. *Letteratura Latina Medievale: Nuovi Saggi e Note Critiche*. Pp. 107–15. Catania: Francesco Battiato, 1909. ["Clericus Adam"]

Petrarch, Francesco. *De remediis utriusque fortunae*. In *Petrarch: Four Dialogues for Scholars*, ed. and trans. Conrad H. Rawski. Cleveland: Western Reserve University, 1967.

Petrarch, Francesco. *Le Familiari*. Ed. Umberto Bosco. Florence: Sansoni, 1942.

Petrarch, Francesco. *Letters on Familiar Matters*. Trans. Aldo S. Bernardo. Baltimore: Johns Hopkins Univ. Press, 1985.

Petrarch, Francesco. *Petrarch: The First Modern Scholar and Man of Letters*. 2d ed. Trans. (with introduction and notes) James Harvey Robinson and Henry Winchester Rolfe. New York: Putnam's Sons, 1914.

Philo of Alexandria. *On the Cherubim*. Ed. and trans. F. H. Colson and G. H. Whitaker. Loeb Classical Library. Cambridge, Mass.: Harvard Univ. Press, 1929.

Philo of Alexandria. *Questions and Answers on Genesis*. Ed. and trans. Ralph

Marcus. Loeb Classical Library. Cambridge, Mass.: Harvard Univ. Press, 1953.

Pizan, Christine de. *The Book of the City of Ladies*. Trans. Earl Jeffrey Richards. New York: Persea, 1982.

Pliny the Elder. *Natural History*. Ed. and trans. H. Rackham. Loeb Classical Library. Cambridge, Mass.: Harvard Univ. Press, 1942.

Post, J. B. "Ravishment of Women and the Statutes of Westminster." In *Legal Records and the Historian*, ed. J. H. Baker, pp. 150–64. London: Royal Historical Society, 1978. [Appendix: Texts of the 1275 and 1285 Statutes of Westminster]

Puttenham, George. *The Arte of English Poesie*. 1589. Rpt. Menston, England: Scolar Press, 1968.

La Querelle de la Rose: Letters and Documents. Ed. and trans. Joseph L. Baird and John R. Kane. Chapel Hill: Univ. of North Carolina Dept. of Romance Languages, 1978.

Quintilian. *Institutio oratoria*. Ed. and trans. H. E. Butler. Loeb Classical Library. Cambridge, Mass.: Harvard Univ. Press, 1969.

Reginald of Canterbury. *The Vita Sancti Malchi of Reginald of Canterbury*. Ed. Levi R. Lind. Urbana: Univ. of Illinois Press, 1942.

Rhazes [ar-Rāzī]. "Ar-Rāzī on the Hidden Illness." Trans. Franz Rosenthal. *Bulletin of the History of Medicine* 52 (1978): 45–60.

Richard of Bury. *Philobiblon*. Ed. and trans. Ernest C. Thomas. London: Kegan Paul, Trench, 1888.

Robert of Basevorn. *Forma praedicandi*. In *Artes praedicandi*, ed. Th.-M. Charland, O.P., pp. 233–323. Publications de l'Institut d'Etudes Médiévales d'Ottawa. Paris and Ottawa, 1936.

Robert of Basevorn. *The Form of Preaching*. Trans. Leopold Krul, O.S.B. In *Three Medieval Rhetorical Arts*, ed. James J. Murphy, pp. 114–215. Berkeley and Los Angeles: Univ. of California Press, 1971.

Robert of Melun. *Oeuvres de Robert de Melun*. Ed. Raymond Martin, O.P. 3 vols. Louvain: Spicilegium Sacrum Lovaniense, 1947.

Rutebeuf. *Œuvres complètes*. Ed. Edmond Faral and Julia Bastin. 2 vols. Paris: Picard, 1959.

Secreta Secretorum. See *The Gouernaunce of Prynces*.

South English Legendary. Ed. Charlotte d'Evelyn and Anna J. Mill. EETS 235. London: Oxford Univ. Press, 1956.

Thomas Aquinas, Saint. *In octo libros Politicorum Aristotelis expositio*. Ed. Raymundi M. Spiazzi. Taurini: Marietti, 1966.

Thomas Aquinas, Saint. *Opera omnia*. Parma, 1852–1873. Rpt. New York: Musurgia, 1948.

Thomas Aquinas, Saint. *Summa contra gentiles*. Trans. Vernon J. Bourke. Notre Dame, Ind.: Univ. of Notre Dame Press, 1975.

Thurot, Charles. *Notices et extraits de divers manuscrits latins.* 1869. Rpt. Frankfurt: Minerva, 1964.

Urbain le Courtois. Ed. Paul Meyer. *Romania* 32 (1903): 70–73.

Victricius of Rouen. *De laude sanctorum. PL* 20:437–58.

Waleys, Thomas. *De modo componendi sermones cum documentis.* In *Artes praedicandi,* ed. Th.-M. Charland, O.P., pp. 329–41. Publications de l'Institut d'Etudes Médiévales d'Ottawa. Paris and Ottawa, 1936.

Wilson, Katharina M., ed. *Medieval Women Writers.* Athens: Univ. of Georgia Press, 1984.

Wycliffe, John. *The English Works of Wyclif, Hitherto Unprinted.* Ed. F. D. Matthew. EETS, o.s. 74. London: Trübner, 1880.

Wycliffe, John. *Select English Works of John Wyclif.* Ed. Thomas Arnold. 3 vols. Oxford: Clarendon, 1869–71.

Secondary Sources

Adelman, Janet. " 'That We May Leere Som Wit.' " In *Twentieth-Century Interpretations of the Pardoner,* ed. Dewey R. Faulkner, pp. 96–106. Englewood Cliffs, N.J.: Prentice-Hall, 1973.

Aers, David. *Chaucer, Langland, and the Creative Imagination.* London: Routledge and Kegan Paul, 1980.

Aers, David. *"Piers Plowman" and Christian Allegory.* London: Arnold, 1975.

Allen, Peter L. *"Ars Amandi, Ars Legendi:* Love Poetry and Literary Theory in Ovid, Andreas Capellanus, and Jean de Meun." *Exemplaria* 1 (1989):181–207.

Allen, Peter L. "Reading Chaucer's Good Women." *ChauR* 21 (1987): 419–34.

Allen, Prudence, R.S.M. *The Concept of Woman: The Aristotelian Revolution, 750 B.C. to A.D. 1250.* Montreal: Eden Press, 1985.

Althusser, Louis. "Ideology and Ideological State Apparatuses (Notes towards an Investigation)." In his *"Lenin and Philosophy" and Other Essays,* trans. Ben Brewster, pp. 127–86. New York: Monthly Review Press, 1971.

Anderson, David. "Theban History in Chaucer's *Troilus.*" *SAC* 4 (1982): 109–33.

Archibald, Elizabeth. "The Flight from Incest: Two Late Classical Precursors of the Constance Theme." *ChauR* 20 (1986): 259–72.

Barkley, Roy Reid. "A Study of the Historical Method of D. W. Robertson, Jr." Ph.D. diss., University of Texas at Austin, 1974.

Baron, Hans. *The Crisis of the Early Italian Renaissance.* Princeton, N.J.: Princeton Univ. Press, 1966.

Barthes, Roland. *The Pleasure of the Text.* Trans. Richard Miller. New York: Hill and Wang, 1975.

Bassnett-McGuire, Susan. *Translation Studies.* New Accents Series. London: Methuen, 1980.

Beauvoir, Simone de. *The Second Sex.* Trans. H. M. Parshley. New York: Knopf, 1957.

Benjamin, Walter. "The Task of the Translator: An Introduction to the Translation of Baudelaire's *Tableaux parisiens.*" In his *Illuminations,* ed. Hannah Arendt, trans. Harry Zohn, pp. 69–82. New York: Schocken Books, 1969.

Benson, C. David. "Chaucer's Pardoner: His Sexuality and Modern Critics." *Medievalia* 8 (1985 for 1982): 337–49.

Benton, John F. "Clio and Venus: An Historical View of Medieval Love." In *The Meaning of Courtly Love,* ed. F. X. Newman, pp. 19–42. Albany: State Univ. of New York Press, 1968.

Benton, John F. "Trotula, Women's Problems, and the Professionalization of Medicine in the Middle Ages." *Bulletin of the History of Medicine* 59 (1985): 30–53.

Besserman, Lawrence. " 'Glosynge Is a Glorious Thyng': Chaucer's Biblical Exegesis." In *Chaucer and Scriptural Tradition,* ed. David Lyle Jeffrey, pp. 65–73. Ottawa: Univ. of Ottawa Press, 1984.

Bibliotheca hagiographica latina. Ed. Société des Bollandistes. Brussels, 1900–1901.

Bloch, R. Howard. *Etymologies and Genealogies: A Literary Anthropology of the French Middle Ages.* Chicago: Univ. of Chicago Press, 1983.

Bloch, R. Howard. "Medieval Misogyny." *Representations* 20 (1987): 1–24.

Bloch, R. Howard. *The Scandal of the Fabliaux.* Chicago: Univ. of Chicago Press, 1986.

Bloch, R. Howard. "Silence and Holes: The *Roman de Silence* and the Art of the Trouvère." In *Images of Power: Medieval History/Discourse/Literature,* ed. Stephen G. Nichols and Kevin Brownlee. *YFS* 70 (1976): 81–99.

Bloomfield, Morton W. "Chaucer's Sense of History." *JEGP* 51 (1952): 301–13.

Bloomfield, Morton W. "Distance and Predestination in *Troilus and Criseyde.*" *PMLA* 72 (1957): 14–26.

Boswell, John. *Christianity, Social Tolerance, and Homosexuality: Gay People in Western Europe from the Beginning of the Christian Era to the Fourteenth Century.* Chicago: Univ. of Chicago Press, 1980.

Bowden, Betsy. *Chaucer Aloud: The Varieties of Textual Interpretation.* Philadelphia: Univ. of Pennsylvania Press, 1987.

Bowden, Muriel. *A Commentary on the General Prologue to the "Canterbury Tales."* 2d ed. New York: Macmillan, 1967.

Braddy, Haldeen. "Chaucer, Alice Perrers, and Cecily Chaumpaigne." *Speculum* 52 (1977): 906–11.

Brinkmann, Hennig. *Mittelalterliche Hermeneutik.* Tübingen: Max Niemeyer, 1980.

Bronson, Bertrand H. *In Search of Chaucer.* Toronto: Univ. of Toronto Press, 1960.

Brooks, Cleanth. *The Well Wrought Urn: Studies in the Structure of Poetry.* New York: Reynald and Hitchcock, 1947.

Brown, Peter. *The Cult of the Saints: Its Rise and Function in Latin Christianity.* Chicago: Univ. of Chicago Press, 1981.

Brundage, James A. *Law, Sex, and Christian Society in Medieval Europe.* Chicago: Univ. of Chicago Press, 1987.

Bullough, Vern L. "Medieval Medical and Scientific Views of Women." *Viator* 4 (1973): 485–501.

Bullough, Vern L., and James Brundage, eds. *Sexual Practices and the Medieval Church.* Buffalo, N.Y.: Prometheus Books, 1982.

Burlin, Robert B. *Chaucerian Fiction.* Princeton, N.J.: Princeton Univ. Press, 1977.

Burns, E. Jane. "The Man Behind the Lady in Troubadour Lyric." *Romance Notes* 25 (1985): 254–70.

Burrow, J. A. *Ricardian Poetry: Chaucer, Gower, Langland, and the Gawain-Poet.* New Haven, Conn.: Yale Univ. Press, 1971.

Bynum, Caroline Walker. *Jesus as Mother: Studies in the Spirituality of the High Middle Ages.* Berkeley and Los Angeles: Univ. of California Press, 1982.

Caie, Graham D. "The Significance of the Early Chaucer Manuscript Glosses (with Special Reference to the *Wife of Bath's Prologue*)." *ChauR* 10 (1976): 350–60.

Cambridge History of the Bible. Ed. P. R. Ackroyd, C. F. Evans, G. W. H. Lampe, and S. L. Greenslade. 3 vols. Cambridge: Cambridge Univ. Press, 1963–70.

Carroll, David. *The Subject in Question: The Languages of Theory and the Strategies of Fiction.* Chicago: Univ. of Chicago Press, 1982.

Carruthers, Mary. "The Wife of Bath and the Painting of Lions." *PMLA* 94 (1979): 209–22.

Carton, Evan. "Complicity and Responsibility in Pandarus' Bed and Chaucer's Art." *PMLA* 94 (1979): 47–61.

Castelli, Elizabeth. "Virginity and Its Meaning for Women's Sexuality in Early Christianity." *Journal of Feminist Studies in Religion* 2 (1986): 61–86.

Chodorow, Nancy. *The Reproduction of Mothering: Psychoanalysis and the Sociology of Gender.* Berkeley and Los Angeles: Univ. of California Press, 1978.

Cixous, Hélène. "The Laugh of the Medusa." In *New French Feminisms,* ed. Elaine Marks and Isabelle de Courtivron. Pp. 245–64. New York: Schocken, 1981.

Cixous, Hélène, and Catherine Clément. *The Newly Born Woman*. Trans. Betsy Wing. Minneapolis: Univ. of Minnesota Press, 1986.

Clanchy, M. T. *From Memory to Written Record: England, 1066–1307*. Cambridge, Mass.: Harvard Univ. Press, 1979.

Coghill, Nevill. *The Poet Chaucer*. 1949. Rpt. London: Oxford Univ. Press, 1950.

Colish, Marcia. *The Mirror of Language*. Rev. ed. Lincoln: Univ. of Nebraska Press, 1983.

Cooper, Helen. *The Structure of the "Canterbury Tales."* Athens: Univ. of Georgia Press, 1984.

Copeland, Rita. "Rhetoric and Vernacular Translation in the Middle Ages." *SAC* 9 (1987): 41–75.

Crane, R. S. "On Hypotheses in 'Historical Criticism': A Propos of Certain Contemporary Medievalists." In his *"The Idea of the Humanities" and Other Essays Critical and Historical*, vol. 2, pp. 236–60. Chicago: Univ. of Chicago Press, 1967.

Crane, R. S. *The Languages of Criticism and the Structure of Poetry*. Toronto: Univ. of Toronto Press, 1953.

Crane, Susan. "Alison's Incapacity and Poetic Instability in the *Wife of Bath's Tale*." *PMLA* 102 (1987): 20–28.

Culler, Jonathan. *On Deconstruction: Theory and Criticism after Structuralism*. Ithaca, N.Y.: Cornell Univ. Press, 1982.

Curry, W. C. *Chaucer and the Mediaeval Sciences*. Rev. ed. New York: Barnes and Noble, 1960.

Curry, W. C. "The Secret of Chaucer's Pardoner." *JEGP* 18 (1919): 593–606.

Curtius, Ernst Robert. *European Literature and the Latin Middle Ages*. Trans. Willard R. Trask. Princeton, N.J.: Princeton Univ. Press, 1953.

David, Alfred. "The Man of Law vs. Chaucer: A Case in Poetics." *PMLA* 82 (1967): 217–25.

David, Alfred. *The Strumpet Muse: Art and Morals in Chaucer's Poetry*. Bloomington: Indiana Univ. Press, 1976.

Delany, Sheila. "The Logic of Obscenity in Chaucer's *Legend of Good Women*." *Florilegium* 7 (1985): 189–205.

Delany, Sheila. "Rewriting Woman Good: Gender and the Anxiety of Influence in Two Late-Medieval Texts." In *Chaucer in the Eighties*, ed. Julian N. Wasserman and Robert J. Blanch, pp. 75–92. Syracuse, N.Y.: Syracuse Univ. Press, 1986.

Delany, Sheila. *Writing Woman: Women Writers and Women in Literature, Medieval to Modern*. New York: Schocken, 1983.

Delasanta, Rodney. "And of Great Reverence: Chaucer's Man of Law." *ChauR* 5 (1971): 288–310.

Delehaye, Hippolyte. *Cinq Leçons sur la méthode hagiographique.* Brussels: Société des Bollandistes, 1934.

Delehaye, Hippolyte. *Les Légendes hagiographiques.* 2d ed. Brussels: Société des Bollandistes, 1906.

Delehaye, Hippolyte. *Les Origines du culte des martyrs.* 2d ed. Brussels: Société des Bollandistes, 1933.

Derrida, Jacques. *The Ear of the Other.* See McDonald, Christie V.

Derrida, Jacques. *Glas.* Trans. John P. Leavey, Jr., and Richard Rand. Lincoln: Univ. of Nebraska Press, 1986.

Diamond, Arlyn. "*Troilus and Criseyde:* The Politics of Love." In *Chaucer in the Eighties,* ed. Julian N. Wasserman and Robert J. Blanch, pp. 93–103. Syracuse, N.Y.: Syracuse Univ. Press, 1986.

Disbrow, Sarah. "The Wife of Bath's Old Wives' Tale." *SAC* 8 (1986): 59–71.

Donaldson, E. Talbot. "Briseis, Briseida, Criseyde, Cresseid, Cressid: Progress of a Heroine." In *Chaucerian Problems and Perspectives,* ed. Edward Vasta and Z. P. Thundy, pp. 1–12. Notre Dame, Ind.: Univ. of Notre Dame Press, 1970.

Donaldson, E. Talbot. "Chaucer's Three 'P's': Pandarus, Pardoner, and Poet." *Michigan Quarterly Review* 14 (1975): 282–301.

Donaldson, E. Talbot. "Cressid False, Criseyde Untrue: An Ambiguity Revisited." In *Poetic Traditions of the English Renaissance.* Ed. Maynard Mack and George deForest Lord. Pp. 67–83. New Haven, Conn.: Yale Univ. Press, 1982.

Donaldson, E. Talbot. "Designing a Camel; or, Generalizing the Middle Ages." *Tennessee Studies in Literature* 22 (1977): 1–16.

Donaldson, E. Talbot. "The Ordering of the *Canterbury Tales.*" In *Medieval Literature and Folklore: Essays in Honor of Francis Lee Utley,* ed. Jerome Mandel and Bruce A. Rosenberg, pp. 193–204. New Brunswick, N.J.: Rutgers Univ. Press, 1970.

Donaldson, E. Talbot. "Patristic Exegesis in the Criticism of Medieval Literature: The Opposition." In *Critical Approaches to Medieval Literature,* ed. Dorothy Bethurum, pp. 1–26. Selected Papers from the English Institute, 1958–59, New York: Columbia Univ. Press, 1960.

Donaldson, E. Talbot. *Speaking of Chaucer.* London: Athlone Press, 1970.

Donaldson, E. Talbot. *The Swan at the Well: Shakespeare Reading Chaucer.* New Haven, Conn.: Yale Univ. Press, 1985.

Donaldson, E. T., ed., *Chaucer's Poetry: An Anthology for the Modern Reader.* New York: Ronald Press, 1958.

Donaldson, Ian. *The Rapes of Lucretia: A Myth and Its Transformations.* Oxford: Clarendon, 1982.

Dronke, Peter. *Women Writers of the Middle Ages: A Critical Study of Texts from Perpetua to Marguerite Porete.* Cambridge: Cambridge Univ. Press, 1984.

Duby, Georges. *Medieval Marriage: Two Models from Twelfth-Century France.* Trans. Elborg Forster. Baltimore: Johns Hopkins Univ. Press, 1978.

Eagleton, Terry. *Literary Theory: An Introduction.* Minneapolis: Univ. of Minnesota Press, 1983.

Eagleton, Terry. *Marxism and Literary Criticism.* Berkeley and Los Angeles: Univ. of California Press, 1976.

Earl, James W. "Typology and Iconographic Style in Early Medieval Hagiography." *Studies in the Literary Imagination* 8 (1975): 15–46.

Ellis, Deborah. "The Merchant's Wife's Tale: Language, Sex, and Commerce in Margery Kempe and in Chaucer." *Exemplaria* 1 (1989).

Fansler, Dean S. *Chaucer and the "Roman de la Rose."* New York: Columbia Univ. Press, 1914.

Felman, Shoshana. "Psychoanalysis and Education: Teaching Terminable and Interminable." *YFS* 63 (1982): 21–44.

Felman, Shoshana. "Women and Madness: The Critical Phallacy." *Diacritics* 5 (1975): 2–10.

Ferguson, Margaret W. "Saint Augustine's Region of Unlikeness: The Crossing of Exile and Language." *Georgia Review* 29 (1975): 842–64.

Ferrante, Joan M. "The Education of Women in the Middle Ages in Theory, Fact, and Fantasy." In *Beyond Their Sex: Learned Women of the European Past,* ed. Patricia H. Labalme, pp. 9–42. New York: New York Univ. Press, 1980.

Ferster, Judith. *Chaucer on Interpretation.* Cambridge: Cambridge Univ. Press, 1985.

Fetterley, Judith. *The Resisting Reader.* Bloomington: Indiana Univ. Press, 1978.

Fisher, John H. *John Gower: Moral Philosopher and Friend of Chaucer.* New York: New York Univ. Press, 1964.

Fleming, John. "Hoccleve's 'Letter of Cupid' and the 'Quarrel' over the *Roman de la Rose.*" *Medium Aevum* 40 (1971): 21–40.

Fleming, John. *Reason and the Lover.* Princeton, N.J.: Princeton Univ. Press, 1984.

Fleming, John. *The "Roman de la Rose": A Study in Allegory and Iconography.* Princeton, N.J.: Princeton Univ. Press, 1969.

Foucault, Michel. "What Is an Author?" In his *Language, Counter-Memory, Practice: Selected Essays and Interviews,* ed. and trans. Donald F. Bouchard, pp. 113–38. Ithaca, N.Y.: Cornell Univ. Press, 1979.

Fradenburg, Louise O. "The Wife of Bath's Passing Fancy." *SAC* 8 (1986): 31–58.

Frank, Robert Worth, Jr. *Chaucer and the "Legend of Good Women."* Cambridge, Mass.: Harvard Univ. Press, 1972.

Freccero, John. "The Fig Tree and the Laurel: Petrarch's Poetics." *Diacritics* 5 (1975): 34–40.

Freccero, John. "Medusa: The Letter and the Spirit." In his *Dante: The Poetics of Conversion*, ed. Rachel Jacoff, pp. 119–35. Cambridge, Mass.: Harvard Univ. Press, 1986.

Freud, Sigmund. "The Dissolution of the Oedipus Complex." In *The Standard Edition of the Complete Psychological Works of Sigmund Freud*, trans. James Strachey, vol. 19, pp. 173–79. London: Hogarth Press, 1953–56.

Freud, Sigmund. "Fetishism." In *The Standard Edition of the Complete Psychological Works of Sigmund Freud*, trans. James Strachey, vol. 21, pp. 152–57.

Freud, Sigmund. "Medusa's Head." In *The Standard Edition of the Complete Psychological Works of Sigmund Freud*, trans. James Strachey, vol. 18, pp. 273–74.

Fries, Maureen. " 'Slydynge of Corage': Chaucer's Criseyde as Feminist and Victim." In *The Authority of Experience: Essays in Feminist Criticism*, ed. Arlyn Diamond and Lee R. Edwards, pp. 45–59. Amherst: Univ. of Massachusetts Press, 1977.

Frowlow, A. *La Relique de la vrai croix: recherches sur le developpement d'un culte*. Archives de l'orient chrétien, no. 7. Paris: Institut français d'études byzantines, 1961.

Fyler, John. *Chaucer and Ovid*. New Haven, Conn.: Yale Univ. Press, 1979.

Gibson, Gail McMurray. " 'Porta haec clausa erit': Comedy, Conception, and Ezekiel's Closed Door in the *Ludus Coventriae* Play of 'Joseph's Return.' " *JMRS* 8 (1978): 137–56.

Gilbert, Sandra M., and Susan Gubar. *The Madwoman in the Attic: The Woman Writer and the Nineteenth-Century Literary Imagination*. New Haven, Conn.: Yale Univ. Press, 1979.

Gilson, Etienne. "Michel Menot et la technique du sermon médiéval." In his *Les Idées et les lettres*. 2d ed. Pp. 93–154. Paris: J. Vrin, 1955.

Ginsberg, Warren. *The Cast of Character*. Toronto: Univ. of Toronto Press, 1983.

Gist, Margaret Adlum. *Love and War in the Middle English Romances*. Philadelphia: Univ. of Pennsylvania Press, 1947.

Glorieux, P. "Le Conflit de 1252–57 a la lumière du Mémoire de Guillaume de Saint-Amour." *Recherches de théologie ancienne et médiévale* 24 (1957): 364–72.

Goddard, H. C. "Chaucer's Legend of Good Women." *JEGP* 7 (1908): 87–129.

Goetzl, Franz R. "Root of Discontent and Aggression." In *Boredom: Root of Discontent and Aggression*, ed. Franz R. Goetzl. Berkeley: Grizzly Peak Press, 1975.

Goodall, Peter. "'Unkynde abhomynaciouns' [*sic*] in Chaucer and Gower." *Parergon* 5 (1987): 94–102.

Goody, Jack. *The Development of the Family and Marriage in Europe.* Cambridge: Cambridge Univ. Press, 1983.

Goody, Jack, J. Thirsk, and E. P. Thompson, eds. *Family and Inheritance: Rural Society in Western Europe, 1200–1800.* Past and Present Publications. Cambridge: Cambridge Univ. Press, 1976.

Gordon, Ida L. *The Double Sorrow of Troilus: A Study of Ambiguities in "Troilus and Criseyde."* Oxford: Clarendon Press, 1970.

Grady, Francis. "Thebes, Troy, and Prophecy in *Troilus and Criseyde.*" Department of English. University of California, Berkeley. 1985.

Greenacre, Phyllis. "The Fetish and the Transitional Object." *Psychoanalytic Study of the Child* 24 (1969): 144–65.

Griffin, Susan. "The Way of All Ideology." In *Feminist Theory: A Critique of Ideology*, ed. Nannerl O. Keohane, Michelle Z. Rosaldo, and Barbara C. Gelpi, pp. 273–92. Chicago: Univ. of Chicago Press, 1982.

Griffith, D. D. "An Interpretation of Chaucer's *Legend of Good Women.*" In *The Manly Anniversary Studies in Language and Literature*, pp. 32–41. Chicago: Univ. of Chicago Press, 1923.

Griffith, D. D. *The Origin of the Griselda Story.* Univ. of Washington Publications in Language and Literature, no. 8. Seattle: Univ. of Washington Press, 1931.

Gubar, Susan. "'The Blank Page' and the Issues of Female Creativity." In *Writing and Sexual Difference*, ed. Elizabeth Abel, pp. 73–93, Chicago: Univ. of Chicago Press, 1982.

Guntrip, Harry. *Personality Structure and Human Interaction.* New York: International Universities Press, 1961.

Hahn, Thomas. "Money, Sexuality, Wordplay, and Context in the *Shipman's Tale.*" In *Chaucer in the Eighties*, ed. Julian N. Wasserman and Robert J. Blanch, pp. 235–49. Syracuse, N.Y.: Syracuse Univ. Press, 1986.

Hansen, Elaine Tuttle. "Irony and the Antifeminist Narrator in Chaucer's *Legend of Good Women.*" *JEGP* 82 (1983): 11–31.

Hartman, Geoffrey. "The Voice of the Shuttle." In his *Beyond Formalism*, pp. 337–55. New Haven, Conn.: Yale Univ. Press, 1970.

Harwood, Britton J. "Chaucer and the Silence of History: Situating the *Canon's Yeoman's Tale.*" *PMLA* 102 (1987): 338–50.

Herlihy, David. *Medieval Households.* Cambridge, Mass.: Harvard Univ. Press, 1985.

Herman, Judith, and Lisa Hirschman. "Father-Daughter Incest." *Signs* 2 (1977): 735–56.

Hermann, John P. "Gesture and Seduction in *Troilus and Criseyde.*" *SAC* 7 (1985): 107–35.

Higonnet, Margaret. "Speaking Silences: Women's Suicide." In *The Female Body in Western Culture: Contemporary Perspectives,* ed. Susan Rubin Suleiman, pp. 68–83. Cambridge, Mass.: Harvard Univ. Press, 1986.

Hill, Thomas D. "Narcissus, Pygmalion, and the Castration of Saturn: Two Mythological Themes in the *Roman de la Rose.*" *SP* 71 (1974): 404–26.

Hollander, Robert. "Babytalk in Dante's *Commedia.*" *Mosaic* 8 (1975): 73–84.

Homans, Margaret. *Bearing the Word: Language and Female Experience in Nineteenth-Century Women's Writing.* Chicago: Univ. of Chicago Press, 1986.

Howard, Donald R. *Chaucer: His Life, His Works, His World.* New York: Dutton, 1987.

Howard, Donald R. *The Idea of the "Canterbury Tales."* Berkeley and Los Angeles: Univ. of California Press, 1976.

Howard, Donald R. "Literature and Sexuality: Book III of Chaucer's *Troilus.*" *Massachusetts Review* 8 (1967): 442–56.

Howard, Donald R. Review of *Fruyt and Chaf,* by D. W. Robertson, Jr., and Bernard F. Huppé. *Speculum,* 39 (1964): 537–41.

Howe, Lawrence. "The Man of Law's Obsession." Dept. of English. Univ. of California, Berkeley. 1984.

Hudson, Ann. "Middle English." In *Editing Medieval Texts,* ed. A. G. Rigg, pp. 34–57. New York: Garland, 1977.

Huppé, Bernard F. "Rape and Woman's Sovereignty in the *Wife of Bath's Tale.*" *Modern Language Notes* 63 (1948): 378–81.

Huppé, Bernard F. *A Reading of the "Canterbury Tales."* Albany: State Univ. of New York Press, 1964.

Irigaray, Luce. *Speculum of the Other Woman.* Trans. Gillian C. Gill. Ithaca, N.Y.: Cornell Univ. Press, 1985.

Irigaray, Luce. *This Sex Which Is Not One.* Trans. Catherine Porter. Ithaca, N.Y.: Cornell Univ. Press, 1985.

Jakobson, Roman. "On Linguistic Aspects of Translation." In *On Translation,* ed. Reuben A. Brower, pp. 232–39. Cambridge, Mass.: Harvard Univ. Press, 1959.

Jardine, Alice, and Paul Smith, eds. *Men in Feminism.* New York: Methuen, 1987.

Jeffrey, David L. "English Saints' Plays." In *Medieval Drama,* ed. Neville Denny, pp. 69–89. Stratford-Upon-Avon Studies, no. 16. London: Arnold Press, 1973.

Jennings, Margaret, C.S.J. "The *Ars componendi sermones* of Ranulph Higden." In *Medieval Eloquence: Studies in the Theory and Practice of Medieval Rhetoric*, ed. J. J. Murphy, pp. 112–26. Berkeley and Los Angeles: Univ. of California Press, 1978.

Johnson, Barbara. "Teaching Ignorance: *L'Ecole des Femmes.*" *YFS* 63 (1982): 165–82.

Jones, Ann Rosalind. "Writing the Body: Toward an Understanding of *l'Écriture féminine.*" In *The New Feminist Criticism*, ed. Elaine Showalter, pp. 361–77. New York: Pantheon, 1985.

Jones, Charles W. *Saints' Lives and Chronicles in Early England*. Ithaca, N.Y.: Cornell Univ. Press, 1947.

Joplin, Patricia Klindienst. "The Voice of the Shuttle Is Ours." *Stanford Literature Review* 1 (1984): 25–53.

Joseph, Gerhard. "Chaucer's Coinage: Foreign Exchange and the Puns of the *Shipman's Tale.*" *ChauR* 17 (1983): 341–57.

Kaske, R. E. " 'Clericus Adam' and Chaucer's 'Adam Scriveyn.' " In *Chaucerian Problems and Perspectives: Essays Presented to Paul E. Beichner, C.S.C.*, ed. E. Vasta and Z. P. Thundy, pp. 114–18. Notre Dame, Ind.: Univ. of Notre Dame Press, 1979.

Kean, P. M. *Chaucer and the Making of English Poetry*. 2 vols. London: Routledge and Kegan Paul, 1972.

Kellogg, Alfred L. *Chaucer, Langland, Arthur: Essays in Middle English Literature*. New Brunswick, N.J.: Rutgers Univ. Press, 1972.

Kelly, Douglas. "Translatio Studii: Translation, Adaptation, and Allegory in Medieval French Literature." *Philological Quarterly* 57 (1978): 287–310.

Kelly, J. N. D. *Jerome: His Life, Writings, and Controversies*. London: Duckworth, 1975.

Kendrick, Laura. *Chaucerian Play: Comedy and Control in the "Canterbury Tales."* Berkeley and Los Angeles: Univ. of California Press, 1988.

Kernan, Anne. "The Archwife and the Eunuch." *ELH* 41 (1974): 1–25.

Kiser, Lisa J. *Telling Classical Tales: Chaucer and the "Legend of Good Women."* Ithaca, N.Y.: Cornell Univ. Press, 1983.

Klein, Melanie, Paula Heimann, and R. E. Money-Kyrle, eds. *New Directions in Psycho-Analysis*. New York: Basic Books, 1955.

Knowles, Dom David. *The Religious Orders in England*. 3 vols. Cambridge: Cambridge Univ. Press, 1957-62.

Kofman, Sarah. *The Enigma of Woman: Woman in Freud's Writings*. Trans. Catherine Porter. Ithaca, N.Y.: Cornell Univ. Press, 1985.

Kristeva, Julia. *Desire in Language: A Semiotic Approach to Literature and Art.* Ed. Leon S. Roudiez. Trans. Thomas Gora, Alice Jardine, and Leon S. Roudiez. New York: Columbia Univ. Press, 1980.

Kristeva, Julia. *In the Beginning Was Love: Psychoanalysis and Faith*. Trans. Arthur Goldhammer. New York: Columbia Univ. Press, 1987.

Lacan, Jacques. *Ecrits: A Selection*. Trans. Alan Sheridan. New York: Norton, 1977.

Lacan, Jacques. *Feminine Sexuality: Jacques Lacan and the école freudienne*. Ed. Juliet Mitchell and Jacqueline Rose. Trans. Jacqueline Rose. New York: Norton, 1982.

Lacan, Jacques. *Four Fundamental Concepts of Psychoanalysis*. Ed. J.-A. Miller. Trans. Alan Sheridan. New York: Norton, 1981.

Lacan, Jacques. *Speech and Language in Psychoanalysis*. Trans. (with notes and commentary) Anthony Wilden. Baltimore: Johns Hopkins Univ. Press, 1968.

Lambert, Mark. "*Troilus*, Books I-III: A Criseydan Reading." In *Essays on "Troilus and Criseyde*," ed. Mary Salu, pp. 105–25. Chaucer Studies, 3. Cambridge: Brewer, 1979.

Landes, David S. *Revolution in Time: Clocks and the Making of the Modern World*. Cambridge, Mass.: Harvard Univ. Press, 1983.

Larbaud, Valery. *An Homage to Jerome: Patron Saint of Translators*. Trans. Jean-Paul de Chezet. Marlboro, Vt.: Marlboro Press, 1984.

Leach, Eleanor Winsor. "Morwe of May: A Season of Feminine Ambiguity." In *Acts of Interpretation: The Text in Its Contexts, 700–1600*, ed. Mary J. Carruthers and Elizabeth D. Kirk, pp. 299–310. Norman, Okla.: Pilgrim Books, 1982.

Le Goff, Jacques. *Time, Work, and Culture in the Middle Ages*. Trans. Arthur Goldhammer. Chicago: Univ. of Chicago Press, 1980.

Leicester, H. Marshall, Jr. "The Art of Impersonation: A General Prologue to the *Canterbury Tales*." *PMLA* 95 (1980): 213–24.

Leicester, H. Marshall, Jr. "Of a Fire in the Dark: Public and Private Feminism in the *Wife of Bath's Tale*." *Women's Studies* 11 (1984): 157–78.

Leicester, H. Marshall, Jr. "Oure Tonges *Différance*: Textuality and Deconstruction in Chaucer." In *Medieval Texts and Contemporary Readers*, ed. Laurie A. Finke and Martin B. Shichtman, pp. 15–26. Ithaca, N.Y.: Cornell Univ. Press, 1987.

Leicester, H. Marshall, Jr. " 'Synne Horrible': The Pardoner's Exegesis of His Tale, and Chaucer's." In *Acts of Interpretation: The Text in Its Contexts, 700–1600*, ed. Mary J. Carruthers and Elizabeth D. Kirk, pp. 25–50. Norman, Okla.: Pilgrim Books, 1982.

Lemaire, Anika. *Jacques Lacan*. Trans. David Macey. London: Routledge and Kegan Paul, 1977.

Lemay, Helen Rodnite. "Human Sexuality in Twelfth- through Fifteenth-Century Scientific Writings." In *Sexual Practices and the Medieval Church*, ed. Vern L. Bullough and James Brundage, pp. 187–205. Buffalo, N.Y.: Prometheus Books, 1982.

Lemay, Helen Rodnite. "William of Saliceto on Human Sexuality." *Viator* 12 (1981): 165–81.

Lerch, Eugen. "Zu einer Stelle bei Eustache Deschamps." *Romanische Forschungen* 62 (1950): 67–68.

Lévi-Strauss, Claude. *The Elementary Structures of Kinship*. Trans. James Harle Bell, John Richard von Sturmer, and Rodney Needham. Rev. ed. Boston: Beacon Press, 1969.

Lévi-Strauss, Claude. "The Family." In *Man, Culture and Society*, ed. H. Shapiro, pp. 261–85. London: Oxford Univ. Press, 1971.

Lévi-Strauss, Claude. *Structural Anthropology*. Trans. Claire Jacobson and Brooke Grundfest Schoepf. New York: Basic Books, 1963.

Lewis, C. S. "What Chaucer Really Did to *Il Filostrato*." *Essays and Studies* 17 (1932): 56–75.

Longo, John Duane. "Literary Appropriation as *Translatio* in Chaucer and the *Roman de la Rose*." Ph.D. diss. Princeton University, 1982.

Longsworth, Robert. "Chaucer's Clerk as Teacher." In *The Learned and the Lewed*, ed. Larry D. Benson, pp. 61–66. Cambridge, Mass.: Harvard Univ. Press, 1974.

Lopez, Robert S. *The Commercial Revolution of the Middle Ages, 950–1350*. Cambridge: Cambridge Univ. Press, 1976.

Lowes, J. L. "Chaucer and the *Ovide moralisé*." *PMLA* 33 (1918): 302–25.

Lowes, J. L. "The Prologue to the *Legend of Good Women* Considered in Its Chronological Relations." *PMLA* 20 (1905): 749–864.

Lubac, Henri de. *Exégèse médiévale*. 4 vols. Paris: Aubier, 1959.

McAlpine, Monica. *The Genre of "Troilus and Criseyde."* Ithaca, N.Y.: Cornell Univ. Press, 1978.

McAlpine, Monica. "The Pardoner's Homosexuality and How It Matters." *PMLA* 95 (1980): 8–22.

McCall, John P. "The *Clerk's Tale* and the Theme of Obedience." *MLQ* 27 (1966): 260–69.

McDonald, Christie V., ed. *The Ear of the Other: Otobiography, Transference, Translation—Texts and Discussions with Jacques Derrida*. New York: Schocken Books, 1985.

MacKinnon, Catherine A. "Feminism, Marxism, Method, and the State." In *Feminist Theory: A Critique of Ideology*, ed. Nannerl O. Keohane, Michelle Z. Rosaldo, and Barbara C. Gelpi. Chicago: Univ. of Chicago Press, 1982.

Machan, Tim William. *Techniques of Translation: Chaucer's "Boece."* Norman, Okla.: Pilgrim Books, 1985.

Macherey, Pierre. *A Theory of Literary Production*. Trans. Geoffrey Wall. London: Routledge and Kegan Paul, 1978.

Manly, John Matthews. *Some New Light on Chaucer*. 1926. Rpt. Gloucester, Mass.: Peter Smith, 1959.

Mann, Jill. *Chaucer and Medieval Estates Satire.* Cambridge: Cambridge Univ. Press, 1973.

Mannoni, O. *Clefs pour l'imaginaire.* Paris: Seuil, 1969.

Marcus, Jane. "Liberty, Sorority, Misogyny." In *The Representation of Women in Fiction,* ed. Carolyn G. Heilbrun and Margaret R. Higonnet, pp. 60–97. Selected Papers from the English Institute, 1981. N.s., no. 7. Baltimore: Johns Hopkins Univ. Press, 1983.

Markus, R. A., ed. *Augustine: A Collection of Critical Essays.* New York: Doubleday Anchor, 1972.

Mauss, Marcel. *The Gift: Forms and Functions of Exchange in Archaic Societies.* Trans. Ian Cunnison. New York: Norton, 1967.

Meech, Sanford Brown. "Chaucer and the *Ovide moralisé:* A Further Study." *PMLA* 46 (1931): 182–204.

Middleton, Anne. "The Clerk and His Tale: Some Literary Contexts." *SAC* 2 (1980): 121–50.

Middleton, Anne. "The 'Physician's Tale' and Love's Martyrs: 'Ensamples mo than ten' as a Method in the *Canterbury Tales.*" *ChauR* 8 (1973): 9–31.

Mieszkowski, Gretchen. " 'Pandras' in Deschamps' Ballade for Chaucer." *ChauR* 9 (1975): 327–36.

Mieszkowski, Gretchen. "The Reputation of Criseyde, 1155–1500." *Transactions of the Connecticut Academy of Arts and Sciences* 43 (1971): 71–153.

Mieszkowski, Gretchen. "R. K. Gordon and the *Troilus and Criseyde* Story." *ChauR* 15 (1980): 127–37.

Miller, D. A. "The Administrator's Black Veil: A Response to J. Hillis Miller." *ADE Bulletin* 88 (1987): 49–53.

Miller, D. A. "The Novel as Usual: Trollope's *Barchester Towers.*" In *Sex, Politics, and Science in the Nineteenth-Century Novel,* ed. Ruth Bernard Yeazell, pp. 1–38. Selected Papers form the English Institute, 1983–84. N.s., no. 10. Baltimore: Johns Hopkins Univ. Press, 1986.

Miller, J. Hillis. "Ariadne's Thread: Repetition and the Narrative Line." *Critical Inquiry* 3 (1976): 57–77.

Miller, Nancy K. "Arachnologies: The Woman, the Text, and the Critic." In *The Poetics of Gender,* ed. Nancy K. Miller, pp. 270–95. New York: Columbia Univ. Press, 1986.

Miller, Robert P. "Chaucer's Pardoner, the Scriptural Eunuch, and the Pardoner's Tale." *Speculum* 30 (1955): 180–99.

Moi, Toril. *Sexual/Textual Politics: Feminist Literary Theory.* New Accents Series. London and New York: Methuen, 1985.

Monfrin, Jacques. "Humanisme et traductions au Moyen Age." *Journal des savants* (1963): 161–90.

Morse, Charlotte C. "The Exemplary Griselda." *SAC* 7 (1985): 51–86.

Morse, J. Mitchell. "The Philosophy of the Clerk of Oxenford." *MLQ* 19 (1958): 3–20.

Murphy, James J. *Rhetoric in the Middle Ages: A History of Rhetorical Theory from St. Augustine to the Renaissance.* Berkeley and Los Angeles: Univ. of California Press, 1974.

Muscatine, Charles. *Chaucer and the French Tradition: A Study in Style and Meaning.* Berkeley and Los Angeles: Univ. of California Press, 1957.

Muscatine, Charles. "The Wife of Bath and Gautier's *La Veuve*." In *Romance Studies in Memory of Edward Billings Ham*, ed. U. T. Holmes, pp. 109–14. California State College Publications, no. 2. Hayward, Calif.: n.p., 1967.

Nichols, Stephen G., Jr. *Romanesque Signs: Early Medieval Narrative and Iconography.* New Haven, Conn.: Yale Univ. Press, 1983.

Nims, Margaret F., IBVM. "*Translatio:* 'Difficult Statement' in Medieval Poetic Theory." *University of Toronto Quarterly* 43 (1974): 215–30.

Noonan, John T., Jr. *Contraception: A History of Its Treatment by the Catholic Theologians and Canonists.* Cambridge, Mass.: Harvard Univ. Press, 1966.

Olsen, Alexandra Hennessy. " 'De Historiis Sanctorum': A Generic Study of Hagiography." *Genre* 13 (1980): 407–29.

Overbeck, Pat Trefzger. "Chaucer's Good Woman." *ChauR* 2 (1967): 75–94.

Owen, Charles A. "The Alternative Reading of *The Canterbury Tales:* Chaucer's Text and the Early Manuscripts." *PMLA* 97 (1982): 237–50.

Owens, Craig. "Outlaws: Gay Men in Feminism." In *Men in Feminism*, ed. Alice Jardine and Paul Smith. London and New York: Methuen, 1987.

Owst, G. R. *Literature and Pulpit in Medieval England.* Oxford: Basil Blackwell, 1961.

Owst, G. R. *Preaching in Medieval England: An Introduction to Sermon Manuscripts of the Period, c. 1350–1450.* New York: Russell and Russell, 1965.

Parker, Patricia. *Inescapable Romance: Studies in the Poetics of a Mode.* Princeton, N.J.: Princeton Univ. Press, 1979.

Parker, Patricia. *Literary Fat Ladies.* London: Methuen, 1987.

Patterson, Lee W. "Ambiguity and Interpretation: A Fifteenth-Century Reading of *Troilus and Criseyde*." *Speculum* 54 (1979): 297–330.

Patterson, Lee W. "Chaucerian Confession: Penitential Literature and the Pardoner." *Medievalia et Humanistica*, n.s., 7 (1976): 153–73.

Patterson, Lee W. " 'For the Wyves love of Bathe': Feminine Rhetoric and Poetic Resolution in the *Roman de la rose* and the *Canterbury Tales*." *Speculum* 58 (1983): 656–95.

Patterson, Lee W. "The Logic of Textual Criticism and the Way of Genius:

The Kane-Donaldson *Piers Plowman* in Historical Perspective." In *Textual Criticism and Literary Interpretation*, ed. Jerome J. McGann, pp. 55–91. Chicago: Univ. of Chicago Press, 1985.

Patterson, Lee W. *Negotiating the Past: The Historical Understanding of Medieval Literature*. Madison: Univ. of Wisconsin Press, 1987.

Pearsall, Derek. "Editing Medieval Texts: Some Developments and Some Problems." In *Textual Criticism and Literary Interpretation*, ed. Jerome J. McGann, pp. 92–106. Chicago: Univ. of Chicago Press, 1985.

Peck, Russell A. "Public Dreams and Private Myths: Perspectives in Middle English Literature." *PMLA* 90 (1975): 461–68.

Perella, Nicholas James. *The Kiss Sacred and Profane: An Interpretive History of Kiss Symbolism and Related Religio-Erotic Themes*. Berkeley and Los Angeles: Univ. of California Press, 1969.

Plucknett, Theodore F. T. "Chaucer's Escapade." *Law Quarterly Review* 64 (1948): 33–36.

Plucknett, Theodore F. T. *A Concise History of the Common Law*. 5th ed. Boston: Little, Brown, 1956.

Poirion, Daniel. *Le Roman de la rose*. Paris: Hatier, 1973.

Pollock, Frederick, and Frederic W. Maitland. *The History of English Law Before the Time of Edward I*. 2 vols. Cambridge: Cambridge Univ. Press, 1895.

Pratt, Robert. "The Development of the Wife of Bath." In *Studies in Medieval Literature in Honor of Professor Albert Croll Baugh*, ed. MacEdward Leach, pp. 45–79. Philadelphia: Univ. of Pennsylvania Press, 1961.

Rashdall, Hastings. *The Universities of Europe in the Middle Ages*. Ed. F. M. Powicke and A. B. Emden. New ed. 3 vols. London: Oxford Univ. Press, 1936.

Reiman, Donald H. "The Real *Clerk's Tale*; or, Patient Griselda Exposed." *Texas Studies in Literature and Language* 5 (1963): 356–73.

Ricoeur, Paul. *Freud and Philosophy: An Essay on Interpretation*. Trans. Denis Savage. New Haven, Conn.: Yale Univ. Press, 1970.

Robertson, D. W., Jr. *Essays in Medieval Culture*. Princeton, N.J.: Princeton Univ. Press, 1980.

Robertson, D. W., Jr. *A Preface to Chaucer*. Princeton, N.J.: Princeton Univ. Press, 1962.

Robertson, D. W., Jr., and B. F. Huppé. *Fruyt and Chaf*. Princeton, N.J.: Princeton Univ. Press, 1963.

Root, R. K. *The Manuscripts of Chaucer's "Troilus."* Chaucer Society, 1st ser., no. 98. London: Kegan Paul, 1914 for 1911.

Root, R. K. *The Textual Tradition of Chaucer's "Troilus."* Chaucer Society, 1st ser., no. 99. London: Kegan Paul, 1916 for 1912.

Rowe, Donald W. *O Love, O Charite! Contraries Harmonized in Chaucer's "Troilus."* Carbondale: Southern Illinois Univ. Press, 1976.

Rowland, Beryl. "Animal Imagery and the Pardoner's Abnormality." *Neophilologus* 48 (1964): 56–60.

Rowland, Beryl. "Chaucer's Idea of the Pardoner." *ChauR* 14 (1979): 140–54.

Rubin, Gayle. "The Traffic in Women: Notes on the 'Political Economy' of Sex." In *Toward an Anthropology of Women,* ed. R. R. Reiter, pp. 157–210. New York: Monthly Review Press, 1975.

Ruggiers, Paul G. *The Art of the "Canterbury Tales."* Madison: Univ. of Wisconsin Press, 1965.

Ruggiers, Paul G., ed. *Editing Chaucer: The Great Tradition.* Norman, Okla.: Pilgrim Books, 1984.

Salter, Elizabeth. *Chaucer: The "Knight's Tale" and the "Clerk's Tale."* London: Edward Arnold, 1962.

Schibanoff, Susan. "Taking Jane's Cue: *Phyllyp Sparowe* as a Primer for Women Readers." *PMLA* 101 (1986): 832–47.

Schibanoff, Susan. "Taking the Gold Out of Egypt: The Art of Reading as a Woman." In *Gender and Reading: Essays on Readers, Texts, and Contexts,* ed. Elizabeth A. Flynn and Patrocinio P. Schweickart, pp. 83–106. Baltimore: Johns Hopkins Univ. Press, 1986.

Schlauch, Margaret. *Chaucer's Constance and Accused Queens.* 1927. Rpt. New York: Gordian Press, 1969.

Sedgwick, Eve Kosofsky. *Between Men: English Literature and Male Homosocial Desire.* New York: Columbia Univ. Press, 1985.

Sejourné, P. "Reliques." In *Dictionnaire de théologie catholique,* vol. 13. Paris: Librairie Letouzey et Ané, 1937.

Severs, J. Burke. *The Literary Relationships of Chaucer's "Clerkes Tale."* New Haven, Conn.: Yale Univ. Press, 1942.

Shoaf, R. A. *The Poem as Green Girdle: "Commercium" in "Sir Gawain and the Green Knight."* University of Florida Monographs. Humanities Series, no. 55. Gainesville: Univ. Presses of Florida, 1984.

Silverman, Kaja. *The Subject of Semiotics.* New York: Oxford Univ. Press, 1983.

Silvia, Daniel S., Jr. "Glosses to the *Canterbury Tales* from St. Jerome's *Epistola Adversus Jovinianum.*" *SP* 62 (1965): 28–39.

Smalley, Beryl. *The Study of the Bible in the Middle Ages.* 3d ed. Oxford: Basil Blackwell, 1983.

Spearing, A. C. *Medieval Dream-Poetry.* Cambridge: Cambridge Univ. Press, 1976.

Spicq, C. *Esquisse d'une histoire de l'exégèse latine au moyen âge.* Bibliothèque thomiste, no. 26. Paris: J. Vrin, 1944.

Steinberg, Leo. *The Sexuality of Christ in Renaissance Art and Modern Oblivion.* New York: Pantheon, 1983.

Steiner, George. *After Babel: Aspects of Language and Translation.* London: Oxford Univ. Press, 1975.

Stevens, Martin. "The Royal Stanza in Early English Literature." *PMLA* 94 (1979): 62–76.

Stock, Brian. *Myth and Science in the Twelfth Century: A Study of Bernard Sylvester.* Princeton, N.J.: Princeton Univ. Press, 1972.

Stockton, Eric W. "The Deadliest Sin in 'The Pardoner's Tale.'" *Tennessee Studies in Literature* 6 (1961): 47–59.

Storm, Melvin. "Alisoun's Ear." *MLQ* 42 (1981): 219–26.

Sumption, Jonathan. *Pilgrimage: An Image of Medieval Religion.* London: Faber, 1975.

Theiner, Paul. "Robertsonianism and the Idea of Literary History." *Studies in Medieval Culture* 6/7 (1976): 195–204.

Toynbee, Paget. "The Ballade Addressed by Eustache Deschamps to Geoffrey Chaucer." *Academy* 40 (1891): 432.

Ullmann, Manfred. *Islamic Medicine.* Edinburgh: Edinburgh Univ. Press, 1978.

Utley, Frances Lee. "Five Genres in the *Clerk's Tale.*" *ChauR* 6 (1972): 217–26.

Van, Thomas A. "Chaucer's Pandarus as an Earthly Maker." *Southern Humanities Review* 12 (1978): 89–97.

Vance, Eugene. "Chaucer, Spenser, and the Ideology of Translation." *Canadian Review of Comparative Literature* 8 (1981): 217–38.

Vance, Eugene. *Mervelous Signals: Poetics and Sign Theory in the Middle Ages.* Lincoln: Univ. of Nebraska Press, 1986.

Vinaver, Eugène. "Principles of Textual Emendation." In *Studies in French Language and Medieval Literature Presented to Mildred K. Pope,* pp. 351–69. Manchester: Manchester Univ. Press, 1939.

Walker, Cheryl. *The Nightingale's Burden: Women Poets and American Culture before 1900.* Bloomington: Indiana Univ. Press, 1982.

Walkup, Kathleen. "By Sovereign Maidens' Might: Notes on Women in Printing." *Fine Print* 11 (1985): 100–104.

Wallace, Kristine Gilmartin. "Array as Motif in the *Clerk's Tale.*" *Rice University Studies* 62 (1976): 99–110.

Warner, Marina. *Alone of All Her Sex: The Myth and the Cult of the Virgin Mary.* New York: Random House, 1976.

Waswo, Richard. "The Narrator of *Troilus and Criseyde.*" *ELH* 50 (1983): 1–25.

Watts, P. R. "The Strange Case of Geoffrey Chaucer and Cecilia Chaumpaigne." *Law Quarterly Review* 63 (1947): 491–515.

Weinstein, Donald, and Rudolph M. Bell. *Saints and Society: The Two Worlds of Western Christendom, 1000–1700.* Chicago: Univ. of Chicago Press, 1982.

Weissman, Hope Phyllis. "Antifeminism in Chaucer's Characterization of Women." In *Geoffrey Chaucer,* ed. George D. Economou, pp. 93–110. New York: McGraw-Hill, 1975.

Weissman, Hope Phyllis. "Late Gothic Pathos in the *Man of Law's Tale.*" *JMRS* 9 (1979): 133–53.

Wetherbee, Winthrop. *Chaucer and the Poets: An Essay on "Troilus and Criseyde."* Ithaca, N.Y.: Cornell Univ. Press, 1984.

Wilden, Anthony. "Lacan and the Discourse of the Other." In *Speech and Language in Psychoanalysis.* By Jacques Lacan. Ed. and trans. Anthony Wilden. Baltimore: Johns Hopkins Univ. Press, 1968.

Williams, Arnold. "Chaucer and the Friars." *Speculum* 28 (1953): 499–513.

Windeatt, B. A. "The Scribes as Chaucer's Early Critics." *SAC* 1 (1979): 119–41.

Winnicott, D. W. "Transitional Objects and Transitional Phenomena: A Study of the First Not-Me Possession." *International Journal of Psycho-Analysis* 34 (1953): 89–97.

Wood, Chauncey. *The Elements of Chaucer's "Troilus."* Durham, N.C.: Duke Univ. Press, 1984.

Wurtele, Douglas. "Chaucer's *Canterbury Tales* and Nicholas of Lyre's *Postillae litteralis et moralis super totam Bibliam.*" In *Chaucer and Scriptural Tradition,* ed. David Lyle Jeffrey, pp. 89–107. Ottawa: Univ. of Ottawa Press, 1984.

Wurtele, Douglas. "The Penitence of Geoffrey Chaucer." *Viator* 11 (1980): 335–59.

Wurtele, Douglas. "The Predicament of Chaucer's Wife of Bath: St. Jerome on Virginity." *Florilegium* 5 (1983): 208–36.

Zimbardo, Rose A. "Creator and Created: The Generic Perspective of Chaucer's *Troilus and Criseyde.*" *ChauR* 11 (1977): 283–98.

Zumthor, Paul. *Langue, texte, énigme.* Paris: Seuil, 1975.

Index